FAST TIMES AND
EXCELLENT ADVENTURES

Fast Times and Excellent Adventures

The Surprising History of the '80s Teen Movie

James King

Constable • London

CONSTABLE

First published in Great Britain in 2018 by Constable

1 3 5 7 9 10 8 6 4 2

A CIP catalogue record for this book
is available from the British Library.

ISBN: 978-1-47212-372-5

Typeset in Stempel Garamond by SX Composing DTP, Rayleigh, Essex
Printed and bound in Great Britain by CPI Group (UK) Ltd, Croydon CR0 4YY

Papers used by Constable are from well-managed forests
and other responsible sources.

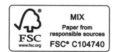

Constable
An imprint of
Little, Brown Book Group
Carmelite House
50 Victoria Embankment
London EC4Y 0DZ

An Hachette UK Company
www.hachette.co.uk

www.littlebrown.co.uk

FAST TIMES AND
EXCELLENT ADVENTURES

Contents

Introduction

We all know what a teen movie is – high-school or college-age characters, youthful issues, maybe a prominent pop soundtrack, definitely an adolescent target audience. But those are just the facts, the boxes to be ticked. What else do they have? What is it that has kept young cinema-goers going to teen films throughout Hollywood's history . . . and keeps them returning, even as adults?

Time certainly plays a part. Whether your teen movie centres on a Saturday detention, an era-hopping DeLorean car or desperate attempts to get laid, it is questions of time that unify the genre and perhaps provide the *real* pull. Life is short, they all say. Adolescence even shorter. So make the most of these few teenage years, this magic time. One day it will all be over.

The 1980s proved especially fertile ground for such alluring stories. Film-makers who flourished in the previous decade – themselves once known as young 'movie brats' – were now hitting

---

1 *New York* magazine, Nik Cohn, 7 June 1976.

middle age, with many facing both personal and professional crises. A new, more focused Hollywood emerged to counter their expensive indulgences and the teen audience that had flocked to see *Jaws* and *Star Wars* – streamlined yarns in which the selling point was the concept rather than brooding Method-acting or an award-winning cast – were ruthlessly targeted.

And, of course, even on the business side, timing was everything. Young writers and directors who came of age during the '60s now found their poignantly autobiographical teen stories encouraged, often by studio executives of a similar age and taste. Meanwhile, relaxed moral codes let them get away with more cheeky rock'n'roll honesty than Gidget could have ever dreamed of.

If many young actors actually just wanted to be taken seriously and were hardly keen to be part of anything deemed a new 'scene', then at least they could take comfort in the fact that if you were a teenager – or even just looked like one – suddenly work was plentiful. Nineteen-seventy-eight's triple teen whammy of *Saturday Night Fever*, *Grease* and *Animal House* had shown Hollywood exactly where it was heading – and it didn't hold back on following up with new youth-centred product.

Over-saturation was inevitable. Surprise successes from the first half of the '80s morphed into more calculated cash-ins, where the presence of a newly emerged star, popular fad or currently fashionable song on the soundtrack often outweighed emotional depth. The emergence of home video as a force to be reckoned with certainly contributed to quantity over quality and some of Hollywood's hottest teen actors and super producers struggled to use their popularity wisely. In a time of heightened consumerism championed by a right-wing president, maybe it was impossible not to?

And then there was the problem of growing up. It happens to everyone (as so many teen movies liked to lament) but, in a youth-obsessed industry, actors maturing in public is no easy task. So if teen films remind *us* of our brief adolescence then they remind many of their stars of something else too: their own moment as the nation's favourite pin-up, eventful but brief.

Happily though, authenticity nearly always won through, marking the difference between, say, *Heathers* (still talked about today) and *Hot Dog: The Movie* (thankfully forgotten). And it was authenticity that would be the natural buzzword come the beginning of the next decade, the packaging of the previous ten years now starting to look too slick – and just too damn *white* – for the 1990s. It was time for teen tastes to go full circle, allowing a grungier, more independent approach that owed much to the '70s to once again find the spotlight.

But the best of the '80s teen movies never entirely went away; forever frozen in time on TV, DVD and download. Their stories might deal with a fleeting period – a day off, a school year, a special summer – but their charm, it seems, is ageless.

This is their story. And it begins two years before the turn of the decade, on a brightly-coloured dancefloor somewhere in Brooklyn.

Chapter One

TRAVOLTA'S '78

Saturday Night Fever and Grease rule the box-office; Hollywood falls back in love with teenagers; and the 'movie brats' struggle with the imminent new decade.

John Travolta was Hollywood's last great star of the '70s. Nineteen-seventy-eight was *his* year. *Saturday Night Fever*, released the previous Christmas, topped the US box-office until Valentine's Day, still filling screens come early April when the actor attended the Fiftieth Academy Awards in Los Angeles, his performance as *Fever*'s Tony Manero up against heavyweight turns from Richard Burton and Marcello Mastroianni for Best Actor. He was just twenty-four years old, the category's third youngest nominee ever.

Richard Dreyfus took home the Oscar that night, for his role as neurotic actor Elliot in Neil Simon's *The Goodbye Girl*, but *Saturday Night Fever* mania wasn't about to go away. Its soundtrack album was still No. 1 – would be for another three months – on its way to shifting fifteen million in the States and ruling charts around the globe. John Travolta, it seemed, had the whole world at his (disco-dancing) feet.

Really though, that was only the start. With barely a pause for breath Travolta was back on the big screen by the summer, this time in *Grease* and between June and October there was only one week when the '50s-set musical wasn't the most popular movie in

America. Its soundtrack, meanwhile, knocked The Rolling Stones from the summit of Billboard's Top 200 to eventually claim the year's second biggest sales figures (behind only *Saturday Night Fever*). In just a few months Travolta had risen from small-screen favourite to the biggest showbiz pin-up on the planet, a one-man film, music and fashion industry, his turbo boost in popularity up there with Elvis post-signing to RCA in '56 or The Beatles after debuting on *The Ed Sullivan Show*. And it all made sense. John Travolta was irresistible; a mix of macho bravado and boyish vulnerability, his masses of dark wavy hair framing a face that could barely contain the lethal combination of sky-blue eyes, sunny grin and the most famous chin dimple since Kirk Douglas.

Yet in just those two movies – films made back-to-back, on screens within moments of one other that fateful year – one phase of Hollywood history was ending, another just starting up. Here was a changeover period in Hollywood so significant that Travolta, the megastar conduit, would struggle for years with the impact.

John had been born to Salvatore and Helen – a tyre salesman and a former actress – in Englewood, New Jersey, on 18 February 1954; the last of six children. Maybe if he'd been a bit older, his rise and fall wouldn't have been so great; a bit younger, on the other hand, and a new age and new decade of teen roles would have surely opened up to him. Yet by the end of 1978 and with his twenty-fifth birthday fast approaching, John Travolta found himself at the top of a pile yet with nowhere to go. Yes, he was Hollywood's last great star of the '70s, perhaps the decade's most sparkling. But he was also the '80s' first victim.

In the early part of the 1970s it had been Travolta's fellow Italian-American New Yorkers Robert De Niro (eleven years his senior) and Al Pacino (fourteen) who had hogged the headlines, turning film-acting asunder by redefining what it meant to be a leading man. Working within the so-called 'New Hollywood' – that group of independent, determinedly cinephile writer/directors such as Francis Coppola, Martin Scorsese and Sidney Lumet – on projects with complex and damaged heroes (*The Godfather*, *Mean Streets*, *Serpico*), suddenly critical acclaim was no longer just about traditional epics boasting glamorous stars. Now that Vietnam,

Watergate and social unrest filled the news bulletins, even the frequently frothy movie industry refocused on the personal and the flawed. The directors might have been nicknamed 'movie brats', a nod to their precociousness, but it was a label that belittled their achievements. Things had gotten impressively intense. '[De Niro] was raising the bar for all of us young actors,' Travolta later remembered, 'and that means if you were going to play a role, you had to really learn how to do the thing you were doing. If you wanted to box, you had to become a real boxer. If you were going to play a saxophone, you had to spend a year learning how to play a saxophone.'[1] The young John could only look on, close but not close enough.

In the summer of '75, with low-budget horror *The Devil's Rain* recently wrapped, his persistence finally paid off. *Welcome Back, Kotter* – a new ABC sitcom about a pupil returning to his old high school to teach – not only gave John an audition but also the winning break he'd been craving, casting him as rebellious student Vinnie Barbarino. Within a few weeks he was getting ten thousand fan letters a week and scripts were feverishly rewritten to give the new heart-throb more screen time. Born too late? It hardly seemed so.

Yet Travolta, mid-decade and no longer a teenager, didn't just want to be a pretty boy, releasing cash-in pop records to lovelorn adolescent fans. It didn't matter that success in *Kotter* led him to having a hit single, 1976's 'Let Her In'.[2] It didn't matter that ABC then cast him as the lead in top-rated TV movie *The Boy in the Plastic Bubble*. It didn't even matter that Brian De Palma's acclaimed operatic teen horror *Carrie* hit cinemas the same week as *Bubble*, with John in a supporting role as school bully Billy Nolan.[3] That actors might kill for that much work wasn't the point. When John's heavy *Kotter* filming schedule reportedly meant he had to turn down the lead in auteur Terence Malick's brooding Texan period piece *Days of Heaven* it was frustrating,

---

1 The Huffington Post, 14 August 2014.

2 Sample lyric: 'I look at her face / and there isn't a trace / of doubt in my mind'.

3 De Palma cast *Carrie* at the same time as his friend George Lucas was choosing actors for *Star Wars*. Amy Irving – Sue in the horror pic – was close to getting the Princess Leia role, whilst William Katt (Tommy) tried out for Luke Skywalker.

pure and simple. The wannabe De Niro desperately wanted a real shot at grown-up film-making.

Then, for a brief moment, the stars aligned. Two sometime business partners – both vastly experienced, both masters of hype and both part of the so-called 'velvet mafia', the gay glitterati whose interests spanned multiple aspects of American showbusiness in the early '70s – got John on their radar.

Allan Carr was the flamboyant one, a kaftan-clad Broadway producer and talent agent who 'thought fast, talked fast, made decisions instantly'.[1] Robert Stigwood was quieter yet arguably more ruthless; a toothy, wavy-haired Australian impresario who looked like an older brother to the Bee Gees boys he managed. Stigwood had played a key role in reshaping the British pop scene of the '60s as a fearlessly independent manager, agent and producer. Now he was expanding into American theatre and film. Carr's client list included the fabulous (Bette Davis and *Playboy*), Stigwood's boasted the serious (supergroup Cream and the EMI corporation) but, ever the showmen, both liked to party. Bee Gee Barry Gibb summed it up: 'If there is reincarnation Robert will come back as Louis XVI'.[2]

Carr and Stigwood clicked. They'd first worked together on Ken Russell's movie of The Who's *Tommy* in '75, Stigwood producing, Carr across marketing and promotion. A surprisingly successful re-dub of a Mexican exploitation flick called *Survive!* had followed, generating good dollars for both of them and for distributor Paramount. They had been aware of the young Travolta's charisma for some time, Carr first meeting him at a recording studio during the teen pop era, Stigwood from that *Jesus Christ Superstar* audition years earlier (the stage musical was one of his productions). Now Carr had a pet project that was crying out for John as lead: a movie version of the show in which the actor had once toured, *Grease*. Stigwood, meanwhile, had just bought the film rights to journalist Nik Cohn's article on Brooklyn clubbers called 'Tribal Rights of the New Saturday Night', a piece

1 *The Big Show: High Times and Dirty Dealings Backstage at the Academy Awards*, Steve Pond, Faber & Faber, 2005, p.4.

2 Interview with Simon Fanshawe, www.simonfanshawe.com

that had first appeared in *New York* magazine a couple of years earlier. He was also desperate for Travolta to topline.

Since *Grease* was still running in theatreland, Carr's movie adaptation of the show was obliged to hold off for another year, allowing Stigwood to get going with his idea first, now renamed *Saturday Night Fever*; a tough look at young, working-class alienation and the weekly release that disco-going gave, to be made with an adult-skewed R-rating.[1] He asked Allan to work on the marketing. More unusually, he signed Travolta to a million-dollar, three-picture deal: first *Fever*, then *Grease*, then a romantic drama called *Moment by Moment*.

Hollywood was aghast. Could a TV pin-up really lead three movies for such big bucks? It was early '77. De Niro had just wrapped on *New York, New York* with Martin Scorsese, having already wowed in *Taxi Driver* and *The Godfather Part II*. Pacino was still basking in the success of *Dog Day Afternoon*. For John Travolta, it was finally time to show everyone what he was really worth.

Within just over a year, of course, he was priceless. *Fever* and *Grease* had shown he could sing, he could dance, he could even get award nominations. *Welcome Back, Kotter* continued on the television too, now as much a show about Vinnie Barbarino as Gabe Kaplan's title character.

Yet as the decade came to a close, changes in Hollywood's output were clear; the brooding anti-heroics of *A Clockwork Orange*, *Mean Streets* and *Serpico* were losing out to the smilier fun-and-games of *Star Wars*, *Superman* and *Smokey and the Bandit*. Steven Spielberg's *Jaws* was at the centre of it all, released in the summer of '75 with unprecedented marketing, merchandising and screen count. Such saturation proved impossible to resist: *Jaws* became the first movie to hit a hundred million dollars in the States. The New Hollywood generation that had relished the complexities of *The Godfather* saga now discovered something much simpler: man versus shark.

It was a shift that made some sense. The constitutional crisis caused by Nixon's Watergate scandal was now a year old and

---

1 'R' officially meant that under-17s had to be accompanied by an adult.

America's involvement in the Vietnam War had officially ended in April 1975. After years of serious, adult-oriented drama that had matched the weighty stories broadcast each day on the nightly news, audiences now not only wanted simpler fun – they *needed* it.

Travolta, however, still needed credibility. 'I want to show that I can do more than play safe, pretty-boy roles,' he always liked to remind journalists when he was starting out.[1] The success of *Fever* and *Grease* had been immense in '78 but it had been a success that overwhelmed the original point of both their stories: gutsy, adolescent angst. Disco tunes, singalongs and John's pin-up status had smoothed out the movies' sharper edges and, whilst modern Hollywood audiences seemed to want more of that mainstream accessibility – the *fun* – Travolta the Method actor had different ideas. How could he stay valuable in a Hollywood that now boasted a new currency? If only he could hold back the '80s a little longer.

Still, if late-'70s Travolta-mania diluted much of his dangerous power, it shouldn't detract from the fact that *Fever* – before saturation turned it into a punchline – had plenty of 'genuine' on offer.

Travolta was determined and dedicated to De Niro-levels of authenticity, filling his spare time learning to dance – nine months training, he later claimed – helped by the snake-hipped choreographer Lester Wilson.[2] For the ambitious actor, Tony Manero was the perfect chance to showcase his 'Method' and he fought with director John Badham to get his dance scenes recut in order to spotlight all that he'd learned: 'I was crying and very angry because of the way the dance highlight was shot. I knew how it should appear on-screen, and it wasn't shot that way. You couldn't even see my feet!'[3] After complaining to Stigwood, Travolta was allowed to recut the scene. Those millions who flocked to *Fever* during the early months of '78 might not have

---

1 See the front cover of Bob McCabe's excellent *Quote, Unquote* book on Travolta, Random House, 1996.

2 Cohort of Bob Fosse, Josephine Baker, Liza Minnelli . . .

3 'Fever Pitch', *Vanity Fair*, Sam Kashner, 15 August 2013.

known about the passions that ran high behind the scenes but they sure appreciated the end result.

Nevertheless, if *Fever*'s popularity threatened to overwhelm Travolta's intensity then the shamelessly mainstream appeal of *Grease* – his second picture of the Stigwood deal and Allan Carr's pet project – smothered it. It was mid-summer '78 and the critics that had praised *Fever* just months earlier now complained that, in the shiny *Grease*, Travolta's charisma had been seriously weakened, watered down from the Pacino-like swagger he'd shown playing Manero. It wasn't the first and it wouldn't be the last of many accusations about a sea change in the industry; a new era of dumbing down.

It's hard to argue. Compared to the blue-collar passion of *Fever*, compared even to the gritty Jacobs and Casey musical on which it was based, *Grease*-the-movie, with its deliberate family makeover – innuendo-laden but ultimately innocent – was always going to be a disappointment for the broadsheets.[1] What had centred, in its stage form, on earthy memories of high school in Chicago had now been retooled by the colourful Allan Carr into a movie fairytale, his own fantasy of what education was like in the late '50s rather than the reality. Barry Gibb's title song might have been sung by Frankie Valli, a former idol of the era, but its production was disco-tinged and slick; pure 1978. Insiders knew the deal: making his new, poppier version of *Grease* (co-written with Bronte Woodard) had been a very personal dose of therapy for producer Carr rather than an attempt at realism: 'Like many kids, I was not too popular in high school. But producing *Grease* made me feel like I was president of my class . . . It was a movie I had to make . . . [and] it turned out to be as perfect a realisation of my dream as I could hope for.'[2]

Still, *Grease* was a huge hit, its 159-dollar box-office million nearly forty million more even than *Fever*. Travolta's dominance seemed unstoppable. So it was perhaps inevitable that after *Grease*'s success with younger teenagers, kids able to see it thanks

---

1 British reviewer Derek Malcolm wrote of Travolta in *Grease* for the *Guardian*, 'He poses like some forlorn young stud in a bedroom full of chastity belts,' 14 September 1978.

2 *Frenchy's Grease Scrapbook*, Didi Conn, André Deutsch, 1998, p.5.

to its family-friendly rating, Paramount looked again at *Fever* and made the obvious decision: release a new PG cut of *that* movie too, aiming squarely at the same youthful *Grease* fans who weren't able to see John in R-rated disco mode the first time around. If the studio hadn't been entirely supportive of either film during production ('The executives at Paramount weren't sure what they had,' claims *Grease* director Randal Kleiser[1]) they were sure as hell going to get their money's worth now they knew there was an appetite. This new *Fever*-lite included forty-seven cuts, forty-three audio changes and thirty-one scenes with alternative, 'softer' takes that Badham had shot in preparation for the film's eventual TV broadcast.[2]

Not that the director had found his actors – all with their De Niro aspirations – exactly keen to offer up gentler, more mainstream interpretations of their feisty Brooklynites. 'Initially, the cast refused to do it. "Oh, that's bullshit, man!" I replied. "Have you guys ever heard of residuals? Every time this is shown on television, you guys will get paid." They were all brand new actors, so they had no idea. Suddenly, they were all very game. In some cases, the TV version is what went into the original because the actors were so much looser and more natural, since they thought it was just a throw-away take.'[3]

The disco focus of *Fever* was always the point, of course; a way for blue-collar immigrant kids to lose themselves for a few hours at the weekend. Yet this new PG cut only made it more so, gutting the dirty talk and angst to highlight the hit songs, the pop and sparkle of the music way more digestible for young teens than R-rated bitterness and rape.[4]

Saturday Night Fever then *Grease* then a *Fever* re-release plus, of course, disco; *endless* disco. Mainstream mania for the guy at the centre of them all – John Travolta, with his contrasting dream of

---

1 Author interview.
2 As detailed on movie.censorship.com
3 John Badham interviewed at thehollywoodinterview.blogspot.com
4 An in-depth look at the film's oft-overlooked moodiness can be found in Nathan Rabin's 'Existential Panic at the Disco: There's an Alluring Darkness Beneath *Saturday Night Fever*'s Disco Floor', *Vanity Fair*, 2 May 2017.

credibility – meant all four were all heading for overkill, scoring huge success whilst simultaneously signing their death warrants.

Come the summer of '79, barely a year after *Fever* had soared and concurrent with the rejigged PG cut of the film getting its first airing ('Because we want everyone to catch *Saturday Night Fever*' ran the new, more inclusive tagline), the infamous Disco Demolition Night took place in Chicago, rock fans snapping and burning disco vinyl, even rioting. It was an over-the-top and reactionary response for sure, but it was clear that the genre was being strangled by ubiquity. If it wasn't actually dead then it was certainly a musical style in need of some medication.

When, in 1980, Paramount reissued the recut *Fever* for a *third* time, this time in a blatant double-bill with *Grease*, the industry's intentions for the new decade couldn't be any clearer: forget serious grown-ups, get the teenage dollar fast – at whatever the cost. It didn't matter that Travolta might have wanted to move on from his teenybopper status. The studio execs weren't ready to let him go.

For Paramount, catching the disco wave just before it crashed had proven to be a vital reboot. As America's oldest-running studio it had long stopped being considered youthful but now boss Robert Evans, who'd overseen adult classics *The Godfather* and *Chinatown* during his tenure, was gone and his replacement chairman, Barry Diller, had hired new execs (nicknamed the 'Killer Dillers') with more experience in television than in film. Paramount's owners Gulf and Western might have had the legendarily demanding Martin Davis at the helm, a bullish businessman who liked to breathe down his studio's neck, but with the no less high-flying Michael Eisner – Diller's former ABC colleague – as Paramount's president, the film company successfully reshaped itself to include more shorter, lighter product that didn't need a prestige movie brat director and that, crucially, would make money even if they didn't win awards. Here was the beginning of a new approach that would change '80s Hollywood for ever: 'high-concept' film-making, where a movie consisted merely of one simple idea which could be summed up as briefly as possible. Eisner, in particular, had that common touch, in tune with the middle-of-the-road tastes of everyday Americans (at ABC he had come up with the idea of *Happy Days*, a huge TV hit). He knew well that in the post-*Jaws*, *Star Wars* and *Grease* world of '78, seventy-four per cent of the movie audience were aged between twelve and twenty-nine[1] . . . and they were targeted ruthlessly. So whilst *Fever* might have started out as much more than simply 'Travolta + disco = hit', that's how it ended up. It had high concept beaten into it. Perhaps the signs were even there from the early days: *Fever*'s original director John G. Avildsen was considered a risk and the suits at Paramount simply fired him. It didn't matter that he'd just been Oscar-nominated for directing *Rocky*.

Late 1980. With the tweaked-clean *Fever* now on cable TV, its origins as a sweary, misogynistic, true 'New York story' were finally swept from people's minds as well as on to the cutting-room floor. Kids at the start of the new decade considered *Fever* to be something very different. It didn't matter that its gutsy roots had always been clearly spelled out in Barry Gibb's downbeat lyrics: 'Life going nowhere, somebody help me . . . ' It didn't matter that John Travolta's performance had been perhaps the decade's most charismatic and influential portrayal of adolescent frustration. Fever had been bleached clean for the young teen revolution just as *Grease* had been by Carr and now it was simply a fun film about disco dancing starring a pin-up in an ice-white suit.

As Hollywood refigured its plans around him, Travolta also found the bright glare of limelight did him no favours. Questions about his private life refused to go away, fuelled in part by the unconventional romance he'd had with Diana Hyland – an actress eighteen years his senior with whom he'd worked in *The Boy in the Plastic Bubble* – and not helped by the campiness of romancing the openly lesbian Lily Tomlin in his third film of the 1978 Stigwood deal, *Moment by Moment*.

Hyland died in John's arms in the spring of 1977 from breast cancer, the star taking a few days off from shooting *Fever* – a movie she'd encouraged him to be part of – to be with her in Los Angeles one last time. He returned to work heartbroken.

---

1 *High Concept: Movies and Marketing in Hollywood*, Justin Wyatt, University of Texas Press, 1994, p.29.

'The pain was on every inch of his body,' Badham remembers, 'but John didn't want people to feel sorry for him. He knew the best thing was plunge completely into what he was doing. Some of the best scenes in that picture were done in that advanced stage of grief.'[1]

Travolta wasn't seriously linked with anyone after Hyland, although the press relished his relationship with Newton-John (fuelled, of course, by Allan Carr's marketing flair) and a platonic friendship with teenage ingénue Brooke Shields, the star of Randal Kleiser's next film after *Grease*, *The Blue Lagoon* ('There are lots of women with physical beauty,' John explained to *People* magazine, 'but Brooke exudes goodness. She's untainted. You don't want anyone to hurt her or say the wrong things, because she's special.'[2]) Travolta was bluntly questioned about his private life in *Rolling Stone* magazine but didn't get annoyed: 'The gay rumour about male stars is such a classic that it didn't surprise me to hear it because I'd heard it about the others,' he explained before answering a clear 'No' to the question 'Are you gay?'[3] One scene in *Fever* certainly didn't do him any favours, the moment where he is lovingly shot grooming himself in front of the mirror, wearing just skimpy black briefs and a gold chain. 'We got all kinds of hassle,' remembers Badham. 'We were letting some man walk around in his underwear, showing his body off.'[4] Production designer Charles Bailey was told to add another poster to Tony's wall to allay any talk: Farrah Fawcett, smouldering.

Yet the gay question never left Travolta, his associations with the openly gay Carr, Stigwood, Kleiser and manager Bob LeMond doubtlessly adding to the debate. LeMond's client list read like a list of pretty boys: Travolta, his Rydell High classmate Jeff 'Kenickie' Conaway, a twenty-something all-rounder from the *Grease* stage show called Patrick Swayze and Jon-Erik Hexum, a blond-haired and blue-eyed model that LeMond 'discovered'

1 McCabe, p.33

2 People, 10 August 1981. Quoted in 'The Many Men in Brooke Shields's Love Life', Laura Lane, people.com, 12 November 2014.

3 'Sex and the Single Star', *Rolling Stone*, Nancy Collins, 18 August 1983.

4 'Fever Pitch', op. cit..

when he came to clean the agent's flat in 1980.[1] It wouldn't be until the next decade that John finally married: to Kelly Preston, an actress who'd once been considered for the Brooke Shields role in *The Blue Lagoon*.

There was also something even more controversial: Scientology. Travolta explained to *Rolling Stone* that although he hadn't been 'audited' (a form of complex interviewing integral to the religion's own 'science', Dianetics) for a year and a half he was still involved in the organisation, something to which he'd been introduced during a low period in his life by actress Joan Prather during the shoot for *The Devil's Rain*. He continued to regularly donate money, especially after crediting the organisation with helping him succeed in his *Welcome Back, Kotter* audition.[2]

Yet under the microscope Travolta's personality could seem confusing, almost empty ('I [first] met with him in his high-rise apartment on Doheny Drive where the most memorable piece of decor was a model airplane suspended over the kitchen table,' recalls Randal Kleiser[3]). With a seeming determination to make unusual lifestyle choices, not to mention the arrival of a new decade suddenly making his star-making disco connotations seem dated, how could Travolta ever be cool again?

In those early years of the '80s John Travolta already seemed filled with regret. *People* magazine of 23 June 1980 described him having 'slipped into disappointment and depression'[4] and as the retro charms of *Raiders of the Lost Ark* energised audiences around the world and the futuristic MTV prepared for its imminent launch, the twenty-seven year old was out of sync with the times; a '70s leftover, trying to grow up. *Moment by Moment* came out at Christmas in '78 . . . and tanked. Critics complained of the lack of

---

1 Hexum would die in a tragic accident on the set of TV show *Cover Up* in October 1984, joking about with a prop gun loaded with blanks, putting it to his head. When he pulled the trigger, wadding from the blank cartridge shattered his skull.

2 According to Lawrence Wright in his book *Going Clear: Scientology, Hollywood and the Prison of Belief*, Scientology teacher Sandy Kent instructed everyone at a group meeting to point in the direction of ABC studios and send out good vibes with the command 'We want John Travolta for the part', (*Going Clear . . .*, Knopf, 2013).

3 Author interview.

4 'Even Cowboys Get the Blues', Arthur Lubow.

chemistry between John and co-star Lily Tomlin, the mature widow with whom his drifter character is supposedly infatuated, and audiences stayed away. Even a theme tune by Yvonne Elliman, the wife of Stigwood's music supervisor Bill Oakes and already a hit-maker with *Fever*'s 'If I Can't Have You', failed to stir up interest. Leading lady Tomlin described the picture in blunt terms – 'a total failure'[1] – and no one disagreed. Was it a low-key character study or a modern romance? Like its star, *Moment by Moment* appeared unsure which path to take. That holiday it had seemed everyone was reverting back to childhood and watching the season's latest post-*Star Wars* blockbuster, *Superman*. If the godfather of the Method, Marlon Brando, would take 3.7 million dollars plus a cut of the profits for a cameo in the comic book movie (he played Jor-El, Superman's father) then the times really were changing.

Summer '81. Travolta's *Urban Cowboy* had been out a year and did OK, albeit almost universally described as merely '*Saturday Night Fever* with country music'. Whilst in Chicago to promote his new thriller *Blow Out* (helmed by *Carrie* director Brian De Palma), John was interviewed, along with co-star Nancy Allen, by Roger Ebert. The film critic for the *Chicago Sun-Times*, Ebert's own national fame was growing, thanks to the PBS-syndicated review show *Sneak Previews* that he presented with fellow film buff Gene Siskel. '*Grease*, of course, started here and should have been filmed here . . . ' the actor pointedly reminded Ebert,[2] in reference to the musical that had begun its stage life at the city's Kingston Mines Theatre ten years earlier, before its Broadway success and that Allan Carr Hollywood rewrite.

Ebert admired Travolta – 'an enormously likeable man whose face lights up when he smiles,' he wrote – but that sense of 'should have' which Travolta briefly voiced in the interview was significant. Things were not going to plan. Such regret seemed to echo in Ebert's writing about the star for several years after, more resonant with each new flop he fronted ('83's *Two of a Kind*: 'This movie

---

1 Quoted on Destined to Denver blog.
2 *Chicago Sun-Times*, 19 July 1981.

should have been struck by a lightning bolt'; *Staying' Alive*, from the same year, 'A disappointment'[1]).

The last thing Travolta ever wanted to be was a nearly man. Yet, as he sat opposite Ebert in the Park Hyatt Hotel that July, just four years since he'd spent '77 filming *Fever* and *Grease* back-to-back, the kind of films he wanted to make were simply, in Hollywood slang, not 'hot' any more. *Heaven's Gate* – an over-budget western epic helmed by De Niro's *Deer Hunter* director Michael Cimino – had been released, in a butchered cut, a few weeks before Martin Scorsese's *Raging Bull* and bombed so big it virtually destroyed United Artists, a studio still recovering from Francis Coppola's *Apocalypse Now* (which *had* been a hit but only after years of draining production difficulties). '*Heaven's Gate* was a movie about a war and was one itself,' admitted the former United Artists exec Steven Bach,[2] a likeable studio man caught at the centre of the storm. So as the post-*Star Wars* era entered the '80s it was no surprise that the straightforward flourished whilst the complex wilted. Spielberg and Lucas, once at the forefront of that free-thinking New Hollywood of the late '60s and early '70s, found success by moving on from the grey areas of their younger work and – in making high-concept action pieces instead – proceeded to kill off the very movement they'd helped to create. Many so-called auteurs still commanded intellectual respect but studios increasingly no longer had the patience to take big gambles on these layered labours of love. Why risk another *Heaven's Gate*? Producers who had once championed the integrity of director-led projects and the power of all-encompassing Method acting began to keep their mouths shut.

Born too late . . . just as Travolta's De Niro dreams got close they were slowly being taken away from him.

Blow Out managed only cult success in '81, not garnering anywhere near the media attention of Richard Gere's *American Gigolo*, released a few months earlier (and which Travolta had turned down). The films he declined – the should-have-beens such as *Gigolo* and *An Officer and a Gentleman* – were making bigger splashes than the ones to which he assented. Feathers had

---

1 Both from Ebert's reviews for the *Chicago Sun-Times*.

2 There's more – much more – in his glorious exposé *Final Cut: Art, Money and Ego in the Making of Heaven's Gate*, Newmarket Press, 1999.

been ruffled when Travolta left *Gigolo* only shortly before filming was due to start, replaced by the cooler, more dispassionate-seeming Philly-native Gere (who had also taken the lead in *Days of Heaven*). The star's discomfort with the material was cited, some say because of *Gigolo*'s homosexual undertones, although writer/director Paul Schrader was ultimately relieved. 'In one day,' he later admitted, 'Richard Gere asked all the questions that Travolta hadn't in six months.'[1] *Gigolo* was another to feature a disco-flavoured soundtrack, by Italian producer Giorgio Moroder, that smartly moved the genre forward from its US soul origins in *Saturday Night Fever*. Moroder fused the synthesiser sounds he had pioneered in Munich – and perfected with Donna Summer – with American rock. Blondie's throbbing theme tune, 'Call Me', was a US No. 1.

An Officer and a Gentleman, meanwhile, had been written by Douglas Day Stewart specifically for Travolta (Stewart had also written *The Boy in the Plastic Bubble*). Larger-than-life producer Jerry Weintraub had tried to whet Paramount's appetite to no avail, eventually offering the project to the keener team at Lorimar. It was their interest which then revived Paramount's; after all, if Lorimar wanted *Officer*, maybe it had something after all? Paramount ultimately won out, although by now Travolta was complaining that the part of Paula (eventually played by Debra Winger) had all the best lines, rather than the male lead Zack, a training naval officer battling with both his drill sergeant and his emotions. Again, Travolta quit the project and again Richard Gere – coincidentally himself an alumnus of *Grease*, playing Danny during its run on the London stage – stepped in with his soon-to-be-trademark style of cerebral detachment. The movie survived considerable on-set tension to strike gold as the third biggest hit of 1982. As it packed out cinemas around the world, Travolta sacked his longtime guru Bob LeMond and signed with the powerhouse Creative Artists Agency. It still wouldn't be enough.

Gere was older than Travolta but image-wise seemed more contemporary; as slick and robotic as the latest '80s computer technology. If John was the friendly guy you knew from high

---

1 BBC news profile on Gere, Chris Jones, 27 December 2002.

school or the nightclub, Richard was more stand-offish and distant; a glamorous modern movie star, not 'one of us'. It was exactly the quality Paramount's thirty-nine-year-old executive Don Simpson was looking for. *Officer* was an old-fashioned story but with a contemporary high-concept edge: big fights and shameless romance, soundtracked by pop artists who could get on radio and MTV to fuel the film's appeal. Here was something with *Fever*-ish grit (that also got a cleaner cut for TV broadcast) yet tidier than Travolta's unpredictable New York bluster; a crisp, white, naval uniform instead of a polyester suit. Gere had just the right coldness hidden behind his smoulder.

Like Allan Carr before him, the persuasive Don Simpson would also use his power in Hollywood to rewrite his own history and transform himself into the player he'd always wanted to be (Simpson grew up in Alaska, described by his classmates as a studious type, although according to his own high-concept polish he was a tough guy, 'the Baby Face Nelson of Anchorage'[1]). For Simpson, unlike Travolta in the early '80s, the time was just right: his bravado plus America's new decade – optimistic, futuristic – proved an ideal match.

It wasn't just Travolta who got left behind; Allan Carr and Robert Stigwood also found themselves increasingly out of fashion. The former ploughed on with his singalong flamboyance, following *Grease* with 1980's *Can't Stop the Music*, a musical starring the gay dance act Village People that flopped thanks to disco overkill (not to mention being terrible). His next project, *Grease 2*, he hoped, would save the day.

Stigwood, meanwhile, watched both his bizarre Bee Gees-starring film of The Beatles' *Sgt. Pepper* album, a project on which he'd focused whilst Carr had worked on *Grease*, and 1980's *Times Square* bomb at the box-office. Stigwood had envisaged the latter as a punk-ish *Fever*, the story of two teenage girls – rich kid Pamela and snarling drifter Nicki – who escape from a mental health institution and live on the streets of Manhattan, wandering the

---

1 Do yourself a favour and find out more about Simpson's self-mythologising in Charles Fleming's seminal *High Concept: Don Simpson and the Hollywood Culture of Excess*, Bloomsbury, 1999.

rooftops, clubs and porno theatres of a city then crippled by violence and poverty. When the duo start writing songs and calling themselves the Sleaze Sisters they gain cult fame, thanks also to regular mentions on the radio show of local nightshift DJ Johnny La Guardia (Tim Curry). Thirteen-year-old Trini Alvarado played nice girl Pamela but it was Robin Johnson, all husky voice and attitude as Nicki, that Stigwood signed up to a Travolta-style deal; a contract that never paid off for either of them. Disputes with Canadian director Allan Moyle also led Stigwood to recut the film himself and *Times Square* eventually came out with little fanfare. Its soundtrack was largely forward-thinking, all new wave acts such as Talking Heads, Gary Numan and The Pretenders but Stigwood's insistence on including a disco-tinged track by Bee Gee Robin Gibb[1] for the film's finale spoke volumes. *Times Square* was unsure whether to be like the R or PG cut of Fever; one eye was on raw anger ('We don't need anti-depressants! We need your understanding'), one was on shifting albums. Cult success beckoned.[2]

Even Travolta's angelic *Grease* co-star Olivia Newton-John found early '80s Hollywood in a state of flux. Her 1980 film *Xanadu* aimed to keep everyone happy by blending vintage MGM musical panache with contemporary roller-disco sparkle. Unfortunately, it didn't know how to handle either. The soundtrack sold but it was the movie's weak box-office and all-round incomprehensibility that landed it the first Golden Raspberry Award for Worst Film of the Year (shared, appropriately, with *Can't Stop the Music*). The Bee Gees, meanwhile, realised the need to ditch traditional disco for their *Fever* follow-ups; albums that met with initial success (1979's US No. 1 *Spirits Having Flown*) before the band's '70s associations proved just too much of a turn-off for young record buyers (1981's *Living Eyes* could only scrape to No.41). Time had simply moved on. The Broadway producing nous of Carr and Stigwood had undeniably helped to make *Grease* the biggest live action movie musical ever and *Fever* the biggest

---

1 The song was called 'Help Me!' and was a duet with one Marcy Detroit, ten years later one half of duo Shakespears Sister.

2 *Times Square* is now a favourite of film festivals and punk bands. Many of its ideas – radical DJs, impromptu gigs – revisited by Moyle himself in his later works *Pump Up the Volume* (1990) and *Empire Records* (1995).

soundtrack but now it was the moment for a different style of entertainment. Don Simpson's tastes were arguably no less camp but in a smoother, sharper, more macho way; as suave as the USA's new president, former movie star Ronald Reagan. Everything suddenly felt so much more modern.

'In my teens, I fell in love with the movies,' Sean Penn once confessed. He was six years younger than Travolta but his influences were the same: the raging bulls of complex '70s cinema. 'And so when I got involved I was a genius in terms of how the movies that were made in the generation that inspired me got made. But the financing wasn't there to do 'em anymore. Trauma. I'm caught in a business that I'm in love with the idea of . . . the whole process that's possible. Only now they're not making movies. They're representing them.'[1]

Come the turn of the decade, Travolta found himself in a similar position; a fan of the old guard, struggling with the new. Unlike Travolta though, Penn hadn't already experienced the highs and lows of fame the way that John had. He wasn't tainted goods. Not so for John Travolta though. Nineteen-seventy-eight already seemed a lifetime ago. Once too young to be part of the 'New Hollywood' crowd he so admired, by the 1980s he was already beginning to look old-fashioned compared to the decade's fresh intake of acting hotshots. Now it was *their* time.

---

1 *Esquire*, Scott Raab, 12 December 2012.

Chapter Two

BABY BOOMERS

All change in the boardrooms of Burbank; American Graffiti *and rock'n'roll nostalgia;* Animal House *delivers retro raunch; and over at the National Lampoon office, John Hughes starts writing.*

As Travolta dealt with the glare of his teen heart-throb status in '78, a thirty-five-year-old journalist was chronicling something going on behind the scenes: the undeniable changes taking place in Hollywood boardrooms that would set the scene for the decade to come. Forget the traditional image of the brash, balding, cigar-chomping producer; suddenly here were twenty-somethings taking charge of studios, liberal and forward thinking in their outlook, fuelled by the social revolution of the '60s to make films in a newer, less formal way. The 'baby boomers'[1] were running the show.

Maureen Orth was the writer of the exposé, a Berkeley graduate and one of the first women at *Newsweek* before becoming senior editor at sister publications *New York* and *New West* magazines (the former of which had first published Cohn's 'Tribal Rites' article two years earlier). Both magazines were bold bi-weeklies, home to much of the so-called 'new journalism' from the early '70s, wanting to pack a punch with their wit and insight. Orth had something of the wide-eyed Diane Keaton look about her yet her writing was anything but flaky. When *New West* published her

---

1 There was sharp rise in births in the US immediately after 1945. Relationships that had been torn apart by World War II were rekindled, marriage rates soared and the image of the 'nuclear family' became an industry as much as an ideal.

article, appropriately titled 'The Baby Moguls', the impact in the summer of '78 was immediate.

'This new breed is young and well-educated,' Orth wrote. 'Many of them come from radical backgrounds and are trying to resolve their past with the present. Their sensibility is already starting to have some impact on the way people at the top live in Hollywood, on the films we see and, at a most critical time, on the future morality of the movie business.' Of the many that could have been mentioned by Orth, seven were singled out: Paramount's playboy Don Simpson, young Universal execs Thom Mount and Sean Daniel, the multi-talented Claire Townsend and Paula Weinstein from Twentieth Century Fox, Warner Bros' Mark Rosenberg (Weinstein's partner, whom she met in New York whilst planning an anti-Vietnam War demonstration) and finally Michael Black, an agent at the recently formed ICM and well known for his sharp one-liners.

'The baby moguls story was the talk of Hollywood, and the industry establishment hated it,' wrote *LA Times* journalist James Bates in a retrospective of the infamous article.[1] 'In the summer of '78, in such Hollywood haunts of the day as Le Dome, Ma Maison and Imperial Gardens, a button appeared on lapels that read "Free the baby moguls". It was an inside joke, or as inside as jokes can be in Hollywood, which is to say a few thousand people probably got it.'

Allan Carr certainly got it and wasn't happy. Thanks to the teen-themed *Grease*, he thought he should also be a baby mogul but really he was way too old. Thom Mount, Carr's friend and colleague, was only twenty-six when Universal's colourful chairman Lew Wasserman put him in charge of the studio. Carr was a full eleven years older.

'When I heard about it [The baby moguls article] I was not thrilled,' remembers Mount. 'But the thing that was important about that article, I thought, is that it really did signal a changing of the guard in the studio system.'[2] Mount had employed the older

---

1 *LA Times*, 22 March 1998.

2 *Interview* magazine, September 1984. Actor Margot Kidder – in Peter Biskind's *Easy Riders, Raging Bulls* – described that change of guard in cheekier terms: 'None of us were prepared for the '80s. Our heads were still in the '70s and we were at sea in a business run by young agents with blow-dried hairdos.'

Carr just after *Grease* to help with marketing Universal's downbeat Vietnam epic *The Deer Hunter*. The fact that he shepherded it to Oscar wins and box-office dollars in the early part of 1979 even led to the boyish executive offering the veteran showman a permanent job with the studio (Carr turned it down). After all, *The Deer Hunter* had been no easy task. Director Michael Cimino – hinting at what would happen with *Heaven's Gate* in 1980 – had run over-schedule and over-budget. Carr had done a good job.

However, like his fellow baby mogul, Don Simpson at Paramount, Thom Mount was also giving Universal bosses big hits with simpler stories. Not everything had to be a weighty award winner. If Paramount's teenage focus in the late '70s was as much to do with perception – Barry Diller and Michael Eisner being seen as TV-influenced, streamlining bosses – then Universal's was more blatant. Mount was Lew Wasserman's *wunderkind,* a Cal Arts graduate who'd previously worked for names as varied as low-rent producer Roger Corman, actress and campaigner Jane Fonda and the high-flying Kennedy brothers, Bobby and Ted. He joined Universal in early 1973 as a reader and assistant to head of production Ned Tanen.

'Mr Wasserman started bringing me to board meetings, as the kind of "house hippy". As the representative of a new generation,' remembers Mount.[1] Wasserman first gave Mount the responsibility of making films for a young black audience and challenged him to win an NAACP[2] Image Award for the studio.[3] Within three years of joining, Mount was president of the company, creating the studio's own stand-alone 'youth unit' along the way, moulding more ground-breaking urban hits such as *Car Wash* ('I like to think I was the only one inside Universal that had actually met anyone who was black'[4]), ultimately moving on to bona fide teen-issue movies.

Mount could see that the landscape needed to change. 'When I got to Universal they were making *W. C. Fields & Me* and *Gable and Lombard*. Creaky, dreadful potboilers. I walked to the commissary and I saw a vaguely familiar older fellow hobbling

---

1 Author interview.

2 National Association for the Advancement of Colored People.

3 Which he did, when Billy Dee Williams triumphed in the Outstanding Actor category for 1976's baseball comedy *The Bingo Long Traveling All-Stars & Motor Kings*.

4 Author interview.

across the lot. And I realised it was John Wayne. I thought John Wayne was dead! The generation gap was so *huge* at Universal. [And] this studio ... had no identity. Warner Brothers owned action ... they were good at it and they had a system, they had people who appreciated action pictures and that's what they did ... that's why it was the home of Eastwood ... Paramount, under Eisner and Diller ... they were making all kinds of films but they were darker, harder-edged ... and Fox owned romance. I looked around the landscape and realised no one was making comedy.'[1]

During his tenure at Universal, Mount increased the studio's output from six to twenty-five movies a year, half of which were comedies. The boss was happy. 'Lew loved it that we disturbed the system in those days. I'm not saying we didn't make mistakes. I mean you are talking to the man who gave *Xanadu* the go-ahead. So we did some stupid things too.'[2] Of the successes though, the hottest was a picture whose contrasts summed up perfectly the mindset of this new group of youngsters – these baby moguls – who were increasingly running Hollywood. The setting was nostalgic, looking back to their own youth in the early '60s, but the mood was chaotic and raunchy enough for Hollywood's new favourite target audience: contemporary teenagers. The film was also branded with a name familiar to the millions of students who read the satirical magazine which bore the same title. *National Lampoon's Animal House* scored the biggest laughs of 1978.

Though released only six weeks after *Grease* in '78, *Animal House* was the anti-Rydell High. Whilst Allan Carr had polished the Casey and Jacobs musical into his own perfectly coiffed teenage dream, *Animal House* – championed by Mount, one of the few Universal execs to 'get' its humour – was a ramshackle riot about college fraternities. The era was similar (*Animal House* was set in 1962, *Grease* 1959–60) and both boasted rock'n'roll as their backbone but Universal's comedy showed how Hollywood's new interest in a teen audience was a varied process. *Grease*'s wholesome revisionism of the past was one way of doing things, perfect for

---

1 Ibid.
2 Ibid.

the entire family. *Fever*'s social punch, meanwhile, was a way of catching the R-rated crowd. Both styles were entirely absent in *Animal House*.

For *Animal House* and the many films that entered the 1980s in its wake, there was a much simpler buzzword: raunch. The mood was raucous, the jokes dirty, the sex cheeky; more than enough to get hormonal teens rushing through the cinema doors. And in his position of power at Universal, Mount was perfectly placed to champion this youthful approach: 'This was where being a founding member of the baby-boom generation was really helpful.'[1]

If *Animal House, Grease* and *Happy Days* showcased a late '70s love of repackaging the past for a young audience, it wasn't a fad that came out of the blue. Perhaps none of the earnest movie brat directors from the early '70s would have made anything quite as frothy as those three, yet the very existence of characters such as Danny Zuko and the Fonz in 1978 owes much to the success of an iconic movie from the early days of the feisty New Hollywood era: George Lucas's *American Graffiti*.

Five years before *Animal House* soared to great heights for Universal, the same studio had seen *American Graffiti* establish its foundations. Here was the story of four teenage friends over one night in 1962, about to head their own way after graduating high school, in a story written and directed by the twenty-eight-year-old former USC (University of California) film student Lucas in order to get rid of frustrations after the failure of his experimental sci-fi pic *THX 1138*.[2] Lucas also wanted to prove to himself and his film-maker buddies Francis Coppola and Steven Spielberg that even a self-confessed nerd could make a film which appealed to a mainstream American audience, especially since commercial movies weren't really his thing. Actually, Lucas wanted to make what he referred to lyrically as 'tone poems' rather than regular stories, yet Coppola told him straight: 'Stop with the artsy-fartsy stuff.'[3] The result? *American Graffiti* was a huge popular success,

---

1 Author interview.

2 A reworking of one of Lucas's student films, *THX* just about covered its 800,000-dollar budget when released in 1971.

3 Interview with Charlie Rose on charlierose.com, 25 December 2015.

setting the stage for *Animal House* and many more. Over the next ten years or so, Hollywood – and beyond – couldn't get enough of revisiting the movie's early '60s rock'n'roll setting.

Despite *Graffiti* being made to prove a point, Lucas also wrote it from the heart, basing the story on his own cherished teenage memories of cruising in cars in his home town of Modesto, California. The plot might have been slight yet *Graffiti* wasn't just a film about how young lives always change. It was also about how America itself would change. In *Graffiti*'s '62, the peak years of the war in Vietnam and of civil unrest were still to come, Kennedy was still alive and the radio had yet to be overtaken by the 'British invasion' of The Beatles and The Stones. Here was a requiem as much as a celebration; a look back at a specific moment in US history that was perched on the edge of a rude awakening with a packed retro soundtrack to match.

Still, if *American Graffiti* was the past then it was the past with a twist; the old days with the benefit of hindsight. Lucas had even managed to turn the relatively mindless teen pastime of cruising in cars into something elegiac. Over at the offices of *National Lampoon* magazine, as the twenty-something writers penned their own cheekily nostalgic articles, many providing inspiration for what would become *Animal House*, they came up with their own less romantic spin on history: use the past to push the limits of taste.

Their reasoning made sense. Sure, life ten or fifteen years earlier might have *seemed* sweeter, more carefree, but it was precisely that carefree attitude that had made fertile ground for all kinds of outrageous pranks and stunts. Just because, for many years, the nation's moral guardians at the Motion Picture Association of America hadn't allowed those teenage pranks to be shown on the big screen didn't mean they hadn't happened. Come the mid-'70s, however, movies could get away with more; way more. Counter-culture had been testing the boundaries throughout the '60s and the new decade boasted a very different mood to its predecessor, with the MPAA loosening its guidelines. Now the baby boomers were in charge and the guys at *Lampoon* wanted to remind everyone that, as much as *American Graffiti* was hugely influential, growing up in the early '60s was a lot more raucous than just sweet-faced Ron Howard and doo-wop.

*

National Lampoon magazine was born in April 1970, the brain-child of former *Harvard Lampoon* editors Doug Kenney, Henry Beard and Rob Hoffman and published by Matty Simmons. Simmons – a wannabe mogul with a penchant for gold jewellery – had originally planned on a counterculture fanzine called *Cheetah* making him his fortune. Instead, when *Cheetah* failed, it was the slightly less rebellious *Weight Watchers* magazine that gave his company Twenty First Century Communications the cash to back *Lampoon*. Ultimately the Harvard boys would be bought out by Simmons but along the way the chaotic, daring and – crucially – hilarious writing that constituted *Lampoon* hit big with the baby-boomer crowd. An early issue featuring a naked Minnie Mouse on its cover got them much needed publicity (and, naturally, a lawsuit from Walt).

Producing *Lampoon* magazine from its tiny New York office often involved writers clashing but Doug Kenney's spliff-soaked charm was always there to soothe the bruised egos. Friends said Kenney was a genius: crazy-haired, eccentric, whip-smart but an outsider, at home and at school. He rewrote his suburban Cleveland childhood in short stories for the magazine, tweaking reality for comic effect, then put months into the creation of the now iconic *1964 High School Yearbook* parody (co-written with P. J. O'Rourke). Childhood friend Robert Sam Anson remembered Kenney's obsession with his teenage years in education, even after they were over: 'High school had always had a special hold on him. In some respects, he had never really left. He still wore his high-school jacket to work, still played high-school games, still told the same dumb high-school jokes. Indeed, he even walked like someone in high school, the step springy, the gait bumptious and jocky. As his classmate and *National Lampoon* collaborator John Weidman put it: "He would have used Clearasil if he could."'[1]

Lampoon was shifting a million, being read by millions more, entirely in tune with the post-Jack Valenti, post-*American Graffiti* sex-and-nostalgia boom. The brand even crossed over to

---

[1] 'The Life and Death of a Comic Genius', *Esquire*, Robert Sam Anson, October 1981.

stage revues, radio shows and albums. Boss Matty Simmons was all too aware that Kenney – the fast-thinking, hard-drinking creative provocateur of middle-American values – needed constant stimulation, else he'd quit. He'd already disappeared on a few occasions, spending a mysterious year in a tent on Martha's Vineyard. A *Lampoon* movie was the obvious next step to keep him busy.

Inspiration struck when Doug Kenney hooked up with Harold Ramis, a Chicago-born Marx Brothers fan in John Lennon glasses who'd worked his way from writing jokes for *Playboy* to scripting *Lampoon*'s *Radio Hour*. Together they tried to get a movie from the *Yearbook* spoof, ultimately deciding to move the action from high school to a raunchier college setting – sex sells, after all – bringing in fellow *Lampoon* regular Chris Miller to add in his own memories. Miller's story 'The Night of the Seven Fires' had already been in the magazine, detailing his former Dartmouth fraternity's bizarre vomiting ritual ('There is sick and then there is sick with elegance, inventiveness and innovation') and the trio hooked it into their story, adding in the 'Animal' of *Animal House* – the silently psychotic character of Bluto – as a part for Second City and *National Lampoon* stage regular John Belushi. Each writer worked on ten pages at a time, then handed them over for one of the others to discuss and polish. Meanwhile, Matty Simmons pitched the idea to studios endlessly. The response was always the same though: the treatment was ramshackle and sprawling, obviously the work of inexperienced film-writers. It also featured *way* too much throwing up.

Thom Mount certainly thought so when he found the idea for *Animal House* in that pile of unwanted scripts at Universal. And yet, there was *something* there; something retro like *American Graffiti*, yet modern too, daring enough for the young audiences who loved to see recognisable institutions from the past mercilessly mocked. After all, thirty-year-old Canadian writer Lorne Michaels had just made his satirical TV sketch show *Saturday Night Live* – a replacement for Johnny Carson reruns – a hit on NBC, proving sharp enough to warrant its position on network television at the same time as being zany enough to feel fresh and dangerous, a middle finger to the establishment.[1] So when Mount read the pages of Kenney, Ramis and Miller's script describing endless vomiting at Dartmouth College he wasn't *entirely* put off. The success of *SNL* convinced him that the mood of the nation felt right. Not to mention, as a fellow baby boomer, reading *National Lampoon* had just always made him really laugh.

Mount was never quite sure how his boss Ned Tanen would react to his ideas ('Today we would say he was bipolar'[2]) and, even though the *National Lampoon* project eventually got a green light, as things moved forward Tanen had his own idea for a director – James Frawley, who'd helmed The Monkees' TV shows. Mount found the choice baffling. *He* wanted John Landis, a Chicago film-maker still only in his twenties but who'd already worked in jobs as varied as mail boy, stunt double and assistant director, as well as helming his own low-budget horror pic *Schlock* in 1971. Landis had also just finished *Kentucky Fried Movie*, a sketch-based movie written by future *Airplane!* scribes David Zucker, Jerry Zucker and Jim Abrahams, featuring improv comics from both Chicago's Second City and LA's Groundlings troupes. In other words, *Kentucky Fried Movie* already had the air of a *National Lampoon* movie – not to mention Monty Python or *Saturday Night Live*. Thom Mount's assistant Sean Daniel also had a girlfriend who'd worked on the set with Landis and thought he was great, so what was the problem?

Mount decided not to outwardly disagree with Tanen, preferring instead to subtly suggest to Frawley that directing *Animal House* wouldn't be the right movie for him. Meanwhile, he got John Landis to begin a charm offensive aimed at Tanen: 'Knowing Tanen's take on life and that he was very interested in "statuesque girls", let's say, I asked Landis to put together a few comic sequences, particularly ones with girls with no tops on, and let me run it for Tanen, ten minutes in a screening room. Tanen saw that and pronounced it genius film-making and we were able to hire John.'[3]

---

1 The young stars of *SNL* – including *Lampoon* show veterans Belushi and Chevy Chase – were rebelliously named the 'Not-Ready-For-Prime-Time Players'.

2 Author interview.

3 Author interview.

James Frawley instead went to Barry Diller at Paramount and helmed *The Big Bus* for them, a disaster movie spoof that predated Zucker, Zucker and Abrahams' *Airplane!* and which Landis himself had once been in discussions to direct. It bombed.

'It had a sense of anarchy and real wit and it was brilliantly funny – but it was kind of hateful,' remembers John Landis of the *Animal House* script he eventually sat down to read.[1] At his suggestion – his main contribution to the writing, he claims – the conflict between rival frat boys in *Animal House* became simpler, a basic good-versus-bad. He also made sure that Belushi's Bluto, the story's comic beast, drifted in and out of scenes rather than being overused ('He's like a meteor, flashing across the sky'). What's more, *Animal House* lost all its barfing jokes. 'Doug Kenney was by far the smartest,' believes Mount of the writing team, 'but Harold Ramis was utterly the heart and soul of the operation. Chris Miller always likes to refer to himself as "the typist" but he's much more than that.'[2] With a new script in place, all that remained was for this bunch of screwy twenty-something film-makers to convince their older bosses that they knew who to cast.

Landis had already had trouble convincing Paramount that *The Big Bus* would be funnier if traditionally serious actors were cast in the comedy roles (Frawley's released version went the other way and featured comedians) and now he had the same problem with Ned Tanen at Universal. Tanen wanted famous names for *Animal House* – Belushi wasn't yet well-known enough to headline a movie on his own – but Landis felt filling his film with well-known comedians such as Chevy Chase and Dom DeLuise would throw the story's earthiness off balance. The compromise came in the form of Donald Sutherland, acclaimed after the success of *M*A*S*H*, *Don't Look Now* and *The Eagle Has Landed*. Landis knew Sutherland from his cameo in *Kentucky Fried Movie* and offered the actor either $40,000 or a cut of profits to leave shooting *Invasion of the Body Snatchers* in San Francisco for a couple of days and head over to the *Animal House* set in Eugene, Oregon to

---

1 'Animal House: The Movie That Changed Comedy', Chris neumer, *Stumped*, 2003.
2 Author interview.

play pot-smoking English tutor Professor Jennings. Thankfully Sutherland agreed, saving Mount and Landis from any more high-level interference for a while.[1] *Animal House* might have been at heart a teen movie about horny students but in the forty-three-year-old Sutherland, they finally had a star.

Filming, though, was often shaky. Aside from Thom Mount and Sean Daniel, Universal wasn't packed with youthful *Animal House* fans and the production was low-budget and under-the-radar (costume designer Deborah Nadoolman sewed togas with Judy Belushi, John's wife, for the infamous party scene). Tanen continued to blow hot and cold, as always, so Mount deliberately kept him in the dark, the Universal boss only discovering at the premiere of the movie that some scenes he'd wanted cut had actually been left in.[2] Still, this was a film with youthful, anti-establishment spirit and the tough filming conditions only added to its confrontational attitude. *Animal House* thrives on its roughness.

Universal released *Animal House* at the close of July 1978 in only twelve theatres but word spread fast. By the end of its run it had clocked an astonishing 140 million dollars, for many years America's highest grossing film comedy of all time. And the formula was simple: a dash of *American Graffiti* with a hit of counterculture rebellion, happily nostalgic whilst simultaneously dealing openly with the issues of sex, generational politics and race that the previous decade had opened up for it. More importantly though, *Animal House* was *funny*, teen cinema's earliest declaration of hilariously arrested development. Even Tony Manero seemed mature by comparison. *American Graffiti* had started a fad for adolescent remembrances but it was *Animal House* that dropped its trousers and pushed the craze into the next decade.

And all around the world. In West Germany, dubbed and re-titled *Ich Glaub', Mich Tritt ein Pferd* (loose translation: *You're Pulling*

---

1 But Sutherland lost potential millions by accepting the flat fee.

2 Tanen had worried that a sequence where the Delta boys turn up at an all-black nightclub was racist but Mount showed it to his friend Richard Pryor who insisted it be left in. By the time of the premiere, there was nothing Tanen could do to change it.

My Leg!), *Animal House* pulled in 800,000 Marks; a decent amount, but such was the popularity there of crazy movie teens obsessed with tits, ass and Bill Haley that *Animal House* actually had competition. Yes, late '70s teen cinema in West Germany certainly enjoyed Bluto, Otter and Boon and their antics at Faber College but actually it was even *more* interested in the boys from *Lemon Popsicle.*

Lemon Popsicle – or *Eis am Stiel,* as it was known in the *kinos* of the Bundesrepublik – was Europe and the Med's own *Animal House*, an Israeli movie written and directed by Boaz Davidson. By 1978 the film-maker was already a veteran of his local industry, sometimes helming as many as three pictures a year, frequently for the well-known showbiz moguls (and real-life cousins) Yoram Globus and Menahem Golan. Tellingly, Davidson was only a year older than Harold Ramis and a year younger than Chris Miller, so when he got the chance to make his own autobiographical take on baby-boom nostalgia, his teenage memories of Tel Aviv were pretty much the same as the *Animal House* boys' all-American reminiscing: rock'n'roll and sex.

But *Lemon Popsicle*'s obstacles were arguably even greater than those that *Animal House* had to overcome. Firstly, it would be filmed in Hebrew, hardly the universal language of teenage horniness. Then Menaham Golan had a sudden change of heart, proudly declaring that he wasn't keen on handing over his money to fund such a lowbrow project, thinking himself a weighty film producer above such teenage smut (he wasn't).

It was Golan's younger cousin, Yoram Globus, who could understand more of what *Lemon Popsicle* was saying about being a teenager and who ultimately gave it the go-ahead. It was a smart move. By the end of 1978, Boaz Davidson's story of his adolescence had not just hit big in Israel but had also miraculously crossed the sea and given Europe something both decidedly ruder and yet – in the story's emotional third act – also something more sensitive than the States had to offer with *Animal House*. Indeed, it was a tough abortion storyline and downbeat conclusion that hindered *Popsicle* ever seeing a major release in America ('The whole making of the movie was like therapy for a little wound that I had,' admits Davidson of the film's melancholy mood[1]). Not that the lack of US interest ultimately hindered Davidson, Globus and Golan. Yes, they worshipped Hollywood movies and dreamed of working there but for a while they could wallow in the fact that *Lemon Popsicle* had played at the Berlin Film Festival, was nominated for a Golden Globe and during its first run alone was seen by over a third of Israel's population.

Animal House was riotous but *Lemon Popsicle* flashed more flesh. America had flirted with porno chic of course, yet it seemed that Europe was the real home of softcore teen comedies in the '70s, sex catching on there in mainstream cinemas in a way that the States could only replicate on the sleazier 'grindhouse' circuit or later with the rise of home video. And in *Popsicle*, nudity was all just part of the nostalgia; simultaneously crude and innocent, authentic fumblings supposedly indicative of gentler times whilst still giving modern teen audiences a cheap thrill. *Popsicle*'s characters were younger than *Animal House*'s and arguably even more horny but there was no moral outrage over its content, just a lot of retro soundtrack albums sold.

Around a third of the movie's budget was used to pay music royalties but it made back over four times its cost in Israel alone. Even the German box-office added up to 2,700,000 Marks; less than *Nur Samstag Nacht* (*Saturday Night Fever*) and *Schmiere* (*Grease*) but still enough to make this little Jewish pic the eleventh biggest of 1978.

Germans, in particular, flocked to see teenage naughtiness that year. *Popcorn und Himbeereis* (*Popcorn and Raspberry Ripple*) was a homegrown sex comedy whose name obviously riffed on *Popsicle*'s and even featured the Israeli film's Zachi Noy. *Summer Night Fever*, meanwhile, was a teen road-trip movie about contemporary lads heading to Ibiza, bearing little resemblance to the Travolta hit it ripped off in its title. Meanwhile, Italy's high-school based *La Liceale* series – known as *Teasers* in English and *Flotte Teens und Heiße Jeans* (*Loose Teens and Tight Jeans*) for the German market – made a star of former beauty queen Gloria Guida that year.

---

1 Commentary on the Blu-ray of *The Last American Virgin*, the US remake of *Popsicle*, also helmed by Davidson.

The UK tended to keep its sex comedies in the private cinemas of Soho but the *Confessions* series was one mainstream hit; a saucier, younger version of the established *Carry Ons*, featuring rubber-faced Robin Askwith as a boyish, randy oik from Clapham called Timmy. It's true that most of these European offerings concentrated more on cheeky smut than genuine youth issues, yet they showed that this new focus on teen sex comedy had gone global. And, outside of Hollywood's big-business restrictions and still relatively tight moral reins, it could be considerably dirtier too. At the end of the decade and flush with their *Popsicle* success, Boaz Davidson, Menahem Golan and Yoram Globus finally crossed the Atlantic to see what they could achieve by buying the B-movie production house Cannon Films in California. At last they were in their dream location and they wasted no time in stating their intentions, splashing press ads all through Hollywood that shone with optimism: 'Cannon Films – with the '80s in mind!'

Over in New York in 1978, a twenty-eight-year-old advertising exec was spending more and more time at the *National Lampoon* magazine offices. He came from Chicago but luckily had clients in the Big Apple that he visited every week and when he eventually got to know the right people at the magazine and showed them his comedy writing, they were seriously impressed. Anyone could see that this chubby guy with a mop of brown hair and round glasses could really tell a story. So it was that *National Lampoon* employed John Hughes.

'Getting into the *Lampoon* was like a Boy Scout initiation or something,' Hughes always remembered. 'They'd be very cruel to you until you made someone laugh, then they welcomed you into the fold. As it turned out, my timing was perfect, because once *Animal House* came out in the summer of '78, breaking all sorts of box-office records and so on, Hollywood, in their infinite wisdom, came knocking and gave every writer at the magazine a development deal, including myself. I looked at that, thought, Hell, this is easy, and flew out to Los Angeles and got four more development deals like that. Again, it's Hollywood jumping on the hot property – tell them you just got a deal, they'll want a part of you sight unseen. "We want to offer you a deal." "Hey, great, I just got two this morning!" I went back home and there was a gigantic snowstorm in the winter of 1979, couldn't leave the house for two weeks, so I just hunkered down and wrote.'[1]

What John Hughes wrote would continue in the vein of *Lampoon*'s focus on family life and hapless adolescents but, on the other hand, he wasn't all about sex and nostalgia. On 13 April 1980, *Grease* the stage show significantly closed its initial run on Broadway after eight years and Hughes was certainly one baby boomer pleased to leave behind that cultural obsession with the past and pick up on the mood change of a new decade. After all, the '80s was a time of fresh music, groundbreaking technology and energising politics so why just focus on how things used to be? *American Graffiti*, *Animal House* and *Lemon Popsicle* had undeniably made their point and put millions in the bank for Lucas, Universal and Golan and Globus . . . but what about teenage life right *now*?

---

1 'John Hughes: Straight Outta Shermer', *Lollipop*, Issue 47, William Ham, spring 1999.

Chapter Three

THE ORDINARY NOW

Discovering Tom Cruise, Sean Penn and Timothy Hutton in Taps; *Ordinary People celebrates the normal (and wins Oscars); and Brooke Shields – 1980s America's (first) favourite girl-next-door.*

Casting directors are part of a film's secret glue, to the outside world virtually invisible. The industry doesn't include casting in the Academy Awards, to the consternation of many, and even a director of casting's film credit is only 'casting by', as the Directors Guild of America have never been too keen on any other crew member using the precious 'D' word.

Then there are many of the movie-goers themselves, thankful for the films but probably unaware of the clandestine process it takes to find the right actors for the right roles; a search lasting an average of three months for a Hollywood movie. Perhaps revealing to the public that *lots* of actors might have been considered for a role spoils some of the mystery of a great movie for an audience? Maybe insiders don't want to let on that it didn't just all happily fall into place in the way we might like to think it did? Rather than be faced with the mechanics, we just prefer the illusion. The *New York Times*, in an article describing casting directors as 'equal parts drama critic, matchmaker and conjurer',[1] clearly didn't just use that last word for the hell of it.

---

1 Shirley Rich, Grand Dame of Casting, Dies at Eighty-Seven', *New York Times*, Margalit Fox, 12 January 2010.

On *Saturday Night Fever*, casting director Shirley Rich had excelled herself at 'conjuring', searching long and hard for boys to play Tony's gang of wise-guy best friends: Joseph Cali (Joey), Bruce Ornstein (Gus) and Barry Miller (Bobby C) etc. They were all rough-around-the-edges supporting actors that never went on to Travolta-level fame but who were nevertheless perfect for that moment in time, ideal smartass buddies who mixed cheekiness with anger. As the new decade arrived, 'smartass' certainly seemed to be a thing; young male characters as feisty as the young male baby-boomer execs calling the shots. Rich, approaching retirement age, now found herself at the forefront of this new demand for cocky hotshots.

Of course, she had her favourites. A nineteen-year-old New Jersey kid called Tom Cruise was one; Jimmy Spader, a twenty-one-year-old school drop-out from Boston, was another, both with a youthful bravado that Rich spotted early during auditions for the 1981 military drama *Taps*. Cruise ultimately won a part in the film – cadet captain David Shawn – although Spader just missed out on playing fellow cadet Alex Dwyer. Still, it was while scouting for *Taps* – the story of a group of army students who forcibly take over their academy in a bid to stop its closure – that Shirley Rich also noticed someone who would go on to be her most acclaimed, *most* smartass, discovery. Sean Penn was the same age as Spader and still working with his home town Los Angeles Repertory Theatre when the veteran casting director first saw him but there was something there, a dynamism, that was enough to beat the Boston boy to the part.

Penn's potential as a future brat of Hollywood was almost too perfect: parents who'd themselves been actors – Eileen Ryan and Leo Penn, the latter blacklisted in the late '50s for his trade union activities and subsequently forced to make a living as a TV director – and an education at Santa Monica High School alongside fellow Hollywood offspring Emilio, Ramon, Renée and Carlos 'Charlie' Estevez,[1] plus up-and-coming young actors Chad and Rob Lowe. Penn has described those years with his friends and his brothers Michael and Chris as idyllic, a mix of surf and fist fights – 'a

---

1 The children of actors Martin Sheen and Janet Templeton.

combination of Huck Finn and *Rumble Fish*'[1] – and they'd all dabble with stage, TV and film roles between classes. Most fun, though, were the home movies they made out of school, with Chris Penn 'the film-making auteur of the neighbourhood' according to Rob Lowe: 'In Malibu in the '70s, it was always time to make a Super 8 film about 'Nam. Oh, and Charlie made a great movie starring his buddy Johnny Depp where the whole premise was blowing up the Fotomat. Remember Fotomats? Anyway, what Laurel Canyon was to music in 1968 and 1970, Malibu was to young actors. The acting coach Peggy Feury lived there.[2] And [author and champion of new journalism] Joan Didion. My brother went to school with her daughter, Quintana. Like, at the Christmas pageant you'd be sitting next to Joan Didion. The place was fucking unreal.'[3] SaMoHi, the school was known as, an acronym as cool as the kids who went there. The building had even been used in *Rebel Without a Cause*, the most famous movie of the teen star to whom Penn bore more than a passing resemblance: James Dean. Shirley Rich can't have failed to see the fire in his genes.

Pre-*Taps*, Sean Penn's screen career was limited to a few TV films, a teen role in an episode of *Barnaby Jones* (about a retired, milk-drinking detective) and a bit part in NBC's soft '70s favourite *Little House on the Prairie*. That particular episode of *Prairie* – 1974's 'The Voice Of Tinker Jones' – was directed by Penn Sr and saw a fourteen-year-old Sean resplendent in check shirt and floppy hat of the old west, helping Walnut Grove's mute outsider Jones build a bell for the local church. *Cute.* Both Penns involved – father and son – must surely have quaked at the show's soppiness, so far removed from their more belligerent attitudes. In real life, Sean was the boy who had a quote from Declaration of Independence author Thomas Jefferson stencilled on to his bedroom door ('Our children are born free and their freedom is a gift of nature and not of those who gave them birth') and who knew, from an early age,

---

1 *Rolling Stone*, Mark Binelli, 19 February 2009. There's more on *Rumble Fish* – Francis Coppola's dreamlike teen gang movie – in Chapter 6.

2 Feury taught Sean Penn four days a week, in four-hour sessions, saying, 'He was always concerned with being physically connected. And that it be really organic', from 'Sean Penn: Bad Boy. Slab Boy. Everyboy', *Rolling Stone*, Christopher Connolly, 26 May 1983.

3 *GQ*, Amy Wallace, 22 September 2015.

his politics: 'I was born in 1960, so the primary television show that my brothers and I grew up watching was the Vietnam War. I grew up in a family that was opposed to it.'[1]

Penn's *Taps* co-star Tom Cruise, by contrast, was nowhere near as radical; nowhere near as *Californian*. Actually Cruise – born Thomas Cruise Mapother IV – had spent his childhood moving around thanks to Tom Sr's job as an electrical engineer, pitching up at fifteen schools in fourteen years, all told. The travelling hit hard and Tom Sr and Mary Lee divorced when their son was twelve. Mary Lee – a special education teacher – took Tom and his sisters to Kentucky for a while and then to New Jersey when she remarried. The teenage Tom finally settled in school but struggled with his dyslexia. Really it was only on the baseball and hockey fields that he excelled, as well as proving a handful on the wrestling mat. 'I look back on high school and grade school and I would never want to go back there. Not in a million years,'[2] he remembers, but Cruise's formative years were right there in his performance in *Taps*: that mixture of discipline and ingenuity that's needed both in sports and the military: '. . . a lot of that character was my childhood,' Cruise told *Interview* magazine.[3] 'I have an aggressive side, absolutely. I need a creative outlet. Now I work out every day. I get up and work out forty-five to sixty minutes. And that's how I start my day. Discipline is very important to me.' And in George C. Scott's character of General Bache there's the firm-but-fair father figure he never had.[4]

Cruise's move from the school gym to the stage came when he played Nathan Detroit in a class production of *Guys and Dolls*. Finally, he felt at home. After the first night he asked his mother and stepdad for ten years to prove himself in showbusiness. In a hint of what determination was to come, he easily beat that goal. Within twelve months the teenage Tom had moved to New York, worked as a busboy at society restaurant Mortimer's, hired and

---

1 From a 2011 interview with CNN, quoted in 'Sean Penn: a firebrand on and off screen', *Guardian*, Peter Beaumont, 18 February 2012.

2 'Tom Cruise: Winging it from *Risky Business* to *Top Gun*', *Rolling Stone*, Christopher Connelly, 19 June 1986.

3 May 1986.

4 A type that would recur in plentiful Cruise films over the years: Robert Duvall in *Days of Thunder*, Paul Newman in *The Color of Money*, even Jason Robards in *Magnolia*.

fired his first manager (Tobe Gibson) and attracted Shirley Rich's attention for a small role in *Taps*. But even then he was poised to over-achieve. After already being cast, he quickly got upgraded to a bigger part – the significant supporting character of Shawn – taking over from another actor. 'Cruise was so strong that the other guy didn't have a chance,' Sean Penn admitted. 'Very intense, two hundred percent there. It was overpowering – and we'd all kind of laugh, because it was so sincere. Good acting, but so far in the intense direction that it was funny.'[1] Yet Cruise was still so green he nearly turned down the bigger role, not wanting to annoy anyone. Once he accepted though, the extra screen time allowed him to really hit hard. It's no surprise he once took his Catholicism so seriously he considered becoming a priest. As Shawn, head shaved and uniform pristine, there's something almost fanatical about him; boyish but fastidious.

The lead role in *Taps*, however, went to an actor who'd already gotten his break from another casting director, Penny Perry. He was also no cocky wise-guy, that type still mainly – at this point – confined to best friend characters like Tom or Sean, as part of an ensemble. Yes, *this* boy was someone resolutely normal, straight-forward and well-behaved. In a word, ordinary.

Timothy Hutton, this archetypal boy-next-door, had been cast by Penny Perry in his first film a year or so earlier: a Robert Redford-directed movie called, appropriately enough, *Ordinary People*. As a result of that debut, right in the middle of filming *Taps* alongside Penn and Cruise in March 1981, the twenty-year-old Hutton found himself leaving the Valley Forge Military Academy in Pennsylvania and heading to Los Angeles for a night. Sure, he and the guys had often escaped the place after hours to go driving: 'We had a great stereo system . . . and we used to play very loud music and drive through the Pennsylvania countryside.' Plus the three had planned – although never pulled off – a helicopter ride over a nearby golf course hosting the US Open, where they would let off smoke bombs and blast out 'Ride of the Valkyries', *Apocalypse Now*-style.[2] *This* outing, though, was something much

---

1 *Rolling Stone*, 19 June 1986, op cit.
2 'Sean Penn: Bad Boy. Slab Boy. Everyboy', op cit.

more grown-up. Hutton was leaving *Taps* for a night to go and win an Oscar.

The Academy Awards that spring of '81 saw Robert De Niro win Best Actor for his archetypal Method performance in Scorsese's *Raging Bull*, a role that required him to not only undertake gruelling boxing training but to also put on thirty kilos for later scenes as the out-of-shape Jake La Motta. 'I feel I have to earn the right to play a part,' he once admitted.[1] It was quite the statement. De Niro rarely revealed *anything*. He hadn't even turned up to collect his Supporting Actor gong in 1975.

As a bold, visceral experience, *Raging Bull* was the crowning achievement of Scorsese and the New Hollywood auteurs; a film that completed the '70s, the decade in which they'd found megastardom, and which was an unforgiving piece of storytelling where dramatic brutality – and levels of commitment to a role – peaked.

Yet for every young star who dreamed of replicating that dedication there was the same old problem, the one that John Travolta knew all about: *Raging Bull* was becoming an exception, an anomaly. So all those hungry teenage performers in awe of the dark passion of De Niro as Jake La Motta (or Pacino as Serpico, Hackman as Popeye Doyle) now found Hollywood in 1981 a very different place. The simpler, teen-focused characters on offer just weren't comparable to the more profound films they dreamed of making, producers unwilling to take chances if audiences weren't. Even *Raging Bull* only just broke even, panicking Scorsese about his future.

So on the very same night that De Niro heard his name announced by Sally Field at the Academy Awards, watched by Timothy Hutton in the audience, the star's *Deer Hunter* director Michael Cimino was facing four years in the wilderness, floundering after the costly debacle of *Heaven's Gate*. Meanwhile Francis Coppola, De Niro's *Godfather Part 2* collaborator, was about to start on *One from the Heart*, the fantasy musical whose budget would balloon so much it would bankrupt him ('in a man,

---

1 'The Shadow King', *Vanity Fair*, Patricia Bosworth, 3 February 2014.

the line between enthusiasm and megalomania is very blurry,' Coppola has confessed of his self-destructive personality[1]). And over at the Golden Raspberry Awards, held that year in organiser John Wilson's house, De Niro's once-celebrated peers Pacino and De Palma – ridiculed following *Cruising* and *Dressed to Kill* – were having their work read out in the same breath as *Can't Stop the Music* and *Xanadu*.[2] Like Travolta's '78, De Niro's '80 was the best of times *and* the worst.

Plus, there was an even darker side to the New Hollywood phenomenon hanging in the air that night, something way more disturbing than simple box-office disappointment. Whilst the whole world knew, as De Niro stepped up to the podium to collect his award, that the day before had seen an assassination attempt on the new US President Ronald Reagan (resulting in the ceremony being delayed by twenty-four hours), what many didn't realise quite yet was how De Niro's acting had played a part in it. Pretty soon though, everyone would.

The subsequent revelations about John Hinckley Jr – Reagan's wannabe killer at the Hilton Hotel in Washington on 30 March 1981 – made it all clear: the twenty-five year old from Dallas had been obsessed with *Taxi Driver*, De Niro's mid-'70s collaboration with Martin Scorsese, watching it a reported fifteen times. Hinckley Jr saw De Niro's character of Travis Bickle as a kindred spirit: another loner, misunderstood by the system, depressed and fascinated by violence. He was also so smitten by Jodie Foster, playing teenage prostitute Iris, that he followed her to Yale University, enrolling in a writing course to be near the eighteen year old, who had gone there to study literature.

Foster had wanted time out of the spotlight, an ordinary life, despite knowing what it might mean for her profile: 'It was probable that my acting career would be over once I got out of college. It was unheard of to leave the business right at that age . . . regardless, there was no way I wasn't going to college. I really loved being a student and hoped that someday (when I was told

---

1 *Rolling Stone*, David Breskin, 7 February 1991.

2 De Palma had originally considered directing *Cruising* himself but delved into the darker corners of human sexuality with *Dressed to Kill* instead. William Friedkin's original choice of lead for *Cruising* was not Pacino but Richard Gere.

my acting career would most certainly come to a grinding halt) I could write scripts, novels and perhaps direct films one day.'[1] Yet with the news about Hinckley Jr, Foster's first year at Yale brought her more attention than any leading role. Authorities were aware of Hinckley Jr's issues but as no arrest ever came, he simply carried on obsessing, convincing himself that only a major crime would get Foster to notice him. So, just like Bickle in *Taxi Driver*, he decided to kill a politician.

Despite the panic that followed the shooting – the Russians were even briefly suspects, due to what was considered an unusual build-up of their submarines off the coast of the Atlantic – the Oscars went off without a hitch that night. Johnny Carson presented for the third year in a row. Dolly Parton, Irene Cara and Dionne Warwick all sang their nominated songs. There was even a video message from Ronald Reagan himself, America's first actor president, recorded several days earlier. The evening was all over in a relatively swift – at least for the Oscars – three and a quarter hours.

Yet whilst *Raging Bull* triumphed in the Best Actor and Best Editing categories (the latter for Thelma Schoonmaker), some felt its missing out on Best Picture and Best Director to Robert Redford's domestic drama *Ordinary People* was a message. For industry voters, *Raging Bull* was easy to be impressed by, difficult to love. The two films had battled during the whole awards season, *Ordinary People*'s frequent triumphs (Golden Globes, Directors Guild, National Board of Review) proving a win for the down-to-earth and normal after a decade where the movie brats had gotten, for many, too dense and too indulgent, letting drugs and ego take over their talent.

'Scorsese is of a generation of movie-makers whose history seems to be composed of the movies they've watched,' wrote Chris Hodenfield in his profile of the director in *Rolling Stone* during the summer of '77. 'They celebrate other film-maker's memories.'[2] When the Hinckley Jr revelation came out, some interpreted it as just more proof that this 'celebration' had gone way too far and

---

1 Author interview.
2 'The Secret Code Between De Niro and Scorsese', *Rolling Stone*, 16 June 1977.

was now so warped it was suffocating reality. *Ordinary People*, the story of a family coming to terms with the death of their oldest son, focused on the everyday and the domestic, where mourning mixed reassuringly with dinner table chitter-chatter about neighbours ('Good God! Not the Murrays!') If Jake La Motta was larger than life, *Ordinary People* was just *life* (albeit a very white, middle-class one). In 1981 lots of young stars in Hollywood no doubt did *still* want to be De Niro. Travolta, for sure. Penn, too, was a vocal champion and – eventually – a friend. Yet times had undeniably changed. Suddenly New Hollywood wasn't looking as much fun to be part of as it once had.

De Niro was thirty-seven when he won the Oscar that night, the first ceremony where all four acting awards had gone to performers under forty. All the New Hollywood big guns, though, were hitting middle age: De Palma celebrating his fortieth a few months earlier, Coppola the year before, Scorsese a few months later. Of course they weren't exactly *old* but they were still all old enough to be the father of Timothy Hutton, that boy who'd left the set of *Taps* to attend the event. The Best Supporting Actor winner – who had been so appealingly wide-eyed and confused as mourning teen Conrad Jarrett in *Ordinary People* – was half their age.

Timothy Hutton might not be the first name associated with '80s teen stars – and he was actually only a teenager for the first seven months of the decade – but he was the first of a new breed of young stars to be rewarded at the highest level. As the movie brat directors, all now at a stage where such a nickname hardly applied, entered their fallow period, they were replaced not just by much younger stars like Hutton but also by more homely, contemporary stories like *Ordinary People*. Divorce drama *Kramer vs Kramer* had taken home the Best Picture Oscar the year before (beating *Apocalypse Now*), family weepie *Terms of Endearment* would do the same a couple of years later, at a ceremony where none of the names so associated with groundbreaking '70s cinema were even nominated. With its middle-class suburban Chicago family, *Ordinary People* had the set-up of the kind of cosy and domestic '80s comedy that was blossoming on TV around the same time – *Growing Pains*, *The Facts of Life* – just without the jokes.

'I think the upper class and middle class have gotten short-changed in our [American] drama,' Robert Redford explained to the *New York Times*, on the set of *Ordinary People*, 'which is one of the reasons this project interests me. The liberal notion seems to be that you're not making anything worthwhile unless it's about the poor. [But] in some of these communities where appearances are everything, somebody who seems to be having trouble mentally or emotionally is cast out. It's death.' Redford was also unequivocally critical of the New Hollywood style that had dominated the previous decade: 'I guess the directors I respond to best are the older ones, from the days when there weren't any cinema schools – the pioneers with fresh approaches who didn't spend a lot of time over-analysing their craft but who operated strictly from their gut. I've always been impatient with directors who over-intellectualise.'[1] It made sense. While it was true that Redford had worked with film school graduate Coppola on the 1974 version of *The Great Gatsby*, Coppola was then the writer rather than director (what's more, his script was significantly changed during filming). Really, Redford's greatest acting successes weren't with any of the movie brats but with seemingly much more straightforward directors such as Sydney Pollack and George Roy Hill.

At the centre of Redford's movie was the teenage Timothy Hutton. He'd been deemed 'supporting' by the Academy but really he was the focus of the story, just not as famous as the supposedly leading actors playing his parents, Donald Sutherland and Mary Tyler Moore. In this new environment of the normal and everyday, Hutton seemed ideally unexceptional, boasting a middle-of-the-road personality that was perfectly suited to the unaffected charm of *Ordinary People* as well as the plea for understanding that sat at the heart of *Taps*.

His father was Jim Hutton, the tall, languid star of detective show *Ellery Queen*, who'd played in a number of movies during the '60s and who was once considered a successor to the down-to-earth Jimmy Stewart. Tim was equally unpretentious: undeniably fresh yet reassuringly old-fashioned. As he gave his Oscar

---

1 'Robert Redford Goes Behind the Camera for a New Image', *New York Times*, Clifford Terry, 27 July 1980.

acceptance speech, looking like a boy uncomfortably wearing a tuxedo for the first time and thanking his dad who had died the year before, young Hutton still wasn't even sure he was in the right job: 'I was interested in sports, I was interested in music, I was interested in maybe going to school to become an architect . . . I know it sounds kinda strange, but I guess it's because I wasn't someone who always wanted to be an actor. It was slow in coming, where I realised, OK, well, this is what I'm going to be doing.'[1]

Despite being the son of a Hollywood actor, Hutton's teacher mother had brought him up on the east coast, before coming back to California when Tim was a teenager, reuniting with his father for the final years of his life. Hutton attended Fairfax High School – a couple of grades above a girl called Demi Moore – then took some drama classes and made a few TV appearances before Penny Perry cast him in *Ordinary People*. It was a giant leap. Redford told the rest of the cast to ignore him, to help the teenager feel as isolated as his depressed character. 'From the moment I got the phone call that I'd got the part, all the way through every day of filming, I just had to keep it out of my head how excited I was and how big it was to me,' he remembered. 'You know, the script, the character, the book [the novel by Judith Guest], the people I was working with . . . I just had to sort of keep myself very focused and have a level-headed appreciation of where I was.'[2]

Hutton's Academy Award win was a landmark, hinting at a new generation of talent, although eighteen months earlier, at the Sheraton Hotel in Universal City, the inaugural Youth in Film Awards had got there first, albeit without the international prestige of the Oscars. Held to recognise the contributions of performers under the age of twenty-one in film, TV, theatre and music and organised by Maureen Dragone, daughter of Golden Globe co-founder Nora Laing, big winners the first year included twenty-one-year-old Dennis Christopher for his performance in coming-of-age cycling drama *Breaking Away* – a *Saturday Night Fever* with racing bikes – and fifteen-year-old Diane Lane for hers in *A Little Romance*. For Dennis Christopher, *Breaking Away*'s

---

1 'Timothy Hutton, from *Ordinary People* and *Taps* to a *Cars* video', The AV Club, Will Harris, 10 March 2015.

2 Ibid.

awards success was his peak. For the already experienced Lane, a Broadway regular who'd struggled with her parents' broken marriage and briefly run away to LA, bigger things were still to come, not to mention a romance with Hutton that would see her as his date on his big Oscar night in 1981. But it was Hutton who hit the biggest awards jackpot first; the polite prince of early '80s Hollywood, America's favourite good-natured teenage son before Penn, Cruise and others exported their feistier charm from supporting roles into leads. If film-makers were searching for a boy who was homely and innocent, he was the first choice. He returned to the set of *Taps* as the hottest young star in Hollywood.

If early '80s casting directors wanted a girl with similarly innocent charms as Tim Hutton, the choice was equally clear. Brooke Shields was younger – just fifteen years old – but she already had the picture editors of countless teen magazines scrabbling to put her fresh face on their covers.

Yet if Shields seemed normal, her childhood had been anything but. Born in 1965, she was taken to New York City to model before she was even a year old. Ten years later, Eileen Ford of the famous Ford Modelling Agency – then home to the in-demand Jerry Hall, Lauren Hutton and Kim Basinger – started up a children's department just for Brooke. It was Shields' single mom Teri who raised her; a 'crazy alcoholic' according to her daughter, 'but she was also fierce in protecting me'.[1] As a result Brooke was clean-cut and well-educated – the archetypal girl-next-door – but Teri's personal issues made for some bizarre decisions. Aged ten, Brooke was photographed naked by fashion snapper Gary Gross, entirely with her mother's consent. At twelve she played a child prostitute in Louis Malle's *Pretty Baby*. By 1980 she was advertising Calvin Klein's new range of diffusion line jeans in a series of commercials shot by Richard Avedon. 'You want to know what comes between me and my Calvins?' she teased. 'Nothing.' ABC and CBS weren't impressed, banning the ads in some areas due to the inference – disputed by Klein – that Brooke was wearing no underwear. True or not, she was still legally a child.

---

1 *Daily Mail*, Louette Harding, 27 April 2010.

Yet it was that contrast between sexiness and purity that made Shields' name. On the one hand, she was no blonde bombshell, ornamented by make-up. Rather her figure was gangly, her demeanour sedate, her hair a serious, scholastic brown. On the other hand, her mother loved to orchestrate high-profile relationships for her – teen actors Scott Baio and Leif Garrett, plus of course, John Travolta, 'names that connoted fame, money, and power'[1] – and for her two biggest films she appeared in various states of undress, playing a virgin experiencing first love and first sex. The mix worked. Whilst Teri's morals might have been questionable, for the few years that Brooke lit up the newsstands on myriad street corners, the look-but-don't-touch darling of teen showbiz, her mom seemed like a publicity genius.

In the June of 1978 Randal Kleiser invited Brooke to the New York premiere of *Grease*, a glittery night at Ian Schrager and Steve Rubell's infamous Studio 54. The club had only opened the year before and would only last a couple more before Schrager and Rubell served time for tax evasion,[2] but it was already a regular celebrity hangout for the likes of Andy Warhol, Farah Fawcett and Liza Minnelli. Newton-John and Travolta wore versions of their Sandy and Danny costumes that evening; Allan Carr partied with Elton John and Grace Jones.

In between the celebrating, Kleiser gave Shields a book he wanted her to read: Henry De Vere Stacpoole's *The Blue Lagoon*. The story of children stranded on a desert island, who grow up and fall in love, had been filmed before but not for thirty years and Kleiser, hot from *Grease*, could now do almost whatever he wanted. And what he wanted was to film this story of 'how humans would develop if they had no nurture, only nature',[3] with Shields as the female lead: teenage innocent Emmeline ('She looked perfect for the part,' Kleiser says, simply[4]).

Filming for *The Blue Lagoon* took place a year later on Nanuya Levu, a Fijian island, working from a script by Kleiser's *Boy in the*

---

1 *There Was a Little Girl: The Real Story of My Mother and Me*, Brooke Shields, Plume, 2015, p.217.
2 In January 2017, Schrager received a full, complete and unconditional Presidential Pardon from President Barack Obama.
3 From *Buffalo Zine*, interview by Vincente Ferrer.
4 Author interview.

Plastic Bubble writer Douglas Day Stewart. For Shields this was already her seventh film role but her co-star was an eighteen-year-old sailing fanatic with no acting experience called Christopher Atkins, surprisingly hired by Kleiser and casting director Vic Ramos to play male lead Richard. Ramos had a hot new discovery on his books called Matt Dillon who he actually thought perfect for the role but Dillon's mom wasn't so keen. So, after over two thousand boys tried for the part, the blonde Atkins from Westchester, New York, found himself pushed into the spotlight. He'd only auditioned on the recommendation of an agent he knew from sailing class. Now he was being encouraged by Kleiser to really fall in love with the famous teen model – even told to put photos of her by his bed, to speed up the process – who was his co-star.

Filming on a remote island for *The Blue Lagoon* proved a bonding experience as everyone stayed in nearby boats or tents on the beach. Sure enough, there were also rumours of an off-screen romance between the leads: 'It was one of the most magical moments of my life, to be on this deserted island for four months and share all that time with her,' Atkins recalled,[1] although Shields was slightly less poetic: 'Chris and I were never romantic.'[2] Instead, she claimed, they bickered and wound each other up, leaving respected cinematographer Néstor Almendros – fresh from winning an Oscar for *Days of Heaven* – to employ his trademark love of natural light to cover up the frostiness and produce a seductively lush sheen. Meanwhile, underwater documentarians Ron and Valerie Taylor filmed the aquatic scenes with relish whilst Brooke and Christopher spent most of the movie with their tops off. Teri kept a watchful eye over her daughter, then partied with the big-drinking Australian crew.

The Blue Lagoon premiered at LA's Cinerama Dome in June 1980, its sensuality easy to see on the screen; for many too easy. The picture was R-rated but Brooke's own age was always going to make it a draw for younger viewers. The film-makers, meanwhile, had to assure the media that an older body double

---

1 'The Blue Lagoon turns thirty-five!' people.com, 3 July 2015.
2 *There Was A Little Girl . . .*, op. cit., p.15.

(actually Valerie Taylor) was used for many of her topless scenes, with Teri gleefully repeating the fact to the press as if to prove that she wasn't a bad mother after all.

'Kids found a way to get into the film. There wasn't a lot of security to keep them out,' admits Kleiser. 'It didn't occur to me that there would be a problem [about the nude scenes]. I was surprised when I heard the attacks that it was kiddie porn. Columbia put a full page ad in the *New York Times* proclaiming it was a "story of natural love".'[1]

Janet Maslin, the film critic over at the same newspaper, wasn't quite so kind: 'Miss Shields' hardest job . . . is to pretend she is giving birth to a baby without ever having wondered why she's put on so much weight. Her second hardest is to keep the wind from ruffling her hair.'[2] Even Shields herself never seemed to deny her Golden Raspberry nomination for Worst Actress was justified, admitting: 'Let's face it, the acting in *The Blue Lagoon* wasn't exactly great.'[3] What might have been a study of how teens coped once their main adult influence is lost (Leo McKern plays Paddy, the children's jovial but drunken mentor who soon succumbs to the ravages of liquor) ultimately failed to go the distance, merely reinforcing traditional roles – Richard the brave hunter, Emmeline the fragile beauty – or just looking the other way. *The Blue Lagoon* was a film that preferred a pretty shot of South Pacific wildlife to any real insight.

For audiences, though, none of that was a problem. It didn't matter that Kleiser's camp sheen, effective in the comically singalong world of *Grease*, had this time been used to gloss over plot-holes and cringe-worthy dialogue (Emmeline to Richard: 'You're always staring at my puppies!') All that mattered was Shields' appeal as everyone's sister, daughter or best friend, a regular girl coming to terms with coy teen sexuality. Even her approach was the very opposite of Method, Atkins telling *People* magazine in 1980, 'She thought I took acting too seriously. I was always trying to get in the mood while she would be skipping off to joke with the crew.'[4]

---

1 Author interview.
2 '*Blue Lagoon*: Coyness in Paradise', *New York Times*, 20 June 1980.
3 'Brooke Shields: This Much I Know', *Guardian*, Shahesta Shaitly, 6 December 2014.
4 Again, Shields phrases it differently, writing in *There Was a Little Girl*: 'I was basically being a brat'.

The Blue Lagoon raked in nearly sixty million dollars at the American box-office, around three times the amount *Raging Bull* would manage a few months later. Shields might have won Worst Actress at that first Razzies for her winsome turn but the public loved her (Favourite Young Motion Picture Performer at 1981's People's Choice Awards). And if Atkins treated his craft too intensely for some, at least his moment in the spotlight briefly paid off. He too dated Diane Lane and got a Golden Globe nomination in the (now defunct) New Star category. Although he ultimately lost – on both counts – to Timothy Hutton.

Summer '81. *Taps* was in post-production, now with the added bonus of its nice guy lead Hutton being an Oscar winner ('You felt that something special was happening,' recalls Tom Cruise of the era[1]). A year after her success with *The Blue Lagoon*, Shields unveiled another tale of everyday teens emerging into the adult world: *Endless Love*.

Endless Love was based on the book of the same name by Scott Spencer and yet, tellingly, its setting was moved from the 'flower power' era of the novel to present day America for the film. In the wake of *Grease* and *Animal House*, the early '60s were still viably nostalgic for movie-makers but that later, more hippy part of the decade? Not yet. Thus the story of adolescent obsession lost its original background of Vietnam and civil unrest in favour of something less controversial, more contemporary.

Although 'flower power' wasn't gone *entirely* from *Endless Love*. Dating teens Jade (Shields) and David (Martin Hewitt) might think that their parents are easygoing about their relationship – their folks had been, after all, young people in the free-loving '60s, with Jade's parents still openly bohemian all these years later – but *Endless Love* highlights the issues that many once-liberal youngsters struggle with when they have teenage children of their own. So whilst David's mother Rose (Beatrice Straight) criticises her son with lines like 'We call ourselves socialists and our son dresses like a Rockefeller!' and Jade's father Hugh (Don Murray) initially appears to be the

---

1 *Interview*, May 1986.

trumpet-playing life-and-soul of the party in his rambling, rococo family home, both parents quickly lose all trace of their 'free-love' background when faced with the reality of their teenagers having sex. It's Hugh whose change of attitude is especially strong, switching from being an easygoing ex-hippy to puritanical tormentor, his sudden militaristic forbidding of his daughter's relationship leading David to the crux of the story, getting his own back on Jade's family with a pile of newspapers and a box of matches.

Endless Love wasn't great. Italian director Franco Zeffirelli had hit big twelve years earlier with his version of *Romeo and Juliet* but, whilst the similarities in plot are obvious, he couldn't quite decide in *Endless Love* whether to be modern and hip (Blondie on the soundtrack, plentiful swearing) or just classical and old-fashioned (lush orchestral score, romantic firelight seduction). Maybe that's what attracted him to the film. In the parent figures, perhaps he saw his own undecided self: open-minded, artistic, but still not a hundred per cent convinced by the attitudes of modern kids? As a result, *Endless Love* played like a movie caught on a cusp, blending the fashionably muted camerawork of British cinematographer David Watkin – part of a trend contemporaneously championed by fellow Brits such as Ridley Scott and Adrian Lyne – with elements much more solidly traditional. The pop music, for example, feels deliberately plonked in rather than cleverly entwined. And whilst Lionel Richie's theme tune, a duet with Diana Ross, became 1981's second biggest selling single,[1] providing the kind of huge push for the film that plentiful teen movies would later try and re-create, it's as old-fashioned a ballad as you're ever likely to hear.

Pre-*Taps*, Brooke Shields' New Jersey neighbour Tom Cruise had auditioned for the male lead in *Endless Love*, whilst Hutton had also been considered before being dismissed as – entirely accurately – too ordinary looking.[2] Both eventually lost to newcomer Martin Hewitt, a twenty-two-year-old drama student making his debut.[3] Cruise did, however, get a walk-on part as David's school friend

---

1 Runner-up to 'Bette Davis Eyes' by Kim Carnes, although both spent nine weeks at the top of the Billboard Hot 100.

2 *Casting Might-Have-Beens*, Eila Mell, McFarland, 2005.

3 He'd actually been making ends meet by working at a car park.

Billy, the very guy who instills in him the idea of deliberately setting fire to Jade's house in order to then raise the alarm and look like a hero. Shirley Rich-favourite Jimmy Spader appeared too, in only his second film yet already stealing scenes as Jade's sour and protective older brother Keith, the vinegar in the salad.

Endless Love was really the story of David – how the actions of others turn his passion into an obsession – but, thanks to Calvin Klein ads and *The Blue Lagoon*, Shields was the star and thus wasn't subjected to the scrutiny of auditions. She was offered *Endless Love* straight out and, despite her having some reservations about it being *another* romance, said 'Yes' because of Zeffirelli's reputation ('He was tough, dramatic, and often insulting or drunk, but he expected your best and would not stop until he got it'[1]). Both Brooke and mom Teri felt they were making something important, the kind of high-class drama you got from a European auteur, although Jade never really says or does anything *that* interesting in the film. Sure, she seemed normal but only because she was so bland.[2]

Shooting took place in New York and Long Island in the autumn of '80, with more body-doubling for Brooke's nude shots under Teri's watchful eye (Tom Cruise claimed she kept a watch over him too). Off-camera, meanwhile, Shields was once again playful whilst her co-stars were serious. In fact, her main concession to the Method-acting craze so many worshipped in De Niro was merely to hum the mournful theme music to Zeffirelli's *Romeo and Juliet* when she needed to look sad. Zeffirelli, meanwhile, pushed for more emotion, ordering reshoots in order for *Endless Love*'s tragic moments to have greater impact. To get Shields to more convincingly express pain, he would ultimately resort to . . . pinching her toes. It was hardly Stanislavski, but it worked. *Endless Love* took over thirty million dollars in the US and Shields found herself nominated for a Young Artist Award. Her profile was sky-high, with more modelling, charity work and a friendship with fellow child star Michael Jackson running alongside her acting. Really, there was no- one else around like her.

---

1 *There Was a Little Girl*, . . . , op. cit., p.171.

2 Zeffirelli did express frustration that the film's sex scenes had to be watered down to virtually nothing after *Endless Love* originally received a prohibitive X certificate from the MPAA. It was still, however, given an R for its release.

But if the public appeared to love Brooke Shields, critics were still unsure. Even Scott Spencer, author of *Endless Love*, disagreed with how the movie played. So alongside a People's Choice Award for Favourite Young Performer came another Golden Raspberry nod for Worst Actress, although at least this time she didn't win.[1] But as Shields approached the age of twenty she knew that her novelty as an ingénue would soon be gone. And, unlike Hutton, she didn't have – or wasn't allowed to have – credibility to help her along the way. Growing up in public was going to be tough.

---

1 In case you're interested it was shared in 1981 by Bo Derek and Faye Dunaway for their turns in *Tarzan the Ape Man* and *Mommie Dearest*.

Chapter Four

FRESH EYES

Foxes, *Jodie Foster and the art of Adrian Lyne; fellow ad man Alan Parker finds* Fame; *MTV brings Europe to the US; and Cannon cashes in with* The Last American Virgin.

East End brothers Keith and Alan Freedman were still teenagers in 1966, the year they rode on the success of England's Wembley World Cup win and the music of the Mods to create fashion label Brutus. Ten years later and a new decade, with their Brutus Trimfit shirt a huge hit, they were now in need of a television campaign to push their latest product: a range of figure-hugging jeans. Though the mood of the '70s was decidedly different to that of its predecessor, once the subsequent ad was launched Brutus found itself not just at the forefront of teen fashion all over again but also right at the cutting edge of where Hollywood film-making was about to go. Watching it now, that thirty seconds of TV airtime that the Freedmans commissioned seems less like an advert for jeans, more like a glimpse into the future.

Londoner Adrian Lyne was thirty-five and working for advertising moguls Saatchi & Saatchi when he directed the Brutus Jeans clip in 1976, a fast-paced onslaught of beautiful people pulling on their denim over shapely bottoms. The background was unfussy but powerful, soft white light flooding in from a single window, illuminating the pale decor. On the soundtrack, singer David Dundas – a Harrow-educated musician and actor – sang 'When I wake up in the mornin' light / I pull on my jeans and

I feel all right'. The whole thing was over in the blink of an eye but even in that short time you felt as if you'd been watching something fresh and modern, hook-laden and immediate; the perfect match of visuals, music and message.

Lyne had spent the '50s at school in Highgate where his father was a teacher, the '60s learning his craft as a commercials director. 'I wasn't remotely interested in whether or not they sold the product,' he's admitted of his time in advertising. 'It was just a fabulous way for me to learn how to do it.'[1] As the highly stylised Brutus campaign wowed the UK, even giving Dundas a worldwide hit with the theme song, Lyne's fellow British commercials directors Ridley Scott and Alan Parker were already readying their debut features: Scott's *The Duellists* followed his glossy promos for companies as varied as Chanel and Hovis whilst Parker's *Bugsy Malone* succeeded spots for Heineken and Cinzano, his cheeky sense of humour a refreshing two fingers up to the more sedate world of traditional advertising. Lyne would have to wait a little longer for his break into movies but when it came, his selling skills – even though he claimed not to be bothered by marketing – would lead to a bigger cultural impact than any of his contemporaries. Just as he did with Brutus Jeans, Lyne could make anything – songs, clothes, *lifestyles* – seem sexy.

If Lyne dreamed of being Truffaut, Alan Parker never really expected to be a film director at all. He just wanted to write ads and meet girls. Parker's '50s childhood had also begun in more modest surroundings than Lyne's, in the working-class Canonbury Court housing estate of north London, before moving up – socially at least – to the local grammar school after passing an entrance exam. It was a big deal: young Alan was the first boy from a flat to go there and the whole street waved him off on his first day. 'It was my cinematic moment,' he remembered, 'and I have put it, at least the sense of it, into many of my films.'[2]

At sixteen Parker got a job in the postroom of a Soho advertising agency, eventually becoming a copy writer. Moving to Collett

---

1 *Movie Maker*, issue 46.
2 'FT magazine', *Financial Times*, Rosie Millard, 23 March 2012.

Dickenson Pearce – the archetypal ad firm of swinging '60s London – proved the boost he needed. Working there with producer David Puttnam proved to be a turning point: 'I had no concerted plan to get into films . . . ended up getting into them due to David Puttnam's ambition.'[1]

Puttnam's determination was certainly legendary. After forming their own company and creating those successful ads for Cinzano and Heineken, Puttnam ushered Parker from TV plays into the world of cinema when he invested in the director's idea for *Bugsy Malone*, a kids' musical starring Jodie Foster and Scott Baio, even fighting to get it shown at the highbrow Cannes Film Festival in the spring of '76. Competing with new films from heavyweight European auteurs Éric Rohmer, Wim Wenders and Roman Polanski – not to mention Jodie Foster's *other* film that year, Scorsese's *Taxi Driver* – *Bugsy Malone* was the working-class oik at a dinner party for the chattering classes. Where Parker had broken the rules in advertising by casting outside of London and filling his commercials with regional accents and naturalistic dialogue, now he was doing the same with the film musical: portraying kids as gangsters with splurge guns. After its first screening *Bugsy Malone* got a standing ovation. *Taxi Driver* eventually won the Palme d'Or but everyone already knew that Martin Scorsese had panache. Alan Parker, though, was the new kid on the block. Suddenly the baby mogul execs in Los Angeles all wanted a British ad director on their books.

Adrian Lyne finally got his Hollywood break in 1979, directing *Foxes*: a post-*Saturday Night Fever* tale of four San Fernando Valley girls from dysfunctional families, producer David Puttnam reteaming with young star of the moment Jodie Foster. The story was written by Gerald Ayres, a middle-aged Columbia exec who'd worked his way up through theatre and television to hit big in the early '70s as producer of Hal Ashby's *The Last Detail*, the bitter road movie for which Travolta had auditioned, losing out to eventual Oscar nominee (and *Foxes* co-star) Randy Quaid. Ayres

---

1 'The British admen who saved Hollywood', *Guardian*, Sam Delaney, 24 August 2007.

had been married young but by the time of *Foxes* was openly gay, a rarity in Hollywood. His script about broken families, petty crime and suicide in an area of LA then attempting to gain independence from the rest of the city was, on the surface, a long way from his own life. Underneath, though, it was really about not fitting in. *That* was something he – and many of the creative team – knew all about.

Foxes brought European style to Californian adolescence; out of place at first glance, inspired at second. 'I had made a lot of movies at that point,' remembers Foster. 'There I was working with a first-time British director doing a movie about adolescent girls in a city he barely knew. I think that was the strength of the movie, its fascination with that place and time. He was an outsider who was captivated by the look, the feel, the energy of one moment in time. It was a curiosity to him. An Englishman discovers the Valley. That really was his very specific lens. Adrian came from commercials so he would shoot endless footage of extras fooling around, inserts on make-up or on snacks being unwrapped . . . ambience. Things that had nothing to do with the plot but were little discoveries for him. I rolled my eyes at the time because it seemed wasteful. But that was Adrian's directorial style emerging. He just got a kick out of being there among young people and wanted to shoot anything that moved. His work always has the sparkle of mischief . . . kind of like him. He's a big kid.'[1]

Alongside Lyne and Ayres on *Foxes* was another 'foreigner': the director of photography Michael Serasin, a Kiwi who'd become a regular in the London commercials world and who brought to *Foxes* the smoky and diffused light that he and others had been using for several years in British advertising. Also behind the camera was veteran English film-maker Leon Bijou, whose son Peter had already worked with Serasin on *Bugsy Malone*. Then there was the music. Largely funded by Neil Bogart's disco label Casablanca, recently merged with Peter Guber's production house Filmworks in a bid to become a movie company, *Foxes* was scored by the record company's in-house team of Giorgio Moroder and

---

1 Author interview.

his German arranger/keyboard player Harold Faltermeyer,[1] with percussion and additional songwriting by Londoners Keith Forsey and Pete Belotte. Their work on *American Gigolo* could still be heard in cinemas, released only three weeks before *Foxes*. 'You bring something new and unique, something European into the American market, the Munich disco scene combined with rock'n'roll elements,' explains Faltermeyer. 'Because at that time that "regular" disco scene was already tapering out. It needed new influences . . . a strong synthesiser riff, guitars . . . '[2]

The pertinence of this group of outsiders coming to California and giving mainstream America a snapshot of its own teenage subcultures wasn't lost on Puttnam: 'There were a lot of interviews around the time of [1969's] *Midnight Cowboy*, interesting interviews done with Jon Voight and Dustin Hoffman, talking about the fact that [director] John Schlesinger was able to observe things that they took for granted, [but] which he found quite extraordinary. Schlesinger's view of New York – and I remember this very vividly from when I first went there in the very early '60s – was an outsider's view. He found it a very extraordinary place in a way that people who lived there didn't find it extraordinary at all . . . Coming from the outside, you do tend to have a different view. In some cases a touristic, slightly obvious view but in other cases you notice things that locals don't notice at all. I think that was true of all of us.'

Foxes was released in February of 1980. Roger Ebert in the *Chicago Sun-Times*, at least, was kind: 'It contains the sounds and rhythms of real teenage lives; it was written and directed after a lot of research, and is acted by kids who are to one degree or another playing themselves. The movie's a rare attempt to provide a portrait of the way teenagers really do live today in some suburban cultures.'[3] For Foster, praise for the film's authenticity made sense. It was a film about teen issues starring teens *with issues*: 'Of course,

---

1 As had been Puttnam's previous film: *Midnight Express*, directed by Alan Parker. The score daringly brought a pulsating electronic ambience to the true story of American Billy Hayes' time in a Turkish prison for smuggling drugs.

2 Author interview.

3 *Chicago Sun-Times*, February 1980.

my memories are going to be coloured by turning sixteen years old, driving around in my new car, coming of age and all the drama and anxiety of that age. I was mad at my mom during that shoot because she was always late driving me to set. There was quite a bit of night shooting on *Foxes* and it was freezing cold in Los Angeles that winter. I got frostbite on my toes from wearing Candie's open-platform shoes.'[1]

Yet despite the re-teaming of Foster and her *Bugsy Malone* co-star Scott Baio (as Brad), *Foxes* made little impact at the box-office. Baio's pin-up status from *Happy Days* – playing Chachi Arcola, the young cousin of Henry Winkler's Fonzie – didn't stop movie audiences being more interested in Richard Gere in *American Gigolo* and Jamie Lee Curtis in *The Fog*. If *Foxes'* style was strong, the story dragged; even Puttnam admitted to its weaknesses: 'The film was funded essentially by a music company and therefore the pressure on us to use music . . . in some ways inappropriately was there. The skateboard chase, for example, was there in order to *advertise* the song. Otherwise I'm not sure what it was doing there. And the other pressure was that the original script was about a girl committing suicide and the studio at the end of the day backed off of that and it had to be an accident. Casablanca wanted an album out of it . . . I had no problem at all with having a song over the end titles for example . . . but the music I think is intrusive and as a result the film loses its authenticity.'[2]

Foxes, though, bottled a moment and bottled it *early,* a blend of chic visuals plus pop soundtrack plus hot young stars that virtually became a blueprint for teen-focused movies by the mid-'80s. It should be much better remembered. Name-wise, it was Jodie Foster who was integral to getting the movie made but casting director Penny Perry – after working with Puttnam on *Midnight Express* – then saw a host of new talent for the supporting role of Annie, many of whom would go on to great success: twenty-year-old Rosanna Arquette, who'd just filmed a tiny role in the misjudged *More American Graffiti*; Arquette's fellow New Yorker Diane Lane; Emmy Award-winning teen star of Aaron Spelling's

---

1 Author interview.
2 Author interview.

TV drama series *Family* Kristy McNichol; and a seventeen-year-old called Jennifer Jason Leigh, the daughter of actor Vic Morrow and screenwriter Barbara Turner.[1]

Eventually Perry cast Cherie Currie, the former lead singer of LA teen punks The Runaways, understandable since an early draft of the script had the four friends actually in their own band. Currie had been spotted by a William Morris agent at a Runaways gig in Huntington Beach and *Foxes* was only her second audition, a fact not missed by Foster's mother Brandy, who considered the rocker too inexperienced. Yet her daughter found a lot to admire in the musician: 'She was very sweet and open. She did macrame and other crafts on set to pass the time, as I recall. Despite the tattoos and the rock star hair, she seemed very naïve, very young. She lacked confidence in her acting ability and was always checking in to make sure she was on the right path with the character. But I thought she was so good, so real, so clearly tapped into the truth of that character.'[2] (As Currie herself says: 'I was pretty much playing myself.'[3])

Puttnam has plenty of praise for the casting of *Foxes* too: 'There are some very, very good scenes in it; there's a fantastic scene between Sally Kellerman and Jodie Foster, a fight between mother and daughter, which is very, very good indeed, extremely well directed, very well realised,'[4] and Foster saw herself rewarded with a nod at the Youth in Film Awards that year.[5] If *Foxes* failed to ignite commercially at the time, looking back it's a fascinating paradox: a film that rallies against emerging Reaganite conservative values whilst simultaneously being very much a corporate product owing much to the music and advertising industries.

'[Before *Foxes*] I rang up Howard Zieff, who was a very famous commercial director and actually quite successful as a feature film

---

1 Morrow's first role had been in archetypal '50s teen delinquent movie *Blackboard Jungle*. Turner had been an actress in the same era, then turned to screenwriting during her second marriage (to TV director Reza Badiyi).

2 Author interview.

3 Legendary Rock Interviews, John Parks, 17 September 2013.

4 Author interview.

5 Other nominees in the Best Young Actress in a Major Motion Picture category were Brooke Shields for *The Blue Lagoon*, Kristy McNichol for *Little Darlings* and eventual winner Diane Lane, rewarded for her performance as a girl with cerebral palsy in *Touched by Love*.

director,' remembers Lyne. 'I said, "What would you tell me? Give me some advice before I start this film." He thought for a long time and finally said, "Be on it at the end." Meaning, don't get replaced – which is certainly the harsh reality of your first film.'[1] *Foxes* hadn't been a hit but at least Lyne didn't get fired. Quite the opposite. Even in a flop he'd managed to create his own distinctive cinematic style.

Summer '79 and, over on the other side of the States, Lyne's fellow British ad director Alan Parker was hanging out at New York's High School for Performing Arts; a gruff Cockney in amongst Big Apple entertainers. Parker's job was simple: to persuade the school's principal to let him film MGM's new teen movie *Hot Lunch* there. There was just one problem though. The city's Board of Education (Principal Klein reluctantly explained to the director) just weren't happy about the grittier elements of the *Hot Lunch* script; a story of music and drama students that featured liberal kicks of sex, drugs and four-letter words. Its writer Christopher Gore had been paid five thousand dollars by agent/producer David De Silva to pen the film and he'd spent time with the students to get the right mood. Then when Parker came on board to helm, he too mingled with the classes in order to better understand the mood of the place. Authenticity was key. Yet the suits on the board still wanted nothing to do with *Hot Lunch* and Parker found himself in an odd position. He'd successfully navigated American union rules to get his British crew work permits but now he wouldn't be able to get that crew into the very location where the story was set. There was really only one thing MGM could do: relocate the entire project to Chicago.

Luckily, Nancy Littlefield wasn't happy. Her job at the New York City mayor's Office of Film, Theater and Broadcasting was simple: to get productions to use the Big Apple. One major movie could generate hundreds of jobs and millions of dollars and she wasn't about to let *Hot Lunch* slip away, no matter what the Board of Education might say. The fifty-year-old former film-maker from the Bronx had already helped *Kramer vs Kramer* and

---

1 *Movie Maker*, op. cit.

Manhattan shoot on the iconic streets, her role created specifically to make it easier to film in the country's spiritual capital. Littlefield was a fighter all right, the first woman to be accepted into the Directors Guild of America. She was determined to find a way for Parker to shoot his story in the proper setting.

Accepting that the *actual* school wouldn't accommodate them, Littlefield showed Alan Parker two abandoned buildings that he might consider, for a few hundred thousand dollars, transforming into something he could use. Creating a school virtually from scratch might not be as entirely authentic but at least it could be kitted out fully as a movie set, rather than having to go with a real school's more restrictive layout. What's more, with the help of Principal Klein – who'd secretly always quite liked Gore's script but had his hands tied – it was announced that current students *could* actually help out with this controversial portrayal of their school . . . just so long as they did it out of official term time in the summer. Parker finally had what he needed: 'The most important factor in getting the film made was that we had the cooperation of the students,' he said in *New York Magazine* around the film's release. 'I told them, "You have to trust me. I'm going to make a film truthful to the spirit of the school, but it's not going to be a documentary; it's a theatrical entertainment. I will push certain things to the theatrical edge."'[1]

If it wasn't exactly what De Silva had in mind for *Hot Lunch*, he couldn't deny that his director had warned him. 'We didn't get off to a very good start because, after mentioning that I would like to write my own version of the script and that I would be making the film with Alan Marshall producing, not him, he began to cry,' remembers Alan Parker. 'I tried to console him as he blubbered into his napkin.'[2] Consequently De Silva didn't have a lot to do with the making of what had originally been his idea. Even the title was changed, to *Fame*, after Parker realised that the original name had its own somewhat unsavoury meaning in the porn industry.

* * *

---

1 '"Chorus Line" Goes to High School', David Rosenthal, 26 May 1980.
2 'Sir Alan Parker on the making of Fame', *Telegraph*, 2 October 2009.

'Truthful' yet 'theatrical': that's *Fame*. It's a movie of two extremes, in which the documentary mood created by following an ensemble cast – many inexperienced and raw – over four years at high school mixes with slickly edited montages and musical brio straight from the worlds of advertising or pop videos (the latter, by 1980, starting to take off). *Fame* kept things real by using the school's current students, former students, even teachers[1] in most scenes. Yet it was also a product, a deliberately heightened snapshot of an educational life backed by a two-million-dollar ad campaign and the biggest free ticket publicity push that MGM had ever known. With no established stars, *Fame* needed its concept to really buzz.

That contrast – truth versus style – is all there in the poster: a seemingly impromptu photo of the kids mid-jam session rather than anything posed or formal, yet also sitting above the highly designed red logo. '*Fame* is the glamour of the Great White Way of Broadway and the squalor of 42nd Street' the tagline reads, further highlighting this world of opposites, ' . . . the dream of instant success and the reminder of failure; the fine line between a Julliard scholarship and dancing topless at the Metropole . . . It's George M. Cohan and the City Ballet, rock'n'roll and Vivaldi. It's New York: vulgar yet beautiful. A dozen races pitching in and having their own crack at the American Dream.' It was a verbatim copy of a note Alan Parker had written to his crew just before filming, summing up exactly what he loved about the story. Like many film-makers from outside America, he'd always dreamed of shooting on the legendary streets of New York and had moved his family to nearby Greenwich, Connecticut, to make it happen. He'd even turned down directing *One from the Heart* in the process, convinced his lugubrious Englishness had something new to say about making it in the most famous city in the world.

What Parker mainly discovered was his distaste for showbiz kids: 'If I'm perfectly honest, I didn't like all of them.'[2] Antonia Franceschi was just turning nineteen and had spent twelve months using the money she earned dancing in the background on *Grease* to study at New York's American School of Ballet. Now she was

---

1 Drama instructor James Moody played Mr Farrell – a drama instructor.
2 *Fame* DVD commentary.

lured back into acting by casting directors wanting her for the role of *Fame*'s rich-bitch dancer Hilary. Franceschi was one of the young cast who actually got on well with the director but she acknowledges a Londoner working in the Big Apple was always going to struggle: 'He was nervous. I think that's a cultural thing. In New York we can be sort of in your face. Sort of wild.'[1] The kids with agents and attitude tended to shun the more inexperienced cast (Franceschi, then still a novice, says simply of several older co-stars, 'They were assholes'), and it was to the quieter newcomers that Parker warmed. Barry Miller, playing wise-guy comedian Ralph Garci, wasn't one of them. He'd already hit big after being cast by Shirley Rich as the tragic Bobby C. in *Saturday Night Fever* and he and Parker frequently clashed. If the resulting edginess in his performance is electrifying to watch it was something that only came from an often painful number of takes and a fractious relationship with cast and crew.

Yet with *Fame*, Parker achieved what he'd always wanted: a different take on showbiz, showing the tough side as well as the fun: 'Sometimes when you're one yard outside of a society, or culture, you tend to look at that culture slightly different from those who are immersed in the middle of it. Things that might be taken for granted are seen with fresh eyes.'[2] Franceschi was only two years out of the real High School of Performing Arts and Parker's take certainly rang true: '*Fame* wasn't that far off, it really wasn't,' she admits. 'At lunchtime . . . some people would get high. We used to shoplift . . . We used to try and hustle businessmen for lunch money. It was really sad.'[3] In fact, Gene Anthony Ray, as rough-hewn street dancer Leroy, was so similar to his feral character that Parker was even a little wary around him. Ray had also once tried the High School for Performing Arts but had gotten expelled after just a year: so nearly the fate of Leroy in the movie. Yet by harnessing the similarities between his performers and their roles, Parker the objective outsider captured the true spirit of teenage wannabes with both a frenetic energy and a

---

1 Author interview.
2 'Sir Alan Parker on the making of Fame', op. cit.
3 Antonia Franceschi interview, op. cit..

pensive style. For the former he was happy to credit his regular editor Gerry Hambling, a collaborator since the advertising days. For the latter he doffed his cap to Michael Serasin, the *Foxes'* cinematographer who'd been inspired as a boy by the noir light of *The Third Man* and who, as a man, wasn't averse to burning incense sticks on set to get just the right sultry, smokey look.

The loose yet exquisitely lit approaches of *Foxes* and *Fame* couldn't fail to get noticed: 'If the character types seem familiar,' wrote Roger Ebert of the latter, 'the movie's way of telling their stories is not.'[1] Yet it was something more easily quantifiable, certainly more immediate, that really hit home with the general public: both featured great songs. As *Foxes* struggled at the US box-office at the start of 1980, its lead track 'On the Radio' was doing the opposite in the Hot 100 and giving Donna Summer her eighth consecutive Top 5 hit. Come August of that year, *Fame*'s title track had given Irene Cara her first.

Without well-known actors in *Fame*, MGM needed the music to be a selling point and to supervise the soundtrack Parker hired Michael Gore, a musician who'd worked across a number of different genres – from collaborations with his '60s teen pop sister Lesley to classical recordings – that mirrored the myriad styles on which the students themselves had to focus. 'Hot Lunch Jam' was exactly what the title said: a freestyle, anything-goes bit of improv, supposedly cooked up by the students as they gorged on bad school canteen food. 'Out Here on My Own' was the movie's heartfelt ballad, feeling lonely under the stage spotlight a suitable metaphor for the kids' plentiful teen angst. Then there was that title track written by Gore and his lyricist Dean Pitchford, a song that had to both perfectly match the choreography of a key scene where the students bring their dance moves out into the streets of Manhattan (which had actually been filmed using Donna Summer's 'Hot Stuff' as a guide track) but which also had to powerfully yet succinctly get to the crux of what the film was about.

For lyrical inspiration, the twenty-eight-year-old Pitchford went back to his own teenage years. 'When I was in high school in

---

1 *Chicago Sun-Times*, 16 May 1980.

Honolulu I competed in speech tournaments and there was one year I used a speech from a British play by Sidney Michaels called *Dylan* and it was the story of Dylan Thomas. And there's one moment in the speech that I used to deliver when Dylan is asked why he is spending his life writing poems and he says "Because in your poems, *you get to live forever*". I had delivered this speech over and over again so it was deeply buried in my mentality. It was part of my psyche.'[1]

After several fruitless weeks of working with Gore on the track, late one night that memory of Dylan Thomas returned: '[Michael] called me about nine-thirty, ten o'clock and he said, "I think I have something." And I went running over to his place – we lived about three blocks away from each other in New York City – and he and I sat down and he played the chorus: "Da da da da da, Fame!" And I said, "I like that! I like that! Go back to the beginning!" And as he played, I sang, "Remember my name – fame! I'm gonna live forever . . . " And he stopped. And he looked at me, like, "Oh! Oh! Oh! Write that down! Write that down!" And I said, "Michael. I'm not gonna forget *that*."'[2]

Initial concerns over whether a song called 'Fame' would get confused with David Bowie's '70s No. 1 of the same name were soon forgotten. Pitchford's determined words and Gore's rousing hooks led the movie's soundtrack album to five million sales on Robert Stigwood's RSO label, the title track itself winning a Golden Globe and Academy Award. Pitchford described *Fame* as a film that 'really felt like the '80s' as he and Gore accepted the Best Original Song Oscar from presenters Angie Dickinson and a rather confused-looking Luciano Pavarotti on that same night in 1981 that Hutton and De Niro triumphed. 'Traditionally the songs that won Academy Awards were cut from the same cloth as Broadway. They were Henry Mancini, Marilyn and Alan Bergman; a throwback to traditional songwriting,' Pitchford explains. 'There hadn't been anything yet that had been a hit on the radio as well as an Academy Award-winning song. It was young and youthful and fresh and it was also a big dance hit, not

1 Author interview.
2 Ibid.

just on pop radio but in discos all over the world. It felt more aggressive I guess, than songs that had preceded it.'[1]

Fame's connection to *Saturday Night Fever* goes deeper than just a soundtrack album on Stigwood's label. Both show, via a mixture of grit and glamour, all the hard work that's needed to turn a fun hobby into a professional success. Both were rated R, tougher and rougher than many remember. Yet whilst *Fame* wasn't sanitised with a PG version, Parker was asked to produce one for a wider audience (having 'final cut' on his films meant he never had to). Even worse, in the director's eyes, *Fame*'s unexpected success – a solid twenty-million-dollar box-office, good for a film without a star – led to a family-friendly TV show in early 1982, set in the same school. Some of the original cast reappeared but Parker and Marshall had no involvement ('Absolutely diabolically awful' is how Parker describes his film's many reinventions on stage and screen[2]). Where the film had dealt with drugs, abortion and homosexuality, the primetime series kept things lighter, told more conventionally. What had once been about the harsh realities of a performer's life now featured fluffier storylines – the boys compete in an athletics contest, Doris gets stuck in a lift – in among occasionally more interesting issues such as the teachers striking and Coco losing a role because of her skin colour.

Parker does acknowledge that the success of the TV show, especially in the UK, where the cast had Top 10 singles and sell-out stage shows, helped to keep his original story alive. Yet the creative difference was palpable; a once audacious concept was turned into something narrative-heavy but lacking real posture. It was the PG reimagining of *Fever* all over again. Gore and Pitchford's title song in the film is a moment of naïve joy in junior year, the kids dancing in the street as Bruno's dad blasts it from his car stereo, unaware that their dreams of 'living forever' through fame are likely to end up in the trash can when they have to make ends meet by waiting tables for a living. What *Fame*'s new television incarnation seemed to suggest, however – and much to the ire of Parker – was that the same song, now playing over bouncy opening

1 Author interview.
2 *Fame* DVD commentary.

credits, was no longer ironic. Those big dreams of fame might actually come true.

It's summer 1982 and, playing on TVs across the USA is the music video for British band A Flock of Seagulls' hit single 'I Ran'. 'We had a meeting with the record company Monday, we met with the director on Tuesday. We filmed it on Wednesday. And it was on TV that Friday,' remembers Seagulls lead singer Mike Score. 'Most bands do New York, Chicago, LA and then go home. Once we were on MTV, we were in every major city at once. Everybody knew what we looked and sounded like, so we were immediately accepted 'cause we were on TV so much . . . We came to America for three weeks and stayed for nine months . . . We weaved ourselves into the fabric of the American new wave.'[1]

Watch the video now and it all seems relatively basic: the Liverpool band playing their instruments whilst revolving inside a mirrored box, two girls clad in what look like bin-bags and sporting seriously heavy eye make-up occasionally walking into shot like a New Romantic version of the twins from *The Shining*. Hardly as evocative as the material Alan Parker and Adrian Lyne had been creating for the big screen but undeniably striking nevertheless. The Seagulls sported red shirts that riffed on Kraftwerk, the mirrors paid homage to an old Brian Eno and Robert Fripp album cover; yet this is also something flouncier, more bouffant and frilly than old electronica. There's definitely no smiling though. In their reflective box, whirling around and around like a machine, A Flock of Seagulls looked like a straight-faced robotic band from the future.

'The first Seagulls album was initially influenced by sci-fi. It was what we were into at the time, watching movies like *Alien* and *Fire in the Sky*,' explains Score. 'It was a great time as sci-fi was just getting into its real stride then and more and more people were starting to believe in aliens and space.'[2] Match that with a new television experience called MTV, dedicated to playing the most memorable pop videos 24/7 and suddenly these arty outsiders

1 *Miami New Times*, Jacob Katel, 7 May 2012.
2 thebigfootdiaries.blogspot.com, 20 February 2013.

from Europe – be they directors, performers, musicians – had found another way of edging their visionary ideas into the American mainstream.

Really, America was playing catch-up. Hollywood had made short musical films for as long as the talkies had been around but many British artists in the '60s – The Beatles, Pink Floyd, The Stones – had blended the idea of recording promotional clips for their songs with fashionable underground film-making techniques, laying the groundwork for the modern music video. Some of it was art but some of it was just practical, a much cheaper way for a European band to be noticed around the world than it was for them to get on a plane and tour for months. It was why Australia had been an early adopter too, the TV music shows *Sounds* and *Countdown* making videos for artists in the absence of any official appearance.

When theatrical British rockers Queen asked local director Bruce Gowers to spend 3500 pounds on their stark, spotlit video for 'Bohemian Rhapsody' in 1975, it certainly wasn't the first time a major band had recorded a promo clip for a single. It was, however, the first time a video hadn't been treated as second best to a live performance. 'Bohemian Rhapsody' was as much about the strong, haunting visuals of the video, where visual feedback created multiple Freddie Mercurys, as it was about the complexities of the song – and the band knew the two would complement each other better than anything they could recreate live on the BBC's *Top of the Pops*. The song was a worldwide No. 1, Top 10 in the States. Within five years Bowie was making a video for 'Ashes to Ashes' that cost half a million dollars.

In America, former Monkees guitarist Mike Nesmith – always the most vocal about the creative constraints of being in a manufactured band – had spent the '70s experimenting. There had been his country-rock solo career, his film-making company Pacific Arts as well as the Countryside record label he'd started with Elektra boss Jac Holzman. It was the latter two that so impressed Warner's satellite and cable operation WASEC – co-funded by American Express – that they asked the forward-thinking Holzman and Nesmith to make a music show for their Nickelodeon kids' channel that would play out many of these new pop promos that they'd noticed springing up across the Atlantic: Squeeze's 'Cool for Cats', Boney M's 'Rivers of Babylon', The Tourists' 'I Only Want to Be with You', as well as early American adopters of the format such as Huey Lewis, Toto and Nesmith himself. In fact, WASEC's chief John Lack, a thirty-three-year-old fresh from working at CBS radio, liked what he saw so much that he then proposed something even bigger to his paymasters: a *whole channel* devoted to music videos.

What would become MTV was to many a tough sell. Nesmith, perhaps still scarred from his days as a mainstream Monkee, thought the whole enterprise too commercial and bailed out. WASEC's own big guns – the ageing president Jack Schneider, AmEx's James Robinson III and Warner's main man Steve Ross – had cold feet too, leaving Lack and his team to reassure them of how much Europeans were already loving music videos *and* – even better – remind them of the fact that they wouldn't have to pay record companies for the clips. Those record companies, however, had their own concerns. *They* were worried that these music videos were just one more expense in a costly industry, not yet understanding how exposure might actually help them shift units. Then there were the reluctant cable operators who needed to be persuaded to carry the new channel. 'When they saw the crazy sex shit from New York and LA we were trying to sell, their attitude was "Who needs it? We got good little communities. We're Baptist. We don't need this crap coming in, corrupting our children,"' admitted Lack.[1]

Lack and his programming head Bob Pittman were left with one final argument to get their idea for music video television going: to trumpet this new channel's groundbreaking nature. MTV's success, they proclaimed, would – like *Fame* – come from selling a *concept* rather than an individual: 'A lot of other people had been playing around, but no one had hit on a winning formula. The concept I had was to have a clear image, to build an attitude. In other words, to build a brand, a channel that happened to use video clips as a building block, as opposed to being a delivery

---

1 'Birth of an MTV Nation', *Vanity Fair*, Robert Sam Anson, 4 June 2008.

system for videos. The star wouldn't be the videos, the star would be the channel.'[1] It was the one thing that really worked: promoting MTV as a lifestyle, summed up by the punky, messed-up graphics that accompanied its futuristic ethos. Advertisers began to show interest. Even better, Steve Ross's teenage daughter told her media mogul dad that the whole idea was seriously cool. After much debate, MTV finally got the green light.

On 1 August 1981, just after midnight, MTV launched, not with the obvious choice of the country's current No. 1 single, Rick Springfield's all-American 'Jessie's Girl', but with a deliberate statement of quirky intent: 'Video Killed the Radio Star', an eccentric three minutes of synth-pop by a Kraftwerk-inspired duo from England called Buggles. 'The British are coming,' Yorkshire screenwriter Colin Welland would famously proclaim less than a year later when picking up his Best Original Screenplay Oscar for David Puttnam's *Chariots of Fire*, but with MTV's championing of British bands such as Buggles – plus Lyne, Parker and Scott already helming *zeitgeisty* Hollywood movies – they'd actually arrived.

MTV had serious style. Presenters – known much more sexily as VJs (ie, video-jockeys, the visual equivalent of DJs) – were diverse and cool: punky former model Nina Blackwood, J. J. Jackson – one of the few African-American radio presenters known for his love of rock – and Martha Quinn, just twenty-two years old. To front shows they stood in what seemed to be a hip New York loft not a million miles away from Montgomery's own West 46th and Broadway apartment in *Fame*; the kind of backdrop that wouldn't interest anyone over twenty-five. The channel's ident, meanwhile, was a ballsy mash-up of a hard-rock melody, graffiti fonts and retro footage of the moon landing. That MTV wasn't even yet carried by cable companies in Manhattan, the very location its kaleidoscopic styling was so obviously influenced by, didn't ultimately matter. Trend-setting kids in the Big Apple were, after all, more used to the radical and strange. Really it was the smaller markets, those often untouched by the latest fads, that gradually got more out of those early days of MTV, eyes and

---

1 Ibid.

minds from more rural locations excitedly opening up to new sounds and visuals. Then there were the vogueish bands themselves, also reaping the benefits of the channel now they were suddenly being seen outside of their usual neighbourhoods. 'We were playing Tulsa, place called Old Lady of Brady, and cowboys with skinny ties and stuff were coming to see us, guys with black leather jackets and big pompadours and motorcycle boots,' recalls Brian Setzer of Stray Cats, a trio of American rockabilly revivalists.[1] Stray Cats were already popular in the UK but had struggled with the vast size of their home market. This new channel changed all that. 'It brought us to the masses, MTV.'[2]

After an ad campaign featuring stars such as Bowie and Jagger proclaiming 'I want my MTV!', cable operators around the country gradually started adding the station to their line-up; record companies in turn realising that what was happening might actually warrant their attention and money. Bands such as A Flock of Seagulls, groups that might previously have been Limey outsiders but who displayed in their videos an artist's eye for memorable style, suddenly flourished.

On 3 July 1982 – over half a year after being a hit in Europe – England's Human League started a three-week reign on top of the Billboard Hot 100 with 'Don't You Want Me', described by the *Village Voice* as 'pretty unmistakably the moment the second British invasion, spurred by MTV, kicked off'.[3] The Human League, like the Seagulls, came from the industrial north of England – in their case, Sheffield – and found glamour in the futurism of *A Clockwork Orange*, Bowie and Moroder. Indeed the League's creativity was such that 'Don't You Want Me''s parent album from late '81, *Dare*, had a sleeve designed to look like a *Vogue* magazine cover. 'Virgin went mental because we made them put a special glaze on it so it would look shiny and glossy, so it cost fifty-five pence more to make per copy than any other album on the shelves that year,' recalls League singer Susan Ann Sulley.[4] Lead vocalist Phil Oakey, meanwhile, was a former

---

1 Named after a fictional band in David Puttnam's *That'll Be the Day*.
2 'Birth of an MTV Nation', op. cit.
3 'One hundred and Single', villagevoice.com, Chris Molanphy, 29 July 2011.
4 The Quietus, John Doran, 14 February 2011.

hospital porter who initially had no desire to get into music but he still styled himself, all long, sleek hair and lip-gloss, as if he was Sheffield's answer to Marie Helvin.

'Don't You Want Me''s video was directed by Steve Barron, an Irishman who'd cut his teeth working with mod revivalists The Jam in the late '70s. But the League clip was on another level. Despite it being the album's fourth single – and Oakey's least favourite – Virgin were convinced 'Don't You Want Me' would be a hit and pumped money into the promo, a sure sign of the new format's growing importance. The result was a lush film-within-a-film tale of romantic obsession, influenced by both classic melodrama *A Star is Born* and Truffaut's *Day for Night*, whose high-art pretensions and ultra-modern synth hooks proceeded to captivate the disaffected youth of America's suburbs just as much as it did Britain's. After all, US radio was dominated by blue-collar rock – '81 was all about Springfield, John Cougar and Joan Jett – so the cosmopolitan MTV saw an opportunity to not only give sophisticated alternative bands a break but also sensitive alternative fans an outlet too. Mirroring what Lyne and Parker had achieved with the lustrous *Foxes* and *Fame* – and Ridley Scott with eye-popping sci-fis *Alien* and *Bladerunner* – British pop culture became a byword for an otherworldly cool, movies and music more closely linked by style than they had been since The Beatles' groundbreaking work with Richard Lester in the '60s.

The acts themselves were also single-minded about breaking that monopoly which macho guitar music had enjoyed for so long, even era-defining punk getting short shrift from Oakey: 'We were never that impressed by the musical side of punk. We loved the rejection of authority but we knew straight away that the records were Eddie Cochran.'[1] It was an attitude that, like that of Parker and Lyne, rebelled against stereotypically macho US style whilst simultaneously respecting the significance of an outsider British band finding success in the vast country; a contradiction that poetically soundtracked the lives of conflicted suburban American youngsters. Back in the summer of '82, with The Human League spearheading the electronic movement, rock radio eventually

---

1 *Scottish Herald*, Teddy Jamieson, 24 November 2012.

caved and added 'Don't You Want Me' to playlists, finally realising its pertinence. MTV had taken the lead and the rest of the media was playing catch-up.

Music videos, like the adverts that Parker and Lyne had been creating, needed to make their impact quickly and the early methods to get those results were varied, from comedy routines to cutting-edge FX (Olivia Newton-John's 1981 hit 'Physical' manages to combine both). Yet the point was nearly always the same: the promo clip neatly summarised the artist or band, it captured everything they stood for, as if they were a pair of Brutus Jeans or a loaf of Hovis. Like the old song-and-dance numbers from movie musicals, videos could also be wildly fantastical, a place to let the imagination run freely past conventional ideas of linear narrative or simple story. In just the first year of MTV, American audiences had been treated to the eccentric futurism of Devo's 'Whip It' (deadpan electro band go S&M in a kitsch cowboy ranch), the sexy choreography of J. Geils Band's 'Centerfold' (leggy models dance around a school classroom), the exotic locations of Duran Duran's 'Save A Prayer' (the band look moody in Sri Lanka) and the Adrian Lyne-esque billowing curtains and shadows of Kim Carnes' 'Bette Davis Eyes', 1981's biggest-selling single. The last two were directed by a twenty-eight-year-old Australian called Russell Mulcahy, who'd also shot 'Video Killed the Radio Star' during his tenure in London, and who went on to become one of the most sought-after directors of the era. 'He always had the vision of a feature film director,' says Duran's John Taylor. 'We had an equal measure of grandiosity.'[1]

Movies, in turn, began to be influenced by the growing popularity of music videos. At first it was simply in getting the right soundtrack: a week after The Human League slipped from the summit of the US singles chart, *The Last American Virgin* – a modern-day, Hollywood remake of *Lemon Popsicle*, produced by Yoram Globus and Menahem Golan's new Cannon Films – included the band's earlier 'Love Action (I Believe in Love)' on its soundtrack, as well as other emerging new wave and electro acts

---

1 *Billboard* magazine, Keith Caulfield, 3 March 2014.

popular on MTV such as U2, The Police and Devo. The result, unlike its '50s-set Israeli source material, was a film refreshingly lacking in nostalgia. The role of high-school ladies' man Rick had even gone to the star of Rick Springfield's 'Jessie's Girl' video, Steve Antin, whilst seventeen-year-old Yonkers newcomer Lawrence Monoson was so desperate to play sensitive lead Gary he used a phony driving licence as ID.

The Last American Virgin, however, also highlighted an early problem with '80s Hollywood's increasing interest in teen cinema: namely, could the adults at business-minded film companies ever be genuinely emotionally connected to modern youth culture? MTV was full of hip New York kids but *American Virgin*'s director Boaz Davidson, from Tel Aviv, was about to hit forty. Whilst he'd injected autobiography into the original *Lemon Popsicle*, basing it on his own formative years, it's a struggle to believe this middle-aged man really had as much heartfelt investment in showing '80s kids listening to The Waitresses' cult new wave hit 'I Know What Boys Like' as he did in remembering how '50s boys listened to 'Tutti Frutti'. It was a question that would return time and again as pop soundtracks became more and more successful and thus – inevitably – more corporate and Cannon's infamous business approach only added to early accusations of opportunism over genuine passion and creativity. Look at their release schedule and you can't help but notice a generous dollop of shameless cashing-in, *The Last American Virgin* coming out directly after their softcore take on *Lady Chatterley's Lover* (starring *Emmanuelle*'s Sylvia Kristel) and a splatter-filled Ridley Scott rip-off called *Alien Contamination*.

Away from the music, *The Last American Virgin* is occasionally a masterpiece of male teenage awkwardness, discomfort perhaps all the more realistic since supposedly girl-hungry leads Monoson and Antin were both gay.[1] Yet *American Virgin*'s parade of hookers and horny housewives really doesn't sit comfortably with other claims that it's a uniquely pensive and hard-boiled coming-of-age tale (co-star Diane Franklin has asserted that 'people want to fluff

---

1 Antin, soon to date showbiz mogul David Geffen, was apparently drunk for his sex scene with man-eater Louisa Moritz.

off *The Last American Virgin* as some kind of teen sex comedy but they can't because the reality is so poignant . . . it wasn't just upbeat and fun. There's some gritty reality you gotta cop too"[1]). Whilst *The Last American Virgin* does admittedly have plenty of adolescent agony, the way it combines that angst with pop tunes and pussy feels more rushed than sophisticated.

Still, *The Last American Virgin* perhaps *can* claim a victory as the earliest and edgiest compilation-style pop soundtrack of the decade, shifting movie music away from its traditional reliance on commissioned orchestral scores and Broadway-style show tunes and attempting instead to capture MTV's contemporary variety on cassette and vinyl. And if its box-office was a puny six million dollars it did eventually find cult success in the same place as the music channel that so influenced its soundtrack. Just like MTV, *The Last American Virgin* became a staple of '80s cable television, the new stations which sprang up from the latest broadcasting technology often including movie channels aimed squarely at a young audience who had been spoilt with TV sets in their bedrooms.

And between the movies and music videos playing on those TVs were the commercial breaks; two minutes full of ads made by sharp-eyed directors all dreaming of becoming the next Alan Parker or Adrian Lyne. The disparate realms of pop, films and advertising had crossed over, often with a distinctly European palette. Soon they would blend even more.

---

1 *The Last American Virgin* Blu-ray documentary.

Chapter Five

BACK TO SCHOOL

Cameron Crowe hides out at Ridgemont High; Porky's *and the lure of the lewd; plus Jennifer Jason Leigh, Nic Coppola and Sean Penn get serious (whilst Phoebe Cates gets topless).*

If *Endless Love* was ultimately more melodramatic than truthful, *Taps* more fairytale than fly-on-the-wall, and *Fame* just too 'jazz hands' to be *entirely* believable, there was one film that took portraying 'normal' contemporary teens to new levels of accuracy in 1981. Its secret weapon was research, starting its fact-finding nearly four years before it even came out. It was in the high-school year of 1978–79 when a twenty-two year old called Cameron Crowe – a baby-faced journalist from San Diego – decided to work extra-hard to make his story of teenagers feel real, honest and ordinary. So, disguising himself as a teenager, the reporter went undercover and *back* to high school.

Crowe's own years in education had been high-achieving but frustrating; he'd skipped grades because of his ability to learn fast yet found being a prodigy in a strict Catholic school made him an outcast. Recurring absences caused by kidney problems hardly helped his status in class. So – just as Allan Carr had realised when adapting *Grease* – this opportunity to have an improved, second crack at adolescence was irresistible, especially at the kind of everyday establishment he'd dreamed of attending as a child: 'There were many of us who believed that all our problems would be solved, all our dreams within reach, if we just went to Ridgemont Public High School,'[1] admits Crowe.

The official reason for his posing as a student, though, wasn't emotional but journalistic: to chronicle the lives of the modern teenager in an essay. The marriage of writing and puberty made sense: Crowe had been penning music reviews for a San Diego fanzine at just thirteen years old before moving on to be *Rolling Stone*'s youngest ever contributor a couple of years later. This was 1973. The magazine was barely half a decade old and, like *National Lampoon*, a student favourite, breaking new ground with Hunter S. Thompson's 'gonzo' political coverage, run out of a Third Street office in San Francisco. Joe Eszterhas was a senior editor, twenty years before *Basic Instinct* would turn him (briefly) into Hollywood's most talked-about screenwriter, whilst contributors included punk's poet laureate Patti Smith, Springsteen's future mentor Jon Landau and Tom Wolfe, the white-suited chief of the new journalism movement that incorporated experimental, literary styles into involved, immersive research. Shooting front covers on her Hasselblad was one Anna-Lou 'Annie' Leibowitz.

When *Rolling Stone* moved from San Francisco to the Big Apple in 1977, however, Cameron Crowe didn't go with them. He had other plans: 'Over a period of time I thought, I'm gonna start interviewing the fans, and it was at a Rod Stewart concert that I just went out into the parking lot and started interviewing the fans and realised, with all due respect to Rod Stewart, that the fans' stories – the people that had been camped out in the parking lot – were almost better than the story of the guy in the hotel room who never left. From that came the idea to do a book about fans and students and high-school life from the inside out. And that became *Fast Times at Ridgemont High*.'[2]

Crowe could sense an ever-growing media focus on youth culture – from disco to *Animal House* to music videos – but what he didn't see was anyone trying to look closer than just the surface. That would be his goal. 'For seven years I wrote articles for a youth culture magazine, and perhaps not a day went by when this

---

1 From the Introduction to the book *Fast Times at Ridgemont High*.
2 Author interview, broadcast on BBC Radio 1, 3 November 2005.

term wasn't used – "the kids". Editors assigned certain articles for "the kids". Music and film executives were constantly discussing whether a product appealed "to the kids". Rock stars spoke of commercial concessions made "for the kids". Kids were discussed as if they were some huge whale, to be harpooned and brought to shore. It began to fascinate me, the idea of The Kids. They were everywhere, standing on street corners in their Lynyrd Skynyrd T-shirts, in cars, in the 7-Eleven. Somehow this grand constituency controlled almost every adult's fate, yet no adult really knew what it was nowadays – to be a kid.'[1]

So, in the autumn of '78, Cameron Crowe gave himself a new name – Dave Cameron – and enrolled at Clairemont High in his home city. It wasn't just his face that looked young enough to still be a student. The twenty-two year old also had the attitude of a teenager, a mix of laidback temperament with a wide-eyed hunger to discover new things. 'He was adorable,' agrees Sarah Lazin, back then Cameron's assistant editor at *Rolling Stone*. 'He was serious about learning stuff. He was a pleasure to work with, a total professional. He was easygoing and eager to learn. Obviously, the bands loved him.'[2] If you could win over Fleetwood Mac at seventeen years old, then charming a bunch of high-school students at twenty-two was a breeze. He had already gotten Clairemont's principal William Gray to agree to the undercover project by entertaining him with tales of interviewing Kris Kristofferson.

Crowe's article first appeared in *Playboy* magazine in September 1981, the name and location of the school changed to Ridgemont High in Redondo Beach, his words hidden deep in an issue more interested in bragging about its new photos of Bo Derek. A few weeks later the piece was published as a book by Simon & Schuster. Over at Universal, Thom Mount had already done a deal with Crowe – brokered by literary agent David Obst – to turn his findings into a movie. To help with filming, Mount hired Art Linson, a producer he knew from making the urban hit *Car Wash* back in 1976. Linson had been friends with the original creator of *Car Wash*, Gary Stromberg, and had helped him deal with his

---

1 Introduction to *Fast Times at Ridgemont High* op. cit.
2 'How Writer-Director's Career Got Rolling', SFGate, Joel Selvin, 10 September 2000.

increasingly crippling drug use during the making of that movie ('Shall we say . . . cocaine was a frequent presence in the creative community,' admits Mount[1]) so felt like a safe pair of hands. What's more, Linson was also friends with Crowe from when the journalist visited the set of his movie *American Hot Wax* a few years earlier, Cameron even earning himself a cameo in the film along the way. To write the screenplay, meanwhile, Mount didn't hire an outsider. He just asked Crowe to do it himself.

The *Fast Times* script that Crowe produced – his screenwriting debut – was an ensemble piece. High-schoolers Linda and Stacy are both fifteen, the former apparently mature and confident around sex, the latter an inexperienced wannabe. Stacy has a square and sensible older brother called Brad whilst other classmates include nerdy Mark Ratner, wide-boy Mike Damone and stoner Jeff Spicoli. To Crowe these characters – real students from his time undercover, but with a few elements fictionalised – were in-betweeners, teens already with the responsibility of part-time work (and harshly judging each other's jobs) but still too naïve to deal properly with the romantic experimentation they now craved. To direct, Mount and Crowe would need someone sensitive to such a moment in teen life.

The answer came in the form of another newbie: a twenty-eight-year-old film school grad (and Joan Jett lookalike) from the Bronx called Amy Heckerling. Mount had already loved her short film *Getting It Over With* but had waited for the American Film Institute graduate to get an agent before talking business with her. So began a shoot that proved to be as frustrating for the headstrong Heckerling as it was for her young stars, ambitious teenagers all dreaming of credibility.

Frustrating . . . although not for everyone. Casting director Don Phillips couldn't believe his luck. Phillips was another *Car Wash* alumnus. He'd also been a producer with Art Linson on Jonathan Demme's 1980 underdog comedy *Melvin and Howard*, during which – legend had it – he stripped down to his underwear in a meeting after it was suggested the film might get scrapped. The

---

1 Author interview. Stromberg is now clean and writes self-help books about his experience.

single-minded casting man refused to get dressed until the decision was reversed (it was, and *Melvin and Howard* went on win Universal two Academy Awards, on the same night as De Niro and Hutton).

For Don Phillips, the supply of talent around when he was casting *Fast Times* in 1981 was particularly rich. 'It was such a time in film-making history, that there were so many young talented actors to come along,' he remembers.[1] He and Heckerling found themselves creating new roles in the story just to squeeze all these newcomers in.

And actually *not* everyone wanted to be De Niro. Anthony Edwards and Eric Stoltz were friends from up the coast in Santa Barbara who'd moved to LA as drama students at the University of Southern California alongside Forest Whitaker (who also appears in *Fast Times* as football hero Charles Jefferson). To Edwards, old-fashioned showing-off seemed of more interest than any kind of Method acting: 'I was insecure and wanted the attention. So I did tons of theatre in school, and then when I was sixteen and got my driver's licence, I started driving to Los Angeles, along with my friend Eric Stoltz, who was a year ahead of me and was doing the same thing. So we had the same manager, and we started auditioning for things and doing commercials when we were sixteen. We were just so micro-focused.'[2]

Turning up at the *Fast Times* auditions ostensibly to hang out with their flat-mate Ally Sheedy (who was auditioning for, but deemed too mature to play, the role of Stacy), the USC boys were spotted by Phillips and asked to read for the Jeff Spicoli role. And whilst they didn't have quite the required charisma, Phillips and Heckerling were so impressed that they added a couple of stoner mates for Spicoli to the story, just so they could be included. Eric Stoltz – like Cameron Crowe, like Allan Carr – relished the chance to redo his time in education: 'I remember that film as being more of a bonding high-school experience than my actual high school was.'[3]

---

1 *Fast Times at Ridgemont High* DVD commentary.

2 'Anthony Edwards on *Zero Hour*, *ER* and being *Top Gun*'s "Mr Lefty Liberal Peace-Lover"', The AV Club, Will Harris, 15 February 2013.

3 moviehole.net, Caffeinated Clint, 8 April 2007.

It was the same for Judge Reinhold, whose real name was the more average Edward but who was so nicknamed because of his serious demeanour, even at just twenty-four years old. Reinhold was actually Heckerling's neighbour over in West Hollywood, having arrived in LA a couple of years earlier; a fortuitous time: 'In a lot of ways, [*Animal House*] was tremendously helpful to my career. Because I arrived in town the same year that movie opened in 1978. And it created this whole new genre of youth-oriented comedies.'[1]

Reinhold could have been Timothy Hutton's slightly cheekier older brother – as normal and unthreatening-looking – but at first Amy Heckerling thought her neighbour looked too old to play Brad. What's more, Don Phillips had been excited by the young Sean Penn he'd seen in *Taps*, even sending Thom Mount to watch Penn in his latest play and consider *him* for the part of Brad. But Penn made it clear he only wanted to play one character: surf dude Jeff Spicoli. So after also dismissing a young TV actor called Tom Hanks, then starring in ABC's little-seen sitcom *Bosom Buddies*, it was Reinhold who grabbed the Brad role. The man with the serious nickname was about to display an unwavering commitment to humiliating himself, from masturbating in a bathroom to – perhaps even worse – dressing up as a pirate.

For many of the performers there was a problem though – a frustration that, ultimately, *Fast Times* was *just* a teen movie. It didn't matter that this was a comedy with female characters as interesting as the males (unlike *Animal House*) or that the research behind the story was unprecedented. Quite the opposite. The fact that *Fast Times* was so dedicated to 'normal life' meant, to some, that it could simply never be as brave or as insightful as *Raging Bull* or *The Godfather*. Certainly, seventeen-year-old Nicolas Coppola – playing one of Brad's teenage work mates at All-American Burger – remembers that era as one in which he was constantly faced with a recurring demon: the need to be taken *seriously*. And whilst *Fast Times* was a useful job it wasn't obviously going to help him on his quest for credibility, a mission that had already seen him consider quitting acting altogether: 'I kept

---

1 thehollywoodinterview.blogspot.co.uk, Alex Simon and Terry Keefe, 22 November 2012.

getting rejected and it got to me. So I wound up in the hospital with hepatitis and mononucleosis. It was horrible. And I said to myself, I'm not doing this again. I'll do one more audition and if I don't get it, I'm done. A lot of my friends from Napa Valley were going up to Alaska and working on the crab boats and coming back with twenty-five thousand dollars and buying sports cars. I thought, I'm going to go and do that. So that was the plan. Sort of a Melville-like existence at sea if I didn't get the job as an actor. And then I did, and everything was changed.'[1]

Perhaps he was feeling the weight of even greater expectation on his shoulders than the others? With a surname like 'Coppola' how could he feel anything else? Here was the nephew of New Hollywood's most ambitious and grandiose visionary, Francis Ford, playing a burger-flipper in a teen pic. Still, the young Coppola's romantic desperation to prove himself did at least open up some interesting performing possibilities, quirks that might not have been there otherwise: 'There's no question that I had a Tourette's-like lack of inhibition in me. I was a punk rocker.' But when he wasn't considered experienced enough for the role of Brad (he hadn't even admitted his real age, knowing the kind of working restrictions placed on under-eighteens making a film), Nicolas Coppola instead was forced into the background – to the mockery of many: 'I was surrounded by actors, whose names I won't mention, who were not very open to the idea of a young guy named "Coppola" being an actor. So that movie was instrumental in me changing my name[2] because of the kind of unfortunate responses to my last name . . . they would congregate outside my trailer and say things, like quoting lines from *Apocalypse Now*, and it made it very hard for me to believe in myself.'[3] Coppola quickly followed his background stint on *Fast Times* with an audition for the role of Rick in *The Last American Virgin* but was told with his Mediterranean colouring and hairy chest he already looked too old. He had just, by then, turned eighteen.

---

1 'You've got to be able to break the wall', *Guardian*, Dorian Lynskey, 16 February 2007.

2 More of which is to come.

3 'Nicolas Cage and the Movie That Made Him Change His Name', *Hollywood Reporter*, Lauren Schutte, 14 February 2012.

Meanwhile, Jennifer Jason Leigh, after her unsuccessful audition for the Annie role in *Foxes*, won the part of confused high-schooler Stacy and was already rivalling Coppola with her need to push the envelope and get into character. Unsurprisingly perhaps, Leigh's early years had mirrored those of her fellow practitioner of the Method, Sean Penn; both were offspring of Hollywood insiders, with a young Leigh appearing in an episode of CBS's cosy drama *The Waltons*, the rival to *Little House on the Prairie* in which Penn had appeared. She might have dropped out of high school but Leigh was nevertheless a disciple of Lee Strasberg's in-depth acting techniques and she'd already turned heads by losing eighty-six pounds to play an anorexic teenager in Aaron Spelling's 1981 TV movie *The Best Little Girl In The World* – replacing Jodie Foster – not to mention having a relationship with actor David Dukes, seventeen years her senior. Playing Stacy in *Fast Times* would see her replace Foster again, the *Taxi Driver* star once considered for the role but by now with her head in her books nearly three thousand miles away over at ale.

Though not as stretching a role as that of someone battling an eating disorder, Stacy's teenage life still allowed Leigh the chance to dig deep and she got a job at a real pizza restaurant in preparation for playing the part-time waitress. Her writer mother, Barbara Turner, might have had reservations about her daughter doing a movie like *Fast Times* but for Leigh, as it seemed to be for many of her co-stars, it was like therapy: 'It's pretty liberating not to be afraid to get angry, or afraid to feel jealousy. So you get to experience all these things in life that you would normally try to suppress, or be more graceful with.'[1] And in Leigh, Heckerling found the kind of bohemian free spirit she loved, someone who cherished risk-taking, especially the topless sex scenes required of Stacy that had upset many in pre-production and would cause a few critics to claim moral outrage.

'She was happy as a clam to have her clothes off,' claimed Cameron Crowe, even hinting that the actress actually wanted the

1 'What You See and What You Get', *Guardian*, Zoe Williams, 12 March 2005.

sex scenes to be *more* graphic.[1] For Jennifer Jason Leigh, such envelope-pushing and Method-acting wasn't just for the sake of it. It was almost spiritual: 'You know, you really do choose your existence in a way. If that stuff appeals to you, which it does to me, you can have a very existential experience in acting.'[2]

Existential . . . but in *Fast Times* still managing to seem just like a regular kid. Because *Fast Times* is 'regular' from the off; everyday teen life. The opening credits alone place the story firmly in the adolescent America of the era: video arcades, hot dogs and girls in tight Jordache jeans. Unlike *Ordinary People*, *Taps* and *The Blue Lagoon*, *Fast Times* didn't use adult characters to ease the audience into the teen story. It was just kids from the get-go.

Just as Cameron Crowe had done, Amy Heckerling and costume designer Marilyn Vance immersed themselves in youth culture during pre-production, visiting local high schools to check the way pupils dressed, relishing the way that cliques tended to look alike; there were the surfers in cutoffs and Hawaiian shirts, cheerleaders in sweaters and skirts or neat jeans, football players with their mohican haircuts and other groups wanting to look European in expensive trendy clothes. In fact, Heckerling never stopped researching: 'I'd go to clubs a lot and I'd see kids dress in great clothes. Then sometimes while location-scouting, I'd see kids in jogging sneakers and backpacks and react strongly about those. We had to settle between what is the cool thing to wear and reality. Spicoli and his buddies were in control of what they wore because they knew what surfers wear. Sean is from Malibu. I'm from the Bronx. I'm not going to tell him what a surfer wears!'[3] If those gangs weren't specifically flagged up in the movie, that was the point. Heckerling and Crowe worked hard to make their research seem casual yet on the money.

It paid off. *Fast Times* felt contemporary from the moment the film's title filled the screen, its shiny pale blue and orange italics glowing with the modernity of a new decade. The Go-Gos – only formed a few years earlier but already with a US No. 1 single and

---

1 DVD commentary, op. cit.

2 *Guardian*, op. cit.

3 DVD commentary, op. cit.

album – played as the credits began whilst in the background there was Ridgemont Mall, filmed at the brand-new Santa Monica Mall. Cut to the interior and we've moved to Sherman Oaks Galleria, twenty minutes north up the 405. Covered shopping malls had really hit their stride in the States in the '60s, after laws encouraging out-of-town development were passed and the rise in car ownership saw customers willing to travel further than the traditional high street. Here were warm, welcoming and soft-muzaked pleasure-domes, where parking was easy and everything was under one roof: shops, restaurants, cinemas, video arcades. Horror director George A. Romero was the first to spot their filmic potential, the giant Monroeville Mall in Pennsylvania the setting for his *Dawn of the Dead*, the 1978 bloody satire on zombie consumer culture. Post-*Fast Times*, the microcosmic shopping precinct would be the standard hang-out for every teen loafer in numerous movies, a locale that immediately lent authenticity to any snapshot of middle-class American pubescent life. If you wanted your film to feel fresh, you needed a mall.

Filming in one was tough though. Heckerling worked closely with her production designer Dan Lomino and cinematographer Matt Leonetti at Sherman Oaks, shooting overnight to avoid crowds and dressing the area to cover a number of different times of the year; back-to-school signs one week, Christmas decorations the next. Hundreds of extras worked as background shoppers whilst restaurants stayed open through the night to feed cast and crew. Yet Heckerling loved it. A self-confessed agoraphobic, the restrictions meant she didn't ever have to go outside.

The sprawling Van Nuys High School campus, one of the oldest in the San Fernando Valley and three miles up the road from Sherman Oaks, was chosen as the location for Ridgemont High itself. Days of filming during school time helped the production team to keep things as realistic as possible, the crew able to shoot without too much disruption to student life thanks to the school's size. Anyway, even whilst shooting in the lunch court – or a history class, a biology class, the boys' locker room or at the front entrance – VNHS students hardly blinked an eye. With Robert Redford as a famous former student, they were already used to Hollywood in their hallways.

As 1981 dissolved into 1982, the *Fast Times* shoot continued to make its way around Los Angeles: the abandoned Morningside Memorial Hospital in Inglewood, where the biology class takes their field trip; the All-American Burger restaurant in Brentwood, where Brad works in the opening of the film; the girls' gym at Canoga Park High School, where the 'last dance' takes place; and several streets in the San Fernando Valley. Then, in the final week of shooting, four small sets were constructed on stage no. 3 at Universal Studios for scenes in various bedrooms: Mike Damone, Linda Barrett, Jeff Spicoli.

But it was a private house at 24124 Welby Way – in West Hills, just on the edge of the lush Bell Canyon park – that hosted the *Fast Times* scene that got all the headlines.

It's claimed the scene where Brad imagines his sister's friend Linda stripping by the pool was so popular on VHS that Blockbuster Video had to frequently replenish their stock, thanks to damage done by eager rewinding. True or not, Phoebe Cates and her red bikini – both on and off – became an iconic moment of teen cinema; an hilarious diversion into teenage-boy-fantasy-land in a film more concerned with the rougher realities of life, as well as an early outing for the artfully lit, slow-motion music-video style of the future[1]. For Phoebe Cates though, the biggest worry was what the neighbours might think. The set was closed that day but you could still see into the backyard pool area from the house next-door. Heckerling, meanwhile, had her own concerns: it was only day two of the shoot but she was dosed up on antibiotics to battle the flu.

Phoebe Cates was a teenage model who, by the time of *Fast Times*, already had four *Seventeen*, three *Elle* and four *Young Miss* magazine covers to her name. Born into an upscale Jewish family in New York, with a father and uncle both big names in the TV industry, Cates was a Julliard pupil who'd originally dreamed of being a ballet dancer but, nixed by a knee injury and soon finding herself bored by modelling, had moved into acting with an

---

1 And indeed expertly spoofed in 2003 for the video to 'Stacy's Mom' by Fountains of Wayne, a song the quartet wrote in tribute to the very band whose music accompanied the original movie scene: The Cars.

unhappy experience on the 1981 *Blue Lagoon*-'inspired' flop *Paradise*. It was so 'inspired' by *The Blue Lagoon*, in fact, that Columbia took low-budget producers Embassy Pictures to court over it, with Cates herself joining in the criticism and refusing to do any publicity. 'I don't consider *Paradise* to be a professional experience,' she told *People* magazine in 1982,[1] just a few months before *Fast Times* propelled her to stardom. 'There was no depth to anything I did in it – and it wasn't entirely my fault.' *Paradise* did, though, not only surprisingly give her a No. 1 single in Italy with the theme tune, it also introduced her to the idea of nude scenes. 'If you've got a good bod, then why not show it?' she admitted in the same *People* interview. Cates was officially old enough to do the more revealing scenes in *Paradise* but, as with Shields, a body double was secretly used. Still, her assertion was undeniable: she definitely had a good bod.

Filming *Fast Times* after the troubles in *Paradise* proved to be a welcome relief for Cates, although Heckerling and script supervisor Marion Tumen mainly remember the pool scene as made difficult by the sun dropping in and out of the clouds the whole time (look closely and you can see the continuity errors). Still, as Heckerling says of Cates, 'It's very easy to make her look good.'[2] What's more, a bit of shade here and there was the last thing audiences noticed when they saw the actress climb out of the pool in her skimpy scarlet swimwear. And *this* time, there were no body doubles used.

Early 1982 and frustration had moved into the Universal board-room. Executive VP Thom Mount was getting annoyed by the producer he had hired, Art Linson ('[his] performance on that picture was perfunctory'[3]), whilst other execs just didn't know what the hell to do with *Fast Times*, this teen movie that was thought neither serious enough to be a hangover of New Hollywood nor raucous enough to be a post-*Animal House* '80s sex-com. The truth is they were more focused on their big budget musical *The Best Little Whorehouse in Texas*, a twenty-million-

1 'Paradise Star Phoebe Cates Hangs Her Own Film with a One-Word Review – "Rip-Off"', *People*, Josh Hammer, 14 June 1982.
2 DVD commentary, op. cit.
3 Author interview.

dollar, big-screen adaptation of a Broadway favourite that starred Hollywood's hottest leading man, Burt Reynolds and singing bombshell Dolly Parton, fresh from the blockbusting popularity of her debut in *9 to 5*. What the heck *was* this thing that Universal's president Ned Tanen – following his success with *American Graffiti* and *Animal House* – had green-lit?

'It's too edgy', 'It's too sexual but not sexy', 'It should be much funnier', 'It should be lighter', 'It should be more pornographic' – just some of the notes handed to director Amy Heckerling.[1] 'Sexual but not sexy' summed it all up. When some Universal staff did bother to look in on the filming, they found the honest portrayal of ordinary teenage hormones more close to the bone than cheeky. *Too* real. The actors might have all been late teens/ early twenties, but these were kids of fifteen and sixteen they were portraying. In the wake of the Brooke Shields' controversies, the studio feared outrage. Veteran character actor Fred Gwynne – a family favourite for his iconic role as TV's Herman Munster – had already declined the film's only significant adult part, the strict history teacher Mr Hand, because of the script's profanity. Art Linson, meanwhile, received an anonymous memo on his desk one night, telling him simply to *not* make the movie. End of. He would end up a pariah if he did.

'Studios would never make that movie today [2016],' believes Thom Mount. 'In this country, in this atmosphere, in this poisonous political climate. A teenage girl gets pregnant . . . she goes to an abortion clinic on her own, she doesn't tell her parents, her brother picks her up and brings her home and life goes on just like life goes on! It seemed to us to be utterly reasonable as a thing to do at that point in time, culturally . . . the baby-boom generation would have no problem with that.'[2] And Heckerling – a tough Bronxite – certainly didn't, determined to keep up the honesty of Crowe's script even as the odds stacked increasingly against her.

Inevitably, the first-time director couldn't help but worry. Mount had initially considered David Lynch to helm the picture; incongruous perhaps, but he was certainly someone with more

---

1 DVD commentary, op. cit.
2 Author interview.

experience. Heckerling, meanwhile, assumed her career was over before it had really begun. 'I thought all the guys were amazing but I was really worried about how the females would come out,' she remembers, hardly surprising since the MPAA – in another blow – had told her she needed to cut out any male nudity if she didn't want the picture to end up with a restrictive X certificate, despite the *female* nudity seeming to pose no problem. How could anyone make a realistic, balanced story with rules like that? But the success of comedy film *Porky's* over the spring of '82 loomed large. Thanks to that surprise hit from Canada, 'sexy but not sexual' – the apparent opposite of *Fast Times* – was now deemed the way to hit big. 'They said it was so sexy to have a funny scene where they're pulling a *schlong* through [a hole on the shower wall],' recalls Heckerling of *Porky's*.[1] Who needed the kind of equality and understanding she was fighting for when you could just make a fast buck with a dick joke?

Porky's. Like it or not, there's an argument for the story of '50s Florida high-schoolers searching for sex being the most influential teen movie of the '80s. Costing little but making loads, *Porky's* had taken the retro raucousness of *Animal House* and honed in on one specific aspect – nudity – and created a storm. Now every film company in Hollywood, like their European counterparts in the wake of *Lemon Popsicle*, saw the cheap and easy potential of teenage flesh. Not that *Porky's* director Bob Clark thought that's all his movie had to offer. He was just trying to do what it seemed like lots of film-makers were trying to do and capture normal teenage life: 'Sure the film was outrageous, it was the most outrageous film of its kind, but it was the truth. *Animal House* is a wonderful film, I love it, but *Porky's* doesn't deserve to be compared to it. *Animal House* was a caricature of college, but *Porky's* was the first one to play us the way we were and I think it did it damn well.'[2]

Somewhere in *Porky's*, amongst the jokey raunch, Clark was telling the 'true' story of his own youth in the deep south of the

---

1 DVD commentary, op. cit.

2 Interview with canuxploitation.com

mid-'50s. So whilst the plot follows a group of boys in the fictional town of Angel Beach, Florida, and the lengths they'll go to just to get laid (hookers, sex clubs, the infamous moment where the boys put their peckers through spy holes in the girls' showers) Clark's adolescence wasn't *just* about popping cherries and peeping toms. He also wanted the racial prejudice he'd witnessed in Louisiana, Alabama and even the sunshine state to be centre-stage in the film. 'It's just telling the plain truth that's the way things were . . . When I moved to Fort Lauderdale in the 1950s, it was a restricted community and I went to a segregated high school. There were "No Jews allowed" signs on the beach and I didn't understand this, it shocked me . . . I've always been appalled by racism – it's part of my nature that human beings are human beings.'[1]

Look closely and that snapshot of outdated attitudes is certainly there in *Porky's*, personified by Cavanaugh (Cyril O'Reilly), the teenage racist who persecutes the school's new Jewish pupil Schwartz (Scott Colomby). It's just that it's sandwiched between jokes about erections and prostitutes. Well-meaning moral outrage, however real and truthful, was always going to struggle to get noticed up against scenes of lithe Miss Honeywell (Kim Cattrall) getting screwed in the gym cupboard and howling like a wolf. *Fast Times'* Brad fantasising about Linda in her bikini was equally comical but, as millions of teenage boys might well attest, it was also a hell of a lot more believable than a nymphomaniac gym mistress.

The cast of *Porky's*, of course, were quick to defend the plentiful accusations of over-the-top sexism: 'I think it's actually pro-women, because every time Pee Wee tries to do something macho he gets slapped in the face,' actor Dan Monahan told *People* magazine in August of 1983. He also played up his own status as a regular Joe, a Cleveland boy who'd enjoyed teenage pranks similar to his geeky character before a taste for drama led him to stage work and – like John Travolta – both a friendship with Brooke Shields *and* a commercial for Safeguard soap. Bob Clark cast Monahan because he reminded him of that archetypal knockabout American teen, Huckleberry Finn.

---

1 Ibid.

During the filming of *Porky's*, the boys lived together at 72 Atlantic Way, a beachside house in Miami. Every morning dog-walkers would look up at the property and notice the after-effects of another party, another bit of damage done. Since much of the film was shot at night, when the cast got back home in the early hours they wanted to keep the adrenaline flowing so competitive pranking was a regular sport for Monahan: 'For a lot of us it was a first time experience of being away from home and being on a set . . . and it was Bob's idea to put us in a house together. We worked our asses off and we partied our asses off too.' Wyatt Knight, who played Tommy, claims Clark wanted the guys to just be natural and playful and to bond like their characters: 'We were encouraged to misbehave . . . '[1]

Yet however regular and genuine *Porky's* claimed to be, female characters were undeniably simplistic, either pin-ups or harridans. It also *sold* itself on the extreme moments rather than the everyday, its blunt poster a mock-up of the much-discussed shower scene – a wide eye peering through a hole at a naked female leg – with the simple tagline 'You'll be glad you came!'. Critics balked, although not without throwing in a few innuendos of their own. 'Bob Clark blows it,' wrote Ebert. 'Peeping Tom scenes can be very funny (remember John Belushi on the ladder in *Animal House*?) Here, it's just smarmy. There's one other problem. None of the male actors in this movie look, sound, or act like teenagers. They all look like overgrown preppies at their fraternity pledge class's fifth reunion. Jokes based on embarrassment never work unless we can identify with the embarrassed character. Here, the actors all seem to be just acting.'[2]

Clark had started out his career making low-budget horror films in Florida, eventually gaining the attention of Quadrant Films some fifteen hundred miles north in Toronto. Quadrant struck a deal to distribute his chiller *Children Shouldn't Play with Dead Things*, turning it into a local hit, so by 1973 the director had moved to Canada full-time. He followed cult slasher favourite *Black Christmas* with *Porky's*, co-produced through

---

1 From On-Screen and Beyond podcast, episode two.
2 *Chicago Sun-Times*, March 1982.

the unlikely partnership of Canada's Astral media empire and Mel Simon, a flamboyant, American shopping-mall magnate with a questionable taste in red suits. After some early screenings on the American west coast, *Porky's* was released nationwide in the States in March of 1982 via Twentieth Century Fox, its cost around 4.5 million dollars. The barbs about racial prejudice were largely ignored by the teenage audience but fortunately for the producers the scathing reviews were too. By the end of the year, despite being mainly filmed in Miami, *Porky's* was officially the biggest Canadian film ever. Its influence both on mainstream teen films *and* the burgeoning home-video market, where increasingly low-budget and exploitative movies could find a young audience, was even more significant. The quick, cheap and star-free flick about boys with erections wasn't going to fade away quietly.

Porky's had something else too, one thing Cameron Crowe definitely hadn't wanted in *Fast Times*: *nostalgia*. 'They used to say nobody will come to see a movie about young people unless it appeals to adults too,' recalls Crowe. 'They were saying, "Can't you have some adult characters, so there's some nostalgia in here? Like *American Graffiti*?" And that was the whole battle, I remember. To convince the studio that young people would actually show up if they had a movie about them.'[1]

Porky's had invigorated the teen movie market but became a burden for those wanting to make films with a little more substance. It certainly put the spotlight on *Fast Times*, Universal even sending John Landis – their golden boy after *Animal House* and *An American Werewolf in London* – on to the set to casually check that Heckerling knew what she was doing. He assured everyone she did. Yet even with the film's release imminent, Crowe and Heckerling were getting pressure to include certain elements in order to increase its appeal to a wider audience. And it wasn't just about the kind of sex on show. The writer and the director were serious music fans and had imagined the likes of rabble-rousing AC/DC, Elvis Costello and Bruce Springsteen on the soundtrack to their film. Certain bosses at Universal, though, just

---

1 *Fast Times at Ridgemont High* DVD commentary, op. cit.

wanted The Ravyns' soft rock anthem 'Raised on the Radio' ('Just an all-American boy / I got my favourite toy') on repeat.

A few weeks before *Fast Times'* mid-August release date, and with the contrasting *Porky's* already a seemingly effortless mega-hit, Amy Heckerling was still arguing over what songs to include: 'I was one of those obnoxious teenagers that thought that the music I liked was great and everything else sucked.'[1] Only after some bargaining with co-producer Irving Azoff did she manage to get new wave bands such as Oingo Boingo on to the soundtrack, allowing in established million-sellers such as Don Henley and Joe Walsh as part of the compromise. Azoff, who would go on to chair Universal's record company MCA the following year (and whose reputation in the entertainment industry earned him the nickname 'poison dwarf') just so happened to manage Henley and Walsh's band The Eagles.

Behind-the-scenes glitches aside, the *Fast Times* soundtrack still proved revolutionary. Since many of the team had worked on *Car Wash*, they already knew the importance of a hit single to accompany a movie (Thom Mount had even had his ass saved on the much ridiculed *Xanadu* by its mega-selling Electric Light Orchestra and Olivia Newton-John soundtrack) and they worked with Danny Bramson, director of Universal's Amphitheatre venue and MCA offshoot Backstreet Records, to fill the album with wall-to-wall contemporary pop, helping to avoid the nostalgia that Crowe was so wary of. Jackson Browne's sweetly melodic 'Somebody's Baby' – written specifically for the film – led the way, heading into the Billboard Top 10 just as the movie started to take off in late summer of '82. Singer/songwriter Browne might not have been the youngest hipster on the block and Heckerling might have been told to use the track twice in the movie (the second time, rather oddly, during Stacy's distinctly unromantic deflowering scene) but his well-known political activism in the era still gave him an edge. As Bruce Springsteen said to Browne: 'You wrote the songs [The Eagles] wished they had.'[2] 'Somebody's Baby' remains his biggest ever.

---

1 Ibid.

2 From Springsteen's speech at Browne's induction into the Rock'n'Roll Hall of Fame, March 2004. Browne had actually co-written The Eagles' hit 'Take it Easy' with Glenn Frey.

Azoff and Heckerling also quickly agreed on certain tracks such as Gerard McMahon's plaintive 'Look in Your Eyes'. 'Irving Azoff came to see me do a show in downtown LA ... as did David Geffen, Maurice White[1] and many record label A&R folk,' says McMahon. 'Irving – as he is – was very convincing on how to shape my career and told me about *Fast Times at Ridgemont High*, that he was involved in its soundtrack and he was confident my song was a perfect fit. He played it for Cameron Crowe and Amy Heckerling ... and within twenty-four hours said, "Your song is going in the film!"'[2]

But as a sign of where much of the industry still was with soundtracks at the time, the shine of *Saturday Night Fever*'s success having been tarnished by musical flops such as Allan Carr's *Can't Stop the Music*, Robert Stigwood's *Sgt. Pepper's Lonely Hearts Club Band* and Cannon's *The Apple*, McMahon was initially warned off allowing his track on to the film. 'Jimmy Iovine was going to produce my album and we both went to an advance screening. Jimmy hated the film and said to me, "I think this could kill your career." He was producing prestigious artists like Springsteen, Patti Smith, U2, Tom Petty and soundtracks back then were somewhat of a "No". Certain artists didn't want to be associated with a particular film.[3] In any event, in all my brattishness I was fascinated with the So Cal youth culture and told Jimmy I'd be allowing my song in the film ... I loved what the film was saying ... and to be validated by Cameron Crowe in his love of my work was quite rewarding.'[4]

And even when an older, classic song was used – such as Led Zeppelin's 1975 rock behemoth 'Kashmir' – it was still pretty cool: the famously fussy Zep only let it in because they liked Crowe's music journalism and, in his original undercover article, many of the characters at Clairemont had been Zeppelin fans, eagerly awaiting the band's upcoming US tour that would ultimately be

---

1 Geffen had just begun his eponymous record label, White was the lead singer of soul band Earth, Wind & Fire.

2 Later known as Gerard McMann, now G. Tom Mac. Author interview.

3 The debacle of post-*Saturday Night Fever* disco pics such as Allan Carr's *Can't Stop the Music* and Cannon's *The Apple* certainly hadn't done the soundtrack industry any favours.

4 Author interview.

cancelled in the wake of drummer John Bonham's death from accidental asphyxiation in September 1980. OK, so 'Kashmir' wasn't the track Crowe originally wanted – *Led Zeppelin IV* was the LP mentioned in the script, not Kashmir's parent album *Physical Graffiti* – but *anything* licensed from Zeppelin was considered a coup. It was all a long way from *Porky's* and girls' locker rooms.

Plus, if not all the attempts to secure music went to plan, there were always other ways for *Fast Times* to look fresh and modern. Bruce Springsteen himself, just crossing over into the mainstream after scoring his first Top 10 hit 'Hungry Heart', didn't make it on to the soundtrack but his younger sister Pamela did appear in the film playing an enthusiastic cheerleader in a school assembly scene (attracting the interest of Sean Penn along the way). New wave queen Debbie Harry didn't have a track in the movie either but *was* represented by a cardboard cutout in a record store scene, whilst another artist discovered by Harry's producer Mike Chapman – the leotard-loving rocker Pat Benatar – was cheekily referenced as the inspiration for a number of the more eccentrically dressed high-school girls. And if Crowe and Heckerling still smart to this day over Elvis Costello not featuring musically in their movie, they at least managed to get a poster of him on the wall of Mike Damone's chaotic bedroom. The resulting hotch-potch of pop culture nods and winks might not have been entirely elegant but even in their scattergun approach they positioned the film as something perfectly in tune with the increasingly knowing but aimless youth of the early '80s. It was MTV on vinyl. Something completely *normal*.

The soundtrack to *Fast Times* featured no original score; any brief orchestral moments came from Universal's musical archive rather than new compositions. The accompanying album came out a couple of weeks before the movie, tellingly on the Elektra label: an outlet that had been merged with David Geffen's Asylum records for several years but was now moving away from singer-songwriter territory into the new wave, with Boston post-punks The Cars in particular propelling them into a new era. Due to rights issues, subsequent home entertainment and TV versions of *Fast Times* have, frustratingly, featured different tracks and not even the album was completely representative of the film-makers' vision, The Cars themselves noticeably absent, despite their song 'Moving in Stereo' accompanying the infamous bikini scene. Still the *Fast Times* soundtrack remains for many the first impactful rock'n'roll compilation soundtrack of the '80s. *Times Square*, *Foxes* and *The Last American Virgin* had all tried but their failure at the box-office meant there had been little immediate attention paid to accompanying albums, however good they sounded. When *Fast Times* hit big at the box-office, the LP followed. The record, with its image of So Cal's iconic Vans slip-ons – beloved of young skater culture – on the cover, wasn't only exactly where Elektra wanted to go. It was also exactly where the movie-going, record-buying teenagers wanted to be taken.

When *Fast Times* came out on 13 August 1982, it wasn't *precisely* the film Heckerling and Crowe had envisaged. The music remained a sore point, whilst the writer had been asked to come up with a 'Where are they now?' coda to the film; not what he wanted since it was too similar to those in the nostalgia-packed *American Graffiti* and *Animal House*. Yet the pair were happy enough. Universal's low opinion of the finished product, on the other hand, meant they only released it on 498 screens – compare that to *The Best Little Whorehouse*'s 1400.

Fast Times also didn't attract glowing reviews, critics seemingly as confused by the whole 'sexual not sexy' issue that had flummoxed Universal's execs during production. So there was Roger Ebert of the *Chicago Sun-Times* famously calling it 'a scuzz-pit of a movie' because of its frenzied obsession with sex whilst at the same time the *New York Daily News* opined that the film was just too mellow: 'The times may be fast, in relative terms, but breakneck they're not.'[1]

Yet not even the naysayers could deny the growing popularity of the film over the following weeks. Forget 'sexual' or 'sexy', at least the audience understood the refreshing, contemporary honesty of *Fast Times*. Nostalgia, all of a sudden, seemed so out of date. As a result of positive word of mouth, a number of new screens were added before Universal finally bowed to an official

---

1 Ernest Leogrande, 3 September 1982.

wide release on over 700 screens come mid-September. The frustrating gestation period had been worth it. *Fast Times* stayed at cinemas for ten weeks in total, grossing over twenty-seven million dollars domestically, six times its production budget.

Less begrudgingly, commentators also praised the host of new talent the picture had to offer: Reinhold, Backer, Cates, Leigh, Whitaker and, most prominently, the surfer with the spliff and the slip-ons, Sean Penn.

While Phillips' ensemble cast of *Fast Times* was almost universally loved it was still the kid from *Little House on the Prairie* that always got singled out. 'All these young actors are relaxed, funny and natural,' wrote Janet Maslin in the *New York Times* review of *Fast Times*, 'but the movie's real scene-stealer is Sean Penn, as a pink-eyed surfer named Jeff Spicoli who wouldn't dream of holding down a job.'[1]

Penn's actual audition for the role hadn't been that hot but Heckerling and Phillips already knew he was the right guy, from the moment they saw him hanging out in the hallway beforehand. And Penn assured his new bosses that when it mattered, his interpretation of Spicoli would be flawless. 'He told us, "I'll bring it. I'll bring that guy. Don't worry. He'll be there,"' remembered Cameron Crowe.[2] 'And then basically the next time we saw him he was in character. And we called him Jeff for the whole movie . . . People say to me, "What was it like working with Sean?" and I say, "I dunno. I worked with *Jeff*."'

Heckerling agreed: 'He was so clear-headed about what he was doing and where he was going . . . [he] came to us with an astounding vocabulary. He had the slang down and just brought so much.'[3]

Such perfectionism came at a cost though. With the actor not wanting to break character, desperate to prove that even in the frivolous days of early '80s Hollywood he could still go for broke, Penn's non-stop Spicoli-like behaviour began to piss off the very

1 3 September 1982.
2 *Fast Times at Ridgemont High* DVD commentary, op. cit.
3 Ibid.

guy he was trying to piss off in the movie: Ray Walston, playing Mr Hand. There were also stories of the young actor demanding that the set be cleared when he filmed his scenes, being over-protective around his girlfriend Pam Springsteen and starting a fight with extras during the prom scene. Penn had previous too. *Fast Times* might only have been his second movie but he had already caused problems on his first, *Taps*, thanks to his self-confessed obsession with creative freedom: 'I was nearly suicidal about it. The director [Harold Becker] . . . I fought with him so much. I must have been a nightmare.'[1] So if *Fast Times* was frustrating for some of its stars in *not* being a weighty '70s movie like *Mean Streets* or *One Flew Over the Cuckoo's Nest*, it is at least – with Penn and Leigh's already fully developed focus on honesty and Method – the *Mean Streets* or *Cuckoo's Nest* of early '80s teen flicks.

It was, in fact, around the same time that Penn was introduced to *Cuckoo's Nest* star Jack Nicholson for the first time by his old friend from *Taps* – 'Tim Hutton brought me up to [Nicholson's] pad . . . It turned out that he and I have a very easy shorthand with each other'[2] – and Nicholson's words of wisdom proved helpful to the newcomer ('he became kind of the angel on my shoulder'[3]). Meanwhile Penn made sure he spread the word about another of his friends from *Taps*, telling everyone on *Fast Times* just how big a star he thought this guy called Tom Cruise was going to be.

Putting down its roots in the summer of '82, *Fast Times'* influence on pop culture spread out in a variety of ways, from its groundbreaking soundtrack to its sexual openness. Yet it's Penn's performance as Spicoli that's still the most talked about, from his popularisation of Checkerboard Vans shoes to the reappearance of similar movie slackers at the close of the decade. The colourful character on the sidelines had stolen the limelight from the straightforward leading men and he wouldn't be going back. His attention to detail had also earned him a nickname amongst his fellow cast members: *Sean De Niro*.[4]

---

1 *Rolling Stone*, Mark Binelli, 19 February 2009.
2 Ibid.
3 Ibid.
4 Penn and De Niro actually share a birthday – 17 August.

OK, so Jeff Spicoli might not have been a role quite up there with his icon's finest, but for a second film Penn couldn't have asked for a better label. He never wanted to be clean-cut like Hutton, sweet and naïve like Shields,[1] or playing some everyday horny teenager in *Porky's*. The angry kid from Malibu never planned to be safe and ordinary. I mean, why be ordinary, when you could be a raging bull?

---

1 The film's coda (that Crowe was forced to add on) tells us that Spicoli supposedly rescued Brooke Shields from drowning – and then blew all his reward money by hiring Van Halen to play at his birthday party.

Chapter Six

THE GANG

Matt channels Marlon in Over the Edge; The Outsiders *sees Coppola head back to basics; plus Dillon, Cruise, Lowe, Estevez, Swayze, Howell and Macchio become Hollywood's big-screen boyband.*

Matt Dillon – or at least, his mother – was wise to turn down *The Blue Lagoon*. Come the turn of the decade, Hollywood was already in awe of Dillon the teenager. Making a movie where he'd have to prance around in a loincloth with a model could have ruined it all.

Casting director Vic Ramos had been introduced to Dillon in 1978, after talent scouts had discovered him in the halls of Hommocks Junior High in Larchmont, New York, not far from eventual *Blue Lagoon* star Chris Atkins' home in Rye. Dillon had been bunking class but it paid off. The scouts loved the kid's persona – the tough guy trying to mask his middle-class background – and Ramos offered to manage him just as he hooked a crucial supporting role in 1979's teen drama *Over the Edge*. The difference between Dillon's east coast life and the Hollywood roots of Penn and Hutton was clear. Dillon could play the rebel but he did it with a mumbling normality. Those brought up in Californian showbiz families acted as if they were never going to do anything else; whether tough or troubled, they were always polished, always powerful. But beneath Dillon's danger there was still a hesitancy, as if he couldn't entirely believe that he wasn't working in construction.

It's that rawness that made *Over the Edge*. Alongside Dillon were a cast of similar unknowns and first-timers, all playing bored teens who've had enough of adult hypocrisy in the fictional town of New Granada,[1] a planned community that promised modernity and comfort but whose blandness left nothing much for the kids to do apart from petty crime. They just want to be understood, their issues to be taken seriously, but when one of their own – Dillon's swaggering Richie, all long hair and crop tops – is shot dead by an over-zealous cop, their plight is dismissed even more. The only thing they can do is riot.

Tim Hunter and Charlie Haas's script for *Over the Edge* had been meticulously researched, starting back in 1973 with the writers meeting real teenagers in new-build towns and listening to their problems: nothing to do, taking drugs to relieve boredom, vandalising half-built properties. A few years later producer George Litto, a former agent who'd worked extensively with blacklisted writers back in the '50s, then latched on to the story's social punch, backing the passion project with some of his own money as well as that of partners Orion Pictures. Orion was still a new deal, formed in 1978 by executives who'd left United Artists and forged a distribution agreement with Warners. Their first picture was Diane Lane's breakthrough (aged thirteen) in *A Little Romance*; their third, Philip Kaufman's 1963-set greaser drama *The Wanderers*. *Over the Edge* would be in the middle.

At first Orion wanted *Over the Edge* to be less blunt and more romantic – to have a little of the *Romeo and Juliet* about it – but Litto held his ground, hiring a cinematographer (Andrew Davis) who was influenced by the measured '60s documentary-making of Frederick Wiseman[2] and a relatively inexperienced thirty-year-old called Jonathan Kaplan to direct. Kaplan had worked with the Sex Pistols and knew the world of authentic teenage rebellion: 'I decided to attack *Over the Edge* from a punk angle: keep it simple. No fancy camera moves, visual effects, nothing fancy . . . When it came to cast *Over the Edge*, we tried to go for that same

---

1 The movie was actually shot in Greeley, Colorado, due to more favourable working practice laws for children but it was loosely based on a news story about a community in the San Francisco area.

2 Such as *High School* (1968) – a day-in-the-life of a high school in Pittsburgh – and *Hospital* (1970), a similar look at New York's Metropolitan Hospital Center.

authenticity. We wanted real teens, as opposed to professional actors – and kids who were also age-appropriate. No twenty-somethings playing fourteen year olds.'[1] He shot the film in twenty days. The young cast partied hard and Kaplan made sure he put the bands they were really listening to – Cheap Trick, The Cars, Van Halen – on to the soundtrack: 'The movie is better for it. I think the soundtrack is ahead of its time. Not many movies used rock scores then. Martin Scorsese's *Mean Streets* had done it, but not too many others.'[2]

Too much too soon? Perhaps. Orion saw the finished picture and worried it could inspire copycat violence, especially at a time when gang troubles were in the news, and of even more concern since the leads were all so young. This was not *Saturday Night Fever*, with its older teens and disco tunes to soften the blow, or even Walter Hill's *The Warriors* from a few months earlier, where a high style made its story of New York tribal warfare feel exciting but not entirely believable. *Over the Edge* was low-key, documentary-like.

In the end, *Over the Edge* released in only a handful of cinemas in May 1979. What little marketing Orion produced tried to place it as a sensational and horrifying juvenile delinquent movie rather than what those involved had intended: something genuine and honest, delving into the troubles of the often-overlooked suburbs. Matt Dillon had wanted to do everything for real: 'Jonathan would call me Marlon – as in Marlon Brando. I was a Method actor and I didn't even know what that meant. And I didn't even know who Marlon Brando was, truthfully. I mean, I only knew him as the old guy from *The Godfather*.'[3] It was a dedication at least noticed by the industry if not, as yet, by film-goers.[4] You can see it in Richie's heart-stopping delivery of the film's most famous line: 'I only got one law. A kid that tells on another kid is a dead kid.' If Dillon the middle-class teen was only pretending to be a

---

1 *Vice* magazine, Mike Sacks, 1 September 2009. Travolta, whose production company were the first to sign a deal with Orion, had of course been twenty-three when playing a high-schooler in *Grease*. Olivia Newton-John was twenty-nine, Jamie Donnelly thirty, Stockard Channing *thirty-three*.

2 Ibid.

3 Ibid.

4 *Over the Edge* would get a limited re-release in 1981 before finally finding appreciation as a regular on cable TV.

rabble-rouser, he still did it with all the swagger of Travolta as Tony Manero or the vulnerability of Stallone in *Rocky*. He was fifteen years old.

Tim Hunter was a scholar of the French new wave and had taught film history at the University of California in Santa Cruz[1] but after the critical acclaim of *Over the Edge* found himself, a little incongruously, pitching movies to the mainstream. After all, even a giant such as Disney still needed to find new hits. Post-*Grease* and *Saturday Night Fever*, in an increasingly teen-focused industry, Disney boss Ron Miller[2] had controversially broken with tradition by deciding to green light more mature PG films as well as their harmless G-rated family fare. When Hunter offered them an adaptation of a book called *Tex* he'd scripted with Charlie Haas, he secured five million dollars to make it – despite *Over the Edge*'s failure at the box-office – and introduced his own, independent way of working into Disney's well-oiled corporate machine. Hunter knew that the story of *Tex* had something. When he'd been researching teen gangs for *Over the Edge*, all the kids were reading the novel – and others – by its author S. E. Hinton. And for the title role, he wanted Matt Dillon back.

By the time of making *Tex*, casting Matt Dillon was no longer *just* about acting. It was also starting to make sense from a box-office point of view. He'd followed *Over the Edge* with growing pains movie *My Bodyguard* in 1980, playing school bully Melvin Moody, then appeared as smouldering eye-candy Randy Adams in *Little Darlings* the same year, an even bigger hit that bluntly dealt with two girls (played by Tatum O'Neal and Kristy McNichol) as they aimed to lose their virginity at summer camp. Both blended comedy with coming-of-age insight, *Little Darlings* an occasionally unfocused but nevertheless intriguing blend of *Animal House* japery – food fights, R-rated swearing – with moments of New Hollywood existentialism ('I feel so lonely,' says McNichol's Angel, after a disappointing lovemaking session with Randy). Dillon's fan base grew, ranging from teenage girls

---

1 where he had been Charlie Haas's professor.
2 Walt's son-in-law.

with posters on their walls to grown-up film journalists in awe of his brooding attitude. 'The magnetism he radiates is very powerful: it is something tangible,' gushed Andy Warhol and Maura Moynihan in *Interview* magazine.[1] 'On his taut physique clothing falls in loose disorder. Buttons seem to come undone and fabric slackens. He is blessed with dramatic Gaelic colouring: glossy black hair, luminous skin with flushed cheeks and enormous liquid eyes. His attention is elusive but, once captured, focuses with great intensity.'

Dillon had five siblings and his little brother Kevin, also an actor, saw first-hand the effect Matt had on people – and had no reason to complain: 'Girls would figure out where he lived, drive by and ring the doorbell. And that wasn't so bad for the younger brother . . . or the older ones.'[2]

Dillon himself had fun with his fame but wasn't entirely comfortable: 'I can't understand it. Looks aren't a big thing to me. I keep reading these articles in fan magazines about me, and I don't even know who they're talking about. It's boring.'[3]

Despite bunking off class that fateful day in Larchmont, what Dillon actually loved was learning. High school might have suffered the moment his acting took off but the hunger for knowledge never went. 'You should always be taking chances,' he told Warhol, explaining why more troubled characters appealed to him. 'When you're playing someone who's sort of seedy, there's less limitation, there's so much space you can travel. There's room to move in.'[4]

Dillon partied at Studio 54 but admitted that his focus on work got in the way of relationships with girls. The rumour ran that he was so keen to be taken seriously that Vic Ramos even vetted photographers' pictures of him, making sure his star didn't look *too* gorgeous. He also, by now, had worked out exactly what it meant to be nicknamed 'Brando' and showed his willingness to experiment by taking classes at the Strasberg Institute. His idol, he unsurprisingly told reporters, was De Niro.

1 *Interview* magazine, December 1983.
2 *Guardian*, Rhik Samadder, 17 June 2015.
3 *Chicago Sun-Times*, Roger Ebert, 25 April 1983.
4 *Interview* magazine, op. cit.

It was almost as if Dillon had clocked what had happened to Travolta and was determined not to crash in the same way. Physical comparisons between the two were obvious: the wavy black hair, the square jaw, the bad-boy, New York swagger that softened with one flash of a disarming smile. Yet Dillon, without a genuine blockbuster – let alone two like Travolta – to shackle him, could take more risks. As teen movies followed either the *Porky's* route and got more overtly raunchy, or the *Fame* route and became shamelessly stylised, Dillon spearheaded a niche that reinvigorated the authentic intensity of '70s blue-collar soul-searching and mixed it with a new, youthful '80s charisma. Whilst his James Dean frown nodded back to adolescent life from over thirty years earlier it wasn't a jokey nostalgia like *Grease* or *Happy Days*, just more of a fresh take on the moody mythology of retro rebels and wild ones. 'Essentially, teenagers are the same now as they were then,' Dillon told Ebert, explaining why that particular moment in the past continued to be so resonant with young audiences. 'Maybe they had a little more innocence then. But right now, I'd say teenagers are about where they were right before the hippy stage of the '60s. Did you ever stop to wonder why today's kids can identify with '50s and '60s teenagers? Maybe it's because high-school society today is more like it was then than like it was in 1970.'[1]

Tex's writer S. E. Hinton – Susie to her friends – knew all about being a teenager in the early '60s. She was born in Tulsa, Oklahoma in 1948, back when the city was still known as the 'oil capital of the world' and grew up a fan of Dean in *Rebel Without a Cause* and Jerome Robbins' teen gang musical *West Side Story*. Books, however, proved a tougher sell: 'At that time realistic teenage fiction didn't exist. If you didn't want to read *Mary Jane Goes to the Prom* and you were through with horse books, there was nothing to read.'[2] So, aged fifteen, she did it herself. 'One day a friend of mine was walking home from school and these "nice" kids jumped out of a car and beat him up because they didn't like his being a greaser. This made me mad and I just went home and

1 From *Chicago Sun-Times*, op. cit.
2 Interview on theoutsidersfanclub.weebly.com.

started pounding out a story ... the beginning of *The Outsiders*. It was just something to let off steam.'[1] *The Outsiders* took two years to fully bloom, worked on between lessons at the city's Will Rogers High School, but eventually Hinton gave it to a friend's writer mother, who then passed it to an agent, who in turn sent the manuscript to Viking Press. By 1967, the eighteen-year-old Susan Hinton – who had once gotten a D in her creative writing class – had her first novel in bookstores.

The Outsiders was a slow-burning success. As a sensitive tale of teenage gangs in the '60s, exploring cliques normally dismissed as mere troublemakers, it struggled in a mainstream literary market dominated that year by Robert Crichton's World War II adventure *The Secret of Santa Vittoria* and Jacqueline Susann's drug-addled soap opera *Valley of the Dolls*. Gradually, though, *The Outsiders* found its place in school libraries and English classes, its nod to the teen rebels of the rock'n'roll era appealing to contemporary young readers, selling enough to help Hinton pay for university in Tulsa and putting pressure on her for a follow-up.

That Was Then, This Is Now was the result of a battle with writer's block in 1971, before *Tex* arrived in 1979, both stories of young Oklahoma boys from broken homes. Between the two was 1975's *Rumble Fish*, bringing more emotional insight into the world of biker gangs and the family bonds and hero worship that sit at their heart. The books featured many of the same characters, lead roles from one appearing in the background of another. It made sense: Tulsa was relatively small. Everyone would know Tim and Curly, Mark and Cathy, Ponyboy Curtis.

Hunter and Haas's take on Hinton's *Tex*, with Dillon in the title role, came out to good reviews but modest returns in July 1982. The hook-up with a new-look Disney might have given the production a decent budget but movie-goers were confused by the Mouse House's move away from its family animation towards teenage angst.[2] Yet as Francis Coppola readied his own adaptation of Hinton's first novel – *The Outsiders* – casting Matt Dillon again

---

1 Ibid.

2 Other underperforming attempts by Disney to branch out into live-action, more mature projects included fantasy horrors *The Watcher in the Woods* (1980) and *Something Wicked This Way Comes* (1983). Both suffered production delays and recuts as the right tone was sought. Both flopped.

was an obvious consideration. Few could match the fine line between brooding outcast and powerhouse movie star that he trod. He had even become friends with Susie Hinton herself. 'She is wonderful,' he told Roger Ebert of the writer, then in her early thirties. 'She was on the set of *Tex* . . . and she really understands the way kids think – especially male kids.'[1]

Even at the height of his '70s success Francis Coppola had always wanted his films to be made away from the studio system and *The Outsiders* fulfilled that dream from the get-go. Rather than having relied on the usual highly paid team of Hollywood readers to find him an interesting project, Coppola had instead been contacted by a school librarian in mid-California whose pupils loved the book. She wrote to him with a straightforward suggestion: 'Make a movie of *The Outsiders*.' And eventually, he did.

This was spring, 1980. *Fame* was about to capture the lives of modern, metropolitan show-offs but there was more to the kids of America than dreams of success in the big city filmed by European outsiders. In the vast mid-west, Susie Hinton's stories of smaller lives from a slower era still resonated. Not knowing exactly where to send her begging letter about *The Outsiders*, Jo Ellen Misakian of the Lone Star School in Fresno had found the address for Paramount Studios in a reference book and hoped that would do the trick. In fact, the note ended up at Francis Coppola's office in New York, a place where he always received less correspondence. As a result, Misakian's letter didn't languish at the bottom of a large pile. Coppola read it, looked at the copy of the book that was also enclosed and smiled. 'I bet kids have a good idea of what should be a movie,' he told his producing partner Fred Roos. 'Check it out.'[2] Roos – a middle-aged former casting director who'd assembled *American Graffiti*, discovered Jack Nicholson back in the '60s and recommended James Earl Jones as the voice of Darth Vader – was not initially keen ('The jacket was so tacky. It looked like the book was privately printed by some religious

---

1 *Chicago Sun-Times*, op. cit.
2 'Making "The Outsiders", A Librarian's Dream', *New York Times*, Aljean Harmetz, 23 March 1983.

organisation'[1]) but, after a few weeks of carrying the novel around he finally read it to kill time on a plane journey. By the summer he was on another flight, this time to Tulsa, to meet Susie Hinton herself and to buy the film rights.

The deal wasn't a big one (five thousand dollars) and Coppola's company Zoetrope had plenty of other things on which to focus first. Their ambitious musical *One from the Heart* was out of control, heading towards twenty-seven million dollars. Shot on Zoetrope's recently purchased studio lot in San Francisco and using expensive hi-tech equipment, Coppola hoped the film would change the way directors made movies, giving them more power to do what they wanted outside of the Hollywood corporations. Instead, it was about to bankrupt him. 'We came to call those last days at Zoetrope "The fall of Saigon"', remembered Coppola's regular casting director Janet Hirshenson,[2] in reference to the Vietnam War he had so grandly portrayed in *Apocalypse Now*.

Michelle Manning was a young production assistant who'd interned at Zoetrope whilst a film student at USC and who, during the filming of *One from the Heart*, had chaperoned local school-children involved in the production. Coppola then gave her a job as his production assistant ('Francis said, "If you can handle these kids, you can handle me"'). Manning had an alternative take on watching the film-maker's financial collapse – 'Remember, I was a kid from Arizona who was just happy to be on the lot. There'd be a party every Friday before we'd have to fire people. It was just wonderful!' – but she could also see how *The Outsiders* might be therapeutic for the struggling director: 'I feel like his reaction to the over-run of money and all of that was to go and be a kid again. So he handed me a paperback book and basically said, "Can you do a budget?" And this was long before any of those computer programs. So I sat down, spent every night in Bungalow C working on a budget that was pretty close. And then we went to Tulsa.'[3]

For everyone worn out by wading through the company's financial quagmire, the opportunity to work with fresh young

1 Ibid.

2 *A Star is Found: Our Adventures Casting Some of Hollywood's Biggest Movies*, Janet Hirshenson and Jane Jenkins, Mariner, 2007.

3 Author interview.

actors on *The Outsiders* – most too youthful to be caught in the bitterness that engulfed Hollywood once the failure of *Heaven's Gate* marked the end of New Hollywood's golden era – proved a welcome dose of optimism. They were hungry and unsullied. Coppola was even reminded of his time as a counsellor at a summer camp and all the fun he used to have. Perhaps working with children again could be the palate-cleanser that he needed after months of worry? He set about tweaking the original script he'd commissioned (by Kathleen Rowell) and began to plan his time getting back to basics in Oklahoma: 'I'd forget my troubles and have some laughs again.'[1]

Darren Dalton was a seventeen-year-old theatre fan from Del Norte High School, New Mexico, who'd driven friends to an open casting for *The Outsiders* at the Hilton in Albuquerque: 'Although I didn't know it at the time, this would be unlike any other audition process for movies.'[2] Dalton ended up being asked by Janet Hirshenson to read the role of Soda Pop for her and Fred Roos ('sitting back on the bed with his shoes off') and the casting director's instincts proved spot-on. Dalton got a call back for some more improv work the next day, then another inviting him to fly – his first time in a plane – to Zoetrope Studios in California. 'I expected to walk into a place filled with unknowns like myself. [But] within the large soundstage was a who's-who of young actors; Scott Baio, faces I knew from television. It was over-whelming ... we would read from the script and improvise different scenarios. I watched some of the best work I'd ever seen. Emilio [Estevez] was there and was amazing. You could see the promise Cruise had in his energetic approach. The most memorable performance of that first trip was Mickey Rourke. He blew everyone away ... he slammed a chair across the room, injuring his hand. They rushed him to the hospital. Amazing.'[3]

Dalton eventually got the part of Soc gang member Rusty Anderson, although originally – like Rourke, who arrived on set

---

1 *New York Times*, op. cit.
2 Author interview.
3 Ibid.

on roller-skates and looking as if he hadn't washed for a week, yet still on a wave of hype that proclaimed him the 'new James Dean' – Dalton had read for the bigger role of greaser gang member Dallas. 'Late in the afternoon, Matt Dillon walked into the audition space. Any hope I felt flew out of the window. I had recently seen him in *Over the Edge* and taking one look, I knew this guy was Dallas.'[1]

Tom Cruise, with *Taps* just released in cinemas, was characteristically eager to hook a part in *The Outsiders*. 'I heard about the movie, and I came out to Los Angeles and stayed at Emilio's house over Christmas ['81]. And I stayed at the Penns' house over the summer ['82]. That's when Sean was doing *Fast Times*.[2] I just went to Francis and said, "Look, I don't care what role you give me, I really want to work with you. I want to be there with all these young actors." That was a hell of a good time.'[3] Just after *Taps*, Cruise had made '60s-set sex comedy *Losin' It* ('I had this small-time agent at the time who said, "Do it, do it." I worked hard, but it was a terrible time in my life'[4]) and the understandably sniffy reviews – 'another example of the Porky the Penis genre,' wrote Andrew Sarris in the *Village Voice*[5] – made him desperate for something more serious than yet another take on horny boys at the beach. Still, despite his eagerness to get into *The Outsiders*, Cruise still risked it all by complaining to Coppola in an audition that he wasn't letting him read for the right parts. The director eventually gave him the supporting role of Steve Randle, a muscly greaser-mechanic complete with the uneven smile of a street brawler, a look achieved by Cruise beefing up for the role and deliberately getting a cap removed from one of his teeth. Cruise's eventual co-star, Santa Monica High School pretty boy Rob Lowe, looked on during the arduous casting process with jealousy and fascination: '[Cruise had] an almost robotic, bloodless focus and intensity that I've never encountered before.'[6]

---

1 Ibid.

2 Presumably Penn was doing promotional work on *Fast Times* since the film was actually shot in the autumn of '81 and winter of '82.

3 *Interview* magazine, Cameron Crowe, May 1986.

4 Ibid.

5 3 April 1983.

6 *Stories I Only Tell My Friends*, Rob Lowe, Random House, 2011, p.101.

Rob Lowe was originally from Dayton, Ohio but, when his parents divorced, he moved with his mother and brother Chad to Malibu where they'd hooked up with the Penns and the Estevez boys – Emilio and Carlos – at SaMoHi. Carlos just wanted to play baseball but Rob knew that, as far as he was concerned, the future was all about being an actor. It was watching *Oliver!* that had done it, subsequently looking up to the handsome charm of Robert Redford and – like everyone else – the cinematic bravura of Martin Scorsese as inspiration. Lowe had never been popular with the girls as a kid and was perhaps a little nervous after being diagnosed deaf in his right ear following a bout of childhood mumps, but his mom supported his dreams of stardom. They worked auditions and agents, the teenager getting bits of screen-time here and there: an ad for burger joint Carl's Jnr, some TV shows. He got more confident, met more girls – Cary Grant's daughter Jennifer, Melissa Gilbert from *Little House on the Prairie* – and found himself pushing for the same parts as Emilio and Sean in *Ordinary People* and *Fast Times*.

Yet whilst *they* got auditions, Lowe got ignored. The Estevez lifestyle was intoxicating, something to aim for, the big house and pool that came with Martin Sheen's acting success in '70s movies such as *Badlands* and *The Little Girl Who Lives Down the Lane* so different to his own. But aged just seventeen, Lowe was already considering quitting. He just wasn't getting noticed: 'In that time that I came up, the anti-leading man was valued. Sean Penn, Mickey Rourke . . . . it was not probably the best time ever for someone like me.'[1] Maybe he was just too traditional-looking? Too clean-cut and contented? Then, just after Christmas '82, Rob Lowe finally got the call he'd been dreaming of: to go and read for Francis Coppola.

Like Darren Dalton, Rob Lowe found casting for *The Outsiders* to be eccentric and overwhelming. Emilio was there – it seemed like *every* male teen actor was there – and the oldest Estevez brother wanted to explain to his friend why this first audition was such a free-for-all, reading for multiple roles and in front of so many others, rather than just the more usual private meeting with

---

1 'Rob Lowe's Tips for Re-Re-Reinventing Yourself', GQ, Amy Wallace, 22 September 2015.

the film-maker. But all he could come up with was 'Hey, it's Francis,' followed by a shrug of his shoulders.[1] Still, Lowe knew it was no time to feel nervous about the legendary director's quirky approach or his own relative inexperience: 'In that situation, you'd better fucking figure out a way to hold your ground.'[2]

Estevez, fresh from working with Dillon on *Tex*, knew Coppola well since his father was still recovering from the film-maker's infamous *Apocalypse Now* shoot. Martin Sheen had starred as Captain Benjamin Willard and had brought over his family to Coppola's set in the Philippines. Sheen, then thirty-six years old, had been drinking heavily at the time and left his sixteen-year-old son Emilio to his own devices in the far east, putting away beer and hanging out in the red light district with *Apocalypse*'s teenage star Larry Fishburne. Relations between Emilio and his father were strained, the actor considering his son cocky, although the youngster did grab some acting work on the war movie (his scenes were ultimately deleted). Really though, Estevez wanted to be back in ninth grade in Los Angeles, enjoying track and field at SaMoHi. A fist fight with his dad eventually ensured that happened, the teenager hurriedly bundled on to the first flight out of Manila.

After school, Estevez dreamed of writing and directing, not just acting, and tried to keep sane by spending some of his time on a ranch in Montana rather than constantly being in the Los Angeles bubble. By '81 Sheen had rediscovered his Catholicism and attempted to straighten out, and father and son worked together on TV movie *In the Custody of Strangers*, aptly a story of strained family relations. Estevez was dating Wilhelmina model Carey Salley but tried to be honest about his situation: 'When I realise there are a billion people in China who don't know I exist, any flightiness is swept away.'[3] After hours of improvising and workshopping at *The Outsiders'* auditions in LA and New York, Coppola eventually cast Estevez as 'Two-Bit' Matthews, the teen drunk with a Mickey Mouse T-shirt and a carefree attitude.

---

1 *Stories I Only Tell My Friends*, ibid., p.100.

2 *GQ*, op. cit.

3 *People* magazine, 28 Febuary 1983.

Meanwhile, Lowe was Sodapop Curtis, a high-school dropout who worked at the local gas station but with movie star looks that turned him into a local hero. The girls couldn't get enough.

The orphaned Curtis brothers were at the centre of *The Outsiders* and, as eldest of the three, Darrel, Coppola and Hirshenson cast Patrick Swayze – 'Buddy' to his friends – a brawny, athletic Texan and Bob LeMond protégé whose ambitions to make it in both sports and dance had been thwarted by injury. Darrel needed to be a surrogate father to Sodapop and his younger sibling Ponyboy and the fact Swayze had already hit thirty – mature and with a long list of life experiences – made him perfect for the role.

After giving up ballet, Swayze had turned to acting coach Warren Robertson whilst working part-time as a carpenter, eventually bagging a part in *Grease* on Broadway then as a roller-skater in *Skatetown USA*, Columbia's ill-fated attempt to cash in on both the dying days of disco and the heart-throb status of *Happy Days* star Scott Baio, written by *Halloween* actor Nick Castle. *Skatetown* was camp and throwaway,[1] frustrating for Swayze since his mother and wife – both dancers – were working down in Texas, choreographing on the higher quality *Urban Cowboy* with Travolta (whose success with *Saturday Night Fever* was the very reason for lame rip-offs like *Skatetown* in the first place). Showing off his moves and his body in the disco pic did at least get Swayze noticed and he was offered a three-picture deal with Columbia, who saw him as a new teen idol. But Swayze, already battling with drink problems, took his manager LeMond's advice and turned it down. Frustrated by missing out on an athletic career, he craved more intensity than being a mere pin-up and what Le Mond was trying to achieve with Travolta gave him some confidence.[2]

The Outsiders offered Swayze the muscular challenge he needed: 'We became like a gang ourselves, hanging out together,

1 Or 'crapola', as Baio has eloquently described it. 'That was that whole time where *Xanadu* and *Roller Boogie* and all that crap was coming out. That was one of those things where they sent me the script and I said, "No", but they just kept calling and offering more money . . . and finally I said, "Well, hell. What is it? Two weeks' work? Whatever, OK, fine." [But] you know sometimes money isn't everything.' The AV Club, Will Harris, 3 April 2014.
2 Swayze was also supposedly introduced to Scientology by Travolta although he didn't stay long with the programme, according to *Going Clear*, Lawrence Wright, Knopf, 2013.

smoking cigarettes, going out for drinks and just generally running wild. Those were crazy days on Hollywood lots – with drugs, alcohol, and testosterone fuelling everything – though the Greasers' drug of choice was beer.'[1]

Coppola wanted his gangs to be aggressive, full of rage, and used local extras keen for a swing at these Hollywood types to add extra severity to the fight scenes. 'Guys were beating on each other, punching and kicking and wrestling in the mud,' Swayze remembered. 'In the middle of it, one guy came charging at me with a wild look in his eyes. He was coming to lay me out and the only way I could keep him from getting hurt myself was to hurt him. I punched him hard in the face and knocked him unconscious.'[2]

Once again, Lowe was stunned by a colleague's enthusiasm: 'He makes Tom Cruise look lobotomised.'[3]

As the youngest Curtis brother – Ponyboy, the sensitive narrator of the story – was fifteen-year-old Tommy Howell. Known professionally as C. Thomas Howell, he had grown up acting in ads and TV shows, splitting his time between his mother's home in Bell Canyon, LA, and his father's further north in Saugus. 'Someone once told me I was a very old soul,'[4] he admitted and Howell's rural interests – horse-riding and hanging out with his grandfather – helped with his softly spoken, doe-eyed portrayal of the bookish Ponyboy. He'd appeared in Spielberg's blockbuster *E.T.* the year before – as Tyler, one of Elliott's brother's friends – but was still the youngest member of the cast and looked up to the caring Cruise, the jokey Estevez and the cool Dillon, who introduced him to the music of The Rolling Stones. Swayze, meanwhile, was like a real brother to his onscreen sibling. Both had the taste for horse-riding and Howell's dad had also worked on the *Urban Cowboy* set, as a stuntman, with Swayze's wife and mother.

Finally, as Ponyboy's best friend Johnny, was Italian-American New Yorker Ralph Macchio – a baby-faced twenty-one year old who had made his debut in failed spoof *Up the Academy, Mad*

---

1 *The Time of My Life*, Patrick Swayze and Lisa Niemi, Simon & Schuster, 2010.
2 Ibid.
3 *Stories I Only Tell My Friends*, op. cit., p.121.
4 From an interview with Orli Kohn in an unnamed 1984 magazine.

magazine's 1980 attempt to replicate *National Lampoon*'s success.[1] Macchio had also been working a while – would even admit to a certain cockiness – but he'd read *The Outsiders* when he was twelve, the first book he'd really loved. Getting the role hit him hard, as did working with a director who might be down on his luck professionally but who creatively was anything but dried up. Whilst the British likes of Adrian Lyne, Alan Parker and Ridley Scott had threatened to make the film-making giant's style look rather outdated, the battle-scarred Francis Coppola was determined to reclaim his crown.

Coppola's methods of creating both bonds and rivalry amongst the gangs of *The Outsiders* were very much those of an unconventional but visionary leader. Over at the Excelsior Hotel in Tulsa the actors playing the more well-heeled Socs were staying on a different floor to the bad-boy greasers, in more luxurious rooms and getting a more generous per diem rate than their enemies in a bid to keep the bitterness between the story's two groups rumbling on even after filming (Tom Cruise was so green he spent the first few days eating frugally, not realising his per diem allowance would be renewed each day). The Curtis 'family' – Swayze, Lowe and Howell – had to spend a night together in a house, fending for themselves, observed silently from the sofa by the note-taking Coppola and Hinton.

Tom Cruise, remembers Coppola's assistant Michelle Manning, was a particular fan of the director's inspirational drive: 'Tom Cruise's character died [in the film] but because Francis created such an atmosphere of inclusion and teaching – we'd have tai chi at the beginning of every day and all these crazy things – and because he'd answer any questions, Tom Cruise wanted to stay on . . . so I'd have him working in the production office xerox-ing for me . . . [Cruise's enthusiasm] was amazing. I mean, like, seriously incredible. He was like a sponge, just soaking everything up.'[2] Meanwhile, to find the perfect take, Coppola would often

---

1 Directed by Robert Downey Sr and featuring his fourteen-year-old son as an extra. *Mad* magazine subsequently paid to get their brand name removed from *Up the Academy* and one of the film's leads – Ron Leibman – publicly disowned it.

2 Author interview.

shoot a scene twenty, sometimes thirty times, exhausting his young stars.

Although they were never *that* exhausted. *The Outsiders* shoot was energetic; a bunch of enthusiastic, optimistic alpha males with raging hormones, fuelled by drinking sessions that spilled out of the hotel rooms and into the hallways, igniting into friendly punch-ups, soundtracked by the raucous tunes of the day on their boom-boxes; for Matt Dillon it was often the brooding rallying cries of Springsteen, for Tommy Howell the thumping British post-punk of Adam Ant. Local girls found themselves the centre of plenty of attention by this bunch of fired-up, horny Hollywood troublemakers, although the already worshipped Dillon barely had to make the effort. His celebrity status did the work for him ('We caused a number of problems when all of us would go out and he was with us. The girls would want to hang around, which didn't make their boyfriends happy,' remembers Darren Dalton[1]).

Ribbing and riding was the order of the day and '70s *Teen Beat* pin-up Leif Garrett, a troubled twenty-two year old whose star was already on the wane but who'd bagged a Soc role in an attempt at reinvention, bore the brunt of it. Garrett was an anomaly in *The Outsiders*: a name from the past, lost in a crowd of faces of the future; an easy target. Plus, as someone who'd already tasted success he had more worldly experience than many of the other cast, not all of it wholesome. He was happy to pass on his knowledge to newbies such as Dalton. 'Our downtime was crazy. Leif showed up and introduced me to multiple bad habits within a single night.'[2] Nevertheless, as Rob Lowe left the chaos of Tulsa to return to his quieter life in LA, he felt positive all the effort had been worth it: 'We all have a suspicion (and a hope) that we've just been part of something special, something that may eventually change our lives.'[3]

The Outsiders certainly tells its story cleanly and wears its influences proudly. The mood is tortured, often melodramatic, full of the anguish and latent homoeroticism that electrified James

---

1 Author interview.
2 Author interview.
3 *Stories I Only Tell My Friends*, op. cit.

Dean and Sal Mineo's relationship so poetically in *Rebel Without a Cause*. Stevie Wonder's plaintive title track begs us to 'stay gold' and the whole movie is soaked in a similarly nostalgic and sunny sheen, soundtracked by Carmine Coppola's sumptuously romantic score. It's a long way from the contemporary clatter and rattle of *Foxes* or *Fame*. Some of the stars deal with that retro artifice better than others, with Howell and Macchio's earnestness seeming more of a performance than Dillon's just-out-of-jail swagger. He, of course, just makes it look easy and even his co-stars had to admit defeat. Whilst Rob Lowe's acting was enriched by Coppola's inspirational leadership, he'd had to really push himself. It had been tough. But Dillon? His New York swagger had the west coast boys like Lowe totally in awe: 'He can just stand there and the camera loves him.'[1]

Rob Lowe's hunches were right. *The Outsiders* did solid business through the spring of 1983 – thirty-three million dollars from a ten-million budget. Even so, distributor Warners wasn't interested in releasing a companion film that Coppola had been scripting during his downtime: an adaptation of another Hinton novel, *Rumble Fish*. That Coppola wanted to use *Rumble Fish* as a chance to get experimental after its more conventional predecessor didn't help. 'I'd rather not explain it because if I did I'd probably mess it up. It's like poetry on film. It's hard to describe,' admitted Matt Dillon to Andy Warhol, when pressed about what could barely be described as *Rumble Fish*'s plot.[2]

Coppola stayed on in Tulsa to shoot *Rumble Fish*, the melancholy fable of smouldering teen Rusty-James and his time wandering the city during suspension from school, mourning the passing of time and reigniting old feuds from the days before drug dealers when his older brother, the Motorcycle Boy, was gangland kingpin. Rehearsing twelve hours a day for a fortnight and hiring many of the same crew from *The Outsiders* – except this time using German expressionism and French existentialism as reference points – Coppola also signed up Stewart Copeland from rock band The

---

1 Ibid, p.130.
2 *Interview* magazine, op. cit.

Police to provide the rhythmically avant-garde soundtrack, whilst Matt Dillon and Diane Lane stayed on to play wide-eyed Rusty-James and his on/off convent school girlfriend Patty. Newcomers included Mickey Rourke, the former amateur boxer who'd so intrigued and impressed back at auditions for *The Outsiders* but who ultimately hadn't quite fitted any role (the rumour was he'd actually had the temerity to *turn down* Coppola's offers) despite being hot from his breakthroughs in Lawrence Kasdan's steamy thriller *Body Heat* and Barry Levinson's autobiographical *Diner*. *Rumble Fish*, however, had the ideal introspective role for Rourke – Rusty's mercurial older brother, the Motorcycle Boy – and the character's inner turmoil and unpredictability allowed the touchy actor to give it his best, softly spoken Marlon Brando intensity.[1]

The brothers' drunken father, meanwhile, was Dennis Hopper, the actor's own history from *Rebel Without a Cause* through to *Easy Rider* and Coppola's *Apocalypse Now* a neat shorthand for the film's highly charged but unconventional leanings. Then there were SaMoHi's younger Penn brother, Chris and Coppola's nephew Nicolas, as Rusty's swaggering friends B. J. and Smokey. Nicolas Coppola couldn't help but feel some trepidation at working in a movie with his famous uncle, especially after the catcalls he'd experienced on *Fast Times*,[2] but as Smokey he at least had several lines this time, an opportunity to properly impress and his distinctive sleepy look and plaintive drawl fitted in perfectly with the picture's poetic air of passing time and mounting regret.

Warners, though, just weren't tempted. CEO Steve Ross was too focused on the company's interests in the nascent MTV and a collapsing Atari[3] to want the worry of a Francis Coppola production, leaving Thom Mount at Universal to jump in.

'I liked Francis very, very much,' said Mount. 'I understood that he'd had problems. That happens to all of us. It's inevitable in

---

1 Although Coppola has said that physically he wanted the Motorcycle Boy to look like Albert Camus.

2 The actor claims he never *really* wanted the role in *Rumble Fish*; he was just helping his uncle and producer Fred Roos out with the auditions. He had, however, been considered for the part of Dallas in *The Outsiders*, losing out – seemingly along with all of Hollywood's young hotshots – to Matt Dillon.

3 Warner Communications had purchased technology giant Atari for twenty-six million dollars in 1976 but, by 1983, the computer company had experienced poor sales of several high-profile games and its latest console, leaving its reputation in tatters. When the flooded home computer market crashed that year, Warners saw its stock price lose two-thirds of its value.

life that things will go up and down. But Francis Coppola's a genius film-maker however you slice it. You can argue that *One from the Heart* is boring and a misfire but you can't argue that he's not alive, awake, ambitious and filled with possibility. For *Rumble Fish*, I thought this was a good fit for Francis . . . I knew he needed to work because he and I shared the same lawyer, Barry Hirsch, for a long time so I was aware of Francis's financial problems which were substantial. He just needed to be working so I thought, Fuck, y'know. Let's take advantage of that . . . I loved the *Rumble Fish* script. I thought it was *really* good. My guys at the studio didn't have the same confidence I had and I ultimately was forced by [MCA Universal chief] Lew Wasserman to make that a negative pick-up, meaning if there were over-runs then a bond company had to pay for the over-runs, not the studio, because they were so terrified coming off *Apocalypse Now* that Francis would burn down Tulsa.'[1]

Tulsa, in fact, survived Coppola's time making two movies there but Lew Wasserman was partially right: *Rumble Fish*, which debuted at the New York Film Festival in autumn '83, ultimately bombed. '*Rumble Fish* was a noble effort at creating a true American art cinema – Francis called it his art-house film for kids,' remembers Hirshenson [2] 'With its off-kilter impressionistic shots, its exaggerated sound effects and its bleak portrait of a dying industrial city, the film took extraordinary risks that the art-house crowd appreciated but that never translated into commercial success.'

Come 1986 a new breed of independent film-makers would find acclaim with their own avant-garde, monochrome debuts, ushering in a fresh wave of American art-house cinema[3] that owed much to the movie brats and it's certainly easy to see their origins in *Rumble Fish*. Nineteen-eighty-*three*, however, just wasn't ready, still in awe of more populist, less self-aware stories. A 'tone poem'[4] – that's how Jack Kroll described *Rumble Fish* in *Newsweek*, echoing the very phrase that George Lucas had used to describe

---

1 Author interview.
2 *A Star is Found*, op. cit.
3 See Chapter 16.
4 7 November 1983.

the types of films he had originally intended to make before *Star Wars* took him into a different realm and galaxy. In *Rumble Fish*, a director who had always considered himself experimental and European-leaning was revisiting his own early days, an era when art had been more important than commerce. Really, it was just too '70s for the '80s, more *The Last Picture Show* than *The Last American Virgin*. And in Rusty-James, Coppola no doubt could see something of himself: the younger brother looking up to his older sibling,[1] intent on not being trapped like the fish he sees in the local pet shop, desperate to always swim free of the pack.

By the final shot of Rusty staring at the sea in California, escaped at last from the shackles of Tulsa, freedom is just what he's found. 'Don't box me in' pleads the song as the credits roll, and it's a demand relevant to both the free-spirited Coppola and many of his restlessly creative stars: Dillon, Rourke, Cage. Escaping those confines, however, wouldn't be easy for any of them.

Still, Coppola's double-bill of teen movies had at least achieved a couple of important things: the director had proven to his industry that he could do relatively modest if he had to and secondly, his bonding with the young cast had helped take his mind off financial worries and remind him of the youthful fun of making a movie. 'I look back and I can see that [Francis] was under incredible pressure,' says Dalton, 'but he never really showed it to us. He would jump onto the catering truck and cook pasta for everyone. He would throw an arm around me when I had any struggles and let me know that he had my back. He was truly amazing.'[2]

What the public saw, meanwhile, was a gang of like-minded boys hanging out together; a new pack of stars exemplifying the mood of juvenile exuberance that had slowly been blossoming in Hollywood via young film-makers revisiting their own adolescence in the teen movies they made. What's more, with S. E. Hinton's sensitivities at their disposal, these boys were boisterous but had a tender side too, discussing emotions in a way that Tony Manero or

---

1 As a child Francis Coppola had hero-worshipped his older brother August (Nic Coppola's father), later crediting much of his own intellectual curiosity to the books his sibling had lent him and the discussions they would have.

2 Author interview.

Jeff Spicoli either wouldn't or couldn't. *The Outsiders* had turned this group into a ready-made teen band, the perfect ensemble for young girls looking for idols: Dillon the moody one, Lowe the charmer, Macchio and Howell the unthreatening brotherly types, Cruise and Estevez the pumped-up bad boys. By 1983 there hadn't been a white boyband in the US charts since the mid-'70s peak of The Bay City Rollers. *The Outsiders* filled that gap.

The paparazzi, naturally, latched on to their lifestyles; lads partying hard and dating beautiful women. Estevez was with Salley whilst Leif Garrett was seeing Nicolette Sheridan, a British model brought up between England and LA by her mother and her partner, the star of TV's *Kojak*, Telly Savalas. Rob Lowe's relationship with Melissa Gilbert recovered from his partying in Tulsa (and the fact that Gilbert's mother didn't like him) whilst Tommy Howell's girlfriend Kyle Richards was another *Little House on the Prairie* alumna, the younger sister of fellow TV stars Kim and Kathy.[1] 'It was a nightmare going out in public with him,' Kyle Richards has said of her time with Howell in the mid-'80s. 'It would be, like, with Rob Lowe and Tom Cruise and Matt Dillon . . .'[2]

'I think Kyle held her own, though,' claimed Dalton, who roomed with Howell for several years. 'She is a powerful person.'[3]

And then there was Matt Dillon, the biggest pin-up of them all, the one that everyone loved. He liked to party, celebrating his eighteenth birthday at Studio 54 alongside Cher's daughter Chastity and fellow actor Mark Patton. 'Girls? Listen, I had a lot of fun – don't get me wrong,' he admitted. But always the cool kid, the beatnik, Dillon never wanted to seem too enthusiastic about such things. 'It felt objectifying, if I'm being honest about it. You wanna be taken seriously for what you do and not just be labelled as some heart-throb. Nobody wants that. Early on, that was a lot of pressure.'[4] Still, soon that pressure would be off. Another of *The Outsiders* was about to take Dillon's place as the most famous

---

1 Kathy Richards married hotel heir Rick Hilton in 1979 and had two young children: future reality TV stars, Paris and Nicky.

2 ET Online, quoting interview from Sirius FM's Andy Cohen Live, 1 December 2015.

3 Author interview.

4 'Matt Dillon on Staying Focused, Surviving Teen Stardom and the Best Advice He Ever Got', *Details*, Logan Hill and Matthew Marden, May 2015.

of the group, the poster boy. What's more, *this* guy seemed to only thrive on the hard work such a position would give him. In fact, he looked as if he loved every minute of it.

Tom Cruise had turned down *Rumble Fish* to take on a role for which he'd auditioned on days off from filming *The Outsiders*. When he heard he had the part, he then asked his *Outsiders* co-star Diane Lane to join him in Chicago and play the female lead. The eighteen-year-old Lane had declined, saying the project was too risqué, and she stayed on in Tulsa with Coppola for *Rumble Fish*. Really though, the nudity in *Risky Business* – that film with which Cruise followed *The Outsiders* – was just part of a bigger message. After the period setting of the S. E. Hinton adaptation, Cruise returned to a contemporary America where – *Risky Business* revealed – even a nervous teenage boy could make big dollars by seizing the initiative and realising that sex sells. And in leaving the gang behind in Oklahoma, Cruise moved away from being indelibly considered part of a pack and began the path to solo fame – just as that very pack were starting to become their own bona fide cultural phenomenon.

Chapter Seven

BIG DREAMS

Grease 2 falters; Risky Business flies (but at a cost); Rob Lowe settles for second best; plus Flashdance sells a lifestyle that leaves Travolta – and everyone – trailing in its wake.

Nineteen-eighty-three. Welcome to the time of Reaganomics. Welcome to the era of big dreams.[1]

Ronald Wilson Reagan – former governor of California, one-time film actor – had defeated sitting President Jimmy Carter in 1980 with promises of fantasies regained: more personal freedom, smaller government, lower taxes and greater international respect. Really, the soon-to-be fortieth president of the United States of America was promising his people the biggest dream of all: the American Dream.

'In this present crisis, government is not the solution to our problems; government is the problem,' the sixty-nine year old told the nation during his inaugural address at the end of January 1981. His nickname said it all: 'The Great Communicator'. Reagan used his leading man charisma to campaign for the necessity to be bold and decisive, when individual initiative trumps state handouts. It was as if he wanted everyone to be a Hollywood hero, everyone to – as he would do just a couple of months after his inauguration – survive whatever assassination attempts were thrown at them. In truth, the retired movie star hadn't retired at all.

---

1 'America is too big for small dreams,' Reagan declared in an address before a joint session of the Congress on the State of the Union, 25 January 1984.

Risky Business, Paul Brickman's sex-as-commodity comedy released in the summer of '83, begins with its own fantasy, Tom Cruise's Joel introducing his recurring erotic apparition of seducing a girl with the line: 'The dream is always the same.' He could have been talking about Reagan's political plans as much as his own carnal ones. Get the girl, win the day; it's as much part of the American Dream as any bill or statute. And dreams for both Ron and Tom – so they wanted us to believe – could come true, however controversially.

By 1982, Allan Carr's dreams were crumbling around him. The fanciful producer's *Grease 2* had been planned as an equally successful sequel to his mega hit from 1978 but a new decade with new politics made such a retro-fabulous musical seem increasingly unnecessary. Huge civil rights and anti-war movements had achieved many of their aims, new laws had been bedded in for several years[1] and suddenly that need for collective nostalgia that dominated the '70s and provided the foundation for *Grease*'s success was less urgent than looking to the future, looking after number one.

Yet the makers of *Grease 2* were faced with a problem: they knew they'd still need a strong link to the original film in order to pique audience interest. Unfortunately all they *actually* had was a small role for Didi Conn's ditzy Frenchie plus Pat Birch – the experienced choreographer of the stage show and first movie – making her debut as a film director. Writers Jim Jacobs and Warren Casey, plus stars John Travolta and Olivia Newton-John, were nowhere to be seen. Even a rumoured cameo from supporting couple Kenickie (Jeff Conaway) and Rizzo (Stockard Channing) came to nothing.

Allan Carr and Robert Stigwood were still confident though, sensing they had an ace up their sleeve that would silence the naysayers: their new leading man. Maxwell Caulfield was a twenty-two-year-old Brit who'd been making waves on the New York acting and modelling scene; straight (indeed, married to

---

1 Nineteen-sixty-seven: bans on interracial marriages outlawed, 1968: Civil Rights Act prohibits discrimination in the housing market, 1973: the military draft ended.

actress Juliet Mills, almost twice his age) yet with a clean-cut James Dean styling that was an instant hit amongst the velvet mafia. So whilst pop star Andy Gibb, the young brother of Stigwood's Bee Gees, *had* been expected to get *Grease 2*'s lead role of Michael Carrington,[1] it was the largely unknown Caulfield who ultimately bagged the part. True, his singing lacked panache but that was less of a problem, Carr reasoned, than Gibb's problems with acting. Michael's love interest, meanwhile – wild Pink Ladies head honcho Stephanie Zinone – was to be played by a twenty-four-year-old model and supermarket checkout girl called Michelle Pfeiffer. A couple of years earlier she'd unsuccessfully tried out for a role in *Raging Bull* but now Pfeiffer wowed at the *Grease 2* auditions overseen by Carr, Birch and Paramount's Don Simpson (the latter wearing his sunglasses the whole time), standing out with her quirky-yet-sexy presence. Pat Benatar, Kristy McNichol and even Brooke Shields – in a mooted reunion with her *Blue Lagoon* co-star Christopher Atkins – were apparently all rejected in favour of Pfeiffer.

Despite Carr's outward optimism, ever the showman, *Grease 2* was doomed to failure. Neither Caulfield nor Pfeiffer had the kind of heat on them that a 1978 Travolta had after *Fever*, whilst the former Danny Zucko had suffered enough flops since *Grease* for anything associated with him – even a sequel in which he didn't star – to be somewhat tainted. The whole project simply felt dated; too little, too late. Then there was Carr himself, battling more than ever with addictions to drink, drugs and sex that had only intensified alongside his professional success. Perhaps that was why Paramount's chief Barry Diller banned Carr from using his studio lot, forcing the movie to shoot twenty minutes away in Norwalk. For Diller, *Grease 2* was little more than a contractual obligation and he barely even wanted to hear Allan Carr's name. He was far more interested in the next *Star Trek* film, *The Wrath of Khan*.

Carr tried to overcome the lack of chemistry between his leads ('The only thing we had in common was discussing our imminent

---

1 Michael is – conveniently – the exchange student cousin of Sandy who enrols at Rydell High two years after she flew off into the clouds with Danny.

stardom,' Caulfield has quipped about his strained relationship with Pfeiffer[1]) by making the movie's party scenes even more outrageous. He also went into publicity overdrive, hyping his discoveries as new teen sensations. Yet audiences could see through the veneer. If the first film had been tweaked by Carr to represent something of his own high-school dreams, at least there was also still something of Casey and Jacobs' original stage show earthiness in there to make it feel authentic. *Grease 2*, however, had lost that safety net. It didn't ring true either as nostalgia or as mirroring present day life. The movie came out in the summer of '82, a long way behind the box-office success of fellow releases *E.T.*, *Poltergeist* and Diller's pet *Star Trek* sequel; fantasy films either modern or futuristic. Diller himself publicly slated *Grease 2*, wanting to make his feelings known about being contractually obliged to pay Carr five million dollars to make it.

Grease 2 coughed and spluttered to fifteen million dollars at the box-office on a budget of over eleven million, only Pfeiffer's Young Artist Award[2] nomination and an eventual cult status offering some compensation. Carr would produce only two more movies, his carefree campiness now at odds with the militarily planned productions of the new decade; a ruthlessness which boasted Paramount, with Diller and his protégés, at the helm. Ideas for further *Grease* sequels and a TV show were quickly shelved whilst Maxwell Caulfield, briefly the apple of Carr's eye, found himself blackballed by those very moguls that had so recently fêted him. Carr even suddenly claimed that he'd never *actually* wanted the young actor to play Michael in the first place. He'd always – he now proudly told everyone – favoured Tom Cruise.

By the end of '82, Cruise was making serious waves. *Taps* and *The Outsiders*, blueprints of the burgeoning teens-versus-adults genre, had showcased his drive and gumption but *Risky Business* now gave him a lead role with a tantalising character arc too: Chicago schoolboy Joel turns from wallflower to player after becoming involved with an escort girl whilst his parents are away.

---

1 *Party Animals*, Robert Hofler, De Capo Press, 2010.
2 Previously known as Youth in Film.

Whilst *Taps* strove for nobility, promoting the importance of fighting for one's honour rather than simply letting it be taken away 'with the stroke of a pen', and *The Outsiders* proudly gave teenage delinquents a voice, *Risky Business* was deliberately less clear-cut; both the pros and the cons of Reaganomics, neatly but unusually wrapped up as a teen sex comedy. Joel's initiative in turning his home into a brothel for school friends is, on the one hand, smart financial thinking. On the other, it's an example of just how low the nation's young 'me-generation' would now stoop in order to get rich. 'Every once in a while you've got to say, "What the fuck?",' was both Joel's mantra and the breakout line from the movie but even that's not black-and-white. To some those twelve words could sound excitingly cheeky and optimistic. To others, they're just reckless and chilling.

Steve Tisch was one person who could afford to say 'What the fuck?' As the son of Bob Tisch, co-chair of the Loews Corporation – the family billion-dollar hotel and cinema conglomerate – he'd dabbled in film production during the '70s[1] and had actually turned down an exec job with Barry Diller at Paramount, recommending his charismatic pal Don Simpson for the gig instead. The *Risky Business* script he'd read from the thirty-two-year-old Paul Brickman – back when it was called *White Boys Off the Lake* – had a refreshingly cool, youthful edge and Tisch couldn't wait to get started on it with producing partner Jon Avnet.[2] He also showed it to a friend of his parents' he thought might be interested: a slightly older showbusiness executive called David Geffen.

David Geffen's dreams – like Cruise's, like Reagan's – were crystal-clear: he wanted to be the biggest and the best, a movie mogul. The results were equally divisive. The '70s had seen the former mail-room worker at the William Morris Agency – a job he obtained with a forged college certificate – move into music management, hitting home runs with the Laurel Canyon sounds of Jackson Browne and Joni Mitchell. Yet like Allan Carr and Don Simpson, this slightly built Elliott Gould lookalike was a high-

---

1 *Outlaw Blues* (1976) was the tale of a songwriting ex-convict trying to make it in country music.
2 Avnet would also shoot second-unit on *Risky Business*.

school outsider with big plans to totally make over his humble Brooklyn background. Why settle for simple management when he could have his own record company too? Geffen's ability to manoeuvre quickly became infamous, his persuasive personality wavering between shouty and insecure, and he set up Asylum Records with Atlantic's fabled boss Ahmet Ertegun, all under the wing of Steve Ross's Warner Bros. empire. Insecure or not, he didn't let romantic ideals get in the way of good business. Within a year he'd sold his portion of Asylum back to Ross for seven million dollars and a bunch of Warner shares.

Ross was always Geffen's cheerleader and, boy, did he need one. The list of Geffen's successes – putting together The Eagles, backing both *Dreamgirls* and *Cats* on Broadway, reuniting Dylan and The Band for a sell-out tour – was matched only by the list of people he was rumoured to have alienated: Mick Jagger, Elton John and, eventually, The Eagles themselves, their own in-fighting well-known but nothing compared to the bitterness between Geffen and their next manager, future *Fast Times* producer Irving Azoff. As the '70s came to an end, Geffen was a millionaire driving a Rolls-Royce, investing in fine art and with a circle of confidants that included Calvin Klein, Steve Rubell from Studio 54 plus both Allan Carr *and* his nemesis at Paramount, Barry Diller. Yet he still wasn't entirely comfortable. A high-profile relationship with Cher inevitably foundered before he fully admitted to his own homosexuality.

It was to Diller – a fellow former William Morris rookie and alleged lover – that Geffen the music-man confessed his goal of running his own film company. Diller, it seemed, was equally competitive. 'Person after person interviewed said Diller's real motivation is being more powerful than Geffen – from business to their sex lives to the firmness of their handshakes,'[1] ran an *LA Magazine* profile of the studio boss. Some say that Barry Diller's eventual move to Twentieth Century Fox in 1984 wasn't simply because he didn't get on with Paramount's new chief Martin Davis. It was also to try and keep pace with Geffen, his even higher-flying friend.

---

1 by Rod Lurie.

Geffen had, in fact, once been given a stint as vice chairman of Warner Bros. Pictures but it ended badly at the close of 1976, the exec made redundant after only eleven months. Yet Geffen knew that Warner's Steve Ross still had faith in him and the studio backed his next project in 1980 – a new label simply called Geffen Records – watching as the thirty-seven year old's legendary persuasion lured Donna Summer away from the team that made her at Neil Bogart's Casablanca Records and convinced John Lennon to get back into the studio. It didn't matter that the former flopped as she attempted to leave behind her disco sound or that Lennon's sales only rocketed after his untimely death in December that year. Ross still had Geffen's back.

When Geffen ultimately got his dream and invested in a movie – Robert Towne's *Personal Best*, a story of athletes in the wake of the US boycott of the 1980 Olympic Games – it was Steve Ross who gave him a production deal at Warner, despite the picture's advance bad word. Towne and Mike Ovitz, his agent from CAA, had fallen out spectacularly with Geffen during a troubled production and *Personal Best* would be an inevitable flop. Yet the wannabe film mogul's wishes had finally come true: the Geffen Company had been born and he was in charge of a movie house at last. The journey had been rocky but he'd ultimately won, a history of well-placed 'What the fuck?'s. With a story like that, he couldn't fail to fall in love with *Risky Business*.

Still, it was only after Steve Tisch had prompted Geffen to read *Risky Business* for a *second* time that he really fell in love with it. Whilst Warner had earlier passed on the film when offered it directly, making the now commonplace suggestion that the sex needed to be more like *Porky's*, Geffen had at first thought entirely the opposite. For him, Brickman's script actually seemed *too* dirty. That second reading, however, really brought out the smart wit in Brickman's words and Geffen said 'Yes'. Now the initially uninterested Warner Bros. would *have* to release it as part of the distribution deal Steve Ross had with the Geffen Company.

As shooting began at the start of July 1982, Paul Brickman – a photography fan who'd worked on the story for seven years so knew exactly how he wanted his film to play out (part-*The Graduate*, part-Bertolucci's *The Conformist*) – was relieved that his paymaster's attitude appeared to be relatively hands-off. David Geffen was from the music world, after all. He'd made his name with bohemian singer/songwriters; he knew how to get the best from creative types. What's more, Brickman was a first-time director and he really needed his boss not to panic, to have confidence in him. The laissez-faire Geffen seemed perfect.

A year later, Brickman would be feeling very different.

It was casting director Nancy Klopper, hot from her work on smash hit *An Officer and a Gentleman*, that suggested Tom Cruise for the role of the hooker-hiring, Porsche-stealing, dancing-in-his-underwear Joel Goodson. Paul Brickman wasn't so convinced. 'Originally, Paul had seen *Taps* and said, "This guy for Joel? This guy is a killer! Let him do *Amityville III*!"' Cruise told Cameron Crowe in *Interview* magazine.[1] Cruise's audition for *Risky Business* took place whilst he was still in bad-boy mode for *The Outsiders*, on a few days off from filming in Tulsa. 'Somehow, my agent, without me knowing, arranged for me to just drop by the office to say "Hello". So I went in wearing a jean jacket, my tooth was chipped, my hair was greasy. I was pumped and talking in an Oklahoma accent, "Hey, how y'all doing?" Paul just sat there, looking at me.'[2] Yet Cruise, of course, was driven and determined, offering his own suggestions for Joel's tics and mannerisms, impressing everyone enough to be invited over to Tisch's house for a second meeting, this time to test alongside the already cast Rebecca De Mornay.

De Mornay was nineteen, had only been auditioning professionally for six months, but she already had life experience that showed through in her coolly confident, iron-fist-in-a-velvet-glove portrayal of call-girl Lana. As a child she'd moved with her mother and half-brother from LA to Europe, educated first at the radically alternative school Summerhill on England's sleepy East Anglian coast, then at high school in Kitzbühel, Austria. Back in California she studied at the Lee Strasberg Institute before hooking a part in Coppola's *One from the Heart*, the draining

---

1 May 1986.
2 Ibid.

flop that had ultimately led the director to get back to basics with *The Outsiders*. Her look was poised and icy, serious but sexy; Grace Kelly meets Debbie Harry. Jon Avnet had considered going to France to find the right Lana, so disappointing was the original US search, but De Mornay's upbringing gave her just the peregrine charm they were looking for, infusing Lana with an integrity that belied her profession. Now she stood in Steve Tisch's lounge being filmed on his video camera, opposite a Tom Cruise who'd overnight shed the image he'd carefully cultivated for Coppola's greaser movie, miraculously turning himself into the squeaky-clean son from the Chicago suburbs that Brickman required. For this second audition, he had morphed into the ideal Joel. David Geffen was so impressed he kept the videotape of the audition, the spine simply labelled 'Tom Cruz'.

Other possible Joels and Lanas were swiftly cast aside: Kevin Anderson, a young actor from Gurnee, north Chicago, who ended getting the supporting role of Chuck; another Chicago native called John Cusack; *Fast Times'* star Brian Backer; the twenty-three-year-old Talia Balsam – already a veteran of TV shows such as *Happy Days* and *Dallas*, as well as being the daughter of actors Martin Balsam and Joyce Van Patten; and Megan Mullally, an LA-born actor who'd studied in Illinois and was starting to make a name on the Chicago theatre scene (she ultimately got the much smaller part of one of Lana's friends).

Cruise and De Mornay's chemistry on set appears to have wavered from white hot to frozen. Brickman talks of how difficult it was to stop their petting during the 'make love on a real train' sex scene yet others suggest Cruise was pushy and two-faced, once complaining to producer Tisch that his female co-star was miscast.[1] Yale graduate Bronson Pinchot – a twenty-three year old making his debut in *Risky Business* as Joel's friend Barry – went further, suggesting that Cruise was 'the biggest bore on the face of the Earth. He had spent some time with Sean Penn . . .[2] [and had]

---

1 Both are mentioned in Andrew Morton's book *Tom Cruise: An Unauthorised Biography*, St Martin's Press, 2008, pp.67–8.

2 Penn had actually visited the *Risky Business* set and – according to Cruise on the DVD's commentary – was secretly in the passenger seat of the Porsche during the scene where Joel first reverses the sports car from the garage . . . and stalls it.

picked up this knack of calling everyone by their character names, because that would probably make your performance better and I don't agree with that . . . he was tense and made constant unrelated comments . . . Very, very strange.'[1]

Pinchot was a theatrical college boy, so too fellow co-star Curtis Armstrong (playing Miles, another of Joel's buddies), an actor who'd already racked up several years on the New York stage. Armstrong auditioned twice for the role – three months apart – and claimed his ability to perfectly replicate a performance time after time, a skill learned from the theatre, is what impressed Brickman enough to cast him. He certainly had no plans to be a film star though.

Cruise's uptight Hollywood ambition, however, was the complete opposite; a long way from a more laidback and liberal stage background. Here was a guy who, according to one-time Glendale girlfriend Nancy Armel, had to leave a Broadway performance of queer musical *La Cage aux Folles* (produced by Allan Carr) at half-time, unable to handle the campiness of the comedy.[2] 'All of the actors who talked about him were like, "What is this guy all about?" And you know, honestly, I never got it, and I don't get it to this day,' Pinchot continues. 'He always talked about himself like he was a mega-superstar; that was weird too . . . It's just a different kind of animal, like a racing greyhound versus a mutt that sits in your lap. I guess I'm a mutt that sits in your lap.' Yet even Cruise has admitted that early fame affected his attitude: 'After *Taps*, I became an asshole. I was the most unpleasant person to be around. My family even said, "Look, cut it out, take it easy, buddy!"'[3]

Still, to millions Cruise was – like Reagan – a hit. 'There's just something about the guy that people like,' House speaker Thomas O'Neill once told the *Los Angeles Times* about the Republican president, his political opposite. 'They're rooting for him and, of course, they're rooting for him because we haven't had any

---

1 The AV Club, Nathan Rabin, 20 October 2009.
2 According to Andrew Morton, op. cit., p.65.
3 *Tom Cruise*, Frank Sanello, Taylor Publishing, 1994, p.42.

presidential successes for years – Kennedy killed, Johnson with Vietnam, Nixon with Watergate, Ford, Carter and all the rest.'[1]

Cruise's own versions of Kennedy, Johnson and Nixon – flawed predecessors to whom he provided an alternative – were movie stars such as his own icon Al Pacino (whose only hit of the era was the controversial *Scarface*), John Travolta (whose success was now becoming a memory) and Burt Reynolds (the charismatic '70s star whose CV was, by 1983, already bogged down with sequels and remakes). What Cruise offered was elements of all three – showmanship, looks, charisma – allied to a sparkling, youthful energy that tried to smooth out complexities in favour of clear-cut optimism. One flash of the smile and you're intrigued, one glimpse of him dancing in his shirt and Y-fronts around an empty house – perhaps Hollywood's ultimate scene of teenage liberation, complete with improvised collar-popping – and you're sold. That Paul Brickman had actually wanted *Risky Business* to be in some way ambiguous wasn't the point. Neither was the fact that Reagan's own claims of economic success were equally debatable. What the public *chose* to see in them was all that mattered; in both cases an uplifting simplicity – a 'Go get 'em' attitude and a winning grin could either ignite the fall of communism or get you a place at Princeton.

It was just that kind of positive veneer that David Geffen wanted for *Risky Business*, even if his director definitely didn't. 'I was writing it in the time just after Reagan had taken office and everyone wanted to be a little capitalist, get their MBAs and wear power suspenders,' explains Brickman. 'I thought, That's all dandy, but life is more complex and darker than that. It's tough out there. Capitalism takes its toll on a lot of people.'[2] Yet whilst Geffen was pleased to see that darkness pushed to the background for the majority of the film, the movie's original ending – those final moments that audiences walk out of the theatre thinking about – was one grey area he couldn't leave be.

'Why does it have to be so tough?' might not seem the most inflammatory of phrases but it was the uncertainty of those words

---

1 From the obituary of Ronald Reagan, *Los Angeles Times*, Johanna Neuman, 6 June 2004.
2 Salon.com, Jake Malooley, 2 September 2013.

delivered by Lana in a tenderly frustrated smirk that lent the original closing scenes of *Risky Business* an enigmatic tone which its producer couldn't handle. Worse still, the story then fully concluded with Joel comforting a confused Lana, undoubtedly more mature than he was when he had started the film but with his own voiceover adding another stinging question: 'Isn't life grand?' Geffen was angry, complaining that this ending felt far too negative. He contacted Brickman to request a change but the director was having none of it. That was the mood, he argued, his story warranted. As a screenwriter, Brickman had already experienced the misery of re-edits[1] and viewed *Risky Business* as his last chance, his very own 'What the fuck?' to an industry that he felt had never respected his talent. He'd even been over to Berlin to work with the soundtrack composers, German electro pioneers Tangerine Dream, to make sure the music was suitably nocturnal and ambient, nothing too upbeat, to match the story's pensive style and content. Now here was David Geffen, previously hands-off, wanting to make his movie feel more like a celebration of the yuppie lifestyle rather than highlighting its uncertainties. Brickman reiterated his answer that the ending stayed but the producer came back with a knockout blow: reshoot it yourself or I'll hire someone else to do it.

Paul Brickman was floored. He certainly didn't want his labour of love ruined by some TV hack. Worn down, he agreed to a compromise. He *would* reshoot the final scene but only if both this new and the original ending were tested in front of an audience. What they liked best, he'd agree to releasing. Steve Tisch supported his director, having been incensed when Geffen revealed that he wanted Tisch himself to pay for the reshoots. Fellow producer Jon Avnet took a deep breath and played the waiting game: 'It was difficult. A very, very difficult time.'[2] Nevertheless, the cast and crew regrouped in June 1983 to shoot a more upbeat finale that Brickman had begrudgingly written – 'just banter'[3] as he would describe it – with Joel and Lana now chatting lightheartedly in an

---

1 Nineteen-seventy-seven's *Citizens' Band* was recut, retitled and rereleased as *Handle with Care*.
2 DVD commentary.
3 Ibid.

anonymous park before Joel's voiceover sums things up with the slightly less brittle, 'The time of your life huh, kid?' To Brickman's dismay, when tested in San Diego it was that new pay-off that got the audience thumbs-up. The ever-ambitious Geffen – a man who always saw *Risky Business* as a story about winning, echoing both his own transformation from geek to mogul and Reagan's own pushing of a new American optimism – had, once again, won.

Moods were certainly sweetened by the film's success: over sixty million dollars at the box-office and golden reviews ('A brief synopsis doesn't begin to suggest what Paul Brickman's fresh, hypnotic and very sexy movie feels like . . . it's a dreamlike version of a boy's sexual awakening'[1]). And whilst Geffen's ending might have ultimately won out, it's clear that plenty of Brickman's original dark tone remained – Cruise's performance was simply too expertly layered to be read only one way.

Cruise, De Mornay and Brickman snuck into a packed public screening in Westwood, no doubt relieved to see the poster on the lobby walls was significantly more chic than an early idea that had featured a winking, cartoon Joel in bed with a bevy of beauties.[2] Cruise and De Mornay also appeared to overcome any early issues by dating in real life before the actor reportedly then moved on to a bigger star – and Geffen's ex – Cher ('It could have been a great big romance because I was crazy for him,' claimed the singer, sixteen years Cruise's senior[3]). The movies, of course, would only get bigger too.

'Tom was like a younger brother on the set. We were very close,' remembers Brickman of the *Risky Business* shoot in 1982 and 1983. 'I was concerned for his own welfare because there's a certain kind of Faustian arrangement with that kind of success.'[4] Perhaps both Cruise and Geffen did have to sacrifice their souls to reach those levels of success? Yet it was the more puritanical Brickman who didn't direct another film for seven years.[5]

---

1 *Newsweek* David Ansen.

2 The actual poster focused on Joel's eyes looking moodily over his Ray-Bans, the title scrawled in hot red neon. Underneath there was still a generic sexy girl – not obviously De Mornay – draped over the bonnet of a Porsche.

3 In interview with Oprah Winfrey, April 2008.

4 Salon.com, op. cit.

5 Nineteen-ninety's *Men Don't Leave*. And he hasn't made another since.

* * *

Risky Business ended up as America's tenth biggest film of 1983. At the head of the list was the *Star Wars* finale *Return of the Jedi* whilst weepie *Terms of Endearment* – Paramount's big Oscar winner – was at two. At three though was an anomaly that would go on to be a blueprint; a dance-heavy teen movie so basic in its 'Follow your dreams' message, few initially predicted great things. This was not a film in which success came with its own complexities, as in *Risky Business*. As it turned out though, *Flashdance* changed the game, as influential on 1980s teen cinema – albeit in a different way – as the previous year's *Porky's*.

In many ways, *Flashdance* mirrored the success of 1983's biggest-selling album: Michael Jackson's *Thriller*. The year had seen continued success for alternative British acts hitting big on the nascent MTV – Culture Club, The Police, David Bowie – but the twenty-five-year-old Jackson's record had decidedly American scope and optimism; an LP made for millions to love. And they did. By the end of the year it seemed that every teenager in the country had watched *Flashdance* and owned a copy of *Thriller*.

Thriller had actually been released at the close of 1982 but didn't reach US No. 1 until the following February, held from the top since its release by rock acts Men at Work and John Cougar. When it got there though, fuelled by the video success of singles 'Billie Jean' and 'Beat It', *Thriller* stayed at the summit for a full seventeen weeks. New albums by '70s giants Pink Floyd, Elton John and Stevie Nicks couldn't shift it, nor could The Bee Gees' follow-up soundtrack to *Saturday Night Fever, Stayin' Alive*. Jackson's success seemed unstoppable, his style perfectly executed. On *Thriller* he wanted to graduate from his disco past yet still acknowledge its influence; he wanted to explore heavy rock yet also create music that made you dance; he wanted to write songs that sounded perfect on the radio but which also made the most of the burgeoning music video world. On *Thriller* Jackson's dreams were boundless.

After more than four months at the top the all-conquering album was *finally* supplanted – by the *Flashdance* soundtrack; a record whose style was equally considered – disco but modern, rock but pop, black but not – and designed to complement a movie that would also cross boundaries in its success. As *Thriller* boasted Quincy Jones and Rod Temperton at the mixing desk, with John Landis and Steve Barron on video directing duties, *Flashdance* had Giorgio Moroder and Phil Ramone across the music – the German disco king and the legendary South African producer[1] – whilst Adrian Lyne, Don Simpson and Jerry Bruckheimer oversaw the visuals. Both *Thriller* and *Flashdance* were concepts; multimedia experiences that sold glamour, fantasy and dreams. Both were so successful that whole industries of stage shows, documentaries and re-releases were born from them.

Flashdance's soundtrack blend was an irresistible one, mixing the uplifting dance of *Fame* alumna Irene Cara with the balladry of singer/songwriter Kim Carnes; the Munich disco of Donna Summer with the driving pop rock of Michael Sembello (the latter a twenty-nine year old Philly musician who'd just had his track 'Carousel' recorded by Jackson for *Thriller*, though ultimately left off the final version). On the cover of the soundtrack LP was the same picture that had graced the movie poster: lead actor Jennifer Beals in her slouchy sweatshirt and high-heels, as exquisitely lit as Jackson had been on the *Thriller* sleeve, looking to camera too, beneath a title written – as on Jackson's release – in an artfully scrawled, glowing italic. And both Jackson and Beals were black.

Jackson's family were African-American, Beals' a mix of African-American and Irish, and both had suffered racial prejudice growing up in the suburbs of Chicago. Crucially though, on *Thriller* and in *Flashdance*, skin colour took a back seat; still inescapable, but also unspecified. After years of damning social commentary via albums by Stevie Wonder and Marvin Gaye, and in the street-smart grit of 'blaxploitation' movies, both *Thriller* and *Flashdance* came up with a new proposition: blending cultures rather than highlighting differences could be the new indicator of success.

It worked for both. *Flashdance* was a phenomenon, the story of an eighteen-year-old 'welder by day, dancer by night' making more than ninety million dollars at the American box-office alone, more than James Bond pic *Octopussy* and Eastwood's Dirty Harry in

---

1 In '83 Ramone was also in the midst of being a spokesman for a new breakthrough in audio called the Compact Disc.

Sudden Impact. That multi-platinum soundtrack, meanwhile, scooped two US No. 1 singles, a Grammy Award and an Oscar. After *Flashdance*, Beals could easily have taken to the stage with Cruise and Jackson as the perfect young pin-ups for Reaganite America.[1]

Yet the bookish Beals didn't toe the line. The nineteen year old had put her Yale literature degree on hold to make *Flashdance* and now she wanted to go back: 'The first thing on my mind was Walt Whitman. What I wanted was still this "mystery inside the story" and the way that I knew how to experience that was through reading and thinking and connecting to other people who were reading and thinking about the same piece of material. And Hollywood at that time seemed . . . like it could get me off my course. Maybe it was all the people on cocaine?'[2] Beals' agent Martha Luttrell, an executive at ICM, respected her client's cerebral dreams and the young actor, panicked by the spotlight that *Flashdance* had suddenly shone on her, returned to the university to resume her studies at Morse College, the same school where Bronson Pinchot had graduated *magna cum laude* a few years earlier. At Yale she befriended another star who'd walked away from the limelight: Jodie Foster ('We were on the same page about our careers,' says Foster. 'We both really believed in academics and wouldn't have missed that experience for anything'[3]). As Cruise and Jackson found themselves bigger stars than ever, Beals and Foster – plus Brooke Shields, now studying French literature at Princeton – found themselves in books.

Yet if the poster girl of *Flashdance* didn't entirely relish the fame the film had given her, many others associated with the movie did. *Flashdance* might have stylishly overcome racial issues by subtly underplaying them but really, that was the only subtle thing about it.

* * *

1 Michael Jackson was actually honoured by the president at a White House ceremony celebrating the pop star's stance against teen drinking. 'Michael Jackson is proof of what a person can accomplish through a lifestyle free of alcohol or drug abuse,' Reagan told press on the lawn in the spring of '84. 'People young and old can respect that.'

2 Off Camera with Sam Jones podcast, March 2015.

3 Author interview.

Flashdance had begun in Toronto in early 1980, where Tom Hedley was a Brit abroad; a film fan and former *Esquire* editor – their youngest ever – working in the Canadian city as chief of a local lifestyle magazine. As journalists are wont to do, he hung out in the odd bar or two, often with a group of artist friends who especially loved one joint – Gimlets on Victoria Street – because of the spectacular show put on by the dancing girls; erotic but not sleazy. They weren't strippers, Hedley would make clear, rather 'more like burlesque: a send-up, a parody of stripping'[1]. What was more, the dancers acted tough and untouchable, confident of their big dreams. Chatting to a few of the girls – there was Gina, Maureen, another called Ann – suddenly Hedley had an idea for a movie. 'I felt that a dance film could be structured musically, with real, written, production numbers and formal dramaturgy, but also giving the appearance that this was happening in real time.'[2] The dancer called Maureen also had a day job that made a potential film an even stronger prospect, a career completely contrasting to her nights on stage: construction worker.

Hedley headed to LA and told his idea to an old friend: former *New York Times* scribe Lynda Obst, now in Los Angeles with her husband David, the literary agent who'd set up the meeting between Cameron Crowe and Thom Mount which had led to *Fast Times* on the big screen. She was hooked ('I was immediately blown away'[3]) and in April of 1980 she called up Casablanca, the record label now launching into the movie world with *Foxes* and which was under the guide of former Columbia exec Peter Guber. *Foxes* had underperformed for Casablanca but Guber was still optimistic, paying Tom Hedley a reported 300,000 dollars, plus five per cent of the net profits, for his story of a sexy dancer with big dreams, provisionally titled *Depot Bar and Grill*.[4]

The clumsy name had to change, of course. Far too downbeat and '70s. But what word could sum up the kind of modern

1 *National Post*, David Berry, 30 April 2014.

2 'On stage, *Flashdance* is in your face and completely alive', the *Independent*, Tom Hedley, 8 October 2010.

3 *Flashdance* DVD documentary.

4 'What Hurt Feelings: The Untold Story of the 31 Year Battle Over *Flashdance*', BuzzFeed, Soraya Roberts, 15 August 2014.

performing the girls were doing? How to describe energies colliding; the glamour of a show where strength, style and passion all meet in the glow of the spotlight, in the beat of the music? Then it arrived: a phrase that meant nothing yet explained everything, a single word whose simplicity mirrored the story's own clear command to 'take your passion . . . and make it happen': *Flashdance*.

Flashdance became the Reaganomics era movie par excellence, an idea – teenage wannabe ballet dancer overcomes social hurdles to make it on her own – that was as happily straightforward as Beals was contentedly academic and as full of determination in its plot as its team was in its production. Hedley and his producer Lynda Obst saw the project battle many an assassination attempt en route to its success yet the single-mindedness of *Flashdance*'s makers was always its greatest shield. That was how it survived the subsequent crash of Casablanca, newly part of Dutch/German giant Polygram, coinciding with the fall of the disco music the label so relied on. It even survived Polygram's draining collaboration with Robert Stigwood's RSO label, which meant bailing out the losses from his flop *Sgt. Pepper* movie project (which was very far from being the repeat of *Saturday Night Fever* everyone had banked on[1]).

Obst and Hedley's secret was to blend the '70s working-class dreams of *Fever* with a contemporary approach to gender politics and choreography, ultimately moving forward in a way that Allan Carr, Robert Stigwood and even John Travolta were all failing to achieve. To appeal to a young audience, the film-makers realised, they might have to embrace a new, more obviously stylish and optimistic future. No wonder Jennifer Beals, happy with her dog-eared copy of *Leaves of Grass*, would end up feeling out of place.

If the plot of *Flashdance* was blatant, it only mirrored the gaudy style of its ever-growing list of colourful contributors. After moving from Casablanca to Polygram's own film departments (where he produced *Endless Love*) Peter Guber teamed up with

---

1 Stigwood's most successful act, The Bee Gees, subsequently sued him for mismanagement.

Jon Peters, a mop-haired Hollywood social climber dubbed 'the luckiest man in the history of film'[1] due to his meteoric rise from being Barbra Streisand's Rodeo Drive hairdresser to becoming her romantic partner and film producer. Peters was an extrovert, a compelling but dangerous mix of Allan Carr's flamboyance (claiming to have once been a 'muff dyer' – i.e. colourist of female pubic hair) and Don Simpson's ego.[2] If Guber was the careful, but hugely successful, college-educated showbiz executive then Peters was the instinctive, rags-to-riches wild boy. *Flashdance* would be their first production together.

Over at 5555 Melrose Avenue, Paramount exec Dawn Steel was excitedly telling her boss Barry Diller all about Obst and Hedley's *Flashdance* idea. It was said she had secretly obtained hold of the script from a rival studio[3] and the thirty-five year old gave an impassioned speech, supposedly standing on the boardroom table as she sang the movie's praises. She showed Diller photos of dancers Gina and Maureen – all Kabuki make-up and gymnastic moves – styled and shot by Tom Hedley's photographer friends to attract distributors. Barry Diller, always impressed by his employees showing a feisty spirit, bought into her pitch.

For Dawn Steel, the *Flashdance* story could have been her own. She had started out in the questionable world of erotic merchandise for *Penthouse* and *Playboy*, working her way up from the Paramount marketing team to vice president of production in 1980. She saw the story of feisty Alex (originally called Raven in the early drafts) as a female Rocky but the comparisons to her own determination to succeed in a tough world, down to *Flashdance*'s setting in Pittsburgh's 'world made of steel' that mirrored her own surname, were clear. With Paramount giving the project a production deal, Steel began assembling a team to work alongside Obst, Hedley, Guber and Peters.

Dean Pitchford had been spending part of his time after his *Fame* Oscar win in writing with musicians Kenny Loggins and

---

1 'Studio Head', *Vanity Fair*, William Stadiem, 4 February 2010.

2 Another claim is that Jon Peters was the inspiration for Warren Beatty's lothario hairdresser in 1975's *Shampoo*, distributed by Columbia whilst under Peter Guber's tenure.

3 As mentioned in *The Barry Diller Story*, George Mair, Wiley, 1997.

Steve Perry[1] and Steel asked for his help on the *Flashdance* soundtrack. 'She had a sound system in her office but she didn't like the way it sounded so for her the real judgement of a song's value was hearing it on her car stereo. So she said, "Get over here! Get over here!" and I went running over to her office and she said, "Come with me!" and grabbed a cassette and we went down to the parking lot and we slammed the doors to her car and she put on "Maniac". And she says, "Am I crazy or is that a hit?" And I say, "No, you're not crazy. That's a fucking great song! Play it again!" And we sat there in her car with the windows cranked up and the stereo blasting and we listened to "Maniac" over and over again.'[2]

Advice was all Pitchford could offer, however. He didn't have time to write new songs for the *Flashdance* soundtrack as he was putting together another teen dance film, from his own script and also produced by Paramount, that was slated for release the following year. 'I didn't want anything but success for *Flashdance* because it would only bode well for us if this music driven movie, coming a year before, did well. And indeed it did and it set an audience up for us.'[3] His movie, about to start filming, was called *Footloose*.

Dawn Steel did, however, sign up her recently sacked colleague Don Simpson – finally fired from Paramount for his excessive behaviour but who 'floated down on his golden parachute' according to Guber[4] – to co-produce the film with his own new business partner, a reserved thirty-nine-year-old Michigan native with whom Simpson had once shared a Laurel Canyon house. Jerry Bruckheimer was the Peter Guber to Don Simpson's Jon Peters, a rising star who'd moved from advertising to hitting big in the movie world working with Paramount on *American Gigolo*, his own personality as slick and insular as Richard Gere's Julian. 'Jerry Bruckheimer is a mastermind. He doesn't know musical terms but he has great ears and he has a great sense of modern combinations . . . Don had a pair of great ears as well. They were larger than life, back then,' remembers Harold Faltermeyer,

---

1 Perry was lead singer with power rockers Journey.

2 Author interview.

3 Ibid.

4 *Shoot Out: Surviving Fame and (Mis)Fortune in Hollywood*, Peter Guber and Peter Bart, Faber & Faber, 2002.

working alongside the producing duo on their soundtracks with Giorgio Moroder. 'They were the golden boys.'[1]

It was Bruckheimer who'd lent Simpson his blazer to wear at his Paramount job interview back in 1976, an event that seemed to sum up their working relationship: Bruckheimer the practical, Simpson the wayward. With larger-than-life Hungarian refugee and former *Rolling Stone* scribe Joe Eszterhas – fresh from a credit dispute with Sly Stallone over their union drama *F. I. S. T.* – brought on board to polish the script, and Adrian Lyne – not hugely keen on the story but needing work after the flop of *Foxes* – hired to direct, the gang was coming together: a ripe mix of focused business heads, high stylists and charismatic risk-takers.[2] It was a combination that seemed to summarise not only lead character Alex's approach to success – work hard, look good, dream big – but also that of the whole era. Maniacs, indeed.

If *Risky Business* and *Flashdance* made '83 the year of aiming high, crossing boundaries and realising your dreams, Rob Lowe still felt he had a long way to go. He might have just worked with the legendary Francis Coppola but even that hadn't worked out entirely how he'd have liked. 'I remember the screening where I saw *The Outsiders* for the first time. Emilio might have been with me, and definitely Steve Burum, the cinematographer. I'll never forget Steve saying, in his dry way, "This movie is going to make a hundred million dollars." And the credits came up and the movie started and it just deteriorated from there. I went from a guy telling me the movie was going to make a hundred million to realising I'm not in the fucking movie . . . I thought it was personal or maybe I must have been bad . . . if that [uncut, original] version of the movie had come out – the version that I thought we were doing, that version that was in the script – I would have had a different, more substantive career and I would have had it quicker.

---

1 Author interview.

2 Simpson and Bruckheimer had offered *Flashdance* to Brian De Palma but he wasn't interested, demanding a ridiculously high salary in order to put them off. When they surprisingly agreed, he walked away. Later he would be attached to another Joe Eszterhas script that wound up being directed by Adrian Lyne, 1987's *Fatal Attraction*.

Without a doubt.'[1] Lowe watched his opportunity to shine in *The Outsiders* slowly dissolve, knowing only that his aspirations aged eighteen remained solid: 'I would have wanted the lead in the next Martin Scorsese movie.'[2]

As it was, he followed *The Outsiders* with *Class*, released in July 1983 and – like *Risky Business* – another story heavily influenced by Mike Nichols' '60s classic *The Graduate*. *Class* recast *The Graduate*'s Benjamin and Mrs Robinson as a scholarship boy (played by Andrew McCarthy) at a prestigious east coast private school having a fling with the mother (Jacqueline Bisset) of his blue-blooded best friend (Lowe). Also like *Risky Business*, *Class* was at once both aspirational and concerned; another cautionary reaction to the undeniable glamour of the Reaganite boom, told via a story of romance across the social divide. Unlike *Risky Business*, though, *Class* couldn't boast what its title promised. Rob Lowe's charisma was undeniable – an early yuppie archetype, all bravado and smiles – but *Class* lacked the flair of the Paul Brickman movie, without a distinctive soundtrack or visual style to help it stand out. Lowe might have complained at the time that his good looks were putting off directors casting him in movies with something to say but Tom Cruise was managing to make statements *and* be cute. It's just that there weren't enough smart projects to go round for both of them. No wonder Lowe was getting frustrated.

Still, *Class* was at least *trying* to make a point. The blue-blood Burroughs clan (Bisset, Lowe and Cliff Robertson, as the patriarch of the family) are as cold as they are rich; son Skip desperate to rebel, father Franklin only interested in business, wife Ellen on the lookout for affairs and alcohol. When McCarthy's quietly middle-class Jonathan finds himself in their refined world, as Skip's friend and Ellen's lover, its elite power and apparent effortlessness seem undeniably seductive, a long way from his own down-to-earth mother and father clucking in their station wagon. *Class* questions the appeal of those surface charms. In a key plot point, Jonathan reveals that he's been so pressured to climb up the

---

1 'Rob Lowe's Tips for Re-Re-Reinventing Yourself', *GQ*, Amy Wallace, 22 September 2015.
2 Ibid.

ladder socially, hoping to advance to Harvard and mix with families like the Burroughs, that he felt forced to cheat on his SATs. Ellen's own stints in rehab, meanwhile, make clear the stress felt even once inside those upper-class circles. When Skip (in a red Porsche, naturally) drives Jonathan up to the family mansion for the Christmas holidays, the latter's reaction to the stately home pithily sums up that conundrum at the heart of *Class*, where money and anxiety go hand in hand: 'I have never seen such a vulgar display of wealth in all my life! How do I get one?'

Class turns radically in tone once Jonathan's affair becomes public; a bold move that makes for a more serious third act. The script, by Jim Kouf and David Greenwalt – Los Angelinos in their early thirties who'd already written a handful of broad comedies – can't deliver a killer punch though, the story's cop-out conclusion feeling more like a laddish pat on the back than a strong statement about the stifling nature of wealth and standing.

Jacqueline Bisset was a thirty-nine-year-old Anglo-French star, a hit in Roman Polanski's *Cul-de-Sac*, cop classic *Bullitt* and sexy *Jaws* homage *The Deep*. Her glamour could add European sophistication and mystique – and arguably more of that than great acting – to anything she touched.[1] Her relationship with Russian ballet star Alexander Godunov, who had hit headlines three years earlier when he claimed political asylum in the States during a Bolshoi Ballet tour of New York, also made her a regular in the society columns. As Ellen in *Class*, however, her struggle is never as fully realised as was Lana's in *Risky Business*. It seemingly doesn't matter that Ellen's conveniently out of the picture come the final moments of the film. At least Jonathan and Skip are still friends.

Andrew McCarthy was feeling Lowe's frustration too. *Class* was the first movie role for the New Jersey teen, a high-school theatre lover subsequently kicked out from his drama programme at NYU but who luckily spotted an ad in a trade paper: 'It was a call for a movie and said, "Wanted. Eighteen, vulnerable and sensitive." And I thought, Well, that's me. I'm eighteen, vulnerable

---

1 Even 1981's campy melodrama *Rich and Famous*, scripted by *Foxes* writer Gerald Ayres and directed by veteran George Cukor.

and sensitive. I went to an open call with five hundred other "Eighteen, vulnerable and sensitive" kids, and twenty or thirty auditions later I was in a movie. It was like winning the lottery.'[1]

McCarthy – like Lowe – didn't feel as if he was making the statements he'd always dreamed of making. 'I was never in the kinds of movies that I wanted to be in. Only in hindsight did they become these iconic films of a generation. At the time they were not these particularly respected films.'[2] Background school kids in *Class* included the gangly Alan Ruck (also frustrated – because he was actually twenty-six and didn't want to be playing so young), plus the quietly ambitious John Cusack and the boyish Casey Siemaszko: 'All the young baby-faced actors in Chicago at that time,' admits Ruck.[3]

However, the very existence of *Class* proved a point: pitch a teen movie and, such was the new mood in Hollywood, now you'd have producers desperate to make it. Great for those young (and young-*looking*) actors. Not so much, recalls Ruck, for those more senior. 'There was this sorta incredulity [amongst older actors], like, "What the hell is going on? Where are the parts? Where are the movies? Where are the stories? It's all high-school stuff!"'

Rob Lowe, meanwhile, would deliberately seek less comical roles post-*Class*, not yet comfortable with what many felt was his most natural ability: to make people laugh. 'Rob is one of the funniest people I've ever met,' claims Jodie Foster, a close friend. 'Did you know he can recite the entire *Wizard of Oz* without any prompting?'[4]

During the filming of *Flashdance*, Jennifer Beals had been feeling uncomfortable. Her innocence was no surprise, really. She'd made a few commercials, done a bit of modelling for photographer Victor Skrebneski, acted in the background of 1980's *My Bodyguard* alongside Matt Dillon, but getting the lead role of Alex in

---

1 'Andrew McCarthy: From Brat Pack Fame to Renaissance Man, an Exceptional Life', Smashing Interviews Magazine, Melissa Parker, 15 March 2016.

2 therumpus.net, Anisse Gross, 14 September 2012.

3 Author interview.

4 Author interview.

Flashdance – after auditioning alongside a young Californian struggling for a break called Kevin Costner – was a new world. A world of hedonism.

At the centre was Simpson, a man whose appetite for drugs, drink and hookers was becoming legendary. He was a regular client of Madam Alex, whose girls he regularly paid for and took Polaroids of, keeping the photo collection in his wardrobe, and his bachelor pad on Cherokee Avenue was *the* weekend party venue for a host of high-powered friends: Jerry Bruckheimer, Steve Tisch and producer and agent Steve Roth.

'In the beginning,' Roth told Charles Fleming for his biography of Simpson, 'we were so hot and rich and there was nothing but cocaine and hookers and millions of laughs.'[1] Heidi Fleiss would soon take Madam Alex's crown as the most infamous Hollywood call-girl operator but back then was still just one of her employees. Fleiss claims she had been 'sold' to Alex by her then-boyfriend, director and gambler Ivan Nagy (which he denies) but the twenty-something call-girl would typify the mood of the moment by showing that even hookers – like welders – had plans to rise up the social ladder. 'It wasn't about sex,' wrote Lynn Hirschberg in her 1994 profile of Fleiss. 'It was about who thought they were winning and who won.'[2]

Beals saw those indulgences of the era bleed into the film: 'In the most banal moments, [*Flashdance*] kind of oozes sexuality. That's Adrian Lyne. He knows how to bring the visceral sexuality to everything. It was a wild ride, to say the least, that movie.'[3] She even claimed that she was getting a lot of pressure to do nude scenes, to the point where she was about to walk away, only finally agreeing to the film if a body double was used. Lyne assured Beals he would protect her but the wide-eyed teenager still felt nervous. An unlikely saviour came in the form of Warren Beatty. Beals met the famously flirtatious actor/director – who had once dated Britt Ekland, the mother of Heidi Fleiss's best friend Victoria Sellers – at a Hollywood party and, when asked about the filming of

1 *High Concept: Don Simpson and the Hollywood Culture of Excess*, Charles Fleming, Bloomsbury, 1998, p.87.

2 'Heidi Does Hollywood', *Vanity Fair*, Lynn Hirschberg, 1 February 1994.

3 The AV Club, Will Harris, 4 August 2015.

Flashdance, confessed her insecurities to him. Beatty understood the game better than most and knew everyone in Hollywood. He told her he would use his influence to make sure she was never mistreated. 'He was my godfather,' Beals remembered,[1] never again asked to do things in *Flashdance* she wasn't comfortable with.

Flashdance still seems like a movie comfortable with *anything*, boasting a suave swagger that came to typify the Simpson and Bruckheimer partnership. It purported to be a film about the hard work of realising your dreams and yet that hard work had never looked more appealing; exquisitely shot and perfectly soundtracked to sell a lifestyle that might have been rather unrealistic (despite Tom Hedley's research) but which sure as hell looked good.

It *had* been hard work behind the scenes, with editors Walt Mulconery and Bud Smith spending seventy-two days and nights straight honing the movie into shape, often watched over by Bruckheimer, Simpson and Lyne. The latter two had also, according to the director, engaged in nine-hour phone calls through the night to discuss the story.[2]

But on screen, things looked alluringly simple. Adrian Lyne had made a feature-length advert and the critics took notice. '*Flashdance* is like a movie that won a free ninety-minute shopping spree in the Hollywood supermarket,'[3] quipped Roger Ebert, with Richard Corliss in *Time* even more florid in his description: 'From every electronic orifice in the US just now – from radio and stereo speakers, from the projectors in 1140 movie theaters and out of the twenty-four-hour mouth of MTV – comes one unavoidable, irresistible message: Flashdance!'[4] It was as if the film had been made for the new music channel, its plentiful soundtrack not sung by characters like in old-fashioned musicals but instead blasted out over fastidiously edited three-minute sequences that were virtually music videos in themselves. Indeed, Irene Cara's title track boasted a promo that was no more than clips of the movie

---

1 Off Camera with Sam Jones, op. cit.

2 'He was someone who could consume you,' Lyne said of the producer, *Flashdance* DVD documentary.

3 *Chicago Sun-Times*, 19 April 1983.

4 9 May 1983.

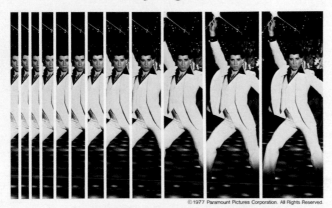

IT IS NOW RATED PG

Because
we want everyone to see
John Travolta's performance...

Because
we want everyone to hear
the #1 group in the country, the Bee Gees...

Because
we want everyone to catch
"Saturday Night Fever."

©1977 Paramount Pictures Corporation. All Rights Reserved.

SATURDAY NIGHT FEVER ™

...Catch it.

PARAMOUNT PICTURES PRESENTS A ROBERT STIGWOOD PRODUCTION JOHN TRAVOLTA
KAREN LYNN GORNEY "SATURDAY NIGHT FEVER" Screenplay by NORMAN WEXLER Directed by
JOHN BADHAM Executive Producer KEVIN McCORMICK Produced by ROBERT STIGWOOD

PG PARENTAL GUIDANCE SUGGESTED **DD** DOLBY STEREO ™ Original music written and performed by the BEE GEES. Read the Bantam Paperback.
SOME MATERIAL MAY NOT BE SUITABLE FOR CHILDREN Soundtrack album available on RSO Records. A Paramount Picture.

An advert for the 1979 PG-cut of *Saturday Night Fever*. John Travolta might have wanted to be Robert De Niro, but Paramount was determined to cash in on his teen heart-throb status.
(© Everett Collection/Mary Evans Picture Library)

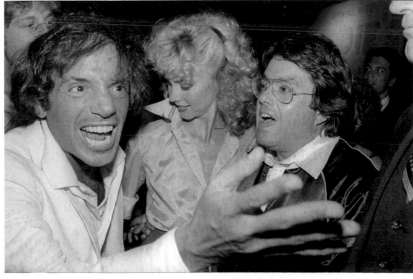

Steve Rubell, Olivia Newton-John and Allan Carr at the June 1978 premiere of *Grease* in Rubell's New York club, Studio 54. Carr produced the film partly to exorcise the ghosts of his own teenage years, partly just to throw some fabulous parties.
(Archive Photos/Getty Images)

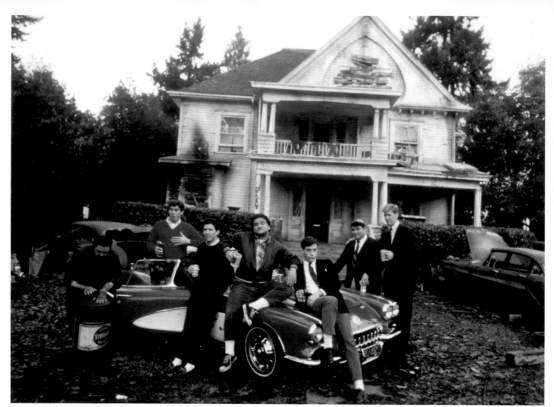

A product of the baby-boom generation, 1978's *Animal House* – starring John Belushi *(centre)* – introduced a raucousness to the retro teen movie following *American Graffiti*'s more poetic approach. Its influence would last well into the next decade. (Universal/Kobal/REX/Shutterstock)

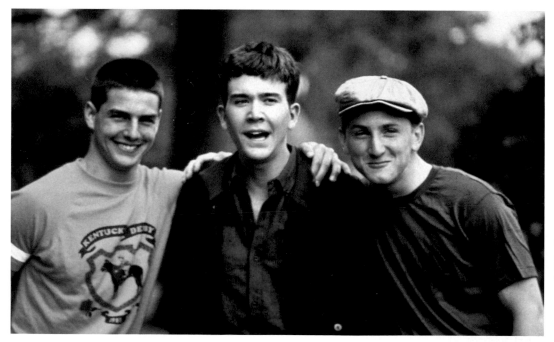

Tom Cruise, Timothy Hutton and Sean Penn enjoying downtime from military drama *Taps* in 1981. Hutton won an Oscar that year as the sensitive son in Robert Redford's *Ordinary People*, but it was Cruise and Penn who would impress Hollywood – and each other – with the intensity of their acting. (Collection Christophel/Alamy Stock Library)

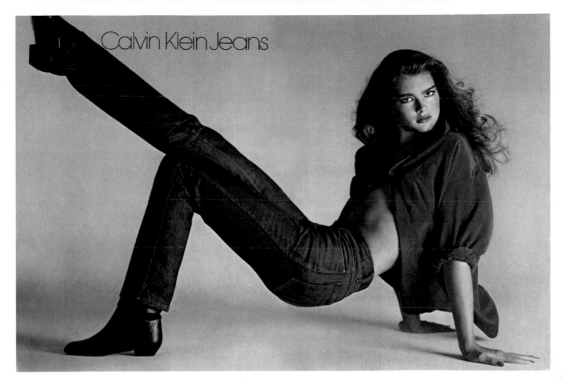

A fifteen-year-old Brooke Shields in Calvin Klein's controversial 1980 ad campaign. Shields had been at *Grease*'s Studio 54 party when director Randall Kleiser offered her a role in his next film, *The Blue Lagoon*. (Courtesy The Advertising Archives)

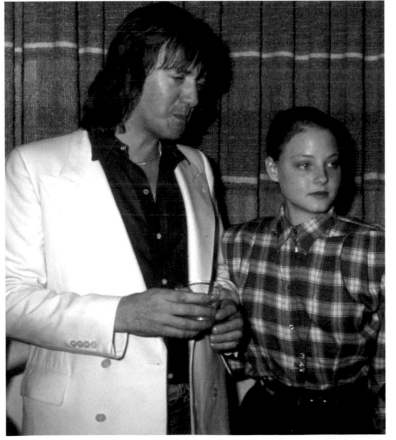

British director Adrian Lyne and a sixteen-year-old Jodie Foster, star of his 1980 debut *Foxes*. With its judicious use of music, lighting and cinematography, *Foxes* hinted at the aesthetic Lyne would use to even greater effect in 1983's *Flashdance*, redefining mainstream Hollywood style in the process. (Ron Galella Collection/Getty Images)

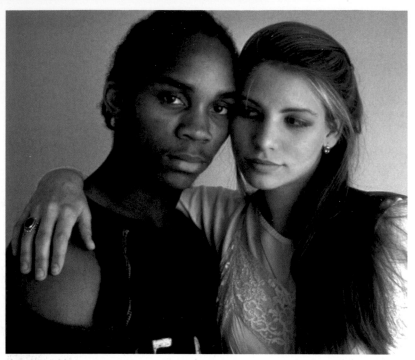

Gene Anthony Ray and Antonia Franceschi, two of the stars of Alan Parker's gritty-yet-chic modern musical, *Fame* (1980). Along with Adrian Lyne, Hugh Hudson and the Scott brothers (Ridley and Tony), Parker used his experience in British advertising to fill *Fame* with strong visuals and memorable set-pieces, a technique also crossing over into early music videos. (© MGM/courtesy Everett Collection/Mary Evans Picture Library)

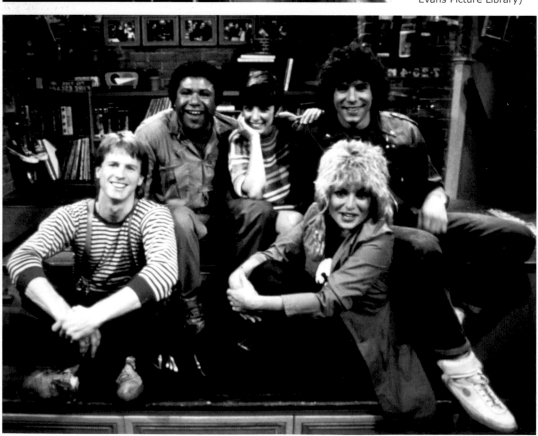

MTV's first VJs *(left to right)*: Alan Hunter, JJ Jackson, Martha Quinn, Nina Blackwood, Mark Goodman. The music channel launched on 1 August 1981 and, as well as playing more traditional homegrown rock, its championing of many British new wave bands gave middle-America a snapshot of teenage European tastes. (© Everett Collection/Mary Evans Picture Library)

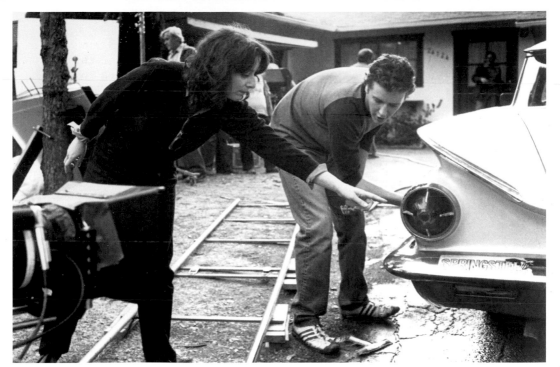

Amy Heckerling directing Judge Reinhold in *Fast Times at Ridgemont High*. The film overcame studio interference and so-so reviews to become a hit in 1982, thanks to a cutting-edge soundtrack and – like the Cameron Crowe book on which it was based – a realistic approach to contemporary teenage life. (Ronald Grant Archive/Mary Evans Picture Library)

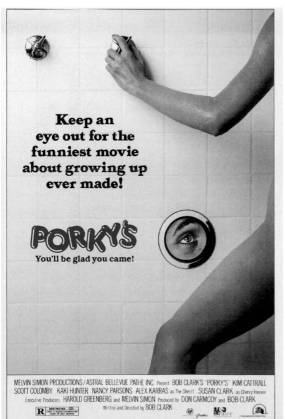

Porky's (1982) took the nostalgic chaos of *Animal House* to new levels of cheekiness. Teen movies in Hollywood would feel the after-effects for years to come and the burgeoning home video market, in particular, thanked its lucky stars. (© 20thCentFox/Everett Collection/Mary Evans Picture Library)

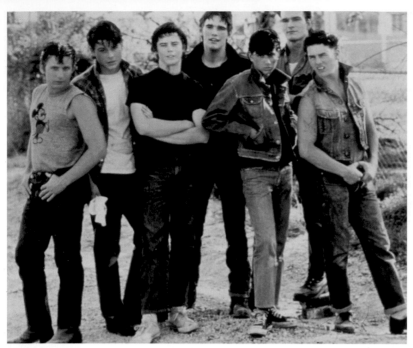

With *The Outsiders* (1983), Francis Ford Coppola successfully rejuvenated his directing career. It was also one of four S. E. Hinton adaptations that came out in the '80s. The cast proved to be instant poster boys *(left to right)*: Emilio Estevez, Rob Lowe, C. Thomas Howell, Matt Dillon, Ralph Macchio, Patrick Swayze, Tom Cruise. (Moviestore/REX/Shutterstock)

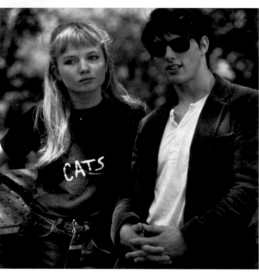

Whilst many of Tom Cruise's contemporaries experienced most fame as a group, he found himself a solo star. *Risky Business* (1983) was his breakthrough, where the money-grabbing politics of Reaganite America are cast in a shady light by writer/director Paul Brickman. Cruise and his co-star Rebecca de Mornay dated both on screen and off. (Time and Life Pictures/Getty Images)

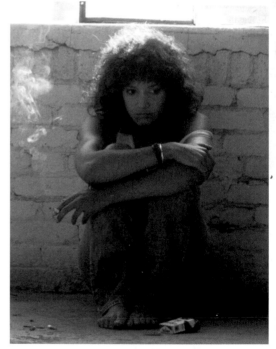

Jennifer Beals in *Flashdance* (1983), Adrian Lyne's exquisite slice of lifestyle porn that shifted millions of tickets, albums and slouchy dancewear. Teenage welder Alex wishes she could be a ballerina and this was the era, *Flashdance* showed, when big dreams come true. Beals, meanwhile, followed her own academic dreams and shunned Hollywood in favour of Yale. (© Paramount/Courtesy Everett Collection/Mary Evans Picture Library)

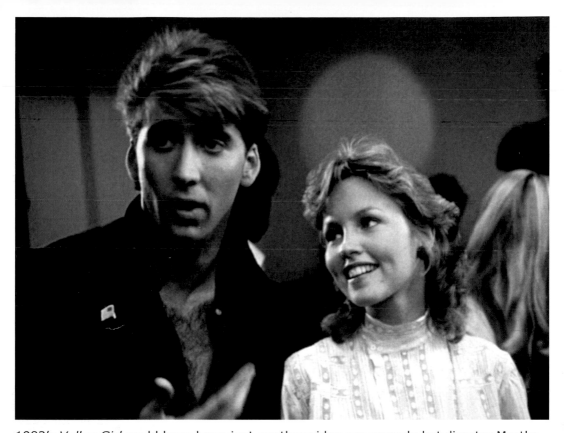

1983's *Valley Girl* could have been just another video sex comedy but director Martha Coolidge had loftier ideas. As the title character, Deborah Foreman personified a new type of Californian mall culture. As her Romeo from the wrong side of the tracks, Nicolas Cage found that changing his surname from Coppola meant people would no longer judge him. (© Atlantic Releasing/Courtesy Everett Collection/Mary Evans Picture Library)

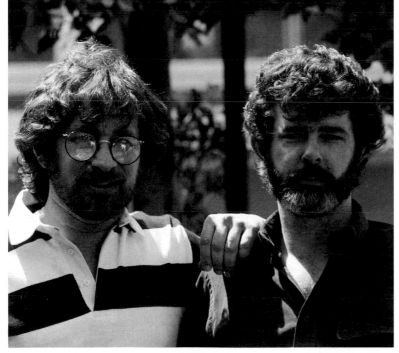

By the mid-'80s Steven Spielberg *(left)* and George Lucas *(right)* were no longer 'movie brats', the former running his production company Amblin from the backlot of Universal, the latter his FX outfit Industrial Light & Magic from Marin County, San Francisco. Spielberg even had the power to encourage the MPAA to introduce a new teen-friendly rating: PG-13. (Wally Fong/AP/REX/Shutterstock)

Mix new computer technology with America's military hardware and what could possibly go wrong? Matthew Broderick and Ally Sheedy – two privileged New Yorkers adept at playing everyday teens – are about to find out in *WarGames*, a thriller that writers Lawrence Lasker and Walter Parkes saw go through many incarnations before its release in 1983.
(Ronald Grant Archive/Mary Evans Picture Library)

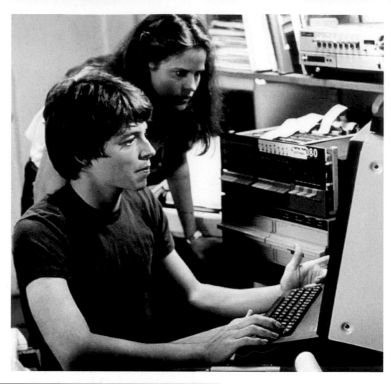

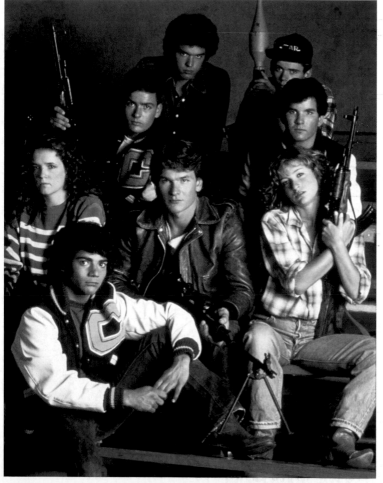

Red Dawn began as a critique of right-wing American attitudes but, by its release in 1984, had been retooled by director John Milius into something more flag-waving. The youngsters who battle a Russian invasion were played by *(clockwise, from bottom)*: Doug Toby, Lea Thompson, Charlie Sheen, Darren Dalton, C. Thomas Howell, Brad Savage, Jennifer Grey, Patrick Swayze.
(© United Artists/Valkyrie Films/Courtesy Ronald Grant/Mary Evans Picture Library)

sewn together, further blurring the boundary between MTV, commercials and the big screen.

It was a defining moment. Early film tie-in hit songs of the decade – 'Up Where We Belong' from *An Officer and a Gentleman*, 'Call Me' from *American Gigolo*, both of them Bruckheimer movies – had videos that focused on the artists, not the movie in which they featured. Within a year of *Flashdance*, big screen tie-in hits such as 'Ghostbusters', 'Footloose' and 'Axel F.' now had videos as full of film clips as they were shots of performers Ray Parker Jr, Kenny Loggins and Harold Faltermeyer.

'We're talking about an era when soundtracks sold millions and millions of records. They supported the movie and sometimes they pushed the movie ... The directors knew it. The producers were demanding that,' remembers Faltermeyer.[1] By late 1984 the music industry's weekly bible *Billboard* had picked up on the phenomenon, devoting a whole article to music video producer Jeffrey Abelson, hot from his success setting up a musical tie-in with *Ghostbusters*.

'If you want your major motion picture promoted by a music video, who do you call? Jeffrey Abelson' the headline ran. Abelson, who had also scored big on MTV with Frankie's 'Relax' in *Body Double* and Phil Collins' title track from *Against All Odds*, was quick to acknowledge that the relationship between pop and movies was no exact science: 'Sometimes a film, its soundtrack and video are destined to be a hit. Other times, only the video or soundtrack become a hit and the movie is a flop, or vice versa. I feel that the video is an entire package that has a synergistic effect on either the movie or the soundtrack or both.'[2]

The downside to the success of records such as *Flashdance*, however, was inevitably an increase in interference from many insiders had previously taken a back seat. Dean Pitchford had helped to usher in the '80s soundtrack album with *Fame* but now found that 'the studio executives who did not until then involve themselves ... suddenly needed to hear all the demos, they wanted to have meetings with the record labels, they wanted to have lunch

---

1 Author interview.
2 'Jeffrey Abelson: Movie Studios' Liaison', *Billboard*, Faye Zuckerman, 10 November 1984.

with the artists, they wanted to be able to hear the earliest stages, they wanted to come into the studio and approve the mixes. Suddenly people who were not in the music industry injected themselves in the music industry. And that was too many chefs in the kitchen.'[1] The result was often a reluctance from producers to sully their soundtrack albums with unproven singles artists, even if those artists had music that featured in the actual film. With expectations now so high for soundtrack sales, it was too much of a risk.

'Nobody wanted to have "Axel F." on the soundtrack,' says Faltermeyer of his instrumental theme from Simpson and Bruckheimer's *Beverly Hills Cop*. 'I remember Irving Azoff's words: "I'm only going to have hit records and hit tracks on the album and that's it. I don't want to have pieces of score which nobody knows. I just don't care about it."[2] So I had a lot of fights to get "Axel F." and "Shoot Out" on the soundtrack or flipsides of various single releases. It was tough.'[3] It was also proof that even experienced industry executives didn't always know what would work. 'Axel F.' ultimately went Top 3 in the USA and was a Europe-wide No. 1[4] as 1984 turned into 1985. Faltermeyer might not have been a natural pop star but by seeming to interact with Eddie Murphy in the video, even a deadpan German in a trilby hat could look cool.

If *Flashdance* rehashed old storytelling tropes – a bit of *Romeo and Juliet* here, some Cinderella there – it knew it had to do so with enough bravado and verve to make them seem fresh. Others fared less well. The sequel to what had once, six years earlier, been the exciting *Flashdance*-size dance hit of its time – *Saturday Night Fever* – was released in July 1983 under the title *Staying Alive* and scooped just over sixty million dollars in total; certainly decent, but thirty million less than *Flashdance* and not even half of what *Fever* had originally made. What happened? On paper at least,

---

1 Author interview.

2 Azoff was, by this point, chairman of MCA Records.

3 Author interview.

4 Worryingly – although perhaps not for its writer Harold Faltermeyer – 'Axel F.' was a Euro No. 1 all over again when 'covered' by novelty ringtone amphibian Crazy Frog in 2005.

Staying Alive was an obvious competitor for *Flashdance*; a similarly music-heavy, rags-to-riches tale of dancers with big ambitions, also distributed by Paramount.

Yet on-screen *Staying Alive* seemed dated, burdened with Travolta's fading star power, Bee Gees overkill and no contemporary musical fad to latch on to in place of disco. Even its story ideas felt flat. Here was a film where the iconic Tony Manero was no longer charmingly optimistic but now an embittered fallen idol, the former king of the Brooklyn dance scene struggling to make ends meet in Manhattan. His big 1983 dream? To get into a Broadway show; hardly as cool as his teenage nights at the Odyssey (now closed down, the film tells us, and turned into a strip club) or as cutting edge as Alex's contemporary, sexy *Flashdance* routines at Mawby's. Even Tony's Manhattan apartment is a pokey, depressing box where he has to wash clothes in the shower; nothing so chic as Alex's artfully mussed Pittsburgh warehouse conversion.

Attempts to give *Staying Alive*'s story some glamour and polish lift things a little at the end, the story concluding with Tony starring in a hi-tech, twenty-minute Broadway dance routine – all pyrotechnics and post-apocalyptic outfits – unappealingly called Satan's Alley. But when The Bee Gees' old disco title track returns for the end credits audiences are thrust back into the previous decade and a now out-of-fashion music style, giving *Staying Alive* the appearance of a film with no idea if it's grimy like the original or glossy for the new decade.

Where *Staying Alive* really gives itself away is with the love triangle at the centre of its story. In Tony's '83, unlike Alex's, the working classes and the rich don't unite. Finola Hughes' posh girl Laura remains a mercurial bitch with only glimpses of warmth, leaving it to Tony's down-to-earth social equal Jackie (Cynthia Rhodes) to win him over; hardly as optimistic as lowly Alex ending up with upwardly mobile Nick.[1] Maybe Laura's punishment is deserved, seeing as she was born with a silver spoon in her

---

1 It's more like, say, Alex deciding to run off with Mawby's greasy cook Jake instead.

mouth, rather than having to work hard for her money[1] as Nick has done in *Flashdance*? In other words, in Reagan's American Dream, it was the not-being-afraid-to-get-your-hands-dirty that made your wealth something to admire. Yet *Staying Alive* offers little hope for change. After Tony wows Broadway with his dancing all he can do is return to his old ways, strutting down the street to his theme tune just as he had opened the original movie six years earlier.

Not that Travolta, now twenty-nine, hadn't worked hard to reprise his most famous role. Contractually bound by Paramount to make the sequel, a consequence of having left their *American Gigolo* so close to production, he had rejected an earlier story idea of having Tony working on social housing projects in the city and so headed to the south of France during the summer of '81 to stay with Robert Stigwood on his yacht and come up with a new plot outline. The Broadway setting was then written up by original scribe Norman Wexler and tweaked by Travolta's choice of director: action man Sly Stallone, who'd impressed the star with his *Rocky* sequels and who was also a client of Travolta's new agent (and David Geffen's old opponent from the *Personal Best* debacle) Mike Ovitz.

As *Staying Alive* was readied, Travolta couldn't sign on to any other projects for fear of annoying an already frustrated Paramount with more delays so instead, he told *People* magazine in March 1983,[2] he flew his plane, studied Scientology and came to terms with parting from his longtime mentor Bob LeMond. More importantly though, he prepared his body. 'Sly is gorgeous . . . to have Sly's kind of body would be beautiful,' he told *People*, the article revealing Travolta had 'waxed the hair off his arms and bronzed the skin with a tanning machine to highlight the lines of his muscles' and piloted his jet to LA every week to show his developing body to a fussy Stallone. Travolta got two million dollars for his efforts, Stallone one million dollars, but the money

---

1 Donna Summer's 'She Works Hard for the Money' came out in May 1983, a US Top 3 hit for the singer, back with Casablanca's owners Polygram after her brief and disastrous stint with Geffen. The video, by British director Brian Grant, was the first by an African-American woman to get heavy rotation on MTV. Its release actually stopped her *Flashdance* track 'Romeo' becoming a single, as they would have ended up competing with one another. In the video, however, Summer nods to the movie: she plays a waitress who has given up her dreams of becoming a ballerina.
2 7 March 1983.

could arguably have been better spent – or just not at all. *Staying Alive*'s total budget of around twenty-two million dollars was three times that of the considerably more impactful *Flashdance*.

But *People* magazine were at least confident, proclaiming 'Stallone is a professional mythmaker. On the set of *Staying Alive*, it's possible to believe that John Travolta, like Rocky, will regain his crown.' Yet younger audiences seemed less impressed by such big name comebacks than by the fresh faces and high concepts of *Flashdance* and *Risky Business*. Travolta could only finish the year with another attempt at rehashing former glories: reuniting with Olivia Newton-John in a bizarre comedy called *Two of a Kind*, playing a bank robber who's given the chance to save the world from God's wrath by showing he can be a nice guy. Some hits on the soundtrack barely made up for the film's five Razzie nominations and lacklustre box-office.

Flashdance, though, had no such baggage, its reliance on great word of mouth rather than star power leading to a rare increase in business in its second week in cinemas, staying on screens into *Staying Alive*'s summer with the help of a soundtrack that worked as an ad for the movie – and vice versa. Bruckheimer liked to recall the time he and Simpson watched audiences leave the Village theater in Westwood after watching *Flashdance* and head straight to the record store next door to buy the album . . . before heading back to the cinema to watch the movie again. Lyne, meanwhile, remembered the cultural impact of Alex's slouchy dancewear: 'I went out into the street and walked up and down Seventh Avenue and I would say every third girl was wearing that stuff. That was a fabulous feeling.'[1]

But it's Lynda Obst's view of *Flashdance*'s 1983 success, as Reagan began his Strategic Defense Initiative[2] after branding Russia an 'evil empire', that is perhaps the most pertinent: 'It was just like a nuclear missile.'[3]

---

1 From the *Footloose* DVD documentary. It was a look – sweat tops, leotards and leggings – also popularised by both TV's *The Kids from Fame* and Jane Fonda's million-selling exercise video around the same time. Travolta's later attempts to cash in on the fad in 1985's aerobics-based thriller *Perfect* were less than successful.

2 Popularly known as 'Star Wars'.

3 *Flashdance* DVD commentary, op. cit.

Chapter Eight

THE JOY OF SEX

Home video takes off (by taking off its clothes); the struggle and success of female film-makers; Nic Coppola becomes Nic Cage in Valley Girl; *plus* Revenge of the Nerds *and* Police Academy *wind up the old guard.*

Not every teen film from 1983 was chic and slick. Not every director wanted diffused light and incense smoke in every shot. Not every producer went on to be a mascot of '80s hedonism. And not every soundtrack became a byword for hitting multiple demographics or gaining wall-to-wall spins on MTV. Theatrical success remained one way of hitting big, of course – *Flashdance* showed that – but so was a newer consumer fad, one that flourished in Reagan's entrepreneurial culture: video rental.

Andre Blay was from the historic spa town of Mount Clemens in east Michigan and had started in the tape duplication business back in the late '60s. It wasn't until a decade later that he wrote to a group of major studios asking permission to transfer their films on to the latest new format that was creating a real buzz: the video cassette. He wasn't thinking about renting these copied tapes out, though; that would come later. For Blay, an avid collector, the idea was simply to sell each copy for fifty bucks to members of his Video Club of America (as advertised in *TV Guide* magazine). After all, cinephiles had willingly paid fairly high prices for 8- and 16-mm copies of movies to play on projectors so, Blay reasoned, why wouldn't they do the same with this newer, easier-to-use format?

Not that there was, as yet, one single video format. The Dutch giant Philips had hit first in Europe, back in 1972, when their bulky, wood-veneered VCR called the N1500 went on sale with its cartridge-style tapes. Around the same time in the States, Cartrivision was a recording system built into the sides of TV sets and sold in department stores, also boasting its own library of pre-recorded cassettes that could be rented via mail order. Cartrivision only lasted a little over a year though, investors losing faith after a well-publicised fault in the tape stock was revealed (simply put, the tape decomposed) whilst the Philips format – its name eventually changed to the sexier-sounding 'Video 2000' – failed to think globally and a version for America's NTSC broadcasting system never materialised. Then, in the mid-'70s, two rival formats emerged from Japan. Sony's Betamax and JVC's VHS would soon stake their place at the head of the race.

JVC was the older company and had built Japan's first television sets, but Sony had made their name globally with transistor radios in the mid-'50s and expected other manufacturers to utilise its Beta technology. JVC wasn't about to roll over though, leaving both corporations to slug it out in an industry war that included pleas to the Japanese government and lawsuits. Away from the mud slinging, each format had its own strengths and weaknesses: VHS tapes were bigger, Beta more compact; VHS tapes had longer recording times, but Beta a better picture. Yet it was ultimately the VHS format that fellow manufacturers such as Toshiba, Hitachi and Matsushita's Panasonic picked up for use in their VCRs and home video-cameras, leaving Beta struggling to find companies outside of Sony to adopt it. And with JVC's baby taking a distinct lead, its popularity then ushered in another irresistible sweetener: lower prices. So whilst the early days of the video market saw Beta claim a respectable twenty-five per cent market share, by 1986 it had crumbled to 7.5 per cent. As the format war drew to a close, consumers who had once been reluctant to purchase a machine (instead choosing to rent one) now decided to deliver the final blow and commit to buying VHS equipment outright. Even the bosses at Sony admitted defeat in 1987 when they began producing VHS machines under licence from their rival, although they determinedly ploughed on with Beta too. To most though, it was clear that Beta was finished, its life preserved for another few years thanks only to its use in the television industry.

Blay's company, Magnetic Video, like most in those early days, hedged its bets and kept both formats going for his new mail-order business. What he hadn't expected were bulk orders from shops who would then rent out the tapes to customers for as little as ten bucks a day; so much cheaper than asking them to buy outright. By 1979 there were around seven hundred such outlets across America. Within five years that number had hit sixteen thousand, renting outpacing buying by ten to one.[1] For an average price of what was now a ludicrously low 2.60 dollars a night, you could watch fairly recent product in your own front room as many times as you could cram in. Just be kind and rewind.[2]

As those figures rose in the first half of the decade, studios that had earlier rejected Blay's ideas now, unsurprisingly, had a change of mind and set up new video arms to release their products in-house: Paramount Home Video, Columbia Pictures Home Entertainment and the joint venture between MGM and CBS that saw not just the former's movies on video but also the latter's small-screen output. Everything, it seemed, was available to repackage and resell. Magnetic was eventually bought by Fox and Andre Blay left in 1982, the studio then merging his original company into its own before teaming up with CBS – who'd left their early partnership with MGM – to form a new distribution double act.

Blay himself wound up at Embassy Home Entertainment, part of a company that had once produced big-screen classics such as *The Graduate* and *The Producers* – and had initially been owned by aerospace giants Avco, investors in Cartrivision. But times had changed. Embassy were now focused on lower-budget TV and film projects perfect for the booming video market, with horrors such as *Phantasm* and *The Howling* proving early home entertainment hits. Phoebe Cates' *Blue Lagoon* knockoff *Paradise* then got

---

1 'Home Video: Home Is Where the Action Is' in *Channels of Communication*, David Lachrenbruch, November/December 1983, p.42.

2 Paramount Home Video also spearheaded a change in video sales by gradually reducing the price, realising they made more money from increased volume than from a high RRP. *Flashdance* alone sold over 200,000 copies when it was put on sale at 39.95 dollars in 1984. Disney's theatrical disappointment *Tex* made back a million dollars from sell-through.

Embassy some notoriety, followed by Scott Baio's remarkably amateurish – but successful – sci-fi sex comedy *Zapped!*, the story of a high-school boffin who develops *Carrie*-like telekinetic powers whilst investigating the effects of cannabis on lab mice.[1]

Nineteen-eighty-three saw the fate of a certain Embassy movie perfectly sum up the way this new technology had changed viewing habits. The intricately produced retro rock'n'roll mystery *Eddie and the Cruisers,* a labour of love co-written and directed by Martin Davidson (who'd made teen-greaser pic *The Lords of Flatbush* in 1974) had originally been funded by indie outfit Aurora Productions, a new company barely a year old. Embassy then bought the rights to distribute but fluffed its big-screen September release; they just didn't have the clout to make it compete in a tough theatrical market where Lawrence Kasdan's baby-boomer comedy-drama *The Big Chill* was grabbing all the buzz. On the small screen though, the film-makers soon found that *Eddie* had a second existence, ultimately popular enough on video and TV to even fund a sequel come the end of the decade. It might not have been the *Flashdance*-style journey they'd have wished for the film, all instant success and capturing the zeitgeist, but the slow burn was certainly better than disappearing altogether.

That movies might now have this kind of ancillary life on video wasn't without controversy. Producers making money from a secondary source such as rental caused much debate in actor and writer unions over residual payments whilst some analysts claimed video was stopping people going out to the movies altogether, leaving theatres out of pocket and blockbusters short on box-office. Others believed that a VCR's recording technology – allowing the copying of rental tapes or movies from television – would lead to widespread piracy (Universal and Disney sued Sony for copyright, merely for *making* VCRs).

Yet there were undoubted advantages too. Video, like the B-movie or rep cinema circuit before, had created a second tier of

---

1 Barney (Baio) uses his powers mainly to magically unbutton girls' blouses and the actor's efforts were rewarded with scathing critical reviews and a Golden Raspberry nomination. Still, *Zapped!* made almost seventeen million dollars at the box-office and Baio claims it was one of the most fun times he's ever had on a film. He was twenty-one, getting paid well and got to hang out with his co-stars Willie Aames (they later both starred in the TV show *Charles in Charge*) and legendary jazz man (and *The Shining*'s creepy chef) Scatman Crothers.

film-making and consumption that insiders couldn't help but take notice of, opening up many studios' back catalogues to new markets and giving them another and more consistent way of making money from classics in their libraries than relying just on big-screen reissues. It was great news too for those misunderstood theatrical flops like *Eddie and the Cruisers* that went on to a fulfilling after-life in rental stores.

Less quantifiable – but arguably most interesting – was audiences' *emotional* connection to the new format. Now they could enjoy the novelty factor of being able to cheaply watch and re-watch a film at home, getting 'closer'[1] to the movie than they could ever at the cinema, an advantage that often outweighed the quality of the story itself. Yes, a bad film was still a bad film but at least on video you paid less for it in the first place, expectations were lower and, if it was a real stinker, you could just fast-forward or switch it off altogether. Such a relationship proved ideal for the time-rich but cash-strapped teen audience. Even better, MPAA ratings that might be strictly enforced at the multiplex could often be overcome at a video store simply by getting a kindly older sibling or parent to rent that horror movie or sex comedy for you.

The result was a new market for low-budget films made specifically *for* video that didn't even need to try and take on their studio rivals – and the last thing their distributors wanted was to get caught up in red tape about residuals, piracy and smaller lines at the multiplex. 'Although the majors scarcely admitted it, these new distributors represented new competition,' wrote Frederick Wasser in his history of the video boom. 'The newcomers were not interested in legislative and contractual controls on the rental stores. They saw that more was to be gained by cooperating with rather than by controlling the stores.'[2] From their business point of view, Ronald Reagan – the ultimate in laissez-faire leadership – couldn't have been cooler.

---

1 As Graeme Turner puts it in *Film as Social Practice*: 'For the return audience, the sense of power and familiarity is strong; no longer do they wait for the narrative to unfold but they confidently collaborate in its gradual development. This aspect of film – its ritual, performative quality – is often ignored but it is invoked every time someone says ... "Here it comes, watch this bit!", Routledge, 1998, p.98.

2 *Veni, Vidi, Video: The Hollywood Empire and the VCR*, Frederick Wasser, University of Texas Press, 2001, p.104.

* * *

Not all the newcomers were actually so new. Nineteen-eighty-three also saw the release of Canadian video hit *Screwballs*, made by Roger Corman's New World Pictures, an indie that had specialised in low-budget B-movies since its inception way back in 1970 (Corman himself had been making them since the mid-'50s). Originally, they had hit big with exploitation movies about nurses, teachers and air hostesses that varied from the interestingly feminist to the entirely shameless, although Corman had started to acquire distribution rights to foreign arthouse projects too, to show he wasn't all sleaze.[1]

With home-video booming in the early '80s, a company such as New World no longer had to rely on backstreet theatres; they now had front rooms too. Genre pics heavily inspired by mainstream successes – always a favourite of the exploitation film-maker – proved especially popular rentals. Thus New World's *Piranha* followed *Jaws*, *Avalanche* followed *The Towering Inferno*, *Rock'n'Roll High School* followed *Animal House* and too many space sagas to mention followed *Star Wars*.

The Slumber Party Massacre was made to cash in on the teen slasher craze after the mainstream success of John Carpenter's *Halloween* in 1978 (which itself had started out a low-budget indie pic distributed by Embassy). Written as a sharp parody of the genre by feminist Rita Mae Brown and directed by Corman's former in-house editor Amy Holden Jones, New World's *Slumber Party* was diluted into something more straightforward during its filming since, as Holden Jones freely admits, 'Roger Corman is a businessman and a film-maker, but probably a businessman first. His movies were designed to cost as little as possible and make the most money. He told me he could make a movie about anything provided it had at least one of the following elements: sex, violence, and humour. All three would be preferable. He would not make any movie that lacked one of these elements.'[2] *Screwballs'* intentions, meanwhile, were equally clear: aim for the *Porky's* market.

---

1 What's more, many of the young directors Corman worked with went on to great things: Jonathan Demme, Francis Coppola, David Cronenberg.

2 Author interview.

Screwballs starred and was co-written by Linda Shayne, a former Berkeley student in her early twenties who'd passed on an academic career to try and make it as a film-maker. Partnering up with Jim Wynorski, a fellow actor and writer she'd met at an audition for Corman's 1981 horror spoof *Saturday the 14th*, together they pitched ideas to the New World boss. Timing was everything. 'The next week *Porky's* hit the theatres and when Roger saw how much money this Fox movie was making, he asked that Jim and I write up a *Porky's* style treatment. [He] called us into his office and asked that before we write anything, we go see as many of the teen comedies playing in theatres that we could and write up why the successful ones made money and what was wrong with the ones that didn't do well at the box-office . . . Jim and I went to the films, discussed the commercial elements and reported them back . . . then we wrote up *Screwballs*.'[1]

Screwballs, like most low-budget video fodder, didn't have money to show off so Shayne knew she would have to punch harder in other ways: 'We pushed the envelope in terms of visuals and satirising the awkwardness of sexuality . . . both the females *and* males are put in awkward and ridiculous situations. There is an absurd irreverence toward them both . . . I thought of our film as a send-up of all previous teen comedies . . . we give the audience that clue early on with the name of the high school and the initials on the cheerleaders' uniforms. Taft & Adams High could be a typical enough school name as both are former US presidents, but their sweaters read: "T & A High". This is in the opening sequence of the film. I think most of the audience understood we were taking this genre to the extreme . . . '[2]

Here were cheap comedies without the need for expensive special effects or stars but with huge potential for profits from multiple markets. Since they could even be pre-sold to TV and video companies, many costs were covered before production had begun. In other worlds, even if they weren't huge on the big screen, it wasn't a problem. As New World saw *Screwballs* take off and turn into a franchise, the company was reportedly making a

---

1 Author interview.
2 Ibid.

modest twenty-three million dollars a year from cinema box-office but a healthy forty-five million dollars from its home video and TV sales.[1]

If this straight-to-video world wasn't exactly producing works of art, it did at least often provide a fertile training ground for new film-makers who'd struggle to get a break in the mainstream. Linda Shayne had big ideas but nowhere to go with them: 'My idea was that I would write a play or screenplay as an acting vehicle, similar to what Sylvester Stallone had done with *Rocky*. [But] back before YouTube and the web, there were basically two options to enter the profession of film-making: nepotism and low-budget movies. I didn't have relatives in the film business, so nepotism was out. Roger Corman was open to women and minorities working in all aspects of film-making, many years before the major movie studios considered it an option. Yes, he produced films in the horror and teen comedy genres, but he also believed in meritocracy at the workplace. He was very specific on what films he wanted to make and that he wanted his films to make money and be produced on limited budgets but he also knew that his company was a teaching studio.'[2]

Amy Holden Jones was another cheerleader, believing the positives of working in the low-budget world outweighed the negatives: 'I found [Corman] heavenly to work for as long as you could accept you'd make almost no money and he would rake in the profits. I made ten thousand dollars for *Slumber Party Massacre*, as I recall. He made a king's ransom. But what made him creatively great was he knew good from bad. Most people in Hollywood do not know good from bad. They try to control artists who should be left alone and hire others who should never have been hired. They choose bad scripts over good or ruin good ones. Creators are always on the hunt for a producer like Roger who can give great notes when needed but recognises and respects talent. These people are few and far between.'[3]

A few miles east from New World's Brentwood office, over at

---

1 United Press International, Bob Webster, 27 July 1986.
2 Author interview.
3 Author interview.

the majors many women were also beginning to make their mark in powerful production roles. By 1983, Dawn Steel was senior vice president of production at Paramount, Sherry Lansing was the first female president of Fox and Lauren Shuler had left her executive role at Motown Productions to become a successful independent. Yet according to Amy Holden Jones there was still a serious equality issue, with only a low-budget outfit such as New World actually giving female film-makers the chance to work: 'It was impossible to work as a woman director in Hollywood when I started. The handful doing it were mainly connected by family and/or actresses, like Penny Marshall. A few, I'm sorry to say, were wives or mistresses of men in power. This was also true of early producers. As Paul Schrader once said, "Greater love hath no man than to make his mistress an executive producer". One early female mid-level studio executive was said to have "fucked her way to the middle". [But] female studio executives never helped me. In fact, they helped few female directors. It was so hard to get where they were, they could not risk hiring one of us in case we failed. Men, by the way, could fail repeatedly and get more films anyway. The early executives all answered to a powerful man above them.'[1]

Valley Girl, released just a fortnight after *Flashdance* in the spring of '83, was filmed for under a million dollars and distributed by another small company – Atlantic Releasing – keen on quickly grabbing their own slice of the growing sex comedy video market. But the pic's thirty-seven-year-old director had very different ideas. Martha Coolidge had been in the industry for a while but was relishing having her first feature finally under way. She wasn't about to let it be just another dumb-and-dirty teen pic and – like Amy Heckerling on *Fast Times* – would have to fight extra hard to get her voice heard.

   Valley Girl might not ultimately have been the sarcastic swipe at a vapid teen culture that the song from which it took its name had been (a hit single in 1982 for psychedelic rock guru Frank Zappa and his fourteen-year-old daughter Moon Unit) but it was still a different prospect to many of its contemporaries. Here was

---

1 Author interview.

something between the studio polish of *Flashdance* and the cheap flesh of *Screwballs*; a classic *Romeo and Juliet* tale of a kind, but one where the social divide wasn't between rival families (or suave boss and glamorous welder) but between LA's rough and rebellious Hollywood neighbourhood and what sat geographically to its north: the San Fernando Valley, a suburban area populated with middle-class kids speaking their own slang, perfected whilst hanging out at the mall.[1]

For many, especially the Zappas, this teen subculture represented by *Valley Girl*'s title character Julie was vacuous, summing up the shallow obsession with consumerism and appearance by which '80s America was becoming engrossed. Real Valley Girls, you sense, would have *loved* a film like *Flashdance*. On the flip side, some saw these kids as a reason to celebrate; here were perky, optimistic go-getters – Reaganomics in a ra-ra skirt. *Valley Girl* the movie pointedly didn't side with either opinion and neither was it just about tits and ass, despite the distributors' wishes. Coolidge just wanted to capture a moment – truthfully, honestly – and get it out there.

Martha Coolidge had actually been capturing moments for a while, starting out making documentaries on the east coast in the '70s before heading to California at the end of the decade to pick up work with Francis Coppola at his Zoetrope studios. When Zoetrope crumbled, so did the rock'n'roll movie Coolidge had planned to make there. She took her idea to Peter Bogdanovich, a former film journalist who'd been hailed a genius for co-writing and directing *The Last Picture Show* and *What's Up, Doc?* in the early '70s but who, like his contemporaries, was now battling both commercial and professional issues. His last film *They All Laughed*, released in the summer of '81, had flopped and his affair with the twenty-year-old model Dorothy Stratten, who appeared in the movie, had ended shockingly when Stratten's husband murdered her and shot himself. Neither Bogdanovich nor Coppola were exactly in a position to hand out money.

Film-making partners Wayne Crawford and Andy Lane were a long way from Coppola's movie brat circles; they'd made *their*

---

1 Notably the Sherman Oaks Galleria, as originally featured in *Fast Times*.

names in the '70s writing, producing and – in the case of Crawford – acting in redneck exploitation pics such as *God's Bloody Acre*, *Tomcats* and *Barracuda*. Their script for *Valley Girl* did offer something different though: a teen rom-com with a strong musical backdrop. When Coolidge met with Lane to discuss it, she realised that all the planning for her aborted rock'n'roll movie with Zoetrope could actually be useful after all: 'I'd spent literally three years in clubs. I knew every club, every band, everybody. I'd prepped for this movie – but I didn't know it was for this movie!'[1]

Not that distributors Atlantic saw the story in quite the same way. The company wasn't even ten years old and its CV consisted mainly of offbeat films from outside the States but taking Crawford and Lane's exploitation background into consideration, plus a desire to move with everyone else into the lucrative world of teen sex comedies with all its cable and video money, executives at the company wanted – yet again – another *Porky's*-style romp, complete with a prescribed and very specific four shots of naked breasts. Coolidge just wasn't that kind of film-maker though and would find herself being handed notes from frustrated bosses that carried one simple and chilling demand: 'More tits!'

Wayne Crawford and Andy Lane fought to keep the out-of-place director on board, convincing Atlantic that she really *was* right for the job. Their work resulted in a movie that ultimately featured the required quartet of boob shots (albeit filmed in a deliberately 'unsexy' way by a belligerent Coolidge) but which also snuck through a lot more range. Cinematography was by Frederick Elmes, Coolidge's former classmate from New York film school and an Ingmar Bergman fan who'd won plaudits for his haunting lensing of David Lynch's industrial horror *Eraserhead*. In supporting roles as hippy parents were Colleen Camp and Frederic Forrest, both Coppola alumni from *Apocalypse Now*, Forrest additionally an Oscar nominee for his supporting turn in 1979's hit musical drama *The Rose*.[2] Then there was the casting of Randy, the punky west Hollywood teen antithesis of Deborah

---

1 Coolidge spoke with film-maker Kevin Smith at his 'SMoviola presents' night at The Lincoln Center on 18 June 2011, following a screening of *Valley Girl*.

2 Frederic Forrest had also just divorced the actress Marilu Henner, a rumoured one-time girlfriend of John Travolta.

Foreman's clean-cut Julie; the Romeo to her Juliet. Coolidge gave the role to an actor who'd been auditioning for movies for a while – had even had parts – but who now also had something noticeably different about him. A new name.

For inspiration in choosing his fresh identity, the eighteen-year-old Nicolas Coppola had looked to his favourite comic book character, Marvel's superhuman anti-hero Luke Cage: 'I needed to re-create myself, re-invent myself. Nicolas Coppola had a hard time believing he could do it. Every time I would go into a casting office or talk about acting with a casting agent, I was talking about my uncle's illustrious body of work and it was getting in the way of the movies. It was making me feel like I was a victim of nepotism and no one would really take me seriously.'[1] If he wanted this new moniker to give him anonymity, it certainly worked. Martha Coolidge had spent years working with Nic's uncle Francis over at Zoetrope but had never crossed paths with the young actor and so, when she saw his headshot and that new name – Nicolas *Cage* – it didn't enter her mind that he was anything to do with her former boss. She was too caught up in the struggle she'd had to find the perfect guy. 'You name 'em, I saw 'em and rejected them,' she remembers. 'I almost cast Judd Nelson[2] but he was tied up . . . in the end I said, "I am sick and tired of seeing these pretty boys" . . . and I literally walked over to the reject pile, looked through it and found this photograph of Nic Cage and I said, "Bring me people who look like this."'[3]

Cage was reserved at first, wrongly presuming he'd only been called on because of Coolidge's ties with his family and shy about the fact that the one gig he'd gotten since *Fast Times* was over in Tulsa on his uncle's *Rumble Fish*. Yet Coolidge really had no idea who this Nic Cage was. She just liked him for his attitude and his look, even calling up her old Zoetrope colleague – and *Rumble Fish* producer – Doug Claybourne in Oklahoma to ask if Cage could get time out of filming to come to LA and make *Valley Girl*.

---

1 *Total Film*, Ceri Thomas, November 2005.

2 A twenty-two-year-old Portland native who'd studied acting with Stella Adler in Manhattan. He was probably working on the 'lost' 3D battle-of-the-bands movie *Rock'n'Roll Hotel* that slipped out into a handful of cinemas in March 1983.

3 Kevin Smith interview, op. cit.

It was Claybourne who revealed to her Cage's surprising family links. They agreed that the actor could fit in *Rumble Fish* before heading back to California to start on *Valley Girl*. Cage was relieved: 'I felt like I had been given an opportunity because of what I did, not because of what he [Uncle Francis] did.'[1]

'I didn't feel like I had a connection with him [at first],' remembers Deborah Foreman, the twenty-year-old former model who'd worked with Emilio Estevez on 1982 TV movie *In the Company of Strangers* (directed by *Xanadu* helmer Robert Greenwald) but for whom *Valley Girl* was a major break.[2] She auditioned to play Julie on a Friday, had got the role by Monday – all remarkably simple. Cage, on the other hand, *wanted* to struggle, remaining dedicated to the intense Lee Strasberg-style Method acting of his hero James Dean, going to great lengths to get into the mind of the rebellious Randy. He insisted on being called only by his character's name and, despite his parents' elevated status in the California arts scene, Cage lived in his car during the filming of *Valley Girl*, parked up in Hollywood, aloof and out of the way.

Yet just like *Fast Times* before it, it was *Valley Girl*'s dedication in the face of adversity that made it stand out in a crowded field; a film that fought to exceed many people's expectations of it and come up with something earthy, realistic, contemporary. The budget was tiny, around 325,000 dollars, and 'an enormous number of people were not paid at all,'[3] admitted Coolidge. The entire art department had only three thousand to play with, many of the actors forced to use their own clothes and props, hurriedly filming in locations without permits. For the prom scene, real college kids were used as extras (unfortunately from rival frat gangs who decided to start a fight and trash the gym). Coolidge eventually got tough on the budget restrictions and squeezed Atlantic for another 150,000 dollars for a soundtrack, although Zappa certainly didn't want his song associated with the movie. Meanwhile Epic – *Valley Girl*'s record label – and Atlantic

---

1 *Total Film*, op. cit.

2 Foreman was also interviewed by Kevin Smith at the same Lincoln Center event.

3 Kevin Smith interview, op. cit.

Releasing clashed over the soundtrack's small print, resulting in no official album ever actually being released and several last-minute music changes ordered for rights reasons. The end credits still claim Bananarama and Culture Club were used but you'll struggle to find them in the film.

That chaos and down-to-earth authenticity ended up *Valley Girl*'s greatest strength; here was a story about dreams of love-across-social-divides but, compared to the fairytale sparkle of *Flashdance*, this was cheekier, friendlier, more authentic and less obviously corporate. Compared to the gross-out gags of *Porky's*, meanwhile, it was virtually feminist ('Maybe because it was directed by a woman . . . this is one of the rare Teenager Movies that doesn't try to get laughs by insulting and embarrassing teenage girls,' wrote Roger Ebert in Chicago's *Sun-Times*[1]). The music that did make the cut was by up-and-coming new wave bands such as The Plimsolls and Modern English, giving *Valley Girl* a cutting-edge, cool feel. Atlantic even rejected the idea of a big studio releasing their movie and instead distributed it themselves. It was a smart move: *Valley Girl* made their money back in its opening weekend. A low-budget quickie with its origins in the throwaway exploitation market had – with the use of a smart cast and crew – found itself insightfully capturing a fashion, going on to stay relevant for longer than expectations thanks to the unique accessibility that video and cable TV had to offer.

Studio players like Simpson and Bruckheimer might not have been impressed with *Valley Girl*'s figures at first glance – a modest seventeen million dollars at the box-office – but a second look would show them a movie that ultimately returned twenty times its budget, before it had even been released on video.

By 1984, video cassette rentals in the States totalled 1.2 billion dollars, a meteoric jump from the two hundred million dollars when the decade began[2] and as *Valley Girl* transferred its success to the small screen, Atlantic had gained enough impetus to ready a horror-comedy starring a baby-faced twenty-two year old from Canada called Michael J. Fox, the breakout star of NBC sitcom

---

1 29 April 1983.

2 'VCRs put entertainment industry into fast-forward frenzy', *Free Lance-Star*, Richard De Atley, 7 September 1985.

Family Ties (in which Deborah Foreman herself had once appeared). The film was to be called *Teen Wolf*.

Foreman, meanwhile, could only watch as *Valley Girl* hit big using a poster and video sleeve that didn't even feature her face, rather that of the actress who plays the bit part of Randy's ex-girl-friend in the movie (Tina Theberge).[1] Cage had at least, by now, become more considerate to his co-star. Before filming wrapped at the end of 1982 he had written a tender poem for Foreman – who was rumoured to be his real-life love interest – touchingly titled 'American Dream Girl'. Glowing from *Valley Girl*'s good reviews ('I came upon *Valley Girl* with low expectations. What can you expect from a genre inspired by *Porky's*? But this movie is a little treasure,' continued Ebert[2]). Cage was also now a giant step closer to being a star.

The home entertainment boom proved a rich environment in which to find work; *any* work. 'The movie industry was in a completely different place than it is now. Video stores had revolutionised it. Suddenly, there were a ton of shelves that needed movies to fill them. There was a lot of work and it did feel like we were invincible,' remembered Darren Dalton, looking to follow up on the buzz he'd gained from appearing in *The Outsiders*. He did so by working with Martha Coolidge straight after she completed *Valley Girl*, on 1984's self-explanatory *National Lampoon's Joy of Sex*. This time, however, the director's desire to take a different path from the usual raunchy comedies didn't work out quite as well as it had done previously. Before the *Joy of Sex* was even finished, Coolidge was fired.[3]

Just as the line between music videos and movies was blurring with the advent of MTV – the former becoming increasingly cinematic, the latter more music-focused – so the demand for teen-centred product meant borders between studio and indie video were becoming more fluid too. If, say, Twentieth Century Fox

---

1 Foreman was unavailable for comment as to why this was.

2 *Chicago Sun-Times*, op. cit.

3 *Lampoon* writer John Hughes had originally written a script for *The Joy of Sex*, intended to star John Belushi and be directed by Penny Marshall, but a completely different story was ultimately used.

scored big with a film then Cannon would try to cheaply cash in.[1] On the flip side, if an indie could have a hit with a low-budget sex comedy, the majors might see the chance to save some money and do the same.

That the teen world's stars were still starting out naturally helped. It didn't matter if you were Columbia or Embassy – getting Tom Cruise in your movie was going to be a hell of a lot cheaper than Clint Eastwood. Even more appealing for many producers, *Flashdance* and *Footloose* had shown that established stars weren't even entirely necessary any more – high concepts were the star now and they didn't have agents demanding money. And such was the teen movie world's love of cheap nudity as one such memorable concept, it was often difficult to tell the difference between which of the ensuing sex comedies came from the mainstream and which from the fringes.

The giant Universal had, of course, financed *Animal House* and the equally established Fox had released *Porky's* but the scores of truly independent rip-offs those films spawned then did battle with studio output, their similarities obvious: low budgets, no stars, plenty of sex and flesh. Popular settings included colleges, summer camps and – most notably – holiday resorts, the seaside location riffing on the old, clean-cut beach movies of the early '60s[2] and infusing them with plenty of modern nudity. Hence, from the independent sector: Crown International's *The Beach Girls*, New World's *Fraternity Vacation*, Cannon's *Hot Chili* and *Hot Resort* plus Spectrum's *Hot Moves*. 'Hot' was clearly the word du jour.

Meanwhile, over at the studios, Columbia came up with *Spring Break* in 1983 (sample dialogue: 'I'm gonna go down to the pool to

---

1 As was the case with their *Conan the Barbarian* rip-off *Hercules* from 1983, starring Schwarzenegger's former Mr Universe rival – and TV's *Incredible Hulk* – Lou Ferrigno.

2 Those 'beach party' movies from the '60s had also seen a simultaneous interest from both established studios *and* low-budget indies. American International Pictures – the double-feature, drive-in specialists – were the kings of the genre with their shameless blend of teen music, girls in bikinis and exaggerated poster claims but major players such as Columbia and MGM also contributed with *Gidget* (1959) and *Where the Boys Are* (1960). The studios' stories might have had higher production values but it was AIP's throwaway films that ultimately proved more popular with kids.

get a beer and a hard-on') and distributed *Hardbodies* a year later.[1] Nineteen-eighty-four also saw Fox attempt to infuse the genre with star power releasing *The Flamingo Kid* – from *Happy Days* creator Garry Marshall and starring Matt Dillon – and Michael Caine's questionable holiday romance with a seventeen year old, *Blame it on Rio* (directed, rather incongruously, by *Singin' in the Rain*'s Stanley Donen).

TriStar got in on the genre in 1985 with *Private Resort*. Its twenty-two-year-old lead Johnny Depp was a Kentucky boy and former gas station employee who'd moved to LA to make it as a rock star. With his music career failing to ignite however, he'd been encouraged to try out acting by his friend Nic Cage, a client of Depp's make-up artist wife Lori Anne. The result? An appearance in Wes Craven's 1984 horror *A Nightmare on Elm Street*, where he'd been unceremoniously bumped off in his bed by knife-gloved bad guy Freddie Krueger in perhaps the era's bloodiest death scene. He was rumoured to have been cast because Craven's teenage daughter liked the look of him and the acting job had certainly put more food on the table than his band Six Gun Method ever had – but Depp still didn't see a future on the big screen. 'It was just a gig y'know. I thought, Well, this will get me through until the music picks up. The first two or three, four films, were just to me a lark.'[2] Following *Elm Street* with *Private Resort* was certainly no more than that, the sex comedy itself a sequel-of-sorts to the similarly themed *Private Lessons* and *Private School*.

Still, despite cashing in on the blockbuster popularity of *Animal House* and *Porky's*, only a few of these films could actually repeat the same kind of success on the big screen. But then, with their producers' focus frequently on the home-video market rather than theatrical, most were happy to settle for modest returns on even more modest budgets.

---

1 Both featured songs by Gerard McMann. Appearing on the *Fast Times* soundtrack hadn't brought him instant stardom but he had become known in the industry as the guy who could write and perform whatever style of song you wanted for your movie. 'If they couldn't get a Prince song such as "Little Red Corvette" into the Tom Cruise film *All the Right Moves* then I got the call to come up with that kind of vibe. Which I did with my song "Mr Popularity"', author interview. *Spring Break* featured his song 'One of These Days' (sounding a little like The Cars) whilst *Hardbodies* boasted 'Smile for the Camera', 'Barbados Rita' and 'Hello, Hello'.

2 *Larry King Special: Johnny Depp*, CNN, 16 October 2011.

Occasionally, though, a new smash hit slipped through, against expectations. In July of 1984 Twentieth Century Fox released *Revenge of the Nerds*, a three-million-dollar college sex comedy directed by Redford's *Ordinary People* editor Jeff Kanew and produced by thirty-year-old media mogul Ted Field, a department store heir and motor racing enthusiast who'd just started his own movie company, Interscope.[1] *Revenge of the Nerds* would be his debut film but, after early preview screenings, it quickly became clear that the folks at Interscope would be wise to curtail hopes of making an immediate splash in America's multiplexes. Video looked to be *Nerds'* natural habitat.

Peter Samuelson – Ted Field's fellow producer – witnessed this early pessimism, present as *Nerds* was tested before release at a shopping mall cinema in Phoenix, Arizona. 'I remember standing next to the head of marketing for Twentieth Century Fox . . . and we're looking at the results – the percentage of audience who rated it good or excellent – and I said to him, "I don't really have a frame of reference because I haven't done any of these screenings before . . . is this any good?" And he put his arm around my shoulder and he said, "How do I put this politely? This is the single worst result I have seen in all my career at Twentieth Century Fox." And I said, "How long have you been at Twentieth Century Fox?" And he said, "Eighteen years." So we were all ready to kill ourselves. I remember no one spoke on the flight back to LA.'[2] As a result Fox swiftly cut back on the already low-budget *Nerds*, reducing the number of prints and advertising spend. Back in LA, the production team tried to be sanguine about the prospects for their first film; they would have to just move on. The Friday that *Nerds* opened, cinemas reported that box-office was, as predicted, quiet.

Then something happened. Word-of-mouth about this new teen comedy surprisingly built, with Saturday's takings decent, Sunday's excellent. By the following Wednesday, Samuelson was getting reports of lines around the block. By the end of the summer, *Nerds* had done business nearly twenty times its budget.

---

1 Field would later start up Interscope's music label and push gangster rap into the mainstream via a deal with Death Row Records.

2 Author interview.

Why? It seemed that for many, *Nerds* was deeper than just *another* video-style sex comedy and was actually a celebration of something more meaningful. Sure, at first glance it appeared to be merely a vaguely interesting blend of new and retro, leads Gilbert (Anthony Edwards) and Lewis (Robert Carradine) dressing like preppy high-schoolers from the '50s – short-sleeved shirts, chinos, hair with ruler-straight partings – but who are also modern computer whizz-kids with their own self-built robot. The influence of the 1962-set *Animal House* was clear to see too, since what plot there is centres on Gilbert and Lewis's attempts to get official recognition for their college fraternity of ramshackle losers,[1] mainly via a series of pranks. Yet away from the outrageous caricatures and questionable attitude towards women, *Revenge of the Nerds* boasted a bolder message that – against the odds – began to resonate with audiences.

'We have news for the beautiful people,' Lewis announces to the crowd at a college pep rally. 'There's a lot more of us than there are of you!' At a time when even the 'outsiders' that S. E. Hinton wrote about looked sexy and cool in their movies, these nerds provided a new, genuinely weedy alternative to the sassy go-getters of Reaganite America. Their numbers included a child prodigy (Wormser), a violinist (Poindexter), a camp African American (Lamar) and a smiley Asian (Takashi); characters not always portrayed in a politically correct light but whose very presence – centre-stage as heroes – gave the studio-distributed *Revenge of the Nerds* the anti-establishment feel of a story from outside the traditional system.

'We sort of invented the word "nerd",' believes Samuelson, who had first seen the idea for the film back when it was known as *Brainz*, before it was moulded into something usable by *Fast Times*' script wizard David Obst. 'At the time we decided to call them nerds, a nerd was one of those very compressed sugared candies that you buy in a little box . . . [2] We were one of the very first to use the word nerd to describe a bright, brainy college student . . . '[3]

---

1 The fictional Lamda Lamda Lamda.

2 First produced only the year before, supposedly taking its name from a character in Dr Seuss's *If I Ran the Zoo*.

3 Author interview.

In truth, Edwards and Carradine had been cast because they were good-looking young guys that could be *made* to look geeky whilst a genuine nerd like actor Eddie Deezen, who'd perfected the type in *Grease* and *WarGames*, was turned down because he was the real deal.[1] What's more, *Nerds'* inclusion of a mainstream artist such as Michael Jackson on the soundtrack – alongside more arty bands such as Talking Heads – meant it wasn't always as much of an outsiders' film as it liked to think it was. But then, could a film distributed by a major film company ever really be?

Still, it's the film's final song that says most about its ethos, 'We Are the Champions' by Queen providing a camp-but-courageous crescendo to a story that always celebrates the underdog; something very personal to Samuelson and his team but which – to the surprise of even the bosses at Fox – then struck a chord with millions of like-minded people around the country: 'The all-time sexual fantasy of nerds is that they will get the girl,' says Samuelson. 'I look back on my own undergraduate and grad student career and I was definitely a nerd. I never got the prettiest girls and all that kind of thing. So there's an aspect that all of us at Interscope . . . felt we were more with the nerds than we ever were with the jocks.'[2] Those early, sneering viewers in Phoenix had obviously been way too cool for this particular school.

The actors, though, combined any social soapboxing with the much more simple joy of being young and having paid work. 'Everybody just kind of decided to go for it on that film and it really felt like summer camp, in a way . . . the weekends on that movie were crazy with the parties. It was not a restrained time,' recalled Anthony Edwards.[3]

Samuelson was a little panicked but ultimately realistic. 'We were supposed to be on best behaviour because the university[4]

---

1 'I did later work on *The Whoopee Boys* for the producer of *Revenge of the Nerds* and he told me I was already like that. I looked geeky in real life. They wanted more regular guys and to dress them up as nerds. I get mistaken for the guys in that film all the time. Just like I still will sometimes be mistaken for Pee Wee Herman,' author interview.

2 Author interview.

3 The AV Club, Will Harris, 15 February 2013.

4 The University of Arizona. Many other colleges had turned down *Nerds* after reading its suggestive script but Arizona agreed on the condition it was never made clear that the film was set there.

[where *Nerds* was filmed] had only just agreed, by the skin of our teeth, to let us in . . . but any time you take a bunch of young people and stick them in a hotel far from home there's going to be quite a lot that goes on in the hotel bar . . . and upstairs.'[1]

The success of *Revenge of the Nerds* unsurprisingly led to three sequels, the first of which – 1987's *Nerds in Paradise* – predictably took the guys (minus Anthony Edwards) to Florida in order to sample the well-worn delights of the beach. Not original, but at least it wasn't called *Hot Nerds*.

Warner, meanwhile, had their own low-budget celebration of outsiders upsetting the establishment in *Police Academy*, a comedy that blended the raucous shenanigans-at-college genre with the sending-up of straight-faced institutions that had been successful for Ivan Reitman's *Meatballs* (1979) and Harold Ramis's *Caddyshack* (1980). It was another studio picture with a video mentality that ended up a massive hit.

'I've always hated uptight snobs,' admits *Police Academy*'s co-writer Neal Israel, a film-maker who'd made his name with zany sketch comedy *Tunnel Vision* in the late '70s and had at one point been approached to direct *Animal House*. He was also married to *Fast Times*' Amy Heckerling.[2] 'And, let's face it, they're easy targets. I love stories about "losers" who turn the social order on its ass; who refuse to take orders from authority figures. *Police Academy* is the ultimate anti-authoritarian comedy.'[3]

Police Academy didn't just nod to *Porky's* with the casting of Kim Cattrall as cadet Karen Thompson (as well as a host of inexpensive young unknowns). According to Israel, *Porky's* also 'showed me there were no limits to how far we could go with sex jokes'[4], and its show-stopper featured bumbling Commandant Lassard (George Gaynes) as the surprised recipient of a blow job from a hooker hiding underneath his microphone stand whilst he

---

1 Author interview.
2 'She always made me laugh. She's extremely witty. My work was broader and more physical, hers more observational and personal. She worked very hard being one of the few "girls" in the "boys" club of directing. And she deserves all the credit for what she accomplished, author interview.'
3 Author interview.
4 Ibid.

attempts to give a speech. The film made over eighty million dollars before it even hit video shelves.

At cinemas just a few weeks after *Police Academy* was another riotous Neal Israel-scripted comedy (co-written with Pat Proft) which proved to be another low-budget hit. *Bachelor Party* featured a twenty-eight-year-old Tom Hanks – then making a name for himself with mermaid rom-com *Splash* – as the fun-loving husband-to-be of well-heeled Debbie (Tawny Kitaen); a party animal wanting the ultimate stag do but also well aware of how little his stuffy future in-laws think of him. Fox bought the script and put the picture into production swiftly, wanting to capitalise on the buzz that was building with *Police Academy*. *Bachelor Party*'s sex-crazed lads and new wave soundtrack racked up nearly forty million dollars. 'We just wrote what made us laugh,' says Israel of his double whammy of smut at the 1984 box-office. 'Fortunately, our sense of humour was stuck at about age fourteen.'[1]

Sure enough, after *Police Academy* and *Revenge of the Nerds* showed that the 'no stars, no style' aesthetic of straight-to-video could also result in box-office success for the studios, the straight-to-video specialists returned the favour. Post-*Police Academy* came a variety of video comedies spoofing similarly serious-minded establishments: *Up the Military* in 1985, *Combat Academy*, *Recruits* and *Stewardess School* a year later, then *The Princess Academy* and *Firehouse* in 1987. *Police Academy* itself, meanwhile, spawned seven sequels, increasingly making their money on tape rather than on the big screen.

Meanwhile, genuine indie video – rather than the studios' version – proved to be many an actor's saviour. Geeky Eddie Deezen scored roles in teen sci-fi horror *Laserblast*, music-heavy beach pic spoof *Surf II* (co-starring Eric Stoltz) plus several films with Fred Olen Ray, the exploitation maestro whose career had kicked off at the start of the decade with the *Evil Dead*-influenced *Alien Dead* and *Poltergeist* 'homage' *Scalps*. '[Independent film] helped me and countless others find work,'[2] admits Deezen. If that work wasn't always good, at least it was plentiful.

---

1 Ibid.

2 Author interview.

Still not every teen and twenty-something found it easy to be in Hollywood, despite this new abundance of big screen and video employment. 'I was fairly culture-shocked for the first few years,' remembers Darren Dalton. 'LA was not the kind of town that I knew. Others that I hung out with like Tom Howell and Judd Nelson were much more comfortable. We all took the place by storm [but] the thing that some people miss is that I was working two or three regular jobs at once when I first came to town. It took a lot of work. That's part of being young, isn't it? The paradox of feeling like a complete alien while also being Superman?'[1]

Universal's parent company MCA, meanwhile, tried to cash in on the success of video by co-funding with Philips a new, superior quality home-entertainment delivery system called LaserDisc. These giant silver disks – overgrown CDs – could handle digital audio, had a sharper picture and didn't need to be rewound like cassettes. But there was a clumsiness about them too – the size of an album, needing to be flipped over halfway through a movie and not capable of home recording. A mid-'80s North American market that was in the throes of a love affair with the much cheaper VHS just wasn't interested.[2] Who really needed to watch *Screwballs II: Loose Screws* or *Police Academy 3: Back in Training* on a more expensive format? Thom Mount was president of Universal whilst his boss Lew Wasserman wrote cheques to fund the new technology and fully admits their failure. 'We lost twenty-five or thirty million dollars fucking around with LaserDisc.'[3]

---

1 Author interview.
2 LaserDisc *was* fairly successful, however, in Asia.
3 Author interview.

Chapter Nine

KIDS KNOW BEST

Spielberg takes on the moral guardians; the many battles of WarGames *and* Red Dawn*; The Karate Kid* shows an open hand; *and it's parents* v. *pop in* Footloose.

Nineteen-eighty-four was a mixed year for the thirty-seven-year-old Steven Spielberg. There was no doubt he was flying high, higher than even E.T. and Elliott on a BMX, thanks to the success of both that extra-terrestrial movie *and* the *Indiana Jones* franchise he shared with George Lucas. His company Amblin Entertainment – three years old and named after his first commercially released short film from the late '60s – had its own offices on Universal Studio lot, run with his former assistant Kathleen Kennedy and her future husband Frank Marshall, a producer who'd spent the previous decade working with Scorsese and Bogdanovich. They were both under forty too. If ever there was a real life revenge of the nerds, it was at Amblin.

But Spielberg wasn't without his critics. A year earlier Amblin had given the green light to a script by twenty-six-year-old Tisch School of the Arts grad Chris Columbus called *Gremlins*, the title riffing on urban myths from the military about cantankerous little creatures getting into bits of hardware and causing them to malfunction. What Spielberg, Columbus and their chosen director Joe Dante – a former editor of movie trailers over at Corman's New World, alongside Amy Holden Jones – ultimately created, however, didn't just have one reference point. *Gremlins* was a blend of multiple winks and conflicting influences: Dante's origins in B-movies versus Spielberg's interest in the mainstream; the teen focus of the youthful Columbus versus nods to vintage Capra-esque ideas of apple-pie America. Plus, most controversially, there was plenty of horror.

Gremlins' story was itself simple enough: youngsters Billy and Kate (played by twenty-year-old newcomer Zach Galligan – a curly-haired rabbit-in-the-headlights – and *Fast Times'* Phoebe Cates) battle truculent lizards in small town America. Yet it was the way in which *Gremlins* mixed the *E.T.*-like cuteness of lead 'creature' Gizmo with cartoonish violence that both wowed and confused audiences. Was this a family movie or a teen horror? A comedy or a fantasy? Even the presence of Cates, still best known for her topless scene in Heckerling's raunchy high-school hit, suggested something stronger than the usual type of kids' movie.[1] Galligan, meanwhile, was a nervy and green leading man who couldn't help but fall for his pin-up co-star, so much more sophisticated than him thanks to her years of modelling and who'd recently begun dating fellow actor Kevin Kline, fifteen years her senior. 'It was my obvious crush on Phoebe that won me the role,' Galligan admitted. 'Spielberg noticed it during my audition and said: "Look at that! He's already in love with her! We don't need to see anybody else."'[2]

When *Gremlins* was released in early June 1984, it came with the host of merchandise tie-ins that Spielberg had first mastered with *E.T.*: from cuddly toys to school lunch-boxes. After all, the MPAA had just rated *Gremlins* a modest PG, a certificate which came with only the vague warning that a film 'may contain some material parents might not like for their young children'. Marketing *Gremlins* to kids seemed natural. Until, that is, audiences actually *saw* it.

'I've no idea how children will react to the sight of a Kingston Falls mom, carving knife in hand, decapitating one gremlin and shoving another into the food processor, head first,' confessed critic Vincent Canby in the *New York Times*. 'Will they laugh when

---

1 Her nerdy *Fast Times'* suitor, career-square Judge Reinhold, also appeared in *Gremlins*, albeit in a role significantly trimmed before release.

2 'Where Are They Now?', foxnews.com, Hollie McKay, 13 June 2013.

Billy Peltzer, the film's idealised, intentionally dopey twenty-year-old hero, is threatened by a gremlin with a chainsaw and then stabbed by a gremlin with a spear gun? Will they cheer when Billy blows up the Kingston Falls movie theatre, where the gremlins, now resembling an average kiddie matinee crowd, are exuberantly responding to *Snow White and the Seven Dwarfs*?'[1]

An answer quickly emerged: yes, audiences *loved* it. Warner released the movie the same week as Columbia's significantly more expensive and more straightforwardly comedic PG-blockbuster *Ghostbusters*[2] but there was more than enough room for both to play to packed houses. *Gremlins* was huge, ending up the US's fourth biggest film of the year, making 148 million dollars, just behind the ectoplasm-blasting scientists, Eddie Murphy's *Beverly Hills Cop* and Indiana Jones' second crack of the whip, *The Temple of Doom*.

Yet the box-office only told part of the story and after *Gremlins'* success the (carving) knives were increasingly out for Spielberg. Yes, he was still the king of friendly movie-making but naysayers also complained that he seemed progressively to be aiming his films – darkly thrilling mash-ups of horror, adventure, comedy and family issues – at a young teen audience who had no corresponding MPAA rating. If these movies were merely given soft PG certificates, as they had been, there was no guarantee that impressionable younger children might not be exposed to them too.

Spielberg, of course, understood the difference between movie violence and real violence and reasoned that young movie-watchers could too. Yet he could also gauge the temperature of the country's older, moral guardians. The boost that home video had given to splatter-filled low-budget horror pics (the most obscene branded 'video nasties' by the UK press) and the appearance of increasingly risqué music videos, pumped to the nation via MTV – Van Halen's 'Hot for Teacher', Duran Duran's 'Girls on Film', Bowie's 'China Girl' – had raised plentiful questions in the media about bad taste and what constituted obscenity. Conservative campaign groups such as the Moral Majority, headed by influential Baptist

---

1 *New York Times*, 8 June 1984.
2 Universal had already passed on *Ghostbusters*, citing expense.

televangelist Jerry Falwell (a major funder to Reagan's presidential campaigns), shouted loudly for a return to Christian family values whilst the Parents' Music Resource Center – a group of politicians' wives led by Mary 'Tipper' Gore – waited on the horizon. They would form in 1985 with dreams of censoring supposedly offensive albums by the likes of Prince and Mötley Crüe, marching on music retailers with their arms full of 'Parental Advisory' stickers.

'I had come under criticism, personal criticism, for both *Temple of Doom* and *Gremlins*, in the same year,' Spielberg told *Vanity Fair*. 'I remember calling Jack Valenti[1] and suggested to him that we need a rating between R and PG, because so many films were falling into a netherworld, you know, of unfairness. Unfair that certain kids were exposed to *Jaws*, but also unfair that certain films were restricted, that kids who were thirteen, fourteen, fifteen *should* be allowed to see [my italics]. I suggested, "Let's call it PG-13 or PG-14, depending on how you want to design the slide rule," and Jack came back to me and said, "We've determined that PG-13 would be the right age for that temperature of movie." So I've always been very proud that I had something to do with that rating.'[2]

Within two months, as *Gremlins* and *Temple of Doom* continued to play in a few cinemas, perhaps freaking out the small children legally allowed to see them, the first of these new PG-13 certifications was stamped on to a movie poster. Spielberg might actually have been making movies for this age group for years but here was an official acknowledgment of a new target demographic for the movie industry; an audience that fitted somewhere between *Star Wars* and *Screwballs* ... although they'd probably managed to secretly watch the latter on video anyway.

'When *Gremlins* first came out, it was mind-blowing. As a kid, you had everything you can imagine thrown at you all at once ... club invites, dates, agency offers,' Zach Galligan remembers. 'But it's not easy to always make the right decisions, even people with a lot of industry experience don't always get it right.' One such wrong decision Zach made was to stay in New

---

1 Valenti was *still* the president of the Motion Picture Association in 1984, eighteen years after being hired.

2 *Vanity Fair*, Jim Windolf, 2 January 2008.

York rather than move to Los Angeles. '[Hollywood] is wildly fickle. When you're out of sight, you're out of mind. My parents wanted me to go to Columbia University and get my degree, which I did . . . but in Hollywood, you have to strike when the iron is hot.'[1] Galligan had reportedly beaten out Emilio Estevez, Judd Nelson and a Philadelphian up-and-comer called Kevin Bacon for the *Gremlins* role – and would soon find himself considered for Spielberg's next producing project, *Back to the Future* – but recording his auditions on videotape in New York then sending them out to California meant he didn't press the Hollywood flesh that he really should have been. His next film, *Nothing Lasts Forever*, featured a host of *Saturday Night Live* stars but its release date of late September 1984 was postponed by MGM at the last minute, never to be reinstated. Zach Galligan wouldn't be seen in another film until 1988.

As part of the fad for teenage rock'n'roll nostalgia that ran from the early '70s to the early '80s, music and movies had been in tune with one another: 'American Pie' and *American Graffiti* were similarly wistful, 'Bat Out of Hell' and *Animal House* both boisterous, 'Stray Cat Strut' and *Porky's* equally cocky. Yet by 1984 neither the successful politicking of Springsteen's anthemic *Born in the USA* album nor the increasingly socially aware European pop crossing the Atlantic alongside were matched with multiple teen movie equivalents.[2] Earnest Irish rockers U2 had scored their first US Top 40 hit with Martin Luther King anthem 'Pride (In the Name of Love)', German power-pop five-piece Nena had taken anti-war fairytale '99 Luftballons' all the way to Billboard's runner-up spot and Liverpool's Frankie Goes to Hollywood, a multi-media project from groundbreaking English label ZTT, combined pumping dancefloor energy with a chilling political punch on global smash 'Two Tribes' (getting its video banned by MTV along the way). Hollywood teen cinema, however, struggled to respond. It could manage style, *Flashdance* had shown

---

1 foxnews.com, op. cit.

2 Springsteen's title track was, even worse, mistakenly adopted as a fist-pumping celebration of national identity – at one point a possible theme song for Reagan's 1984 presidential campaign – when it was in fact written about a working-class Vietnam veteran; ignored, unloved and isolated.

that, with Simpson and Bruckheimer's similarly high-concept successor *Beverly Hills Cop* following its formula of simple plot and slick soundtrack to even greater success. But in this time of military escalation, where was Hollywood's rebellious soap-boxing to match the ire of the music world?

WarGames was an exception of sorts; a movie version of 'Two Tribes', albeit with the thumping Linn drum machine turned down a notch. Even better, as America's nuclear defences caused passionate debate both on Capitol Hill and around the world in 1983 and 1984, *WarGames* took that era-defining Cold War paranoia and blended it with *another* social concern. Here was a thriller that undeniably riffed on a youthful dread of nuclear annihilation – a threat shown as very much the fault of chest-beating adults, not easygoing kids – but which also provided Hollywood's first insight into a new teen phenomenon, one that Reagan himself had worriedly enquired about in a meeting of Congress: computer hacking.

Hacking had been known about in the technology world since the late '70s, a logical next step after the 'phreaking' subculture of the '60s that saw telephone systems tampered with in order to make free calls. Hacking had even been referenced in Disney's neon techno-romp *Tron* from 1982, about a software programmer drawn into his own arcade game, but it wasn't until the summer of '83 – as *Flashdance* caused queues at both cinemas and record stores – that hackers in the shape of the so-called 414s, a gang of computer-obsessed teenagers from Milwaukee, made mainstream headlines when they broke into a host of big business computer systems. Reagan, between dealing with rival high-profile military exercises by NATO and Russia, demanded to know what measures could be taken against future cyber-attacks.

WarGames' release that season couldn't have been more prescient: the story of a Seattle teenager David Lightman (Matthew Broderick) who hacks into the computer system of an already nervous American military, almost sparking war with Moscow. Like the unconventional methods through which money is made in *Risky Business* and dreams are realised in *Flashdance*, David's youthful ambitions also challenge the status quo: he just wants to do stuff that grown-up society says he shouldn't. And as with Joel, those methods are as exciting as they are dangerous (had *WarGames* not been rated PG, you can bet your life Lightman would have piped up with a well-placed 'What the fuck?'). But David has also got something more. With the new and untethered power of a home computer, he has the technology to seriously upset the adult establishment from the comfort of his own bedroom.

As *WarGames* played on movie screens across the USA, the home computing market was new and booming. Nineteen-eighty-two had seen the launch of the revolutionary Commodore 64 in the USA – sold in department stores as well as electrical outlets, all for under six hundred dollars – and competitors such as IBM's Personal Computer[1] and Steve Wozniak's Apple II all had their passionate supporters. By 1984, IBM had four billion dollars in annual revenue from its so-called PC, the very name soon becoming a byword for any non-Apple computer product, whilst the Commodore was shifting around two million units a year. It seemed as if demand for this new technology was unstoppable.

So too, many feared, were the computers themselves. *WarGames* inevitably raised newsworthy moral questions relating to the stockpiling of nuclear arsenals and hacking into secret files but actually its main concern was the machine itself. With the average suburban teenager able to have their own watered-down version of *2001*'s HAL sat on their desk and with super-computers now increasingly running America's defence system by themselves, what would happen if that technology became uncontrollable, unable to identify what was real and what was just a game? It was no longer a problem just for futuristic astronauts in outer space. Now it could affect even geeky kids in Seattle.

'We were surprised to hear you could plug the phone in and reach other computers,' admitted Laurence Lasker,[2] who – along with his co-writer Walter Parkes – came up with the idea of *WarGames*. Surprised, because computers hadn't even been their story's original hook, which concerned a high-school science prodigy taken to meet a disabled professor – mentally alert but physically deteriorating – who wants him to be his successor in

---

1 Using Charlie Chaplin in its ads in a bid to humanise and simplify what to many was a confusing new invention.

2 Writers' Guild of America talk, 26 April 1984.

the programming of a deep-space laser system. Lasker and Parkes had looked to Cambridge's celebrated theoretical physicist Stephen Hawking as their main influence, an early draft of what would become *WarGames* initially called *The Story of a Genius*.

Lasker had been a script-reader in the industry, the son of actress Jane Greer, whilst Parkes' documentary work had got him an Oscar nod for the neo-Nazi investigation *The California Reich*. Neither, though, were experienced scriptwriters. Yet when producer Leonard Goldberg first saw their story in late 1979, he liked the idea of this new kind of hero: a slacker kid who might just be a genius. Goldberg was also someone with enough small-screen hits – *Starsky and Hutch*, *Charlie's Angels*, Travolta's breakthrough TV movie *The Boy in the Plastic Bubble* – to help get the boys a deal with Universal. They started to write, tweaking the plot to include hacking after visits in 1980 to young computer boffins at nearby universities ('We had a kid from UCLA who took us through the steps of breaking into the UCLA computer. This was in 1980, the spring. This was common knowledge,' said Lasker[1]). After meeting with a twenty-one-year-old real-life hacker called David Scott Lewis they took the idea even further, folding both his story and another from the news about a boy breaking into computers belonging to NORAD[2] into their script. Ultimately, the idea of the military's WOPR[3] computer no longer responding to human commands emerged, the story now fully morphing into a cautionary tale about cold robotic thinking in a militarised world. Yet it was the unpredictability of *human* behaviour – the very opposite of that robotic thinking – that ironically threatened to scupper *WarGames*' production before it had even got going.

The first unpleasant surprise for Parkes and Lasker was a simple one, worryingly common in Hollywood: execs at Universal brought in a new writer – Walon Green[4] – without their approval and ordered the main character change from being a school kid to

---

1 Ibid.
2 What was then the North American Air Defense Command.
3 War Operation Plan Response.
4 Oscar nominee for co-scripting Sam Peckinpah's *The Wild Bunch* in 1969.

a college kid. The next shock was more macabre: the duo's original plan to cast John Lennon in the film – who they'd already contacted through his record label boss David Geffen – were dealt a tragic blow at the hands of gunman Mark Chapman in late 1980.[1] Finally came the knockout punch: a gobsmacked Lasker and Parkes were suddenly told by Universal chiefs that they were now off the *WarGames* script entirely, staying on only as names on the production credits.

When *WarGames* finally began shooting a year later it was at a different studio – MGM, after Universal belatedly decided the project was too expensive – and with a hotshot named Martin Brest behind the camera; a capricious thirty year old who'd impressed the industry with his American Film Institute student film in the late '70s (that had featured Orson Welles) and had gone on to helm 1979's OAP-robbery romp *Going in Style*.[2] Yet there was still more trouble ahead. Just three weeks after starting, it was Brest who was now publicly fired from *WarGames*. He had been involved in hiring the key personnel, had even shot some scenes that would go on to be the film's most famous (David hacking a public telephone with a ring-pull from a soda can; David visiting the professional computer 'nerds' – one unsurprisingly played by Eddie Deezen   for advice). Yet Brest's vision for the film had been quickly deemed by MGM too dark and serious, the film-maker's personality ironically too aloof and robotic for a film about the dangers of the aloof and robotic. 'I shed all my humanistic characteristics when I'm working,' Brest later told the *LA Times*. 'I don't eat a lot, don't sleep much and, other than what I'm addressing in the film, don't carry on too many conversations.'[3] *WarGames* was in jeopardy all over again.

Over at Columbia, *Saturday Night Fever*'s helmer John Badham was busy putting the finishing touches to his own cautionary tale of military technology – the hi-tech helicopter thriller *Blue Thunder* – when he got the call asking him to take over on the long-troubled *WarGames*. Producer Leonard Goldberg showed

---

1 The role of reclusive boffin Dr Falken eventually went to British actor John Wood.

2 Although Brest's most recent work at this point had been playing Dr Miller in *Fast Times*, director Amy Heckerling was an ex-girlfriend.

3 Leonard Klady, 20 July 1988.

him some of the scenes already shot to try and tempt him and Badham immediately saw there was a crucial element missing from the footage: fun. 'If I could change somebody's grades on the computer,' the director explained, 'I'd be peeing in my pants with excitement to show it to some girl. And the girl would be excited about it!'[1] After he'd said 'Yes' to the job, Badham had one important call to make: to a surprised Lawrence Lasker and Walter Parkes, finally rehiring them to work on what had been their idea all along.

The movie that Badham envisaged – and which he and Lasker and Parkes now sculpted from both their original draft and a new one – was the key to the film's success; a balance of social commentary about a modern, computerised world with more of the adventure that Badham demanded and that Brest had shied away from. True, *WarGames* wasn't the jaw-dropping military satire with which Frankie Goes to Hollywood had bombarded the pop charts but it was a cleverly Hitchcockian think piece; a nuclear age *North by Northwest*.

Even working with John Badham, the situation on *WarGames* was never ideal for Lasker and Parkes, the former claiming he and his co-writer had to hang around the shoot almost in secret, studio executives never acknowledging them and with no one but the main cast and crew seeming to know who they were, even as they hurriedly rewrote scenes in the morning, ready for filming in the afternoon. Yet despite uncomfortable circumstances, their words added up to a brilliantly succinct screenplay. From the first scene, where nervous US military men are faced with the task of turning the keys that will fire American nuclear missiles, the story's main issue is powerfully visualised: what role is there for emotion in a hi-tech world? Their masterstroke was to drop into the middle of this conundrum a type of person not only at the forefront of modern technology but one that's also constantly dealing with their own fluctuating emotions: the teenager. And even with a lack of life experience, that teenager might still know better than his elders.

* * *

---

1 '*WarGames*: A look back at the film that turned geeks and phreaks into stars', *Wired*, Scott Brown, 21 July 2008. Brest went on to successfully helm the distinctly lighter-in-tone *Beverly Hills Cop*.

Matthew Broderick was big on emotions. 'I hate those movies because it's not like that,' he told the *Pittsburgh Press* in the summer of '83 when asked about the current flood of teen sex comedies. 'High school is not a big fun party where you're trying to see a naked girl all the time. High school is going on your first date and you're terrified and you kiss her and every time you see her again at school you're terrified.'[1] Tellingly, the interview with Broderick appeared above adverts for the just-released sex comedy sequel *Porky's 2: The Next Day*,[2] as well as that year's other disappointing follow-up: Travolta's *Staying' Alive*. If you want a perfect snapshot of Hollywood's teen scene in 1983, it's all there on one newspaper page: hangovers from *Animal House* and disco mingling with Broderick – the one hint of an exciting future.

Matthew Broderick was exciting because he was different. Here was a twenty-one year old – then starring in Neil Simon's coming-of-age comedy drama *Brighton Beach Memoirs* at New York's Alvin Theatre – who didn't claim De Niro and Pacino as his acting idols but the much more colourful, occasionally frivolous Peter O'Toole instead. If John Badham wanted fun to mix with *WarGames'* imminent threat of World War III, here was a lead actor who knew just how to get the balance right.

'The best thing to be in Hollywood these days is one of the boys. In 1983 the new kids in town staged an unexpected coup that threatened the longstanding Redford/Beatty/Reynolds regime,' stated *People* magazine boldly at the end of that year, even hinting at the nickname this gang would go on to be known by. 'It was a good year for such charter members of the brat pack as Sean Penn and Tom Cruise, but none in that crowd can claim the double whammy of mild-mannered New Yorker Matthew Broderick.'[3]

It's true that whilst the alumni of SaMoHi partied on the west coast, Broderick's life on the east was uniquely cultured. His mother Patricia was an artist and playwright, his father James an

---

1 Gene Siskel, 19 July 1983.

2 'The first hit in the Big Leagues is an amazing experience. The second hit . . . it can't feel the same way,' claimed the already-jaded *Porky's* star Dan Monahan of his experience filming *Porky's II*, On Screen and Beyond podcast, episode 2.

3 Author unknown, 26 December 1983.

actor and, from his home in the liberal mecca of Greenwich Village, Broderick would head up to Central Park West on 88th Street to his classes at the Walden School, a progressive private education establishment founded by art therapist Margaret Naumburg. An early stage role in the school's production of *A Midsummer Night's Dream* sparked his passion for acting, followed off-Broadway by *Torch Song Trilogy*, a gay-themed drama scripted by Harvey Fierstein (who would go on to write the hit adaptation of *La Cage aux Folles*, produced by Allan Carr and soon to be walked-out-of by a disgruntled Tom Cruise). Broderick had made his movie debut in *Max Dugan Returns*, scripted by Neil Simon and filmed at the end of 1982 when he played alongside his father's friend Jason Robards. Robards comforted Broderick when his father died in November of that year, the beginning of an intense few months for the young actor. By the summer of '83, both *WarGames* at the movies and *Brighton Beach Memoirs* at the theatre – the *double whammy* – had turned him into a star. 'It's a little dreamlike,' Broderick admitted.[1]

'Matthew Broderick is one of the funniest people I have ever met . . . he loved musical comedy, he loved the stage and he loved Neil Simon. A delight,' remembered his *WarGames* co-star Ally Sheedy.[2] That they got on shouldn't be a surprise. Here was another prodigious New York liberal expertly playing the kid-next-door. Like Broderick, Sheedy also went to school off Central Park West – the Columbia Grammar, just a few minutes' walk from the Walden and the alma mater of Warner mogul Steve Ross – but even at a young age school couldn't contain her talents. Writing and dance were Sheedy's passions – she performed with the American Ballet Theater at six years old and aged just twelve her picture book *She Was Nice to Mice*, a relatively grown-up tale about a rodent who travels back to the time of Queen Elizabeth I, was picked up by her mother's friend, the editor Joyce Johnson and published by McGraw-Hill.

As a teenager she combined homework with writing for high-profile magazines, at fifteen appearing in the *New York Times* in

---

1 *Pittsburgh Press*, op. cit.
2 Den of Geek, Simon Brew, 20 May 2008.

an article about a children's literary group held at her mother's house, a club full of kids with parents in the book world.[1] As the new decade arrived and Sheedy turned eighteen she headed to the University of Southern California to study performing arts, roles following in local theatre, TV (*Hill Street Blues*) and – in the summer of '82 – alongside Sean Penn in the unflinching detention centre drama *Bad Boys*, the story of teen gangs filmed in the style of a '30s Cagney crime pic and where Penn showed once again how he could electrify the screen with simply a scowl, glance or clench of the jaw.[2]

Auditions for the role of *WarGames'* Jennifer, the only person who can get David Lightman thinking about something other than computers, were spread over four months but both Sheedy and Broderick seemed natural choices. Their backgrounds might have been more bohemian than the characters they were playing but both had the air of normal teens; approachable, suburban and bemused by the global political climate. Matt Dillon's movie star appeal knowingly nodded back to Dean and Brando, Penn's intensity to De Niro and Pacino, whilst Brooke Shields was the groomed princess who'd grown up in the public eye; a young Elizabeth Taylor in hip denim. *WarGames'* happy couple, however, lived in the present moment rather than harking back to the past. Sheedy, for one, empathised with her character: 'I couldn't make heads or tails of the script. It was easy for me to do the part where she's asking the questions.'[3]

Yet Sheedy wasn't without ambition and dreams, her rise to fame having already included modelling for the front cover of *Young Miss* magazine a few months earlier, where she was pictured cuddling the canine movie star Benji alongside the proud proclamation: 'News about Chris Atkins, Brooke Shields and

---

1 Sheedy's mother Charlotte was a writer and literary agent who had split from her father – advertising executive John J. Sheedy Jr – in 1971, subsequently coming out as lesbian.

2 'He kinda showed up fully formed . . . ' remembers *Bad Boys* co-star Alan Ruck of Sean Penn. 'He wanted to be called by his character name when he was on set . . . he knew what he wanted in terms of his performance, his direction, where he wanted his character to go. He wasn't even twenty-one years old but he was standing up for himself to the director on set, basically saying "I understand what your idea is – but I prefer mine"', author interview.

3 *Wired*, op. cit.

Kim Fields . . . "[1] Her performance in *WarGames* wasn't just a financial success either (nearly eighty million dollars at the US box-office). Ally Sheedy's breezy-but-smart appeal saw her nominated in the Best Young Motion Picture Actress category at the fifth Youth in Film Awards. It was a breakthrough year that she experienced in a similar dreamlike haze to Broderick: 'It was like a fairytale.'[2]

In 1984, a year after *WarGames*, came another World War III teen movie; a film to which Matthew Broderick had also once been attached. Yet really his manner was far too smooth, too big city, for this story about small-town teenagers ('Wolverines') fighting back against a communist invasion of America. The liberally educated stage star just wouldn't have looked right roughing it in the Colorado wilderness of *Red Dawn*, a film that *is* perhaps the movie equivalent of 'Born in the USA' – albeit the jingoistic misinterpretation of the song, rather than the bleak poem The Boss had originally intended. If *WarGames* displays a relatively complex nervousness about the morality of stockpiling nuclear weapons, all able to be triggered by heartless computers, then *Red Dawn* countered much more simply: never trust those damn Russkies in the first place.

Not that *Red Dawn*'s stars appeared to mind its blunt politics. Sean Penn, you sense, would never have made something so reactionary but a lot of young actors, like Ally Sheedy getting cast in *WarGames,* were just happy to be living the fairytale of getting paid to be in movies. Darren Dalton was called up by his casting directors from *The Outsiders*, Jane Jenkins and Janet Hirschenson, and was given a role as local mayor's son Daryl: 'It was one of those times when you meet the director and he gives you the job in the room. I loved [director] John Milius right away . . . having been cast early, I helped in the screen testing to find the main role, Jed. That's where I first met Charlie Sheen[3] . . . when I went to the airport to board for New Mexico and begin training, stretched

---

1 The teenage star of TV drama *The Facts of Life*.
2 Den of Geek, op. cit.
3 Carlos Estevez had now anglicised his first name to Charlie and taken his father's stage surname of Sheen. In *Red Dawn* – his first film – he got the supporting part of Matt, Jed's younger brother.

out across a row of seats with his head in Kyle Richards' lap was C. Thomas [Howell]. I had really known him mostly as "the little kid that was always working" on *The Outsiders*. We bonded on *Red Dawn* right away. By the end of the shoot, Tommy, Charlie and myself had grown very close... we were a bunch of kids making a war film. I don't think any of us really saw the Cold War connections that people would make... we knew it as a kind of survival. It was bitter cold and challenging. John Milius was a larger-than-life figure throughout [but] there was no greater storyteller.'[1]

Milius was the forty-year-old 'teddy bear with a machine gun'[2] who had been a lesser-known part of the movie brat gang from the '70s, albeit one who'd picked up huge pay cheques for both original scripts and rewrites. Yet the stocky, bearded Milius styled himself not so much as a boffin, more as a tough guy; a Hemingway-esque adventurer who liked to show off his growing gun collection. His peers both looked up to this gutsy flamboyance and kept their distance from it, leaving Milius – by the late '70s – rich from the cut of *Star Wars* profits his friend George Lucas had given him but also at odds with Francis Coppola after the director had turned his snarling script for *Apocalypse Now* into a dreamlike anti-war movie.

Milius had a history with coming-of-age tales, already having tapped into the youthful post-*American Graffiti* mood as writer/ director of *Big Wednesday* back in 1978, where the despondency of being a guy growing up in Vietnam-era America was set against the constant search for perfect waves in Malibu. Warner had pressured him to make it more of an *Animal House* frat boy movie but Milius stuck to his guns – probably literally – fashioning a film about male loyalties which turned surfing's complex relationship with the sea into something mythical. Yet *Big Wednesday* flopped, leaving it to the muscular *Conan the Barbarian* to give Milius his next hit in 1982. *Conan* was much more straightforward than the surfing pic, being the story of a fantastical fighter seeking revenge for his parents' murder, but its success was significant,

---

1 Author interview.
2 Ibid.

selling huge amounts of tickets as well as changing perceptions of its thirty-five-year-old star, an Austrian called Arnold Schwarzenegger. Suddenly the former Mr Universe was no longer merely a charismatic bodybuilder. Now he had turned into a leading man.

When John Milius followed *Conan* with *Red Dawn*, Schwarzenegger was already in Mexico shooting the fantasy movie's sequel, *Conan the Destroyer*, without him. Yet there's still something of *Conan* in *Red Dawn*'s bullish teenage attitude. Schwarzenegger's thick accent and giant stature made him seem otherworldly – half-rural, half-futuristic, all powerful – and different to America's own muscle man, Sylvester Stallone, who was simultaneously celebrating the go-get-'em ingenuity of beefy blue-collar America in films such as 1982's *Rocky III* and *First Blood*. But what they both achieved when *Conan* and *First Blood* released to substantial US box-office returns[1] was incredibly simple: Arnie and Sly gave America a new type of hero.

Here were action men who just got on with things alone and on their terms, as distrustful of officialdom as Reagan supposedly was of 'big government'. John Rambo was a disillusioned Vietnam veteran who uses his combat skills to overpower corrupt cops in small-town Washington state, whilst Conan was a legendary warrior whose violently individualist stance earned him respect ('In time he became a king by his own hand . . . '). But whilst Stallone and Schwarzenegger were, at first glance, opposites – downtrodden local boy versus European *übermensch* – together they represented an appealingly clear-cut new take on male (*very* male) heroism. By the time Milius got his hands on *Red Dawn*, that blunt tough-guy attitude would find a natural equivalent in Reagan's equally straightforward foreign policy of 'Russians bad, Americans good' – and this time it was up to teenagers to clean up the mess their elders had made and battle for the future.

Red Dawn wasn't always thus. Originally called *Ten Soldiers*, the story had been conceived by a history graduate from Texas called

---

1 *Conan*: forty million dollars, *First Blood*: forty-seven million dollars. The scripts for *First Blood* and *Conan* had actually been around for almost a decade, getting multiple rewrites and possible directors along the way. Milius himself had initially been approached to helm *First Blood*.

Kevin Reynolds, writing it as his student thesis when studying film at USC: 'This was at the height of this resurgent Cold War fervour . . . I noticed there was a lot of jingoism going on and everyone wanted to kick the Russkies' butts. But people in this country had no idea what it would be like to fight a war in their own backyard.'[1] *Ten Soldiers* was quickly sold to MGM, getting Reynolds an agent and a meeting with Spielberg along the way. Spielberg openly championed a student film called *Fandango* that Reynolds then shot using his MGM money[2] and with such associations, the young film-maker found himself with heat in Hollywood.

Still, it wasn't enough for some. Kevin Reynolds desperately wanted to direct his *Ten Soldiers* script but the budget, MGM reasoned, was too big to rest with a first-timer. What's more, the studio's president Frank Yablans sensed the mood of the cinema-going public and demanded a *Rambo*-style story rather than a complex study of teenagers forced to fight on home soil ('After all, *First Blood* grossed a lot more than fucking *Lord of the Flies*'[3]). With John Milius brought on board to helm and Alexander Haig, the former army general who had recently resigned as Reagan's secretary of state following several controversial decisions, joining him as a rumoured military advisor (he had also just joined the MGM board), *Ten Soldiers* – now rebranded *Red Dawn* – went off in a very different direction to the one its writer had planned. Unlike Lasker and Parkes with *WarGames*, Reynolds would never get back his pet project whilst Milius, the man who had lamented his own *Apocalypse Now* script getting radically rewritten in the late '70s, was now doing exactly the same to someone else's baby.

Following the hiring of Darren Dalton and Tommy Howell, Milius – along with casting directors Jenkins and Hirschenson – chose another alumnus of *The Outsiders* to play lead Wolverine Jed: Patrick Swayze. Swayze, now thirty, had made a few episodes of cop show *The Renegades* since working with Francis Coppola

---

1 The *Austin Chronicle*, Marc Savlov, 8 May 2009.
2 Reynolds would eventually direct the feature-length version of *Fandango* in 1985.
3 *Shoot Out*, Peter Bart and Peter Guber, PenguinRandomHouse, 2003.

but without the luxury of youth that his co-stars enjoyed he was back battling a drinking problem brought on by multiple insecurities: 'Who was I? Was I just some teen idol, a piece of beefcake who'd never be taken seriously as an actor?'[1] *Red Dawn*'s military machismo and enforced authoritarian atmosphere on set proved to be his saviour, helping Swayze shift focus away from those demons. Milius – who liked to be referred to on set as 'the general' – even gave the older actor the responsibility of looking after the young members of the cast, simultaneously continuing to indulge his own fascination for the military lifestyle by hiring real mercenaries to teach his actors authentic survival techniques, pitting them against the National Guard in a game of trench warfare out in the New Mexico wilderness.

'Charlie Sheen and Tommy Howell loved it – they were as gung-ho as I was,' remembered Swayze. 'But Lea Thompson and Jennifer Grey [the only two females in the cast] seemed taken aback by my intensity. In fact, it's probably true to say that Jennifer couldn't stand me once I started barking orders at everyone.'[2]

Milius's strength – writing characters with guts and drive – infused its right-wing politics with a wild poetry. 'Don't cry! Let it turn to something else,' Jed repeats, mantra-like, to his small corps of youthful soldiers, teenagers forced to become men. Hard-bitten coming-of-age moments arrive thick and fast: Howell's Robert drinking the blood of a moose he's just killed;[3] the boys witnessing the mass-shooting of local men by enemy soldiers; Jed and Matt reduced to communicating with their father (Harry Dean Stanton) through the wire fence of the internment camp in which he's imprisoned ('You can't afford to be crying now,' he tells them. 'I don't want either of you to ever cry for me again.') Through each unsettling scene, Basil Poledouris's persistent score spins and weaves, capturing the horror in its web.

Reviews were sniffy. Even fans of Milius's trademark *Conan* theme – radical, weapon-toting, male drive – labelled the picture 'a childishly simplistic masturbatory fantasy for right-wing hebephrenics that's

---

1 *The Time of My Life*, Patrick Swayze and Lisa Niemi, Simon & Schuster, 2010.
2 Ibid.
3 It was actually just Hershey's chocolate and food dye.

mostly safe enough to play the White House'[1]. You'd never see *that* on the poster. Yet what might have been an unexpected letdown – Milius clearly aiming his story at a younger audience than his previous work – soon seemed less of a mistake. That 'hebephrenic' teen audience, full of unsettled emotions and worries – especially about the anti-capitalist Russia – was a hot new target market that would bewitch Hollywood not just for the rest of the decade but for the next thirty years. With its PG-13 label – *Red Dawn* being the first film released with the rating – that market now even had a name. Here was the new normal.

Janet Maslin, at least, acknowledged the pros as well as the cons of this gung-ho adolescent swagger – '[it] may be rabidly inflammatory, but it isn't dull'[2] – and theatrically *Red Dawn* appealed, getting close to the box-office of those Stallone and Schwarzenegger vehicles whose moods it aped (thirty-eight million dollars in the US). And if Milius appeared to be dumbing down, playing to the whims of an ever younger audience, he wasn't the only former '70s star doing so.

When *Rocky* helmer John G. Avildsen accepted his Best Director award at the Oscars in March 1977 he summed up why he thought his movie had won so many fans: 'I guess what *Rocky* did was give a lot of people hope and there was never a better feeling than doing that.' It made sense. That original *Rocky* movie, before the ever more overblown sequels began to tarnish its reputation, wasn't just the *story* of a supposedly underwhelming boxer given another chance. It was also predicted to be an underwhelming performer itself; hurriedly shot, low-budget, Sylvester Stallone not even yet a star. That *Rocky* made over two hundred million dollars around the world and nabbed the Academy Award for Best Picture remains one of the industry's greatest real-life fairytales.

Yet for Avildsen, the riches soon returned to rags. He was bumped from *Saturday Night Fever* then turned down *Rocky II* to instead make the barely released romantic drama *Slow Dancing in the Big City* in 1979, following it with fellow flop *The Formula*

---

1 *Austin Chronicle*, Steve Fore, 7 September 1984.
2 *New York Times*, 10 August 1984.

a year later. *Neighbors*, in 1981, re-teamed *Blues Brothers* double-act Dan Aykroyd and John Belushi, chalking up a decent thirty-million-dollars at the box-office but proved to be a dark time for the director. His stars didn't believe he could 'do comedy' and wanted him off the project, whilst Belushi's drug problem was so out of control he wouldn't live long enough to make another movie. Avildsen licked his wounds by making a short documentary (actually Oscar-nominated), but wouldn't release another feature film for the next two years. Finally, in 1984, the story of a bullied teen who takes up martial arts gave the Oscar-winner the belated follow-up hit he'd been looking for, albeit one that was essentially a rewrite of the movie that had given him that Best Director gong eight years earlier.

The Karate Kid is *Rocky* with hormones. Even its climactic song, Joe Esposito's 'You're the Best', was originally written for *Rocky III* before being rejected by Stallone in favour of Survivor's 'Eye of the Tiger'.[1] Despite being a teen movie about individual ingenuity and the power of discipline, *The Karate Kid* also – like *Rocky* – never overtly celebrates violence. It might have come out in the era of '80s bombast, just six weeks before *Red Dawn*, but its downtrodden Italian-American hero – engaging but persecuted – was more in the mould of a Balboa or a Manero from the previous decade. Like boxing in the Stallone picture, or even the dancing in *Fever*, karate is a means to an end; a regimented art form that's a route to respect. Those who see it purely as fighting for the sake of fighting are the bad guys. Get too proud of your punches and you'll end up, title character Daniel is told, like maniacal martial arts 'tutor' John Kreese, the former military man from the pumped-up Cobra Kai dojo ('Strike hard! Strike first! No mercy!'). Daniel's trainer Mr Miyagi, on the other hand, is a super sensei just as happy tending his bonsai trees.

As *Red Dawn* tightened its right-wing grip on the communist bad guys, *The Karate Kid*'s more enlightened, open hand – modern but with a social conscience – was certainly at odds with Stallone and Schwarzenegger's snarling contemporaneous action

---

1 Stallone had also wanted Queen's 'Another One Bites the Dust', even using it as a temp track during editing, but failed to license it. So whilst the geeky *Revenge of the Nerds* succeeded in getting the British rockers into their film, tough guy Sly failed.

hits *Rambo: First Blood Part II* and *Commando*, even more so with the continuing video success of mumbling sixty-something hard man Charles Bronson in mid-'80s revenge movies such as *The Evil That Men Do* and *Death Wish 3*. Compared to the meditative qualities of *The Karate Kid*, even a family-friendly television hit such as *The A-Team* – a watered-down take on the 'misunderstood Vietnam veterans' hook of *Rambo* – seemed all too eager to throw a punch or shoot a submachine gun just to give its audience a quick thrill.

The Karate Kid's writer, Robert Mark Kamen, earned his first onscreen credit for *Taps*, another film about military dedication more concerned with questions of fairness than simply getting off on two tribes going to war. Kamen had developed an interest in martial arts as an alienated teen growing up in a New York housing project, training in Goju-ryu with teacher Meitoku Yago, the inspiration for Mr Miyagi.[1] It was the true principles of karate, rather than an over-emphasis on violence that the west had latched on to via exploitative martial arts movies, that he championed: humility, learning, determination.

His resulting script for *The Karate Kid* was a story subtly drawn. Its heroes weren't just two random immigrants; one actually originated from a country that only forty years earlier had battled America in World War II. But then Miyagi's Japanese heritage is made even richer when we learn that he actually fought *for* the States in the 442nd Infantry Regiment, a unit made up almost entirely of Japanese men who had been living in the US at the time of Pearl Harbor and who were drafted to fight whilst their families were held in internment camps. His wife had even died in such a camp, giving birth to a stillborn son. So whilst Daniel himself never appears to misjudge Miyagi or treat him with anything but respect it's easy to see that, in his many years in the States, the man with the bonsai has suffered from plenty of others not being so willing to deal with the complexities of his past.

But then, Daniel's background is complex too: a working-class, New Jersey boy from a single-parent family whose mother moves him to Los Angeles so she can make it in the burgeoning computer

---

1 Miyagi was actually the surname of the legendary Okinawan Goju-ryu practitioner, Miyagi Chogun.

companies of Silicon Valley, but who ends up waiting tables. His condo in Reseda is only around four miles away from the grand suburbs of Encino, home to his high-school girlfriend Ali (Elisabeth Shue), but their lifestyles are poles apart. Ali's Ayran ex, Johnny (William Zabka), drives a sports car; Daniel bums lifts in his mom's station wagon or, more often, just rides his pushbike.

Daniel understandably gets pissed off with his situation, initially fighting – and losing to – Johnny when the rich kid starts giving Ali a tough time at a beach party. Yet the film is as much about tolerance and training as it is about combat, Miyagi introducing Daniel to karate via a series of long-winded and seemingly random tasks that will ultimately help him to master fighting techniques: cleaning cars, painting fences. Just when our bile towards Johnny threatens to overwhelm, Miyagi is there once again to preach calm ('Fighting always last answer to problem'). When the inevitable fight does finally occur it's in the official, controlled environment of a local competition and Daniel – unlike rivals from the Cobra Kai – plays by the rules. Even when he defeats Johnny he does it with a move – a scissor kick from the 'crane' pose – that's as acrobatically artful as it is powerful. The defeated Johnny can't help but congratulate him. If only real warfare was as noble.

The part of Daniel had been offered to renowned anti-war campaigner Sean Penn but he turned it down, saying he wanted more mature roles. It made sense. He looked his age – twenty-three – so why play a teenager? Ralph Macchio was himself twenty-two by now but still seemed fifteen, maybe younger. No one would believe him as anything but a scrawny high-school kid.

Macchio was relishing the fame that working with Coppola had brought him: 'You never forget that moment, you know, when you come around the corner and *The Outsiders* [billboard] is up right above the Chateau Marmont . . . '[1] – but was also trying to prove himself as an actor. He signed on for dark educational satire *Teachers*, alongside growling barnstormer Nick Nolte and even took on a cheekily nicknamed 'disease of the week' TV movie in

---

1 laist.com, Shelby Howard, 23 January 2009.

1984 called *The Three Wishes of Billy Grier* – ironically playing a teenager who ages *prematurely* – because of the opportunity to stretch himself.

Whilst *The Karate Kid* would ultimately offer Macchio the challenges he craved, it took a while for him to realise it. As he auditioned in front of John Avildsen at his New York apartment – fellow young actors queuing outside – he wasn't even that keen, more concerned about the film's name than anything else: 'There was a ton of guys out on the hallway, all joking about the hideousness of the title, about how corny it was . . . '[1] Avildsen called Macchio the next day, not officially offering him the part but giving him some loaded advice: 'Learn karate'. After screen tests for producers in LA, Macchio found Avildsen true to his hint and was confirmed as Daniel LaRusso – the lead role in a movie whose title he still didn't like. Finally sitting down to read the script properly though, he was relieved to see that *The Karate Kid* might not quite be the cheesy children's movie he'd first worried it was. *And* he would be doing all his own stunts.

Cast as Daniel's love interest Ali, twenty-year-old co-star Elisabeth Shue was the opposite of all those boys obsessed with movie-making and Method-acting. If anything, her attitude was more akin to that of Jennifer Beals, now back at Yale: 'I had never been in school plays or had any interest in performing apart from sports. A friend of mine was interested in doing commercials in New York City so for fun we would take the train in and go to visit agents. Living close to the city was probably the biggest reason I got into the business at all. At the time I had braces [but] when they were off I tried again and got a manager based on nothing more than some mediocre singing talent and possibly "looking commercial". I realised pretty quickly that taking acting lessons would be a good idea. One commercial led to the next, [then] five years of doing commercials before I got a break and was hired for the pilot *Call to Glory* with Craig T. Nelson . . . When I had finished and was back in New York I had an audition to meet John Avildsen. I brought still pictures from the pilot, clearly shocked I finally had an actual role in a production. That just

---

1 From a Q&A with Macchio hosted by the 92nd Street Y in Tribeca, 19 July 2012.

shows how green I was. Actors don't bring stills from past work to auditions! Anyway, I ended up screen testing with Ralph and was pretty surprised I got it. When it came out I never knew how much money it made until years later. I remember being amazed my name was even on the billboard. I don't remember it changing my life too much. I did highlight my hair for the first time and my brothers made fun of me saying that I'd "changed"! But other than that not much at all . . . I decided I should transfer to Harvard and get back to school . . . At the time I was not the "It girl" or stopped on the street. No one was banging down my door . . . looking back I can see that being the only girl in a family of boys I am sure led to some need to differentiate myself and find ways to express my individuality. But at the time I was interested primarily in paying for college.'[1]

Writer Michael Kamen – who had used the money *he'd* made from movies on buying a winery in the North Bay area of California so beloved of Francis Coppola and Sean Penn – was pissed off that Columbia weren't throwing more at *The Karate Kid*, especially after he and Avildsen had also fought with them to keep in some of the movie's slower moments, such as Miyagi's hard-hitting back story. 'They put nothing into the advertising of the movie. They advertised the first two weeks and then it just carried itself by word of mouth,'[2] he complained, but the picture nevertheless ended up in the Top 10 biggest earners of the year. Macchio saw that success first-hand when he snuck into a preview screening at Manhattan's Coronet Theater on 3rd Avenue, mid-May in 1984. As the audience milled about on the sidewalk afterwards, nearly everyone was trying to do the crane kick.

Deliberate or not, *The Karate Kid* hit big by cleverly appealing to two opposite audiences: *Red Dawn*-ers and *WarGames*-ers. Its tagline was pretty clear – 'He taught him the secret to karate lies in the mind and heart. Not in the hands' – yet the story of Daniel's victory was still open to interpretation, as jingoistic as it was mellow if looked at in a certain way. Take the Cobra Kai's approach to training: humourless and uniform, the martial arts equivalent

---

1 Author interview.
2 *San Francisco Gate*, Peter Hartlaub, 11 March 2004.

of Nazi Germany or Stalin's Russia. Daniel, on the other hand, had a cocky American swagger reminiscent of umpteen teen Hollywood idols. So whilst Daniel's approach was actually liberal-minded, *The Karate Kid* could be – and was – just as easily read as a celebration of laidback US idealism over hardline dictatorships. A year later, *Rocky IV* would play on the same oppositions, contrasting the title character's wild and unconventional fight training with the computerised, ruthlessly efficient programme followed by his Russian nemesis, Ivan Drago (played by Dolph Lundgren). *The Karate Kid* got there first . . . *if* you wanted it to.

The biggest movie battle of 1984, however, used no violence at all to win the day. *Footloose*'s blend of pop culture and social punch may not have boasted the artistic rage of British politico pop from Heaven 17 or Depeche Mode,[1] or the US military concerns of *Red Dawn* and *WarGames*, but it was a story that took political rebellion straight to the heart of the nation's headlines: America's Bible belt, home of conservatism, evangelism and Jerry Falwell's Moral Majority campaign. And as its weapon of choice to take on these interfering adults, *Footloose* had kids *dancing*.

'I began writing the movie four years before it came out, when there was no Moral Majority. It just happened to be that I was working on something that joined up with the zeitgeist,'[2] remembers *Footloose*'s screenwriter Dean Pitchford, the Oscar-winning 'Fame' songwriter who'd penned the script during time off from his day job as a pop lyricist. Like Parkes' and Lasker's *WarGames* and Milius's version of *Red Dawn* – other teen movies that chimed with prevailing political moods – *Footloose* had also experienced a painfully drawn-out journey from page to screen. If Pitchford's story itself, the tale of city boy Ren bringing his liberal ways to a sleepy southern community,[3] didn't radically change its focus during that long gestation, it did witness several of the incendiary boardroom shake-ups that were beginning to characterise the era.

---

1 Touching social nerves with 'Crushed by the Wheels of Industry' and 'Everything Counts' respectively.

2 Author interview.

3 'A little outrageous but on the edge of believable,' according to Pitchford, author interview.

Footloose had begun at Fox courtesy of producer Dan Melnick, a former TV, Broadway and MGM executive with a soft spot for playing card games with Barry Diller and for musicals, once even married to the daughter of legendary *Oklahoma!* and *South Pacific* composer Richard Rodgers. But when in 1981 Fox was bought for over 700 million dollars in a complex deal by investors Marc Rich and Marvin Davis, a commodities trader and an oil baron,[1] Melnick fell out of favour.

It's not hard to see why. Marvin Davis was a tough man to get on with, a giant in both bulk and ego, fascinated by the celebrity of Hollywood whilst still seeing his new film studio acquisition as a cold business deal rather than an artistic statement; understandable perhaps, but tough for creative producers such as Melnick in their liberal bubble. On Davis's first day at Fox, the head of production Sherry Lansing was sent to see him. Such was his outlook, Davis was expecting a man to be in that kind of senior post – a *Jerry* Lansing – and, on seeing a woman, shooed her away from the office with a dismissive, 'No, I don't need any coffee now, honey.'[2] In his defence, Davis did champion *Taps* – one of the early films under his tenure – when others in the studio were nervous about its prospects but his quick dismissal of *Footloose* led Dan Melnick to take the project to Paramount, a move that soured his relationship with the new Fox studio owner further. Davis had bigger names to mingle with though. He claimed that at a dinner with Ronald and Nancy Reagan he was asked by the president if he could make movies with less sex in them.[3]

Don Simpson was brought to *Footloose* to give notes and oversee revisions but his subsequent focus on *Flashdance*, followed by rumblings around the future of fellow executives Jeffrey Katzenberg and Michael Eisner, once again meant *Footloose* was at risk of getting lost in the fallout.[4] Dawn Steel remained to shepherd *Footloose* but the studio's favoured director, Broadway

---

1 Davis was rumoured the be the inspiration for Denver oil baron Blake Carrington in TV's glossily iconic soap opera *Dynasty*.

2 'The Man Who Ate Hollywood', *Vanity Fair*, Mark Seal, 1 November 2005.

3 Ibid.

4 Paramount's Chairman and CEO Barry Diller would leave Paramount in 1984, heading to the same role at Fox (and a fractious relationship with Marvin Davis). When Eisner subsequently wasn't given the vacant Paramount role, he and Katzenberg left for Disney the same year.

musical veteran and former choreographer Herb Ross, quit when a contract couldn't be agreed. Dean Pitchford's story had survived several years of boardroom crossfire at two different studios but now with the respected Ross gone it faced its toughest challenge in the shape of the new director hired by Paramount: Michael Cimino, making his controversial post-*Heaven's Gate* comeback.

'I was terrified,' remembers Pitchford. 'I had had friends on the ground at United Artists when he made *Heaven's Gate*; one of those things where you just sort of watch a ship slowly sinking. I was terrified the same thing was going to happen [to *Footloose*] . . . an entire studio had not been able to stand up to Michael Cimino as he slowly took it down and I'm on meetings with him where he's asking me to do more and more elaborate things. He wants me to fly to Chicago and rent a car and stay in a particular area because in the movie Ren came from Chicago so he wanted me to suck up the atmosphere . . . all the while I'm feeling like I don't know how to say "No" to this guy or if it's my place to say "No" . . . . during all that time I'm getting noted and rewriting. I think I wrote twenty-two drafts.'[1]

Luckily, with Cimino's every move under the microscope following the *Heaven's Gate* debacle, it wouldn't take long before he became the second director to leave *Footloose*, fired from the movie when executives at Paramount were no longer able to ignore the high costs he was clocking up with his demands (including wanting to add in a John Steinbeck-esque element to the plot, where wandering peasants battled for respect from the local preacher). Adding to Pitchford's relief, original directing choice Herbert Ross was then brought back on to the project. Now that the battle to get the story on to the big screen was finally settled, they could begin looking for actors to play *Footloose*'s very particular type of fighters.

Herb Ross, casting director Marci Liroff and Dean Pitchford already had someone in mind for *Footloose*'s lead role of cosmopolitan hoofer Ren: 'We'd been told a lot about this young man named Tom Cruise and we were allowed into the editing

---

1 Author interview.

room to see some of the cut footage for *Risky Business*. We went, "Oh, my gosh, wouldn't he be fantastic?! He's so sexy and so funny . . . " so Herbert Ross asked for a meeting with him. Well, by the time *Risky Business* was being edited, Tom had already started to get pumped up for *All the Right Moves*[1] in which he played a football player. So he'd bulked up and put on some pounds and some more muscle. Herbert met with him and instead of being tall and lean and someone who could photograph dancing well, he was more like a fireplug, much more sturdily built. Herbert's background was in dance and he knew how a body looked on film and he came away from that audition and said, "There might be another time, if he were in different shape, when I could see it but he's not somebody that the camera would want to film dancing."[2]

Matthew Broderick was also briefly considered for the Ren part whilst Rob Lowe claims to have auditioned so hard he injured his knee dancing. But it was another actor that Ross met who had something extra special. Well, *two* things in fact. 'When Herbert was in New York and met Kevin, one of the things he first talked about was how long Kevin's legs were. . . ' remembers Pitchford. 'You look at the movie and Kevin has got a great body for the camera. Herbert was all-consumed about line. The line of the dancer. And it bears out. Kevin looks terrific doing what he does in *Footloose*.'[3]

Kevin was Kevin Bacon, a twenty-five-year-old Philadelphia native who'd been in New York since the late '70s, determined to emulate – if not beat – his father's considerable success in their home city as an architect and town planner. In the Big Apple, Bacon alternated theatre with waiting tables and was first seen on the big screen as a bit-parter in *Animal House* but was finally beginning to get noticed via roles in *Slab Boys* (with Sean Penn) on Broadway and *Diner* (with Mickey Rourke) at the movies. That Paramount weren't interested at first, citing Bacon as more of a character actor than a lead, only made him all the more keen: 'I

---

1 A movie that had also been cast by Liroff. She had previously worked with Spielberg on *E.T.* and *Poltergeist*, as well as *Porky's II: The Next Day*.

2 Author interview.

3 Author interview.

wanted it. I really did want it. It was an exhausting screen test because I was doing a play at the time and I went in on a Sunday night after the show – late, until twelve o'clock because we were working on costumes and hair and stuff like that. Then the next day I got up in the morning and we blocked it out for cameras and we rehearsed for about twelve hours. Then I got up on Tuesday and shot for about twelve hours. So it was really very tiring. I'd never done a screen test . . . not as extensive as the one for *Footloose*. I was charged when it came through. I was happy.'[1]

He was also happy to be playing alongside Chris Penn, since Sean's younger brother – fresh from turns in *All the Right Moves* and *Rumble Fish* – turned out to be as jokey in real life as he was playing *Footloose*'s hapless hick Willard. Penn Jr was bulkier than his famous sibling; another bruiser but with less of the beatnik poet about him and more of the classroom show-off, a routine he would roll out again a few months later in Cameron Crowe's ill-fated *The Wild Life*.[2] Mirroring Penn's cheeky supporting role in *Footloose* from a female perspective was eighteen-year-old Sarah Jessica Parker playing high-school scruff Rusty; a last minute piece of casting after Tracy Nelson – whom Parker knew from their time starring in TV show *Square Pegs* – pulled out. Parker couldn't hide her crush on Kevin Bacon – 'We'd just kind of smile at each other,' she coyly told an interviewer at the time[3] – but it was Chris Penn who, during filming in Utah, became her first proper boyfriend.

The final role in the teen quartet was Ariel, the daughter of the town's bible-bashing pastor Rev Shaw Moore and the flighty object of Ren's affections, despite her already being in a relationship with town tough guy Chuck. If Ren had his anger issues then it was important to Dean Pitchford that Ariel be just as complex:

---

1 Interview with Bobbie Wygant for *Footloose* release, NBC 5 in Dallas.

2 *The Wild Life* was another ensemble teen movie – a post-high-school comedy – with Crowe's script directed by *Fast Times* producer Art Linson and with Eric Stoltz, Lea Thompson and Ilan Mitchell-Smith starring alongside Chris Penn. Crowe was so unhappy with the results he has since tried to forget the experience altogether: 'That was a lesson in why it's good to direct your own screenplays. That was a group of people that came together and decided that this screenplay that wasn't really a sequel to *Fast Times* was going to be made so that it *kinda was*... and sold that way,' author interview, BBC Radio 1, 3 November 2005.

3 James Sanford, who thirty years later reprinted parts of his interview as 'Let's Hear It For The Girl: Sarah Jessica Parker On The Making Of *Footloose*' at birthsmoviesdeath.com, 9 April 2014.

'Very early on I knew what Ren's wound was going to be – that his father had walked out and completely destroyed his life on Chicago and they had to move . . . it took me a little bit longer to realise that if I had Ariel's brother – Shaw's son – die then the two of them had a family secret . . . something that would be discovered later on by Ren. Giving her that as a wound and then turning her into the kind of firebrand who would jump out the window of a car and transfer into her boyfriend's truck and carouse around with Chuck like she did, it kind of gave her a bit of a death wish.'[1] It worked. Whilst *Footloose* came at a time when teenage leads were mainly guys dealing with peer problems such as losing their virginity or beating bullies, Ariel was a girl with real world issues to battle: grief and guilt.

Casting Ariel came down to two: perennial contender Jennifer Jason Leigh – who'd just finished *Grandview USA* with Tommy Howell and Patrick Swayze – and Lori Singer, a Julliard-trained musician best known for playing prodigious musician Julie on TV's *The Kids from Fame*. If it had been Bacon's legs that helped bag him *Footloose* in New York then Singer's casting – according to Pitchford – was down to a similar physical trait. 'For one weekend we were convinced it was going to be Jennifer Jason Leigh. The decision had been made on a Friday. Then on Monday morning . . . Dan Melnick walked in and announced that he'd been watching footage of the two of them and Jennifer is about six inches shorter than Lori. And he said that's Lori's tall and beautiful and will look fantastic opposite Kevin Bacon. So the decision was made then and there to go with Lori Singer.' Singer was already in her mid-twenties and married when she played high-schooler Ariel, having wed lawyer Richard Emery – twelve years her senior – back in 1980, the same year that her respected conductor father Jacques Singer died. But Pitchford saw her life experience as a valuable asset: 'She was in person a kind of wild spirit, very funny and risk taking [and] she did a wonderful job of bringing that to the motion picture.'[2]

* * *

---

1 Author interview.
2 Author interview.

With Dean Pitchford's background in musicals, the *Footloose* soundtrack was always in the forefront of his mind. He wanted a compilation-tape feel, a diverse line-up of songs that could be used to anchor the story's pace and rhythm like a Broadway show, but mainly reflected his diverse personal taste. The album would be released on Columbia Records – home to Kenny Loggins, with whom Pitchford had already been writing – and with the increasing sales of soundtracks the label bosses demanded more of their own artists on the album, only allowing two 'outside' acts if their last release had gone gold. Why should they help out an up-and-coming newcomer from a rival company? Alongside Columbia stars such as soul singer Deniece Williams, Canadian rock act Loverboy and Welsh power ballad queen Bonnie Tyler, Pitchford signed up Sammy Hagar from Geffen and Solar Records' dance act Shalamar:[1] 'When the soundtrack was finally compiled and it was sent over to Walter Yelnick, who was president of Columbia at the time, he called Michael Eisner [at Paramount] and said, "This is one of the most exciting albums I've ever seen here at my time at Columbia because we can put records on every radio format." And that's what happened. We had dance records and adult contemporary and pop and rock and pretty much every chart that Billboard had in those days had a place for our songs.' So too did MTV.

In the year since *Flashdance*'s success the music TV station had become available virtually all over the country, certainly helping to push both *Footloose* the movie and the soundtrack. Indeed, the album knocked *Thriller* from its fourth stint at the top, sold seven million and generated two No. 1 singles whilst the movie itself beat middling reviews to score eighty million dollars. If *Footloose* had been released any other time it might not have struck the chord it did; a year earlier the moral debate it centred on was not nearly so newsworthy, a year later its music TV-friendly soundtrack would have been less of a novelty. For *Footloose*, the spring of '84 was a perfect storm.

But it wasn't *just* good timing. Those accusing *Footloose* of being clichéd[2] missed its many plus points, those strengths that

---

1 Later that year Shalamar were also featured on the *Beverly Hills Cop* soundtrack.

2 '*Footloose* is one part Mickey Rooney musical, one part teen-movie cliché, one part rock video, and all trash,' ran the subheading to David Denby's *New York* magazine review, 27 February 1984

went beyond its good marketing and great music to connect it to a massive audience. As the story of a boy who had lost his father and a man who had lost his son, *Footloose* was ultimately measured in its anger, open-minded about those who closed themselves off, such as Rev Moore. 'We didn't want to make the minister a bible-thumping, fire-breathing zealot. It was very important he be a flesh-and-blood human being who had his reasons for believing in and clinging to the things that he clung to. John Lithgow is an incredibly, deeply human being – he's got such humanity about him. It didn't fall into any of the clichés that it could have. At that time the Moral Majority was very black-and-white . . . if you turned on the television in the United States on a Sunday morning you saw a lot of people pounding on podiums and screaming their faces red and talking about the demise of America. We fortunately didn't tip over into that area.'[1]

And if *Footloose*'s kids-versus-adults storyline did nod to the past, it wasn't stuck there. In capturing the dual worlds of city and backwater, youth and age, conservatives and liberals, *Flashdance* actually highlighted the twin moods of contemporary America, where in November of 1984 the seventy-three-year-old Ronald Reagan would win a second term as Republican president, beating fifty-six-year-old Democrat Walter Mondale, a former vice president who had run on a campaign of less spending on nuclear weapons, championing women's rights . . . and being considerably younger than his rival.[2] It appeared to be an easy victory for Reagan, capturing even traditional Democrats thanks to the economic growth he'd overseen in his first term, but *Footloose* was a reminder that not everyone believed in the power of age and tradition. It was like *WarGames'* David Lightman teaching the ageing military about modern day conflict all over again. For Rev Moore's parish of Bomont to progress, the pastor finally realised they had to leave the past behind . . . and think more like the town's young folk.

Kevin Bacon was now a star but he also knew he didn't want to get tarnished with the past, however recent. 'What's right for John

---

1 Dean Pitchford, author interview.

2 Unsuccessful Democratic hopeful Senator Gary Hart was even younger – forty-eight – and was known as 'the yuppie candidate'.

Travolta isn't necessarily right for me,' he told NBC 5 during promotion for *Footloose*, all too aware of the complicated position the star found himself in post-*Saturday Night Fever*. Like Travolta in his breakthrough year of 1978, Bacon wasn't a teenager any more – despite playing one – and his focus was less on being a heart-throb and more on being taken seriously: 'I certainly like to be appreciated as an actor and that's really what's important to me . . . I don't have any desires to be idolised by young girls. It's very sweet and very flattering but it's really not my life's goal.'[1] Considering he was already in a relationship with fellow actor Tracy Pollan, who he met during their time together in a Broadway play, being a pin-up for 1984's new PG-13 crowd was really the last thing he needed.

1 NBC 5, op. cit

Chapter Ten

TRIPLE THREATS

*Sean Penn meets his match; Prince and Madonna – desperately
seeking credibility; plus Coppola and Scorsese get a helping
(gloved) hand from Michael Jackson.*

On 10 January 1985, on a break after filming real-life spy story
The Falcon and the Snowman with Timothy Hutton, Sean Penn
met America's hottest new pop star. Over the next three years his
world – the *whole* entertainment world – would explode.

Madonna was a cannonball; twenty-six, flush with success,
bristling with attitude ('I'm tough, ambitious and I know exactly
what I want. If that makes me a bitch, OK'[1]). Her single 'Like a
Virgin' had just hit No. 1 and an album of the same name was Top
3. Now here she was filming the video for her next release,
'Material Girl', at Lucille Ball's old Desilu Studios on North
Cahuenga in Hollywood. The clip would be the singer's glossiest
yet: an immaculate re-creation of Marilyn Monroe's 'Diamonds
Are a Girl's Best Friend' routine from Howard Hawks' Technicolor
camp fest *Gentlemen Prefer Blondes*, its bold visuals perfect for an
MTV-obsessed public and – as in Hawks' original – an ideal
partner to the song's money-loving lyrics ('Only boys that save
their pennies make my rainy day'). Madonna had risen to fame
over the previous two years playfully mixing sex with innocence,

---

1 *People* magazine, 27 July 1992.

then standing back to watch the fallout.[1] Paying homage to Monroe, who'd perfected her own flirty routine thirty years earlier, made total sense.

It was former art student Mary Lambert who'd got the gig directing, having already helmed a couple of earlier Madonna videos, and she'd invited some friends of friends to hang out on set and witness this new pop phenomenon. One was Penn. The actor watched from the gallery, clocking this girl in a pink evening dress throw herself into the role, sashaying around her male dancers, toying and teasing; Monroe but harder, more knowing. He was wearing sunglasses but they had little effect. Madonna was dazzling.

Success had been a while coming for the Bay City-born Madonna Louise Ciccone. She'd left the dance programme at her home state university in the summer of '77 and headed to New York to make it as a dancer, her head full of lively attitude and impatient ambition. Such determination – bravado masking insecurity – got her a mix of work: dancing for French disco star Patrick Hernandez; starring in micro-budget underground movie *A Certain Sacrifice* and, after deciding to pursue music rather than dance, featuring in a few bands that began to make a name for themselves on the city's alternative scene.

Madonna had no money, of course, but still she wilfully refused to ask her father to help her out (he'd always been cynical about the move to the city) and her focus on her career was single-minded. When she signed a contract with record studio owner Camille Barbone – after the singer cornered her and demanded a meeting – there was one condition: Barbone wanted to focus solely on Madonna, not the band she'd been hanging out with. The results were undeniable. 'I brought her into the mainstream music business in a way that she didn't have to fuck for it,' says Barbone. 'Word got around that someone was investing money in her, someone with a studio and contacts. As a result, within the indus-

---

1 'Like a Virgin' is perhaps the filthiest-seeming love song ever, its video paradoxically showing a punked-up, writhing Madonna – all dangling crucifix and brash Boy Toy belt – on an elegant gondola as it ambles through Venice's genteel Renaissance waterways.

try, they began to take her seriously too.'[1] And as the city's opposing punk and disco sounds started to blend into an early '80s electronic hybrid, producing something no longer so obviously
concerned with working-class alienation but more about celebrating a street-smart hedonism, Madonna would be at scenester
hangouts Danceteria and the Mudd Club, partying with the hip-
pest DJs and producers in town: Mark Kamins, Arthur Baker,
John 'Jellybean' Benitez.

The deal with Barbone quickly fell through but the clubs were
always a reliable source of optimism. Back in Detroit, Madonna
had escaped her childhood issues – the death of her mother, her
father remarrying – by partying at the city's gay club Menjo's but
in the Big Apple the dreams were even bigger, where clubbers
liked to show off their creativity via almost weekly reinventions
and makeovers and with both eyes always on the future, the next
big idea, the newest place to be seen in; a touch of Evelyn Waugh's
jazz-age London in '80s hi-NRG Manhattan.

When Madonna finally got a new manager plus a deal for a
single from Seymour Stein at Sire Records (for 'Everybody', a cute
electro invitation-to-dance released in late 1982), she was initially
pushed as a 'black artist', her club sound still too cool for a
notoriously compartmentalised American music industry. Yet
between her bouts of brattishness there was always that blue-
collar Detroit work ethic and the singer diligently went to the right
places – radio stations, clubs (where Kamins played 'Everybody'
from a cassette) – to push the song to an audience as wide as the
one she sang about, then religiously rehearsing her act for the
subsequent video filmed at Paradise Garage, Michael Brody's gay
club in Hudson Square. As she began a relationship with hip New
York artist Jean-Michel Basquiat, she found herself in the Top 10
of the dance-club chart. Within a year – and now partnering up
with producer John Benitez both professionally and personally –
Madonna was finally a proper pop star, with her infectiously
optimistic third single 'Holiday' in the mainstream Top 20 and,
out of the blue, movie producer Jon Peters on the phone.

---

1 'Madonna: For the First Time, Her Friends and Lovers Speak Out', *Independent*, Lucy O'Brien,
  1 September 2007.

In the second half of 1983, Jon Peters and Peter Guber were still basking in the remarkable success of *Flashdance*, although they'd followed it with something completely different: *DC Cab*, an urban comedy film about a Washington taxi company that starred Mr T and Adam Baldwin, directed by flamboyant former fashionista Joel Schumacher. *DC Cab* was essentially an update of their '70s hit *Car Wash* (for which Schumacher had written the screenplay) by the same company, Universal but, despite another soundtrack featuring *Flashdance* alumni Giorgio Moroder and Irene Cara, it only raked in a modest sixteen million dollars at the box-office.

The *next* Peters and Guber production on the cards, however, would be a return to the polish of *Flashdance*, another dramatic face-off between big dreams and romance, being the story of high-school wrestler Louden Swain and the two challenges that face him: training for a big match with a local rival and falling in love with Carla, the new lodger staying at his home. Whilst this film's grand name – *Vision Quest* – might sound like a rip-off of *Flashdance*'s similarly charged title (it was also written in almost identically artful italics on the poster), *Vision Quest* had actually been an award-winning book first, a late '70s coming-of-age tale by Terry Davis.

Guber and Peters wanted to keep the grit of the book's Washington State setting – Spokane, rather like *Flashdance*'s Pittsburgh, a city distinctly lacking the usual movie glamour of LA or New York – but the soundtrack on Geffen Records would be a slick compilation of power rock from Journey, Foreigner and – despite his ongoing tensions with David Geffen himself – former Eagle Don Henley. With a view to making the album sound more contemporary, whilst also needing someone to play a bar singer, Peters had his eye on the up-and-coming Madonna. He'd already considered her for a part in his Bette Midler comedy *Ruthless People* but *Vision Quest* felt more suitable ('They didn't want to get an actress to pretend she's a singer. They wanted someone with a lot of style already,' Madonna modestly quipped[1]). It helped that the pop star was also desperate to be in films too.

---

1 'Papa Don't Preach: Madonna as Phenomenon', *The Madonna Companion: Two Decades of Commentary*, editors Carol Benson and Allen Metz, Schirmer, 2000, p.107.

Ultimately Madonna claimed to have been bored and cold filming her scenes for *Vision Quest*, shot by *Taps* director Harold Becker up at Spokane's Big Foot Tavern at the end of November 1983 (performing the ballad 'Crazy for You' and a new Benitez collaboration called 'Gambler'). Yet there were at least two compensations. First up she got to meet Peters' legendary girlfriend, Barbra Streisand. Secondly, appearing in *Vision Quest* successfully crossed her over into the movie arena in which she was hungry to succeed. The wrestling pic itself did unremarkable business, its twenty-four-year-old star Matthew Modine already a married man with a serious demeanour that was at odds with the rebellious sparkle of his contemporaries. Simply put, he was a harder sell to teenage girls than Tom Cruise or Matt Dillon. Yet Madonna scored hits with her *Vision Quest* songs, even with the contractual restrictions of being released via Geffen Records rather than her official label Sire. In some countries the title of the movie was even changed to *Crazy for You* to reflect the singer's mushrooming popularity. In short, her *Vision Quest* role had been minor but ended up being hugely influential. By spring '84, as casting began for a new comedy from Orion Pictures about a Manhattan party girl who becomes embroiled with a square New Jersey housewife, producers saw Madonna as not only cheaper than original first choice Diane Keaton, but more importantly as someone younger, sexier and – in the eyes of many teenagers – way cooler.

Over in LA and still several months before he would watch Madonna channel Marilyn for 'Material Girl', Sean Penn was in love again. His relationship with *Fast Times* co-star Pamela Springsteen was over[1] and the object of his affection this time was Elizabeth McGovern, a twenty-three-year-old actress he'd met filming romantic drama *Racing with the Moon*, the story of Henry and Nicky (Penn and Nic Cage), best friends in early '40s California who have both been drafted into the military. Henry falls for Caddie (McGovern) just weeks before he has to leave the country, whilst Nicky faces the reality of becoming a father; all in

---

1 Penn and Springsteen had lived together in a Californian apartment owned by her famous brother.

a script by twenty-three-year-old UCLA dropout Steven Kloves. Former actor Richard Benjamin – a serious-looking leading man in the Dustin Hoffman mould, star of '70s hits *Goodbye Columbus* and *Westworld* – directed.

'It was so amazing to me, because in this age range at that time, I saw people that are now huge stars, just one after the other kept coming in there,' recalls Benjamin, 'but there was something about Sean that just felt to me that he was the real thing, and there was such deepness in there and there was just something about him, as certainly we all know ... I'd seen *Valley Girl* and Nicky [Cage] came in. I read one person after another of these terrific people; but the minute I saw Nicky, I stopped. Elizabeth, who I had always just absolutely loved, I just cast her ... there's something about Elizabeth that is like that kind of '40s girl in the Coke ads or something.'[1]

But McGovern was much more than just a Coke girl. Born to academic parents, her family tree included diplomats and politicians and she'd studied at the prestigious American Conservatory Theater in San Francisco and at Julliard in New York. By the time she was filming *Racing with the Moon* she'd already appeared alongside Tim Hutton in *Ordinary People*, garnered her own Academy Award nod for a supporting turn in Miloš Forman's turn-of-the-century epic *Ragtime* (1981) and was about to be seen at 1984's Cannes Film Festival in Sergio Leone's even weightier *Once Upon a Time in America*, where – in a role originally considered for her lookalike Brooke Shields – she starred alongside Robert De Niro.

For Penn here was someone decidedly different to Springsteen ... and to himself. McGovern was poised, smiley and educated; the elegant opposite to his scowling roughneck: 'I thought he was kind of goofy and filled with a passion that was sort of ridiculous but endearing to me at the same time,' McGovern said of her new colleague. '... he would argue, "If I'm playing a guy who stays out all night on a beach, I have to in fact stay out on a beach all night." Whereas I would go home and get a good night's sleep.'[2]

---

1 Conversations at the Cinematheque, text by Felicia Tollette, 8 August 2010.
2 *Sean Penn: His Life and Times*, Richard T. Kelly, Faber & Faber, 2005, p.122.

Despite its on-the-rise young stars, *Racing with the Moon* struggled to get going. Originally backed by Fox, the studio soon got cold feet at the lack of comedy in the subtle story and wanted to cut the budget. Kids wanted jokey sex they reasoned, so why throw money at romance? Eventually *Racing with the Moon* found itself with *Taps* producer Stanley Jaffe and former studio boss Sherry Lansing, who'd left Fox to run an independent company with a deal at Paramount. At least they understood what the movie was trying to do.

Even better, when production started up in Mendocino, three hours north of San Francisco, the director noticed an on-set romance: 'Way in the distance, we see two people walking, and they're holding hands. And I say, "Boy, if that's Elizabeth and Sean, it's good for the movie." And it was. I thought they're a little more than friends. Excellent! Now this has got to last for the whole film . . . and it sure did.'[1] Penn had once asked Pam Springsteen to marry him but even though that relationship ultimately foundered, he remained romantic about the idea of lifelong commitment. He and McGovern got engaged.

Yet despite the real-life romance at the heart of *Racing with the Moon*, the naysayers at Fox were ultimately proven right. Out of touch with current tastes, its bygone feel was simply not where teen movies were heading and it stumbled to a six-million-dollar US box-office in late May 1984; disappointing, although still an insignificant loss compared to *Once Upon a Time in America*'s five-million total against a budget six times that.[2]

Penn and McGovern – two twenty-three-year-old rebels with a cause – found themselves battling not to be reduced to a mere celebrity couple. Penn, in particular, hated the media glare, refusing not just to do a cover shoot with McGovern for *People* magazine but also all interview requests to promote *Racing with the Moon*. He wasn't hugely involved in the creative process, he argued, so what could he be expected to say? Stanley Jaffe was furious; publicity was exactly what this kind of a film needed.

'Sometimes I think it's a miracle that Sean's still with us,'

---

1 Conversations at the Cinematheque, op. cit.

2 The movie's box-office failure wasn't helped by the controversial 139-minute-cut that producers re-leased in the States, carved from the original's 239 minutes against the wishes of Sergio Leone.

McGovern once confessed, her relationship with Penn eventually ending when she just couldn't keep up with his incendiary spirit. Certainly if there was a tide going one way, he'd swim against it. After *Racing with the Moon*, Penn drowned his sorrows over the break-up by partying with Mickey Rourke in New York (where he was filming Adrian Lyne's *9½ Weeks*), then with Harry Dean Stanton at the Cannes Film Festival, with Tom Cruise in London (where he was shooting *Legend* at Pinewood) and finally on his own in Belfast. It was late spring '84. Over the previous few weeks Penn's co-star from the *Slab Boys* play, Kevin Bacon, had been at the top of the box-office with *Footloose* before it was usurped by the likes of *Police Academy* and a fourth *Friday the 13th* slasher pic. But Sean Penn dreamed of making something moodier.

His pet project was a script by Nicholas Kazan called *At Close Range*, the true story of father and son criminals in Pennsylvania, and he'd already been in contact with iconic '70s director Bob Rafelson about directing. Rafelson had won plaudits working with another of Sean's heroes – Jack Nicholson – and they shared an uncompromising attitude that the actor admired. But there were two problems. Rafelson's behaviour had meant his reputation had suffered, studios now less willing to work with him. *At Close Range* would never get off the ground with *his* name attached. Secondly, the film's darkness was even more at odds with fashion than *Racing with the Moon*'s. Penn was fighting against the tide again, his youthful attempts at contemplative film-making struggling to stay afloat whilst many cinemas that summer now enjoyed sell-out crowds for a movie featuring a pop singer in his mid-twenties who was still happy to play – as his character was called – The Kid.

Purple Rain – released at the end of July 1984 – starred the enigmatic singer/songwriter/multi-instrumentalist Prince, a puzzling but adored teen icon full of contradictions: part soul-singer, part rock-guitar-god, so reclusive in life but on stage a gregarious sexual showman. Songs such as 'Head' and 'Sister' were funk-filled jams that left little to the imagination, both from a 1980 album whose title was self-explanatory: *Dirty Mind*. It would be his track 'Darling Nikki', from the *Purple Rain* soundtrack album, that would supposedly influence Tipper Gore to start up the ultra-conservative Parents' Music Resource Center when she found her eleven-year-old daughter listening to its *Penthouse*-letters-page lyrics. Others welcomed such a libertine spirit. After all, there were much worse things going on in the world: 'It certainly sounded safer to a lot of us than the drugs of the Lower East Side or the disillusionment of presidential politics,' argued Prince's tour manager Alan Leeds.[1]

Prince had been releasing records longer than Madonna but was only a couple of months older and a recent surge in his mainstream success, fuelled by music television finally 'accepting' certain black music coincided with her own arrival on the scene. If Penn bemoaned cinema's increasingly marketing-led, style-over-content approach of films such as *Purple Rain*,[2] then over in New York his future girlfriend Madonna could only look on at Prince's movie success in admiration. *Purple Rain* hit cinemas just a few weeks after *Racing with the Moon* but its story was awash with the simpler teen angst, latest tunes and MTV visuals that *Racing with the Moon*'s quiet romance was missing. A day later, 28 July 1984, Los Angeles began its hosting of the twenty-third Olympic Games: opened by Reagan, boycotted by the Russians, sponsored by McDonald's. That summer, both events – the Prince movie and the sporting spectacular – celebrated a similar attitude, one at the heart of Reagan's sweeping moves towards a more deregulated, proudly capitalist economy. Content is one thing, they confidently shouted. But in contemporary America, it's the *way* you sell it that really matters.

'It sizzles! You don't have to be nineteen to have uninhibited fun at *Purple Rain*,' Sheila Benson glowingly wrote in the *Los Angeles Times*.[3] It sure helped, though. *Purple Rain* was Prince's teenage autobiography, albeit one that mixed facts with myth-making. Set in his home town of Minneapolis, The Kid was a local rocker: a

---

1 In his liner notes to Prince's 1993 best-of compilation, *The Hits Vol.2*.

2 Comparing the '70s New Hollywood era to the modern one, Penn claimed: 'It was more of a golden generation. Now it's comforting. We're fed familiarity and so we get to see the same movie over and over again. I only want to do dramas that say something about the human spirit. Something real and serious, something John Cassavetes would be proud of,' *Total Film*, Hilary Morgan, April 2004.

3 A quote that decorated the *Purple Rain* DVD cover.

monosyllabic showman permanently clad in frilly shirts and frock coats, gliding around on a majestic purple motorbike, adored on stage at the iconic First Avenue Club where the real Prince had himself played over the years. The Kid is a hero, apparently already sure of himself and his act, a confident grown-up. He was, in other words, exactly like the real Prince of 1984, just without the star's success.[1]

Still, in a bid to make the character more relevant to the film's target young audience, The Kid lived at home with his abusive parents. Whilst he lived a life outside of the home like that of a flamboyant twenty-six-year-old millionaire rock star, back in his bedroom he suffered with the same problems as plenty of teens across the country: family fallouts, emotional insecurity. Underneath all the purple posturing, he was vulnerable. If that sounded corny, it made no difference. *Purple Rain* – the movie debut of its director, producers and star – announced itself to the world with an audacity that could paper over any cracks.

The story of *Purple Rain* originated in Prince's head, ideas then scrawled into an appropriately purple notebook he carried with him whilst touring. The initial concept was tentative – loose memories of his own Minneapolis childhood with his tough father – and an early title hardly clarified things; *Dreams*. Yet in some respects the singer was always entirely sure of what he wanted. He told his management team of Bob Cavallo, Joseph Ruffalo and Steven Fargnoli that he wanted to make a film with the support of a major film studio and with his name above the title. Simple. It was down to them, coming to their last year on their contract and looking to renew, to find him something.

A script was put together by William Blinn, who'd worked on TV's *The Kids from Fame* and originated *Starsky and Hutch* for Aaron Spelling, but Cavallo initially struggled to drum up studio interest. He was also still looking for a director. First choice James Foley was about to make ripples with his debut *Reckless*, a star-crossed teen lovers pic that starred Aiden Quinn and Daryl Hannah, with smaller roles for Jennifer Grey and Pam Springsteen.

---

1 Prince's crossover had begun a couple of years earlier, with the release of his 1982 album confusingly called *1999*.

Reckless would also boast an up-to-the-minute new wave sound-track featuring INXS and Romeo Void. *Purple Rain*, however, wasn't for him.

But Foley had a suggestion: why not ask his friend Albert Magnoli, editor on *Reckless* and a music fan who'd made a movie about jazz only a couple of years earlier at USC? Magnoli knew how to sell himself, impressing the *Purple Rain* team not only with his visual experimentation but also with tweaks to the script, pitching ideas to Prince during a meeting at the famous Du-Par's restaurant[1] on Ventura Boulevard. The singer was so taken, albeit in his own quiet way, he offered Magnoli not just the job of helming his entry into the movie world but also access to his hundred-song archive to find exactly the right tracks for the movie.

Bob Cavallo would still have his work cut out; a film set in icy Minneapolis, helmed by a first-time writer/director and starring an up-and-coming black pop star meant this wasn't the obvious project to excite a studio. Yet in hiring Magnoli, *Purple Rain* gained a youthful stylist. 'When I made this movie, I did not have a television so I was unaware of MTV completely,'[2] Magnoli has confessed, but he at least understood what Prince was selling: a sexy, Byronic funk. The way Magnoli utilised his editing skills to preserve that, combined with a rich and sultry cinematography from *An Officer and a Gentleman*'s Don Thorin, captured musical lightning in a bottle; up there alongside Adrian Lyne's shepherding of *Flashdance* in terms of its cultural influence on pop videos. Sean Penn may have wanted serious content in his movies – and *Purple Rain* did, in its own way, attempt that – but now style was serious too. Magnoli shot the film with nods to Bob Fosse's 1971 Oscar-winner *Cabaret*, which itself had been a hymn to the decadent spirit of Weimar-era Germany. In *Purple Rain*, no moment was left untouched by opulence.

At the centre of that flamboyance was *Purple Rain*'s real selling point: the freewheeling excitement of a Prince live performance. It was there from the start, the movie opening with a full seven and a half minutes of attitude, acrobatics and dry ice. 'Let's Go Crazy'

---

1 'Home of the legendary buttermilk hot cakes!'
2 *Purple Rain* Blu-ray commentary.

indeed. The ensuing drama of the plot might have verged on the clumsy but there was still an authenticity to the showbusiness side that hit hard: glamour, eroticism and competition, no place for shrinking violets. The nine hundred extras were real local kids, the venues were real Minneapolis hangouts and – thankfully for Magnoli, working on a tight schedule – the bands were close-knit outfits who had their sets down pat from relentless touring. That sheer razzamatazz of their live performances made up for any blips in the story.

Yet the bosses at Warner, where *Purple Rain* eventually found financing, still weren't convinced that the project as a whole had a future. Despite CEO Steve Ross's interests in MTV, his film execs Terry Semel and Bob Daly worried that Prince was no superstar and certainly no actor (neither was leading lady Apollonia Kotero – an eleventh hour replacement for Prince protégée Vanity, from whom he'd recently split). Meanwhile head of production Mark Canton complained about the film's brash violence. Prince countered: 'Violence is something that happens in everyday life, and we were only telling a story. I wish it was looked at that way, because I don't think anything we did was unnecessary,'[1] but certain scenes were altered to lighten the mood.

Still, it was down to Prince's publicist Howard Bloom to make a bold speech to the suits at Warner in order to convince them they had something special. 'I got pissed off . . . everyone saying it wasn't a movie,' he remembered, so he proclaimed it as something of a cultural landmark. 'I also said that killing *Purple Rain* would be a sin against art!'[2]

Purple Rain might not be art of the most intellectual kind but the point is, it tried. This was pop looking to match its razzle-dazzle with declarations of creative credibility; claims that Prince could in fact justify, being a writer as well as a pop star, his tracks already covered by the likes of Cyndi Lauper ('When You Were Mine') and Chaka Khan ('I Feel For You'). As a multi-instrumentalist and a self-proclaimed artist, Prince suffered for his songs and for control of his own career, battling Warner for his

---

1 In an interview for MTV in late 1985, recorded at the Theatre de la Verdure in Nice where he was filming a video.

2 *Brooklyn Paper*, Jacob Kleinman, 28 July 2009.

publishing rights and creative freedom as far back as his first album, *For You*, in 1978.[1] *Purple Rain* the movie was a high-concept, high-style way of restating those pleas, a self-eulogising melodrama wrapped up in the form of a teen-friendly pop pic.

Bowie had been the most recent singer to do the same thing, 1976's *The Man Who Fell to Earth* an experimental sci-fi story that fed from his extra-terrestrial stage persona. But *Purple Rain* was more flagrantly sexual, more openly cross-cultural and, ultimately, more unashamedly mainstream. *The Man Who Fell to Earth* went virtually unseen in the States as Barry Diller at Paramount reneged on his initial deal to distribute it, citing the film's wilful obscurity. *Purple Rain*, though, *wanted* to be adored. As with Jennifer Beals in *Flashdance* (who had been considered for the female lead in *Purple Rain*, but who was now at college) Prince's blackness isn't commented on once in the movie. That would be too niche. Instead, *Purple Rain* dealt with something universal: professional ambition and the quest for respect. Wrapping that up in seductive visuals and pouting glamour just reinforced the point that the Olympics marketing men were simultaneously making that summer, rebranding the LA games as a celebratory showbusiness event. Credibility wasn't something to be embarrassed about. It could also be majestic.

Test screenings of *Purple Rain* backed up the theory, with stories of joyful reactions – clapping, singing, the ageless 'dancing in the aisles' – leading Warner to release the movie on to more screens than they'd first planned. 'When Doves Cry', a last-minute addition to the soundtrack when director Magnoli requested a dramatic song for a montage sequence, was released eight weeks before the movie and hit No. 1. Film bosses had earlier complained that the track sounded unfinished[2] but its frequent plays on MTV, using footage from the film, soon shut them up. Life was imitating art. Just as the movie showed The Kid proving his unique showmanship to a local audience, in the real world Prince was doing the same to a national one.

Purple Rain earned more than sixty-eight million dollars at the

---

1 And he would famously refer to himself as the label's 'slave' in the mid-'90s.
2 It remains one of the only US chart-toppers not to have a bassline.

US box-office and at one point it simultaneously gave Prince the top movie, album and single (with its second release, 'Let's Go Crazy') in the country. Comparisons with Michael Jackson were inevitable. Here was another black prodigy showcasing his influences. But the *Purple Rain* album, much of it recorded live and rougher around the edges than the super-smooth R&B of *Thriller*, is the epitome of a magical pop record; an amalgamation of multiple influences – soul, rock, disco, psychedelia – polished to a melodic whole that's both immediate yet unquantifiable. Listen closely and you can pick out the sound of a hundred other records but, when they're blended together, Prince still manages to sound like no one else. 'I was brought up in a black-and-white world . . . [but] I listened to all kinds of music when I was young,' he told MTV, 'and when I was younger I always said that one day I would play all kinds of music and not be judged for the colour of my skin but the quality of my work, and hopefully I will continue.'[1] In 1984, Prince was showbiz's most persuasive magpie.[2]

Back at the shoot for 'Material Girl' in early 1985, its homage to classic social climbing comedy *Gentlemen Prefer Blondes* was reinforcing Madonna's own ruthless ambition. Her relationship with John Benitez was coming to an end, not helped by their now being on opposite sides of the country and made considerably more sensitive by a rumoured pregnancy that had been terminated. So, spending time with her new-found fame in California, Madonna moved on with her life by getting to know the moody guy in the sunglasses to whom she'd just been introduced.

Sean Penn had been staying at James Foley's house, having befriended the director after hanging out with him at various parties following the split from Elizabeth McGovern. The timing was perfect: Penn had been looking for a film-maker he could work with in the same way De Niro did with Scorsese, as soul brothers. In Foley he saw a kindred spirit, even offering him his pet project *At Close Range*, despite not especially liking what Foley had done with *Reckless*. Now, in the days after meeting

---

1 *Brooklyn Paper*, op. cit.

2 Brian Rafferty's 'The Oral History of *Purple Rain*', from July 2009's *Spin* magazine, was of great help for this section.

Madonna on 'Material Girl', he left Foley's couch to romance the singer, taking her on tours of his home city. Like millions in the States, Penn had been aware of Madonna before they met, his assistant often playing a cassette of *Like a Virgin* in the car as they travelled together, despite his own musical tastes being somewhat more understated. Now as he drove past the sights of LA, the pop star was sat next to him for real.

Penn fell hard. Madonna's belligerent attitude – that sexiness born from a mix of hostility and flirtation – was intoxicating and he wanted to introduce her to his Hollywood friends Mickey Rourke and Jack Nicholson. He was even keen to show her – unusually for such a political liberal – his not insignificant gun collection.[1] There was just one problem though: for a brief period it looked as if Penn had competition for Madonna's attention. More frustratingly, it was from a star whose movie had done considerably better business than any of Penn's own: Prince.

Prince and Madonna were both at the American Music Awards at the end of January 1985, where she presented him – whilst chewing gum – with *Purple Rain*'s award for Best Black Album on a night where he won an armful of gongs. Stories about their relationship blossomed in the gossip columns alongside conflicting rumours of her romance with Penn, much to the latter's annoyance. In many respects, Prince was certainly more like Madonna than was the serious actor: flowery yet focused, flamboyant yet coy. The bullish Penn, on the other hand, was rumoured to have found it hard to even accept Madonna's New York circle of friends, full of underground artists and gay club-goers.

Yet it was precisely that ice to her fire that ultimately made Sean Penn irresistible to the Material Girl. Penn was surprisingly old-school, as gentlemanly as he was rebellious, and even his macho attitude could be used to brutishly fight for creative expression. If a tendency to recklessness sometimes got him into trouble then it only reinforced that intoxicating conundrum at the heart of his behaviour and that of friends such as Rourke, Estevez and Cage; yes, they were wild, but they were also undeniably passionate about their work, frighteningly talented. Penn smoked four packs

---

1 As reported by Andrew Morton in his book *Madonna*, Michael O'Mara, 2001.

a day, drank heavily and looked like her father but to Madonna, he was a hot-blooded artist who was, even in his rash scuffles with the press, chivalrously defending her honour. The delicate five-foot-two Prince needed a tattooed six-foot-eight minder called Charles 'Big Chick' Huntsberry to accompany him in public but the surly Penn was his own bodyguard. Madonna's bond with Prince did eventually prove fruitful professionally[1] but no romance ever bloomed, the pair quickly retreating back to their individual spotlights as all too similar colleagues rather than lovers. Penn had won another fight.

Nevertheless, if serious Sean was depressed by the state of the entertainment world then he was now involved with the wrong person. Within a few months, as he finally got to make *At Close Range* with James Foley in Nashville, he was engaged again and this time to the epitome of what he hated most: a modern, fame-loving star with a screaming teen audience.[2]

Spring '85. Another month, another Madonna music video. Still, this new one – for a driving, dancefloor thumper of a single called 'Into the Groove' – was nowhere near as high-concept as some of her previous mini-movies. Despite her success, Madonna's bosses at Warner didn't want to pump yet more money into an expensive promo and risk over-saturation. After all, it was only a couple of months since 'Material Girl' had hit No. 2, even less since 'Crazy for You' went one better. So instead 'Into the Groove' was released in the States as B-side to another *Like a Virgin* track, 'Angel', and the accompanying video was simply a compilation of clips from a new film in which it featured: *Desperately Seeking Susan*.

'Into the Groove' barely even needed promotion. *Desperately Seeking Susan* saw Madonna star in her first proper lead role and when both the movie and the song released that spring, at exactly the moment her relationship with Penn was blowing up around the world, interest could hardly have been bigger. So even though the 'Into the Groove' video was basic and – if you hadn't seen the film – a little incoherent, none of that mattered. The prospect of

---

1 They would work together on 'Love Song' from her 1989 *Like a Prayer* album.
2 And one whose song 'Live to Tell' featured on the *At Close Range* soundtrack.

the attitude-filled Madonna, so striking and stylish on stage and in photos, now properly on the big screen was impossible to resist. Here was someone who seemed to have studied the power of playing sexy dress-up; girly but gutsy. One look at her and you got the message: punky confrontation with a disco pout and a postmodernist wink. Thus with heavy rotation on MTV many of those random *Desperately Seeking Susan* moments which featured in the video quickly became iconic: Madonna rolling around, scantily clad, on a hotel bed; dancing, hands aloft, at a club; in a public toilet, hands still aloft, airing her armpits under a dryer. They might not have made much sense but they were certainly memorable.

Desperately Seeking Susan the movie has a plot, of course; a slightly more grown-up take on the female friendship storyline of *Times Square* from five years earlier. Rosanna Arquette played New Jersey girl Roberta, a wife so bored that she has to get her kicks from reading personals ads in the local paper. One keeps reappearing: a romance played out in print between the mysterious Susan (Madonna) and Jim (Robert Joy), intriguing Roberta so much that she heads to Battery Park to spy on their planned rendezvous. Her obsession with the cool city chick Susan – the hipster opposite of her suburban life – leads Roberta to mimic her style, enough that she gets mistaken for her. And when Roberta suffers memory loss after a bang to the head, even *she* starts to think that she's actually this lace-clad party girl – this Holly Golightly with a ghetto-blaster – rather than just a valium-popping, neglected wife from Fort Lee.

Plot aside, what the success of the 'Into the Groove' video proved was just how striking *Desperately Seeking Susan* is visually. *Purple Rain* had been similarly stylish and successful but with a palette rich with dark velvety tones; unsurprisingly heavy on the purple. *Desperately Seeking Susan* might have also set itself up for instant MTV playability but this time the look was more bright, more brash, more chaotic. Back in 1982, the film's director Susan Seidelman had made the low-budget indie pic *Smithereens* about scenesters from the Big Apple's underground (as Madonna herself had once been) and now she relished championing their audaciously eye-catching fashions all over again for her mainstream debut.

As Roberta finds herself in trendy Manhattan, her eyes are our eyes; widening at the city streets bustling with random styles, races and languages; opening up to the unsophisticated grandeur of graffiti-splattered walls, B-movie theatres and tenement blocks.

The music in *Desperately Seeking Susan* was crucial – a suitable melting-pot compilation featuring not just 'Into the Groove' but also English new wavers The Fixx and some retro Motown – yet so much of the film concerns what we're shown rather than what we hear. Even Susan doesn't have pages of dialogue; her black-and-gold, Egyptian-themed jacket and rhinestone-studded pixie boots tell us everything we need to know. The stickers on her suitcase say 'Atlantic City', the kitsch Vegas of the east, but it's Manhattan that's her real playground, from the shabby magic shows of Harlem to the disco lights of Danceteria, Madonna's real-life hangout. An 'empress of trash', that's what *Rolling Stone* called Susan.[1] So if the singer's bosses didn't want much from the 'Into the Groove' promo, video editor Doug Dowdle at least had the best raw materials to work with, cutting Seidelman's celebration of Susan's patchwork subculture into a four-minute explosion of mid-'80s pop life; a million miles away from the videos he'd worked on for Phil Collins and Bonnie Tyler.

It's one of those rare lines of a dialogue though, rather than an outfit or a location, that best summed up the appeal of Susan – and in turn, Madonna. 'Fortunately for everybody,' she announces, 'I'm here and I'm *thinking*.' Madonna's arrival on the entertainment scene hadn't been a quiet one; it was a grand entrance. Like Prince's regal behaviour on stage and in *Purple Rain*, as much Louis XIV as James Brown, Madonna also hit big with a pre-formed confidence. Being worshipped, it seemed, was her right, not just a hope.

Yet, as with her idol Marilyn Monroe's marriage to playwright Arthur Miller, the tabloids found her relationship with new boyfriend Sean Penn easy to dismiss. What would a ditzy blonde and a serious actor possibly have in common? Neither Penn nor Madonna, now with a summer '85 wedding planned, felt little need to win over a public with warmth or humility. Their routines were apparently different – bright party girl versus moody bruiser

---

1 'Madonna and Rosanna Arquette Get Desperate', *Rolling Stone*, Fred Schruers, 9 May 1985.

– yet they also shared a sneering, sexual strength that seemed perfectly pre-formed for movies; a confidence that said, 'You owe us respect', rather than modestly admitting the need to earn it. 'I never met anyone who has such a focus,' Rosanna Arquette said of Madonna at the time, her own personality more obviously jittery, brought up as she was by peripatetic, free-spirited acting parents and, by the age of twenty five, already divorced and recently out of rehab following a public break-up with Toto drummer Steve Porcaro. 'She goes right for it,' she continued, 'and she gets what she wants. I admire that a lot. But I think behind all that is a little tiny girl inside.'[1]

Desperately Seeking Susan could have played much older, had the bosses at Orion got their way and cast Goldie Hawn alongside Diane Keaton as a forty-something Susan and Roberta.[2] Seidelman, though, wanted fresher faces and luckily, even if Orion didn't think Madonna was as famous as other possibles Rebecca De Mornay, Melanie Griffith or (of course) Jennifer Jason Leigh, one executive's teenage son – a huge Material Girl fan – convinced them otherwise. And if Madonna's increasing popularity as a bubblegum-pop star meant trimming scenes to get a PG-13 rather than an R, then so be it. Arquette might have struggled with 'Into the Groove's rather blatant insertion into the film, even Madonna feeling that it distracted from her attempts to be taken seriously as an actress, but from behind its mask of teen-friendly screwball laughs *Desperately Seeking Susan* still shouts loud about sex, marriage and gender politics; a bold combination. And like *Purple Rain, Desperately Seeking Susan*'s focus on youth culture's high style didn't stop it from throwing in some biting social commentary too. Madonna and Prince were utilising movies as vehicles of self-expression, an extension of music videos. They were pop stars – both films reminded us of that – but they still had plenty to say.

By the time of Penn and Madonna's not-so-secret wedding on 16 August 1985 (her twenty-seventh birthday and a day before his twenty-fifth), the paparazzi's helicopters circling the ceremony at developer Karl Unger's Malibu home showed just how big a name

---

1 Ibid.

2 The picture would also have cost way more than its eventual 4.5 million dollars had it starred Annie Hall and Private Benjamin.

Madonna had become; bigger than her *Susan* co-star Rosanna Arquette (increasingly irritated by her leading role being overlooked), bigger than her new husband (who took time out of the wedding to fire warning shots from a balcony and scare off the snappers), bigger than nearly *everyone*. Penn acknowledged the chaos of the day by announcing to the crowd of big names – Cruise, Geffen, Warhol – 'Welcome to this year's remake of *Apocalypse Now*.' In the outside world, *Desperately Seeking Susan* won good reviews and almost thirty million dollars at the box-office, plus 'Dress You Up' and 'Gambler' had given Madonna two more worldwide hits. Not even Prince could compete.

But then, did he want to? Following *Purple Rain*'s success, Prince seemed to shed the overblown style of his act and discover modesty – albeit a rather false one – U-turning in an attempt to reinforce his artistic credibility. His follow-up album, 1985's *Around the World in a Day*, didn't match the success of its predecessor but in a way that seemed deliberate – the singer refused publicity and only released singles after the album had come out. Meanwhile, Prince's next movie, *Under the Cherry Moon*, was announced as a black-and-white, jazz-age drama set in France; an homage to European art cinema rather than another gaudy celebration of success. Warner Bros. could hardly expect a repeat of *Purple Rain*'s lengthy queues. After triumphing with the 'Material Girl' video, it was Mary Lambert who was hired to direct *Under the Cherry Moon*. By the autumn – a month into shooting – Prince himself had given himself helming duties. His new-found modesty only extended so far.

Whilst Madonna and Prince threw themselves into attracting teenage cinema-goers, the biggest-selling pop star of the mid-'80s was more tentative. Michael Jackson – the youngest of the trio, albeit by just a few weeks[1] – had already appeared in *The Wiz*,[2] 1978's flop urban remake of *The Wizard of Oz*, but didn't seem in a hurry to capitalise on the record-breaking success of *Thriller* by making a movie. True, he had worked with Spielberg on a song for

---

1 All three were born in the summer of 1958.

2 Written by Joel Schumacher, produced by Lauren Shuler at Motown Productions.

the *E.T.* audiobook in 1982 and confessed to the director his dream of starring in a *Peter Pan* reboot. Later, Jackson then discussed with *Flashdance*'s Tom Hedley the possibility of a *Hunchback of Notre Dame* remake, the writer also offering him the title role in a film he was planning with producer Lynda Obst called *Street Dandy*, about a mime artist. Yet nothing came to fruition.

Instead, Jackson stayed within the realms in which he was more comfortable: the world of the music video, albeit in ever more expensive and creative ways, further blurring the boundaries between MTV and cinema. And whilst Penn bemoaned the loss of a '70s gutsiness in contemporary cinema, two of the directors who'd been at the forefront of that decade's film-making now found themselves surprisingly working in the new pop medium, and alongside the childlike Jackson and his fairytale ideas. The fact that Martin Scorsese and Francis Coppola were collaborating with the world's biggest music star might, for some, have been a reason to celebrate; proof that Jackson's modern, unashamed pop was – like Prince and Madonna's – actively seeking artistic credibility. But the truth from the film-makers' points of view was much less romantic: they needed the work.[1]

Despite some commercial redemption with *The Outsiders*, Coppola's dream Zoetrope Studios project collapsed after the disaster of *One from the Heart*, leaving him to sell off the company's vast lot and become a director for hire. When he was approached by George Lucas to helm a project for Disney – a mini sci-fi spectacular called *Captain Eo*, starring Michael Jackson – he couldn't refuse. Disney, for their part, needed a boost too. After years at the forefront of film technology they'd been pushed back by the likes of Lucas himself, his sci-fi space operas shunting their traditional family animations into a black hole. Michael Eisner had just left Paramount, frustrated that he wasn't given Barry

---

1 Coppola and Scorsese's colleague Brian De Palma had already shot Bruce Springsteen's video for 'Dancing in the Dark' – he was friends with The Boss's manager Jon Landau – at the end of June 1984, albeit in a fairly straightforward live setting at the Saint Paul Civic Center in Minnesota. The stage is lit in De Palma's trademark blood-red but, apart from that it's the least complex, most mainstream thing that either he or Bruce have ever done. There was also De Palma's mock video for Frankie Goes to Hollywood's 'Relax' that featured as a movie-within-a-movie in his porn world thriller *Body Double* from the same year. That was much more in his trademark style: lots of tracking shots, lots of mirrors and *lots* of sex.

Diller's recently vacated job as studio chief, and his move to Disney as a CEO came with forward-thinking plans to blend all the company's well-known interests – films, theme parks, technology – into one high-profile extravaganza; the perfect way for the Mouse House to re-stake their claim in the entertainment industry. And Jackson, a star whose achievements made even Prince and Madonna's look flimsy, was the obvious choice to help. Plus, of course, Jacko *loved* Disney. But Coppola wasn't his first choice. Jackson had wanted Steven Spielberg, his friend from *E.T.*, to help make *Captain Eo* but the director wasn't in a position to take time out of his feature-making schedule to helm a seventeen-minute 3D novelty. Even George Lucas, credited as executive producer, wanted to take a back seat, busy as he was with developing his Industrial Light and Magic effects company and a third *Indiana Jones* picture with Spielberg.

Coppola, on the other hand, was most definitely available. It didn't matter that *Captain Eo* wouldn't be high art, not even showing in proper cinemas but rather at Disney's theme park in Anaheim. He just wanted a job. Plus, of course, Lucas was an old friend and the idea of pushing his special effects technology – as Jackson was demanding – was an interesting one, even if the film's story was hardly the most ambitious. '. . . the film industry doesn't want to finance every movie that aims to be different,' Coppola once complained. 'They want it to be like Coca-Cola. You get it and it's Coca-Cola and you drink it and they make it again and again and again and they make good money.'[1] Coppola was a wine connoisseur, of course, complete with his own vineyard in California's Napa Valley. But in 1985, approaching bankruptcy, he knew that even *he* would have to make the odd can of Coke.

Coppola's two weeks on the *Captain Eo* shoot actually saw him as conductor rather than composer, his son Gio ultimately directing a fair chunk for him, although the *Apocalypse Now* helmer can claim to have come up with the film's title, riffing on the Greek word 'eos' that means 'light'. Breaks in filming, however, were used by Coppola Sr to sit in the hot-tub in his Airstream

---

1 the-talks.com, 8 February 2012.

trailer and watch audition tapes for his next project: time travelling rom-com *Peggy Sue Got Married*.

After pre-production meetings in April 1985, George Lucas had also done his fair share of delegating, handing over the day-to-day running of *Eo* to Rusty Lemorande, a producer who'd hit big alongside Jon Peters on 1980's golf comedy *Caddyshack*, the last film scripted by *National Lampoon*'s Doug Kenney before his death aged just thirty-three.[1] It was Lemorande who oversaw *Eo*'s July shoot in Culver City, responsible for an ever-growing host of complex effects created by *Star Wars* alumnus Harrison Ellenshaw. What Lucas and Coppola did inject into the project was scale; a grandeur with which their names had become associated – and which was matched by Jackson's own ambition – even if they weren't always the ones that had to deal with the practicalities of achieving it. *Captain Eo*'s final budgetary figure was kept hidden from the press, estimated at somewhere between fifteen and thirty million dollars. On a dollar-per-minute basis, *Captain Eo* can claim to be one of the most expensive movies ever made.

Yet the main problem with *Captain Eo* was that which also affected *Purple Rain*: if Jackson wanted to prove himself as a leading man as well as a pop star he was still clearly most comfortable during the film's musical moments (the main one being a big finale – Jackson singing 'We're Here to Change the World' – which Coppola believed looked too much like a stand-alone music video. He was right). Some at Disney were also worried about Jackson's high-pitched speaking voice, others about his crotch-grabbing. For his part, Jackson had wanted *Captain Eo* to be scary, having already publicised his love of chilling tales with the ghoulish John Landis video for 'Thriller'. Yet his was still an innocent, fairytale love of horror, like a child giggling nervously through *Scooby Doo* rather than an adult appreciation of H. R. Giger's surrealist macabre. All of which meant *Captain Eo* was *a bit* like *Alien* . . . just with a heavy dose of *The Muppets* too. The pop star liked to think he was a tough guy but space had certainly never seen a heroic adventurer quite so fey. Only Anjelica Huston

---

1 The critical mauling that *Caddyshack* received saw Kenney escape to Kauai, Hawaii, on the orders of his friend Chevy Chase, to take time out and deal with his depression. His death falling from a cliff top was ruled accidental but few believed he hadn't been looking for somewhere to end his life.

as the feisty Supreme Leader roused the project into anything approaching excitement. But by the time of its belated release in September 1986, Disney needed *Captain Eo* to wow the world.

The intervening year, however, had seen Jackson leave the relative simplicity of being a pop star and move into a new realm as tabloid favourite, dubbed 'Wacko Jacko' following (often untrue) stories about sleeping in oxygen tents, buying the skull of Joseph 'Elephant Man' Merrick and hanging out with his pet chimp Bubbles. As a teenage brand he was peerless, but he now showcased not only classic pop and eye-watering dance moves but also rumours of seriously eccentric behaviour. Seeking solace from the press, he didn't even turn up to *Captain Eo*'s razzy premiere, hosted for a live TV broadcast by *Dallas* star Patrick Duffy and Justine Bateman from hit sitcom *Family Ties*. If Jackson had wanted to branch out and break new ground he found himself forcibly trapped in his own comfort zone. He couldn't really be a movie star any more, even if he tried to butch up his voice and made a vow to never grab his crotch again. He'd simply become too famous to be anything apart from Michael Jackson.

So when Jackson hooked up with Coppola's contemporary Martin Scorsese the following year, it was for something that required even less acting and even more singing: the music video for his new single 'Bad'. Scorsese's agreement to direct might not have been purely a financial one like Coppola's but he still needed to say 'Yes'. For him – despite his success in the previous decade – it was all about proving he could be responsible. 'The industry is now run by businessmen,' the director would claim, just as Coppola had suggested. Yet he was also more understanding of the situation. 'If I want to continue to make personal films, I have to show them I have some sort of respect for money and that it will actually show on the screen.'[1] Directing the video for 'Bad' would allow him a certain creativity, playing out some more of his Vincente Minnelli musical fantasies that he'd started in 1977's *New York, New York* but, more importantly, it was to show everyone that he still had something many feared he'd lost in a sea of awards, bloated budgets and cocaine: modesty.

---

1 *Scorsese on Scorsese*, editors David Thompson and Ian Christie, Faber & Faber, 2003, p.114.

Whilst Scorsese's name remained a buzzword for cinematic guts and bravura, what he and many of his fellow '70s movie brats now represented to many was risk. He had followed *Raging Bull* with *The King of Comedy*, a bitterly satirical drama about a star-obsessed stalker that opened the Cannes Film Festival in May 1983 (the same year that it closed with *WarGames*) but which made back barely a tenth of its budget on its US release. It didn't matter that *The King of Comedy* was brutally hilarious, featuring not only another impressively warped turn from Robert De Niro but also a revelatory one from funnyman Jerry Lewis, a comedian best known for dopey '60s slapsticks such as *Cinderfella* and *The Bellboy*. It didn't make money – and that was enough for its visionary director to become *persona non grata*.

Produced during a period of physical exhaustion for Scorsese, *The King of Comedy*'s mixed critical reception didn't help with his state of mind either. Barry Diller and Michael Eisner at Paramount had offered him more mainstream product as an olive branch – *Beverly Hills Cop* when it was still a Sly Stallone project, Harrison Ford in *Witness* – but the increasingly troubled film-maker was still holding out for his pet project, something that connected with him spiritually, an intense biblical biopic called *The Last Temptation of Christ*. The film studio, though, were jittery about his demands to film the movie in the Middle East and he knew why: 'After all, Paramount had spent very little on *Flashdance*, which was a big hit and had control because it was shot in LA. If something went wrong, they could go right on to the set and stop the production or fire the director.'[1]

Plans for *The Last Temptation of Christ* unsurprisingly foundered, still too much of an overblown gamble for the studios, leaving Scorsese to begin his road to redemption with a low-budget indie screwball comedy made with David Geffen called *After Hours*, starring *An American Werewolf in London*'s Griffin Dunne (who also produced)[2] and *Desperately Seeking Susan*'s

---

1 Ibid, p.95.

2 Dunne's family included father Dominik, Uncle John and Aunt (by marriage) Joan Didion – all celebrated journalists and authors. His younger sister Dominique had appeared in *Poltergeist* but died a few months after its summer 1982 release, strangled by her ex-boyfriend John Sweeney (who was later convicted of voluntary manslaughter).

Rosanna Arquette. It was hardly a blockbuster – just over ten million at the US box-office – but at least that was more than double its cost *and* it handed Scorsese a Best Director win at Cannes. Plus, with thirty-year-old Dunne in the lead role rather than the usual De Niro, *After Hours* was Scorsese moving into more youthful, modern territory; changing with the times and proving himself all over again. The world of *After Hours* was no longer that of a middle-aged Italian-American hoodlum but rather that of an entirely '80s yuppie, the young up-and-coming professional tied to a workaholic attitude and routine. What *After Hours* probes – as did other 'yuppie nightmare' films of the era such as John Landis's *Into the Night* from 1985 and Jonathan Demme's *Something Wild* a year later – is what happens when the uptight male lead has to abandon his businesslike lifestyle and dive into female-led chaos. It was *Risky Business* for the post-college generation.

Following the refreshing *After Hours* with 'Bad' reinforced this mid-'80s renaissance for Scorsese, interpreting Jackson's song as a graffiti- and breakdancing-packed call-to-arms, bursting with the bluster and bravado of a strutting rabble and featuring a clad-in-black Jackson back in tough guy mode; all youthful yells, hollers and handclaps as he leads his street gang through a Brooklyn subway. 'Bad' was like a singalong from an updated, urban *West Side Story*, achieving what both star and director were after: Jackson was in a movie without actually being in a movie whilst Scorsese had made an MGM musical without the pressures of an epic production (although the full-length clip of 'Bad' ran to an eye-watering eighteen minutes). Still, Jackson's lack of proper movie roles somehow made him look rather limited in comparison with his contemporaries. Yes, he might have been working with the critically lauded director of *Raging Bull* but, despite those defiant album titles *Thriller* and *Bad*, here was someone who seemed more content to skirt around movies rather than take the risk of ever making a proper one.

Martin Scorsese, at least, was back. Working on a music video might not have been his dream job but it injected the still-new medium with its greatest shot of credibility so far, following on from Jackson's groundbreaking work with John Landis on

'Thriller'. Both he and Coppola had successfully done something neither had ever wanted to do back in their movie brat days: they had played the Hollywood game. But such was the climate – they realised – they now *had* to.

Scorsese's next project, whilst he waited for someone to have the nerve to finance *The Last Temptation of Christ*, did involve him taking another pay cut as a measure of his still-wobbly reputation but at least with *The Color of Money* he was working again with the most exciting actors in Hollywood, nodding to his past by using Paul Newman (the film was a sequel to Newman's *The Hustler*, from 1961) but also casting the breakout star of the new generation: *Risky Business*'s own Joel Goodson, the all-winning, all-grinning Tom Cruise.

Cruise's pal Sean Penn, meanwhile, was finding life with a pop star had its professional downside, dragging him further away from his principles. Penn and Madonna had moved in together in Malibu – at Olivia Newton-John's former house – but a decision to film a retro comedy with her called *Shanghai Surprise* in late 1985 had stopped him working on a project with which he was far more in tune, an adaptation of beat writer Charles Bukowski's booze-soaked memoir *Barfly*.[1] *Shanghai Surprise* was little consolation, ultimately proving more of an alcoholic experience than even *Barfly*, albeit for different reasons. 'It's the only movie I ever did drunk . . . ' admits Penn. 'It was torture. *Torture*.'[2] That Penn and Madonna had progressed to playing grown-up roles – a conman and a nurse in 1937 China – rather than rebellious kids made no difference. *Shanghai Surprise* was a leaden comedy starring people who just couldn't deliver the light touch needed (or, in Penn's case, who didn't even want to), with a script that couldn't decide if it was truly a Marlene Dietrich throwback or something saucier for an MTV sex-kitten. Penn and director Jim Goddard worked together like oil and water. Press intrusion on set, even out in Hong Kong, only added to the chaos.

Meanwhile, Sean Penn's reputation as a punch-slinger was

---

1 *Barfly* was eventually made with Penn's drinking buddy Mickey Rourke in the lead role.
2 *Sean Penn*, Richard T. Kelly, Faber & Faber, 2005, p.167.

growing. He'd already hit a probing reporter and photographer who'd been hanging around down in Nashville during the filming of *At Close Range*, then in April 1986 he attacked Madonna's old friend David Wolinski in a club in LA. The result was a thousand-dollar fine and a year's probation and the list kept growing. August 1986, Penn punched two photographers outside his New York apartment; April 1987, he broke probation when he assaulted an extra on set; May 1987, he broke probation again when charged with reckless driving, this time given sixty days in jail (although he served around half of that). Meanwhile the rumour mill turned at hyper-speed: Penn was apparently jealous of Madonna's new musical protégé, pretty boy Nick Kamen; and, mainly, the actor's drinking was now out of hand.[1] 'The Poison Penns – or S&M, as they are known to some – have never been an Astaire-Rogers sort of match. He's art; she's commerce. He hates publicity; she attracts it the way velvet draws lint,' summarised *People* magazine at the end of 1987 in an article written in conjunction with the latest dramatic news about the stars' relationship: after just over two years of marriage, they were getting divorced.

One fellow actor interviewed for the *People* piece was sympathetic. Judd Nelson told writer Joanne Kaufman: 'I understand what Sean has gone through . . . it's tough on him and it's gotta be tough on his marriage. We've both had people follow us on the street and say, "Hey, man, come on and hit me." It's like this big snowballing effect.'[2] What frustrated Penn the most was the way that the circus around his wife had interrupted his determination to be taken seriously as an actor. He wanted to be known for his movies, not his personal life. Perhaps he was more like the increasingly intense and reclusive Prince than he might have realised.

Shanghai Surprise dented Penn's reputation but didn't ruin it. Over at Orion, boss Mike Medavoy reassured him that he wanted to continue working together and Penn took on *Colors*, the story of two cops and the brewing intensity of gang warfare in LA's

---

1 Penn's thoughts on his drinking have been relatively sanguine: 'I'm not an alcoholic. I'm just a big drinker and there's a big difference,' he told Lynn Hirschberg of the *New York Times* magazine, 27 December 1998.

2 'Everyone Said It Wouldn't Last', *People* magazine, 14 December 1987.

'projects', hoping that his friend James Foley would continue their partnership and direct. Foley, though, threw a curveball: he was going to work with Madonna instead, teaming up for another yuppie nightmare pic called *Slammer* (later retitled *Who's That Girl*). A crestfallen Penn reworked the *Colors* script to get his hero Dennis Hopper – whom he'd wanted for *Barfly* – interested in directing and it worked, the movie eventually shooting with the actor safely back in Method mode, riding around South Central with real cops, just as Prince released his densest music yet: the double album *Sign O' the Times*.

The controversial lyrics to *Sign O' the Times*' title track could almost be *Colors*' plotline: 'At home there are seventeen-year-old boys and their idea of fun / Is being in a gang called The Disciples / High on crack, totin' a machine gun.' Both Prince and Penn were no longer just flirting with getting serious; now they were using their high profile in the entertainment world to wear their politics on their sleeves. Madonna was maturing too yet was always relentlessly commercial, aware of her target market.[1] Michael Jackson, meanwhile, retreated further into childlike fantasy, his only other film of the era being *Moonwalker*; essentially a series of elaborate music videos strung together.[2]

Prince and Penn, however, used their power in the industry to make statements with little apparent thought for blockbuster success. If it was a little ironic that they only found themselves in a position to dismiss mainstream fame by being mainstream famous in the first place, their new status in these defiantly post-pin-up years was undeniably idiosyncratic. *Under the Cherry Moon*'s off-putting stateliness summed up Prince's passion for the unorthodox – making only around ten million dollars in the US and winning multiple Golden Raspberry awards – but Penn had always been more direct: 'I think a movie like *Raiders of the Lost Ark* is just like taking drugs. I'm against the whole idea of, "Oh, it's good entertainment."'[3] It was late 1987 and as the dust settled

---

1 'Like a Prayer', for example, was an innovative gospel pop single from 1989 but it was still part of a deal with Pepsi.

2 Madonna hinted to James Corden in December 2016 that she and Jackson once shared a kiss. More details than that, however, weren't forthcoming.

3 *Rolling Stone*, Christopher Connolly, 26 May 1983.

on the previous three years, the Californian actor and the Minnesotan rock star whose attitudes had once seemed so different were now, as they approached thirty, both outsiders looking in.

Chapter Eleven

BIG BUDGETS,
HIGH CONCEPTS

MTV goes mainstream; Absolute Beginners *proves too much, too soon;* Top Gun *ruthlessly hits its target and* Back to the Future *crowns Spielberg the king of Hollywood Inc.*

If age makes some rebels, like Prince and Sean Penn, more single-minded then for others it represents a mellowing. In 1984 MTV became a publicly traded company; a significant move, making something that once boasted a youthful, underground mindset now seem all grown-up. While MTV's earlier backers American Express and Warner Bros. had never exactly been bohemian spirits, as soon as what once seemed like authentic teenage rebellion hit the serious stock market, it lost a certain craziness.

Bob Pittman had nurtured the channel through its colourful and creative infancy: 'We were a bunch of kids and when you are a kid, you are just completely sure that you are right. You are maniacal . . . someone would say, "Let's buy a house and give it away in a contest." And it would be, "Hey, why not?"'[1] But when the money finally began to flow into MTV, helped in no small part by the success of Michael Jackson and *Flashdance*, those kids had to quickly grow business heads.

---

1 'Birth of an MTV Nation', *Vanity Fair*, Robert Sam Anson, 4 June 2008.

As a sign of its increasingly mainstream status, MTV presented its first Video Music Awards that September, held at the historic Radio City Music Hall in New York and hosted by established thirty-somethings Dan Aykroyd and Bette Midler. The night saw both David Bowie and The Beatles honoured with Video Vanguard gongs for their pioneering work in the field, although what really got people talking was Madonna in her sexy wedding dress, jumping out of a cake and singing 'Like a Virgin'. But not everyone was happy with how MTV had grown exponentially and caught the nation's attention. Bleached British rocker Billy Idol[1] found solo success after leaving his early punk band Generation X and heading to New York to record with Giorgio Moroder collaborator Keith Forsey. 'White Wedding' and 'Rebel Yell' were big video hits in 1982 and 1983 but Idol was annoyed to find the primitive and provocative spirit of early MTV disappearing when the mass market beckoned. 'Suddenly you were competing on a level that was ridiculous. People like Michael Jackson moved everything up. Instead of $200,000 it was $2 million. It stopped the homegrown effect – it became video hell.'[2]

MTV began to court older viewers with its spin-off channel VH1 and then, in 1985, American Express left the set-up entirely, leaving Warner to soon sell everything off to the media con glomerate Viacom, a company that had made its name distributing CBS shows to local TV stations. Music videos had become pure mainstream, an integral – and showy – part of an album's promotional campaign[3] and now the young directors that had made their name via MTV found themselves either working with those significantly bigger budgets that Billy Idol despised or – ready or not – were seeing their short-form success rewarded with full-length projects.

Steve Barron had been at the top of the music-video game thanks to his iconic work on 'Billie Jean' and 'Don't You Want Me', as well as early Madonna track 'Burning Up'; success that led to his feature debut *Electric Dreams*, released in July 1984.

---

1 Real name William Broad, from Stanmore in Middlesex.
2 *Vanity Fair*, op. cit.
3 Duran Duran's *Mad Max 2* homage, the video for 1984's 'The Wild Boys', cost over a million pounds.

Distributed by MGM, *Electric Dreams* was funded by Richard Branson's Virgin Films – an offshoot of his record label that was flush with fourteen million pounds to invest in movies – and was written and produced by Rusty Lemorande[1] just before he worked on *Captain Eo*. Its ultra-contemporary story of a home computer that starts thinking for itself was, on paper at least, a kind of rom-com *WarGames*.

But whilst Barron shot the screwball plot with as much hi-tech nous as he could muster – all dynamic camera moves, digital gadgets and flashing lights – *Electric Dreams*' connection to the music world ultimately overwhelmed its thin concept (man battles his computer for the hand of a girl). Its soundtrack, laden with Virgin artists such as Culture Club, Heaven 17 and Phil Collins – plus a Giorgio Moroder score – led to a seemingly endless stream of musical montages that felt more like a series of pop videos. This wouldn't have been an entirely bad thing if there was something else to steady the balance but *Electric Dreams* didn't have back-up, its weak lead performance by Lenny Von Dohlen (desperately riffing on Cary Grant's nervy *Bringing Up Baby* routine) not strong enough to fight back. All of which saw dramatic tension take a back seat to something much more blatant: its desperation to create a new *Flashdance*-style soundtrack. In some respects it succeeded: Phil Oakey and Moroder's title song was a global hit, complete with a music video that was ninety per cent clips from the film. Yet the movie itself flopped, perhaps the only thing of real interest being a subplot where Edgar the tearaway computer 'sampled' old TV shows and movies and turned them into songs; a hint of things to come, not just in the world of music production but also in Moroder's restoration and re-editing of 1927 German sci-fi *Metropolis*, released the same year.[2] The second most interesting thing? The reappearance, in a supporting role as a slimy musician, of *Grease 2*'s Maxwell Caulfield.

Some music video directors fared better, with performances

---

1 Lemorande knew Barron's mother; she'd been in charge of continuity on Lemorande's Barbra Streisand picture *Yentl*.

2 Moroder recorded a new soundtrack for *Metropolis* in order to blend its original black-and-white story with contemporary power pop sung by Freddie Mercury and Bonnie Tyler – with unsurprisingly mixed results.

and plots to back up their undeniable visual flair. Russell Mulcahy – who'd directed Duran Duran's most extravagant outings – released his Aussie horror *Razorback* the same year as Barron's computer romance and with considerably greater critical success, resulting in six Australian Film Institute nominations and the chance to helm big-budget action pic *Highlander* twelve months later.[1] Meanwhile Julien Temple, a thirty-something Londoner who'd made his name filming the Sex Pistols, saw success with video hits for Stray Cats and Dexy's Midnight Runners land him his biggest opportunity yet: helming the UK's own attempt to get a slice of Hollywood's music-heavy teen movie market, *Absolute Beginners*. After all, Temple's many promos for bands had reaped great rewards on MTV. What could possibly go wrong?

Temple's plan for *Absolute Beginners* was simple: 'Let's make a British film for British kids. Music videos were reaching that kind of audience but cinema wasn't.'[2] But the road to hell – or at least, to bankruptcy – is paved with good intentions. What the making of *Absolute Beginners* proved once and for all was the vast difference between what works on MTV and what works at the multiplex.

Sure, Temple's eye for style was clear to see, early '80s work with ABC on 'Poison Arrow', Sade on 'Smooth Operator' and Culture Club on 'Do You Really Want to Hurt Me?' showing a love of mixing exotic, jazz-era theatricality (all three feature moodily lit nightclubs) with crime-themed plots, sitting somewhere between *grand guignol* and pantomime. Even directing the clean, modern electro of Depeche Mode's 'Leave in Silence' there was a strong element of performance in the video, the band 'playing' random objects that passed in front of them on a conveyor belt – deadpan and Kraftwerk-like – before proceeding to bounce around on Space Hoppers. Unexpected shifts into broad comedy were never far away in Temple's videos. After all, one of his earliest collaborators – punk agitator Johnny Rotten – had been as much music hall as malcontent.

---

1 With a soundtrack by Queen.

2 From the documentary *Absolute Ambition*, as featured on the *Absolute Beginners* Blu-ray.

What Temple planned for *Absolute Beginners*, based on the book by Colin McInnes about London's teen culture in the late '50s, was to make use of a longer running time to squeeze a thin story about a nineteen-year-old Soho photographer through even more filters than he could with a video. The result mixed the shiny corporate glamour of '80s pop with the clashing political belligerence of punk, the smokiness of his favourite bohemian cabaret clubs and the colourful, graceful chic of classic Hollywood musicals. The finished product was as arresting to watch as it was confusing to follow; a story told through multiple scriptwriters (Don Macpherson, Richard Burridge, Chris Wicking) that was, in the words of its producer Stephen Woolley, 'like trying to pour a quart into a pint pot'[1].

That carnivalesque mood would work fifteen years later for Baz Luhrmann's postmodern musical *Moulin Rouge!* In 1986 the appetite was different. *Absolute Beginners* was a film unashamedly about teenagers, starring teenagers and for teenagers but it crucially misjudged just what contemporary teenagers really wanted. Temple's re-creation of Soho in '58 – 'when the teenage miracle hit full bloom' we're informed in voiceover – was studio-bound and artificial, more *Funny Face* than *Flashdance*, filmed as an MGM-style song-and-dance movie simply because the non-conformist film-maker believed that the 'maximum cinema' razzle-dazzle of those old days was alluringly unhip and out of the ordinary. Impressively *outré*, perhaps – but not a great commercial decision. Huge sets, indoors and out, were created with Coppola's *One from the Heart* in mind – surely an early warning sign – leaving producers Palace Pictures having to excessively talk up the movie as the next big thing in order to secure more financing to fund such spectacle. *Absolute Beginners*, the world was told via taste-making publications such as *The Face* and *NME*, would outdo Hollywood's current offerings and be the coolest teen movie in years.

Patsy Kensit was a seventeen-year-old Londoner desperate to get in on the action. She was in a band, Eighth Wonder, but had found

---

1 Ibid.

more work as a child actor in respected BBC costume dramas such as *Silas Marner* and *Great Expectations*, roles at odds with her background as the daughter of Kray brothers associate, Jimmy 'The Dip' Kensit. Still, Julien Temple wasn't interested in someone more known for wearing a corset than a mini-skirt, despite Kensit's rising status as a London scenester and her undoubted keenness to bag the role. Eighth Wonder ploughed on with their music, sharing their manager Steve Dagger with the significantly more successful Spandau Ballet.

Dagger, however, had an ace up his sleeve. He knew Stephen Woolley and invited him to a gig Eighth Wonder were doing at the YMCA on London's Tottenham Court Road. Woolley remembered Kensit – she'd tested for a role in his breakthrough film, Neil Jordan's adaptation of Angela Carter's *Company of Wolves* – but seeing her in pop star mode, all blond bob and little black dress, gave her a new contemporary cool; enough for him to persuade Temple that she was in fact perfect to play *Absolute Beginners'* hip ingénue, Crepe Suzette. Eighth Wonder would even get a song on the movie's sure-to-be-massive soundtrack. Kensit's dream of teen stardom was starting to come true.

Production on *Absolute Beginners* didn't start well. Delays meant the film was over budget almost as soon as it commenced shooting whilst Kensit and her co-lead, newcomer Eddie O'Connell, were rumoured to have not exactly bonded off-camera. Still, that was nothing compared to the tension between film-makers and financiers. As the movie progressed, Temple's expensive vision for *Absolute Beginners* was deemed radically out of sync with its relatively modest six-million-pound budget, forcing bean counters from the bond company to be brought in to oversee production.[1] Then, as shooting drew to a close – and with Temple disgruntled that he'd not been allowed to finish what he started – the director was sacked from the project entirely, locked out of the cutting room as four editors began the mammoth task of finding some coherence in his flamboyant curiosity. Not even buzz in the teen mags could cancel out the horror stories that leaked to the press.

---

1 *Fame* producer Alan Marshall was installed on set to try and manage the sticky situation.

The British film industry braced itself, in no mood to be taken down by a video director's costly folly. Following *Electric Dreams*, Virgin had put money into *Absolute Beginners* but found themselves simultaneously caught in a well-publicised and damaging fight with director Michael Radford, recent helmer of their adaptation of George Orwell's *Nineteen Eighty-Four*, over the label's insistence on using a Eurythmics pop soundtrack in the movie rather than Radford's preferred score. Meanwhile *Absolute Beginners*' co-producers Goldcrest, despite having won plaudits working with David Puttnam on *Local Hero* and *Chariots of Fire*, was under the cosh with Hugh Hudson's nineteen-million-pound misfire *Revolution* – in which the bloody American War of Independence had been re-created with Al Pacino in rural Norfolk – and *The Mission*, a Puttnam award-winner which struggled to turn its undoubted luminosity into much of a return on its 16.5-million-pound budget.

Absolute Beginners cost less than half *The Mission* but Nik Powell and Stephen Woolley at Palace sensed that, as the new kids on the movie scene, it would be their poppy teen film that would bear the brunt of their colleagues' many frustrations. Palace had begun as a video distribution company only a few years earlier, Woolley a charismatic and pony-tailed former cinema manager and Powell previously an executive at Virgin, where he'd helped fund Temple's Sex Pistols' satire *The Great Rock'n'Roll Swindle*. At a time when British film seemed to focus more and more on prestige historical productions, Palace had made their name releasing cult foreign language and arthouse movies on video. *Absolute Beginners*, they hoped, would take them into the big league. Ultimately they were made to pay for such youthful moxie.

Absolute Beginners was released in April of 1986 and whilst it did well with its music – including Bowie's big title track, other songs by Sade, Paul Weller and, of course, Eighth Wonder – and even performed OK at the UK box-office, what it crucially *wasn't* was the worldwide phenomenon everyone had been told it would be. If it was a phenomenon at all, it was one of hype rather than material success. Kensit, who'd already made the front of *Tatler* whilst shooting the movie, was plastered all over bestselling teen magazines but, simultaneously, critics were plunging their knives into the actual film ('All that noise, all that energy, so little govern-ing thought,' wrote *Time Out*[1]). American reviewers, perhaps less aware of its filming problems and more encouraging of ambition, were kinder – 'a Felliniesque crossview of styles and social types'[2], wrote Caryn James in the *New York Times* – but the many companies that had turned down US distribution rights – Geffen, Fox, TriStar – were proven right when Mike Medavoy's Orion failed to make *Absolute Beginners* a hit stateside. At least Temple, unable to now get work in his homeland after the film's troubles, could head to LA with some acknowledgement of his talent. But Virgin could only lick their wounds and gradually wind down their interest in the movie industry, whilst Palace struggled on, inspiring and surprising as ever, yet on their way to bankruptcy by the early '90s. Goldcrest, meanwhile, was put up for sale.

Even if, in a parallel universe, *Absolute Beginners had* enjoyed a smooth production, it's hard to imagine the finished product ever connecting with a young audience in the way that it really needed to. It tried too hard. While Temple wanted to entertain and provoke, making it clear how London's racial problems from the late '50s had gone nowhere nearly thirty years later, the social issues teenagers were actually responding to in movies had no such historical leanings. America's *Flashdance* and *Footloose* showed where musicals were now; impassioned yes, but seamlessly incorporating modern pop into the background fabric of the film rather than being sung out loud by characters, the issues they tackled – social inequality, religious small-mindedness – presented in unashamedly contemporary settings, even if the problems were themselves nothing new.

The failure of Temple's vision proved to be a turning point in teen cinema, a sign that the indulgences that had affected older directors such as Coppola and Cimino had crossed over to the very film-makers once seen as their young, cool polar opposites. Excessively stylised moments in teen movies had become commonplace, of course, scenes that seemed to be included merely for audiences to gawp at their composition and bravado rather

---

1 by 'CPea'

2 18 April 1986.

than for any narrative purpose – the *Fame* street-dancing, Alex directing traffic in *Flashdance* – and they frequently worked. But *Absolute Beginners*, like the less high-profile *Electric Dreams*, had too many of them, coldly thinking in four-minute music video chunks and leaving character development behind. Yes, music videos had a huge – and swift – impact on pop culture but ambitious MTV directors didn't necessarily have the story-telling rigour needed for the big screen. The resulting 'style-over-content' issues of *Absolute Beginners* might have been interpreted as Felliniesque by some . . . but it certainly wasn't the universally lauded Fellini of *La Dolce Vita* or *8½*, films as well known for their intellect as their flamboyance.

And anyway, did modern teenagers really want to watch Fellini?

A month after *Absolute Beginners* was released to a largely un-interested world, America found a film that achieved the exact opposite, where technical ambition and storytelling simplicity were perfectly matched. It was a movie also directed by a Brit – the forty-two-year-old former ad man Tony Scott – yet this wasn't a tale full of English quirks or knowing eccentricity. Here was something essentially little more than a dynamic recruitment ad for the US military, a glossy and macho two hours as interested in fetishising all its aeronautical hardware and flogging its soundtrack as in its cursory romantic storyline.

Yet *Top Gun* soared. Scott's previous film, vampire romance *The Hunger*, had – like *Absolute Beginners* – starred David Bowie but this move from idiosyncratic horror to an assertive, sassy American buddy pic proved to be his making. Producers Don Simpson and Jerry Bruckheimer knew that visual showiness and mainstream success weren't mutually exclusive; the success of certain memorable ad campaigns, music videos and their own work with Adrian Lyne on *Flashdance* was proof of that. In *Top Gun*, Scott's frenetic artistry was paired with an endlessly honed script and the result was a jingoistic behemoth. Simpson and Bruckheimer chose stories that, really, were just old-fashioned fairytales. Yet mixing those traditional feel-good narratives with modern pizazz meant they'd practically become the teen world's in-house film-makers, giving young audiences what they actually wanted rather than what someone thought they *should* want. *Top Gun*'s success (177 million dollars in the States) suggested that the aesthetically brazen simplicity of action, pop music and romance was all they were really after.

Tom Cruise wanted simplicity too. The twenty-four year old had spent a frustrating year working with Tony Scott's brother Ridley on the curious-but-ambitious fantasy *Legend*, a big-budget fairytale shot in London's Pinewood Studios that had ultimately suffered multiple cuts, a ditched soundtrack and delayed US release; another punch in the guts for the British film industry.

The shooting of *Legend* had also coincided with the death of Cruise's estranged father Thomas Mapother III, as well as interrupting his relationship with Rebecca De Mornay, so it had been a time of much soul-searching. 'It was hard for Cruise to explain, but the year he spent in London filming *Legend* was really important to him. The isolation of the set, the disruption of his personal life, even the profound innocence of the character he played – each of these seemed to rekindle some of the pain and fear of his childhood and enabled him to develop new strength,'[1] revealed *Rolling Stone* in a profile from June 1986. *Top Gun*'s return to the tough military world of *Taps* saw Cruise relieved to be back in his favourite environment, using the single-minded discipline required to be a fighter pilot as a way to work through his issues. Matthew Modine had turned down the lead role of Lieutenant Pete 'Maverick' Mitchell – his politics just didn't line up with the story's pro-military stance – but really he was too mellow for the role anyway. Cruise's hotshot acting style, all perfectly placed smiles and blunt charisma, found its ideal partner in Scott's willingness to go all out with the no-nonsense, flashy patriotism.

Now playing a man with the serious responsibility of defending his country, *Top Gun* also saw Cruise successfully mature on screen, moving on from the high-school roles. Yes, Maverick lived up to his nickname – as unpredictable as a teenage rebel – but in both *Top Gun* and *Beverly Hills Cop*, Simpson and Bruckheimer

---

1 Christopher Connolly, 19 June 1986.

showed how the adult world might actually benefit from a typically adolescent style of defiance, both essentially anti-establishment *Police Academy* stories but with bigger budgets and more panache. And really, who needed buttoned-up squares in law enforcement and the military when there was a president so jokey and down-to-earth – at least on the surface – in the White House? Simpson and Bruckheimer could look to *Top Gun*'s Maverick or *Beverly Hills Cop*'s Axel Foley and see both Ronald Reagan *and* themselves: non-conformists right at the heart of the grown-up mainstream, supposedly 'everyday folk' showing the stuck-up elite just how things are done. It didn't matter that deep down their rebellion was paradoxically conformist, endorsing old chestnuts such as nationalism, female subversiveness and capitalist values. What they really knew how to do was *entertain*.

Not every former London ad man was having such a great time entertaining as Tony Scott. His brother Ridley was still recovering from *Legend* whilst David Puttnam licked his wounds after the Goldcrest debacle. Adrian Lyne, however, continued the hot streak kindled by *Flashdance* with the blockbusting erotic thriller *9½ Weeks*, a marathon of S&M naughtiness even more fancifully shot than his previous films and which starred Mickey Rourke and Kim Basinger. So whilst coming from the European ad world wasn't a copper-bottomed guarantee of success, what Tony Scott and Adrian Lyne confirmed was that when they tapped into the clean focus and stylish simplicity that had made their commercials so successful, they could make entertaining 'watercooler' movies like nobody else; certainly they had more disciplined narratives and a greater willingness to play the corporate game than their rock'n'roll music video counterparts.[1]

And really, Scott hadn't moved on from his advertising background at all. *Top Gun* was the peak of Simpson and Bruckheimer's high concept chic begun at Paramount with *American Gigolo* and *Flashdance*; pictures discussed for weeks after you'd seen them and that made you want to buy ... *stuff*. *Top Gun* not only increased applications to be a US navy fighter pilot by five hundred

---

1 In addition to the failures of Temple's *Absolute Beginners* and Barron's *Electric Dreams*, Mulcahy's *Highlander* was also a commercial disappointment, criticised for its weak narrative, despite eventual cult success.

per cent, it also gave a meteoric boost to Maverick's choice of sunglasses, Ray-Ban.

'The narrative of each film relies on style in order to progress,'[1] wrote Justin Wyatt in his analysis of high concept, a book in which he focused closely on Simpson and Bruckheimer's box-office bonanzas. 'Alex's unique dancing style places her outside the world of both the strip clubs and the ballet, Maverick's renegade flying style causes his disciplinary problems with his superiors in *Top Gun* and Julian Kay's choice of clothes and image separates him from all the other gigolos in Los Angeles. Furthermore, the reliance of bold images in the films reinforces the extraction of these images from the film for the film's marketing and merchandising.' Combine this with a similarly extractable pop soundtrack in a plot that's easy to convey and you've got a feature-length commercial, something that was selling specific, outside products (leggings, Aviator shades, Armani suits) as well as something more general: a cool *lifestyle*. Essentially, a Simpson and Bruckheimer film was an advert for itself.

It's true that other films had style too but there was always something that marked out the hits like *Top Gun* from the misses like *One from the Heart*. Coppola revived an artificial sheen previously associated with classic musicals with *One from the Heart*, but what selling points did it really have? No pin-up young actors,[2] an off-beat plot and a soundtrack that mixed Tom Waits with country star Crystal Gale. It was chic, yes – but muddled. *Absolute Beginners*, meanwhile, oddly combined romance with race riots, '50s jazz with '80s pop and – weirdest of all – David Bowie with Lionel Blair.[3]

But Simpson and Bruckheimer? They sold something much more artfully straightforward. You buy a ticket to watch a film that spends two hours convincing you to do something very

---

1 *High Concept: Movies and Marketing in Hollywood*, Justin Wyatt, University of Texas Press, 1994, p.17.

2 Instead it had thirty-five-year-old Teri Garr and forty-six-year-old Frederic Forrest; respected but hardly idolised.

3 Born Henry Ogus on 12 December 1928, in Montreal. He moved to London as a child and found fame in the '60s as a dancer and sometime actor but, by the time of *Absolute Beginners*, was best known as a team captain on charades-based TV game show *Give Us a Clue*. In other words, he was *not* David Bowie.

simple: go back and watch it all over again. Such shamelessness might have been too much for some (*Top Gun* was criticised as 'juvenile' and 'superficial' in the *Daily News*[1]), with the producers' calculated business focus not leaving much space for the raw or unexpected in their pictures. Their success also led to, in the case of Simpson, an ostentatious personal life that was headed for melt-down. It didn't stop their hook-up with the world of advertising being an era-defining one, though. Capitalism had never looked so good.

Several former Hollywood giants were finding life difficult in this new high-concept atmosphere. George Lucas had quit directing to focus on producing but by the mid-'80s found a significant chunk of the *Star Wars* money he'd earned from carefully holding on to merchandising rights was disappearing. The space trilogy had now ended, he'd divorced Marcia Griffin at a reported cost of seventy million dollars[2] and movies he'd overseen such as *Labyrinth* and *Howard the Duck* (both 1986) had under-performed. Scorsese and Coppola, meanwhile, continued to claw back their reputations and bank balances as directors for hire, the latter's *Peggy Sue Got Married* a return to the retro teenage setting of *The Outsiders* albeit this time with a body-swap set-up that allowed for a more knowing and comedic adult take on the genre.

Spielberg, on the other hand, had no such issues. Setting up his Amblin Entertainment production company on the backlot of Universal Studios – complete with its own '*Jaws* Lake' – Spielberg, Kathleen Kennedy and Frank Marshall saw Amblin as not just a company that would continue the director's fascination with films about childhood, families and spectacle. It would also change the way films were sold. At the helm of Amblin Spielberg generated his own take on high-concept – hangovers from the previous decade's big-budget blockbusters that were admittedly shot with less swagger than Simpson and Bruckheimer's movies but still had epic scale, cutting-edge effects and aggressive promotional campaigns. Amblin managed to maintain significant control when

---

1 Kathleen Carroll, 16 May 1986.
2 'The secret weapon behind *Star Wars*', news.com.au, Frank Chung, 17 December 2015.

marketing its products too, laying the ground rules for the timing and nature of advertising. *E.T.* and *Gremlins* had begun the process and, by 1985, Amblin's *Back to the Future* was said to have earned three million dollars in promotions alone.

Still, one thing Simpson and Bruckheimer's and Amblin's approaches did have in common was their ability to make and sell a movie without attaching a traditional star. Now that the *idea* was the star, the producers' names on a poster or trailer were enough in themselves to tell an audience all they needed to know. In Simpson and Bruckheimer's case, their brand meant elegantly OTT contemporary fairytales – MTV the motion picture – with one half of the team increasingly well-renowned for living a life as flashy as his films. Don Simpson was never the sexy pop star pin-up he dreamed of being (despite much cosmetic surgery) but, according to *Top Gun* and *Beverly Hills Cop* composer Harold Faltermeyer, that insecurity only drove the producer to live a rock'n'roll lifestyle all the more.

'Don was a crazy guy, y'know? One time he was supposed to come into a listening session for *Cop* and he'd just run over a fire hydrant with his Ferrari. And in no time the Ferrari was filling with water and he couldn't open the door . . . he almost drowned. He came into the studio soaking wet and swearing and we knew, in one way, he was crazy. But on the other hand he was the guy with the great ears and with the great connections in the business. Bruckheimer and Simpson was the perfect match: Jerry, absolutely straight and on the money and Don being a wild guy but getting the great connections together.'[1]

Spielberg's brand, on the flip side, brought with it much safer, more family-friendly expectations, albeit tied to stories that often had a melancholy heart.[2] He was in the business for the films, not the Ferraris and in his personal life had just married old-flame Amy Irving, the actress he first met when Brian De Palma cast her

---

1 Author interview.

2 It was the slight deviation from this formula that had caused Spielberg so much trouble over the certification of *Gremlins* and, to a lesser extent, the 1982 horror film *Poltergeist* that he produced (and, some say, co-directed). *Poltergeist* was released by MGM in the same month as *E.T.* and also featured a child – seven-year-old Heather O'Rourke – in the lead. It was not, however, a kids' film – although Spielberg successfully campaigned for it to get a PG rating, this being a time before the more suitable PG-13 came into being.

in *Carrie* and who, in mid-1985, gave birth to their son Max. As such, Amblin's 1985 hit *Back to the Future* – the biggest teen movie hit of the decade – was as much a Spielberg film as it was a Bob Zemeckis and Bob Gale one, despite the latter two being the originators of the story. With its blend of youth issues and fantasy storyline, a dissection of family life masquerading as a blockbuster caper, *Back to the Future* could have come straight from Spielberg's high-concept *Close Encounters* and *Jaws* playbook.

Spielberg knew Gale and Zemeckis well: the twenty-something writers from USC film school had worked on the director's war comedy *1941*, a rare flop from the end of the '70s that tried (and failed) to bring the zaniness of *National Lampoon* and *SNL* to the aftermath of Pearl Harbor by casting John Belushi and Dan Aykroyd as contrasting military men. Spielberg had also produced Zemeckis's early directorial efforts: 1978's *I Wanna Hold Your Hand* was a teenage love letter to The Beatles and their iconic '64 debut on American TV that featured Nancy Allen, Marc McClure and Eddie Deezen[1] whilst 1980's *Used Cars* was a dark comedy starring Kurt Russell. Yet since both were commercial disappointments, Zemeckis was reluctant to hassle Spielberg about taking on another of his projects. Instead he and Gale showed their *Back to the Future* idea to the team at Columbia and they liked it. A deal was set.

By February 1981 Gale and Zemeckis found themselves in an unenviable situation: they were acknowledged by the industry for the inventiveness of their early movies but unloved by ticket-buyers. So, after Columbia's initial interest, the inevitable happened: the studio put *Back to the Future* in turnaround.

'They thought it was a really nice, cute, warm film, but not sexual enough,' confessed Gale, the early '80s curse of *Animal House* and *Porky's* success striking once again. 'They suggested that we take it to Disney, but we decided to see if any other of the

---

1 'Steven hung out a lot on the *I Wanna Hold Your Hand* set, helping Bob with his first film. Spielberg is a very cool guy – regular, unpretentious. Both Bob and Steven were like fathers to me,' Eddie Deezen, author interview.

major studios wanted a piece of us.'[1] They didn't. Everyone rejected the story of young Marty McFly time-travelling back to his parents' teenage years, even with the script going through two more drafts. With nothing to lose, Gale and Zemeckis finally decided to take Columbia's advice and pitch their idea to Disney. After being criticised by Columbia for not being risqué enough they now found themselves at the other end of the spectrum, politely informed that a mother falling in love with her son was not appropriate for a family film under the Disney banner.

A full two years later and *Back to the Future* was still struggling. In the meantime though, Michael Douglas had asked Zemeckis to helm a comedy thriller he was producing and starring in called *Romancing the Stone*. Make a hit of that, Zemeckis thought, and investors would surely take another look at *Back to the Future*. Yet distributor Fox's expectations were so low for *Romancing the Stone* they even nixed Zemeckis's next job, replacing him on their expensive sci-fi drama *Cocoon* with the less-fanciful Ron Howard, whose mermaid movie *Splash* had been cheaply and efficiently filmed for Disney's new adult division, Touchstone.

Fox were wrong to be so negative about Zemeckis. Whilst both *Splash* and *Romancing the Stone* were significant hits when released in the March of 1984, it was the Zemeckis movie that actually made more money, confounding Fox's expectations. And sure enough, those doors that had once been closed now opened for Zemeckis and Gale and the duo found themselves more confident of pushing *Back to the Future* all over again, this time even taking the picture to the one place they had originally tried to avoid: Spielberg at Amblin.

When Amblin and their distributors Universal gave *Back to the Future* the go-ahead, Zemeckis and Gale's pet project finally found life breathed into it. Even better, Zemeckis hoped to show up Fox for a second time since *Back to the Future* and *Cocoon* – the project he'd been fired from – were set to open within a month of one another in the summer of '85. Sure enough, whilst Ron Howard's *Cocoon* did give Fox another big hit – nearly eighty million dollars

---

1 *Back to the Future: The Official Book to the Complete Movie Trilogy*, Michael Klastornin and Sally Hibbin, Hamlyn, 1990.

in ticket sales – *Back to the Future* boasted eleven weeks at No. 1 and over 200 million dollars at the box-office. *Cocoon* had been big but this was something else; a phenomenon.

The bosses at Universal could breathe a sigh of relief. Nineteen-eighty-five had seen theatrical business decline by ten per cent, largely due to video, but *Back to the Future* proved the studio's saviour. Its soundtrack, released on Universal owners MCA's label, went Top 20, fuelled by the huge success of lead single 'The Power of Love' by Huey Lewis and the News. Amblin also handled a huge merchandising push – tie-in books and toys – plus significant product placement for Pepsi and Nike; all extra entry points into the film for audiences and all things that made them money.

Even George Lucas got in on the *Back to the Future* action, his Industrial Light and Magic outfit on visual FX duties. It was all a big leap from his youthful dream of making those anti-commercial 'tone poems' with Coppola out in San Francisco, away from the finance-obsessed machine of traditional LA film-making. Everyone grows up, of course, but Lucas's abandoning of those avant-garde dreams in favour of business has always seemed a particular letdown, not least because the man himself has expressed his own regret at such a move. Yet the George Lucas of the 1980s was an increasingly disillusioned one,[1] creator of the monster *Star Wars* franchise that had changed the industry – and made him rich – but which wasn't what he'd always dreamed of.

And maybe that's part of *Back to the Future*'s power, its time-travelling concept carrying with it the sadness of realising how Marty's once-vivacious teenage parents became disillusioned adults themselves. Its story was certainly part of a trend, a fad for time travel and body-swapping plots which allowed toilworn adults to relive their carefree childhoods through bold plot devices. Some like *Peggy Sue Got Married* (1986) and *Big* (1988)[2] were fantastical,

---

1 'At the end of nine years of making *Star Wars*, I was not ready to continue it. I was completely burned out on it. I was more passionate about raising my kids than making movies and especially making *Star Wars*', *Empire*, Ian Freer, 15 March 1999.

2 Between October 1987 and June 1988 there were actually four male body-swap movies, Fox's *Big* preceded by TriStar's *Like Father, Like Son*, New World's *18 Again* and Columbia's *Vice Versa* (starring Judge Reinhold). But it was the Tom Hanks movie that got the best reviews – and a subsequent 116-million dollar box-office. Hanks was Oscar nominated as was the script, co-written by Spielberg's sister Anne.

others like *Back to School* (1986) and *Hiding Out* (1987) gave more practical reasons for why their adult stars might be given a second chance to get things right at high school. All were part of what Roger Ebert disparagingly referred to as the 'Generation Squeeze', films given the green light simply because their young-and-old characters would theoretically appeal to more than just one demographic (*Back to the Future* also manages to 'squeeze' science-fiction, comedy, retro music and romance into its story – really, something for everyone). Yet these films' charming of older audiences carried with it something more melancholy too, the age-old philosophical conundrum: '*What if?*'

Not that the team at Amblin claimed their output was quite so considered: 'We were just making what we felt we wanted to see,' believed Kathleen Kennedy. 'It's interesting 'cause nowadays it feels that people approach these things in a much more calculated way because there is so much at stake, frankly. There is so much more money being spent. But when we were doing it, it was completely instinctual.'[1] True or not, for Amblin and Universal those instincts could mean millions of dollars.

Back to the Future was a film about the past with its politics in the present. ILM and Amblin's production involvement, a sign of Lucas and Spielberg's continuing development from creative brats into corporate businessmen, was one thing but even casting the teen pic had political connotations. America in 1985 made it almost impossible not to have.

Despite the financial boom, Reagan's opinions in the mid-'80s were frequently divisive, many feeling the president's vocal championing of a market economy over government interference was leading to a cutback in crucial health, education and welfare funding ('I believe the best social programme is a job,' he had famously declared). The split nation was clear to see. In the 1984 election against Walter Mondale, Reagan gained only nine per cent of the black vote yet did little to help himself, refusing sanctions against a then divided South Africa which surely would have helped his standing with the civil rights movement.

---

1 *The Hollywood Reporter*, Kim Masters, 15 June 2016

As a result, the campaigns of both 1984 and 1988 saw Martin Luther King's former colleague Jesse Jackson run for Democratic candidate on a platform of reversing tax cuts for the rich, beginning nuclear disarmament talks with the Soviet Union and creating a 'rainbow coalition' of minorities; the bluntest, most liberal anti-Reagan policies in the mainstream. Jackson gained plentiful media attention as the second-ever black politician to make significant inroads towards the White House but ultimately fell short of the Democratic nomination both times. Reagan's harsher conservative side, meanwhile, continued to be softened by his jovial, jokey personality.

Television tapped into such oppositions with *Family Ties*, an NBC sitcom starring Michael Gross and Meredith Baxter as ex-hippy, liberal-thinking baby-boom parents amusingly at odds with their children; specifically their neo-conservative son Alex with his picture of Richard Nixon on his bedside table. Alex was a yuppie archetype, his attitude a twist on the usual 'liberal teen versus uptight parents' dynamic that films such as *Footloose* played on, and it was Matthew Broderick who had been first attached to the role. When his deal fell through though, casting director Judith Weiner knew there was someone who could be a more-than-worthwhile replacement. A penniless young Canadian called Mike – she persuaded *Family Ties* executive producer Gary David Goldberg – had *exactly* what the role needed.

Mike was Mike Fox. Whilst 'Michael *J.* Fox' was written on his Screen Actors' Guild card, the J. didn't actually stand for anything. It was just put there to sound different to a veteran TV bit-parter with the same name. Still, the twenty-two-year-old Clash fan was hardly doing any better than TV bit parts himself. Whilst it was Broderick's big-screen success that had scuppered his involvement with *Family Ties*, Fox had only ever come *close* to a significant film lead, auditioning for the hotly contested Conrad role in *Ordinary People* (while Redford was apparently flossing his teeth). Most of Fox's early years in LA, fresh from leaving his family in Edmonton, Alberta, were spent trying to cope with a long-distance relationship with his childhood sweetheart Diane and battling an empty bank balance. Even when Goldberg found himself agreeing with Weiner and falling for Fox's comedic charms, the bosses at NBC weren't convinced that Mike had what it takes. They reluctantly kept him in the show once the pilot was picked up but privately grumbled he'd never be a heart-throb. He was, they reasoned, just too damn short.

Family Ties debuted modestly at the end of 1982. Just like Travolta's Vinnie Barbarino in *Welcome Back, Kotter*, Alex Keaton was a supporting character; the show was really *about* the ex-hippy parents (actually based on Gary David Goldberg and his wife). But by its third season in the autumn of '84, screening directly after NBC's megahit *The Cosby Show*, *Family Ties* had grown to be a fixture in the Top 10, watched in over twenty million US households. What's more – and against NBC's expectations – Alex had become the star. The show's unyielding depiction of a schism in America had struck a humorous chord and at the centre of it all was Fox's right-wing but clumsy, good-looking but approachable boy-next-door. He was *Risky Business*'s Joel cleaned up and smoothed out for a primetime audience; another Reagan in miniature.

Bob Zemeckis, finally on the hunt for his Marty McFly after all those years of *Back to the Future*'s limbo, couldn't help but notice. Yet when Goldberg told the film-maker that he couldn't use the young star (with Goldberg not even mentioning his decision to Fox himself) a frustrated Zemeckis knew he wouldn't be able to hang about. Universal had invested big in *Back to the Future* and now they needed to get going, Michael J. Fox or no Michael J. Fox. So as the Canadian carried on filming season three of *Family Ties*, his Republican dynamism a perfect Marty-McFly-in-waiting, over at Amblin Zemeckis had to decide between two next best choices: Tommy Howell, hot from *The Outsiders*, and Eric Stoltz.

Soon, two had become one. It would be a big deal carrying a huge movie like *Back to the Future* and Stoltz – in his early twenties – was a few years older than Howell and more mature. The guy had performing in his blood too, coming from a musical family, although really he'd stumbled into movies. Watching from the orchestra pit as a kid, playing piano for endless local stage productions, the young Californian figured he might give acting a try just because it looked kind of fun. His first work was mainly in the theatre, with occasional roles in '80s TV shows *Knots*

Landing, The Waltons and *The Fall Guy* but Cameron Crowe saw something there, becoming a friend as well as his director after casting him and Anthony Edwards as Spicoli's stoners in *Fast Times*. Whilst Edwards hit big with leads in *Revenge of the Nerds* and *Gotcha!*, Stoltz was left to serve his time in low-rent video movies (beach film spoof *Surf II*) and horror pics (*The New Kids*, alongside James Spader).

But by 1984, with Zemeckis on the verge of making his casting decision, Stoltz was also starting to be talked about. His role in Peter Bogdanovich's *Mask*, the biopic of teenage craniodiaphyseal dysplasia sufferer Rocky Dennis, was rumoured to be seriously impressive, even as Bogdanovich argued with distributors Universal over why he couldn't get the Springsteen songs he wanted for the soundtrack. So whilst Zemeckis worried that Stoltz might not have the lightness of touch he wanted for Marty – the very lightness he'd seen in Michael J. Fox – he couldn't deny that the guy's profile was on the up. Stoltz was finally cast and, four years after Columbia had initially shown interest, filming for *Back to the Future* began at last.

Just a month in, everything changed. Eric's *Back to the Future* co-star Lea Thompson, playing Marty's mother both in the present day and the mid-'50s, struggled with his intense approach, finding him difficult to work with. 'It was a time when we were emerging from the '70s. All the young actors wanted to be like De Niro and Pacino, which was good in a lot of ways.'[1] Good – but not what Zemeckis needed for his teenage lead. Stoltz looked serious and spoke softly, more of a boffin himself than the friend-of-a-boffin that Marty needed to be. Here was a character who had to embody the '80s in a look, a glance, a mannerism – represent the mood of a decade as he finds himself lost in a completely different one. Eric Stoltz was a good-looking guy and a talented actor but, after a few weeks playing Marty, it was clear he just couldn't be *cocky* enough.[2]

---

1 From *We Don't Need Roads*, Caseen Gaines, quoted in 'Back to the Future: 13 things you may not know', *Daily Telegraph*, author unknown, 21 October 2015.

2 Eddie Deezen worked with Stoltz on 1984's spoof *Surf II* and, conversely, remembers him as jokey and lighthearted: 'We played poker together all the time back in those days. He was dating Ally Sheedy at the time. Ally was a doll. Eric was a very funny guy. He loved pizza at those poker games,' author interview.

Bob Zemeckis instinctively knew what was up: he'd made the wrong decision. He still wanted Michael J. Fox and was prepared to fight for him but any changes at this late stage would have to be handled with care: 'We had [Universal executive] Sid Sheinberg who had a very close relationship with Steven [Spielberg] at Amblin. And we presented the situation to him and we felt that we could pull it off and he trusted us. I'm not sure that today, in today's corporate world, we would be able to pull that off because there's just too many people involved in making a decision. Back then it was very, very clean cut. And Sid had the foresight and the guts to make the call.'[1] It was a call that put a month's worth of shooting in the dustbin, Eric Stoltz back into unemployment and – as had been originally intended – Michael J. Fox's name at the top of *Back to the Future*'s cast list.

Stoltz had to be pragmatic: 'I went back to acting school, I moved to Europe, I did some plays in New York and I actually invested in myself in a way that was much healthier for me.'[2]

Over at the Universal lot, Lea Thompson awaited her replacement 'son'. The petite, brunette former ballet dancer from Minnesota already had plenty of experience of film-making, from a Burger King commercial alongside Elisabeth Shue and Sarah Michelle Gellar to roles in *All the Right Moves*, *Red Dawn* and *The Wild Life*. It was whilst making the hardly romantic *Jaws 3-D*,[3] however, that she met twenty-nine-year-old Texan Dennis Quaid, six years her senior, forming a relationship that survived both the movie's bad press,[4] Quaid's break-up with his actress wife P. J. Soles and his self-confessed bad-boy lifestyle where cocaine was a daily presence. By the time of *Back to the Future*, Thompson and Quaid were engaged.

Michael J. Fox, meanwhile, had spent the last few months feeling frustrated. He'd actually seen some of *Back to the Future*'s crew scouting for locations in Pasadena whilst he was out there

---

1 Bob Zemeckis, slashfilm.com, Peter Sciretta, 19 June 2015.

2 moviehole.com, Clint, 8 April 2007.

3 *Jaws 3-D* was, at one point, planned as a spoof with *National Lampoon*'s Matty Simmons overseeing a script co-written by John Hughes. Universal, perhaps unfortunately, soon got cold feet.

4 Including multiple Golden Raspberry nominations. Box-office, however, was solid enough for the much-ridiculed sequel *Jaws: The Revenge* to get the green light.

quickly shooting *Teen Wolf* for Atlantic, the small film company keen to make the most of their hot-streak after *Valley Girl*. The guys from Amblin had told Fox that their movie featured Crispin Glover, one of his former co-stars from a TV movie called *High School USA*, in a supporting role. 'While it was unusual for me to feel competitive with my peers, it did sting a little to know that crazy Crispin was gearing up to do a Spielberg film while I, layered in latex, toiled away on a B-grade, high-school werewolf comedy.'[1]

But when Stoltz was pushed from *Back to the Future* and Zemeckis approached Goldberg all over again, all that changed. This time the TV producer didn't keep the request from his golden boy; he knew the movie guys must be really serious to come back. Eventually Fox and Goldberg made a deal: if the actor agreed to taking on *Back to the Future*, he would have to film it at night and at weekends, working around shooting *Family Ties*. The sitcom's leading lady Meredith Baxter was on maternity leave at the time so Goldberg couldn't risk losing another star. Fox took the movie script back home to consider his options but deep down he knew this was the film break he'd been yearning for. 'The character of Marty McFly – a skate-boarding, girl-chasing, high school rock'n'roll musician – seemed like the kind of guy I could play in my sleep. That very nearly turned out to be the case.'[2]

Saying 'Yes' was the easy part. Filming *Back to the Future* meant Michael J. Fox was picked up from the *Family Ties* studio at Paramount at six in the evening every weekday, driven to wherever the movie was shooting, working through the night to get as much done as possible before getting a couple of hours sleep and heading back to Paramount at half past nine the next morning. He was exhausted but wired, the whole process feeding into his performance as the manic and dynamic Marty. Could the careful Eric Stoltz, the man now happy with his 'healthier' alternative life away from *Back to the Future*, ever have been so gung-ho? On *Mask*, he didn't let anyone see him without his substantial make-up, in order to make it feel like he really *was* Rocky Dennis. *Back to the Future* had no place in its script or time in its shooting

1 *Lucky Man*, Michael J. Fox, Ebury, 2003, p.106.
2 Ibid, p.109.

schedule for such solemnity. This was a romp, not *Raging Bull*. And most importantly, Michael J. Fox didn't mind.

Crispin Glover – playing Marty's dad George both in the present and the past – wasn't so sure though. If Marty himself never makes his politics as clear as brash Alex Keaton might on *Family Ties*, *Back to the Future*'s plot conclusion – in Glover's eyes – *did* wear its politics on its sleeve. And he didn't like what it said. 'I think it's a bad message... propaganda,' claimed Glover of the film's resolution that saw the McFlys – their lives changed by Marty's actions in the past – miraculously wealthy and confident rather than the crumbling, downtrodden family that began the film. 'The characters should be in love and the *love* should be the reward,' he complained.[1] The movie's title song was, after all, 'The Power of Love'[2] not 'The Power of Cash'.

Glover made his feelings known to Bob Zemeckis. 'I was asking questions that the producers and director didn't like,'[3] – but the ending remained, Glover now insistent that Universal's ties to the global MCA corporation meant they were too entrenched in capitalist principles to ever try a more socially radical storyline. In fact, he believed, Universal championed *Back to the Future* all the more because what it said – money equals happiness – only served to uphold the free market status quo on which it thrived.

After the film's success, Crispin Glover didn't return for the sequels ('If you question propaganda it has serious consequences'[4]) although the semantics of his absence are disputed. He suggests he wasn't being offered a fair salary in comparison to his equally billed co-stars Lea Thompson and Tom Wilson,[5] whilst Bob Gale claims Glover was just asking for too much (a million dollars). When Glover's facial image was used in mask form, worn by his replacement Jeffrey Weissman in 1989's *Back to the Future Part II*, he sued the film-makers for using his likeness without his

---

1 Sirius XM interview with Anthony and Opie, 6 June 2013.

2 'You don't need money, don't take fame / Don't need no credit card to ride this train'.

3 Sirius XM, op. cit.

4 Ibid.

5 Tom Wilson played bully Biff Tanen, named after Universal's quixotic executive Ned Tanen, with whom Gale and Zemeckis had clashed as far back as *I Wanna Hold Your Hand*.

permission as well as for the reuse of scenes from the original that were briefly replayed. He won an unconfirmed 760,000-dollar payout,[1] if not actually rewriting the law books then at least forcing a landmark decision for actors' rights. It was a case of the artist versus the conglomerate, like *Family Ties'* liberal Steve and Elyse Keaton fighting with their Reaganomic son Alex all over again.

Yet Crispin Glover had a point. In a time of increased corporate ownership, it's no surprise that storytellers might have been reluctant to bite the hand that feeds. *Family Ties*, for example, was careful never to select one political viewpoint over another: 'We dealt with it [political disagreement] like it was just a generational thing and . . . love would conquer it,' remembered Michael J. Fox. 'There was an understanding that could be reached.'[2] Romantic-sounding, yes – but NBC could hardly appear too left-wing seeing as it was itself part of the giant RCA electric corporation, boasting investments in Arista Records, Columbia home video and Hertz car rental and which, in 1986, was bought by the even bigger consumer company General Electric.[3] It was all part of the process, like MTV's buyout by Viacom; a cog in a gargantuan machine. And NBC wasn't alone.

Nineteen-eighty-two had seen the purchase of Columbia Pictures by Coca-Cola for 820 million dollars, as a result of which the beverage firm created[4] an entirely new sister studio for Columbia, Tri-Star, in order to up its output without – on the face of things – monopolising the market. Essentially Coca-Cola was diversifying its new film business in the same way that it was with its ever-growing range of soft drinks.[5] By the time that Columbia/TriStar was subsequently bought for nearly five billion dollars by Japan's Sony Corp behemoth at the end of the decade, four different studio heads – including David Puttnam and Dawn Steel – had foundered under the Coke regime. Peter Guber and Jon Peters were deemed to be the right replacements

---

1 '*Back to the Future Part II* from a legal perspective', *The Hollywood Reporter*, Eriq Gardner, 21 October 2015.

2 NBC *Today* show, 7 October 2015.

3 In 2003 NBC was in fact united with Universal – Glover's *bête noire* – when it was merged with French giants Vivendi, by that point owners of the film studio.

4 Along with television partners HBO and CBS.

5 The original, basic Coke spawning Diet, caffeine-free and Cherry versions in 1982, 1983 and 1985 respectively.

for a new era, albeit for a significant fee that included not only a buyout of their own production company but also to take care of the fact that they had an ongoing deal with Warner Bros. that had produced recent hits *Batman* and *Tango and Cash*.[1] The power of love only got you so far. Credit cards were, in fact, essential.

As *Back to the Future* passed 200 million dollars at the 1985 US box-office, the singer of its theme song – New York blues man Huey Lewis – was himself getting frustrated by the corporate side of the business. The reason was simple: he was certain that fellow artist Ray Parker Jr had copied one of his songs – 'I Want A New Drug' – and passed it off as the title track to the previous year's sci-fi blockbuster, *Ghostbusters*.

Outside of the songs' similarly playful melody and chugging beat there was some logic to his argument. Lewis, who had a cameo role in *Back to the Future* as one of Marty's teachers in the talent show audition scene,[2] claimed that he had originally been asked to produce the title track for *Ghostbusters* but turned it down because of his commitment to Spielberg and Zemeckis on their time-travel film. Nineteen-eighty-four had been Lewis's breakthrough, the album *Sports* (with his band The News) the second-highest seller of the year.[3] His fun-loving, rootsy sound was big business. Who wouldn't want that in a movie?

When Columbia failed to win him over, however, what second choice Ray Parker Jr was eventually asked to produce for *Ghostbusters*, insisted Lewis, was a song that simply tapped into his band's popularity by mimicking one of their songs. 'Ghostbusters'' subsequent million sales, Oscar nomination and near ubiquity on MTV[4] only made him more angry. 'The offensive part was not so much that Ray Parker Jr had ripped this song off,

---

1 The giant new Sony media monster found itself facing an even more high-profile artist-versus-corporation row when pop singer George Michael refused to cooperate with the company after treatment that he described as 'professional slavery'. He took Sony to court in late 1992, claiming 'unreasonable restraint of trade' and that they didn't want to market him as a credible artist, only a sex symbol. He lost the case.

2 'I'm afraid you're just too darn loud!'

3 Behind Michael Jackson's *Thriller*.

4 The 'Ghostbusters' video, helmed by the film's director Ivan Reitman, made much use of the movie's stars Dan Aykroyd, Bill Murray, Ernie Hudson and Harold Ramis.

[more that] it was kind of symbolic of an industry that wants something – they wanted our wave and they wanted to buy it . . . it's not for sale [but] in the end I suppose they were right. I suppose it was for sale, because, basically, they bought it.'[1]

Columbia eventually settled with Lewis, out of court,[2] but increasing debate about the renumeration of writers in the ballooning and avaricious showbusiness industry led to much unrest in the decade. In the music sector, Lewis's claims of deliberate mimicry morphed into something even more complex when songwriters found their tracks being cheekily sampled by burgeoning house and hip-hop acts, often with huge chart success. Meanwhile, in Hollywood, three Writers' Guild of America strikes over secondary earnings from pay-TV and home video mirrored Glover's complaints about the integrity of entertainment corporations. A 1981 strike had resulted in a healthy deal over residuals that some scribes said was so good it led directly to a clash in 1985 where producers were determined to grab back some of the financial sway they felt they'd lost. After three weeks of refusing to work, this time the WGA caved in. Come 1988 and further testy contract negotiations, the WGA were on strike for a record twenty-two weeks until concessions were made on both sides. But the mood between writers and producers remained fraught. When everything seemed available for reusing, remixing or recycling, who should reap the rewards?

There was also some irony in the situation. Back in 1960 the head of the Screen Actors' Guild was a middle-aged Ronald Reagan, then committed to making sure his colleagues were paid their dues from TV showings of their films; so much so he led a strike which resulted in a victory.[3] By August 1981, the now-US president had decided to fire over eleven thousand striking federal air traffic controllers as a show of strength against union interference in the free market he so loved.[4] He had moved from ally to agitator. Backing him up in the controversial decision was

---

1 VH1's *Behind the Music*, 2001.

2 The feud was reignited again in 2001, when Parker Jr claimed that Lewis's discussion of the case on the episode of VH1's *Behind the Music* broke a confidentiality agreement.

3 Although films made before 1948 were, controversially, exempt from the decision.

4 The air traffic controllers' union, PATCO, had actually supported Reagan in the 1980 election.

Transportation Secretary Andrew 'Drew' Lewis, a career businessman who, in 1983, would take over as CEO of Warner Amex, effectively running MTV.

Away from the financial debate, Lea Thompson went to see *Back to the Future* for the first time at the Cinerama Dome on Sunset Boulevard, on a date with her boyfriend Dennis Quaid: 'It was completely full and we stood at the back and watched the whole movie. People were just ecstatic! I was like, "Oh my gosh . . . this is spectacular!"'[1] Michael J. Fox was now propelled into the A-list, the once-broke actor suddenly revelling in the spoils of fame: a house on Laurel Canyon, a drive full of sports cars, plenty of female attention. But seeing his face staring back at him from the cover of countless magazines freaked him out, its hall of mirrors effect 'a perfect metaphor for what my life had become as I found myself in the labyrinthine fun-house of America mega-celebrity – a place where, I discovered, it's easy to get lost'[2]. Come February 1986 *Back to the Future*'s influence had gone even further, from fun-house to White House, with the septuagenarian Ronald Reagan attempting to attract the teen market by quoting it – albeit rather unnaturally – in his annual state of the union address:

'Tonight I want to speak directly to America's younger generation because you hold the destiny of our nation in your hands. With all the temptations young people face, it sometimes seems the allure of the permissive society requires superhuman feats of self-control. But the call of the future is too strong, the challenge too great to get lost in the blind alleyways of dissolution, drugs, and despair. Never has there been a more exciting time to be alive, a time of rousing wonder and heroic achievement. As they said in the film *Back to the Future*, "Where we're going, we don't need roads".'

Uplifting perhaps, but for many Reagan reaching out to the young was disingenuous. He'd battled with the University of California when he was governor of the state and had repeatedly opposed new funding for basic education. As president he'd seen a

---

1 *US Weekly*, Stephanie Webber and Ingrid Meilan, 25 November 2014.
2 *Lucky Man*, op. cit., p.114.

comprehensive study titled *A Nation at Risk: The Imperative for Educational Reform* published in 1983, stating in no uncertain terms the issues facing the nation's schools: falling SAT scores, limited literacy and numeracy. The causes were, naturally, debated by both sides. Was it underfunding and social inequality or just lazy students and unaccountable teachers? The message, however, was clear: there were serious problems. Reagan, for his part, proposed the mandatory reintroduction of prayer back into schools as a partial solution. It failed to get through Congress but – as shown by his later quoting of *Back to the Future* – here was a president who made sure he at least *looked* as if he was interested in young people's welfare. 'The whole situation is replete with irony,' the educational researcher Dennis P. Doyle told the *New York Times*. 'The most anti-education president in our history has succeeded in making education an issue.'[1]

It was Reagan's final line of that speech in 1986 that perhaps said the most though. After a rousing celebration of America's economic growth, thanks to – he claimed – 'quiet courage and common sense', the world's most powerful capitalist decided to end by declaring: 'Let us go forward to create our world of tomorrow in faith, in unity, and in love.' The country was in mourning, since only a week earlier its *Challenger* space shuttle had exploded just after take-off, killing the seven-person crew.[2] Whatever other problems America was facing – an increasingly irresponsible financial market, worsening social inequality, the imminent exposure of the government's illegal arms sales to Iran – the power of love seemed like a good idea to hang on to.

---

1 'Top objectives elude Reagan as education policy evolves', *New York Times*, Edward B. Fiske, 27 December 1983.

2 The state of the union address had in fact been postponed because of the tragedy.

Chapter Twelve

SINCERELY YOURS

The Brat Pack are christened (and not happy about it); John Hughes finds his princess of the suburbs; The Breakfast Club get in touch with their feelings; and Joel Schumacher gives St Elmo's Fire *some serious heat.*

For Ally Sheedy, it was all a joke gone wrong. Writer David Blum might have planned to write a profile solely of Emilio Estevez for the summer '85 issue of *New York* magazine but Sheedy remembers being asked by Estevez to come along to the interview too, to hang out at the newly hip Hard Rock Café with a bunch of their friends and to play at being hot shots, cockily performing in the way a journalist like Blum might expect them to. After all, the article was to be about Estevez's huge success and lofty ambitions; an actor who didn't see his youth getting in the way of his dreams of writing and directing. Blum would want to see some of that popularity on show, right?

Sheedy wasn't that kind of party girl though – she didn't even drink – so she passed on the invitation, as did fellow actress Demi Moore, leaving Blum to instead chronicle Emilio alongside his male friends Rob Lowe and Judd Nelson, the three of them milking their playboy reputations that night and giving Blum exactly what they *thought* he wanted.

But by the time of publication, Emilio's idea had misfired. In print those high spirits didn't look fun-loving any more, they looked like plain arrogance. Even worse, Blum had decided to give these young stars a group name, something that he thought perfectly summed up the youthful bullishness he'd witnessed. *New York* magazine liked it so much they splashed the phrase on their cover that July: 'Hollywood's Brat Pack'.[1]

The 'Brat Pack' was a term no actor wanted to be a part of; not those who were deemed by David Blum to be at its centre like Rob Lowe ('We were totally minimised – like we were indistinguishable pretty people'[2]) or on its peripheries like Andrew McCarthy ('It's all just some lazy fucking journalist lumping it all together'[3]). Not even those the same age who *could* have been part of the scene, such as Jodie Foster,[4] wanted to be involved – or at least her mother made *sure* she wasn't: 'My mother really wanted to keep my career separate from groups. She wanted me to be seen as an actress first, not an age group, so that my career had the opportunity for more longevity. So she didn't let me participate in any publicity that lumped me into a group . . . so I really avoided the teen movies of the '80s, all the John Hughes-style films. I went to college instead and waited for dramatic roles.'[5]

Still, few could deny the existence of this new breed of young Hollywood stars: names made famous by the industry's relentless pursuit of a teenage audience over the previous few years, and by the ensemble movies such as *Fast Times* and *The Outsiders* that brought many of them together in the same film; cheaply at first, although with each hit less so. Sure there were individual personalities but it was as a unit that they had most resonance; ebullient and ambitious. Even Foster looked on from her dorm room at Yale with a certain amount of wonder: 'I knew all the actors in the Brat Pack, of course. I made *Hotel New Hampshire*[6] with Rob Lowe. He was best friends with Emilio Estevez, who I had known as a kid through working with his dad. He had great,

---

1 *You Couldn't Ignore Me If You Tried*, Susannah Gora, Three Rivers Press, 2011, p.119.

2 'Rob Lowe's Tips for Re-Re-Reinventing Yourself', GQ, Amy Wallace, 22 September 2015.

3 'Andrew McCarthy Is Bitter About His Brat Pack Past', observer.com, Andrew Goldman, 30 August 1999.

4 Foster is eight days younger than Demi Moore.

5 Author interview.

6 In 1984, alongside Nastassja Kinski, Matthew Modine and Beau Bridges. Tony Richardson directed, based on the book by John Irving.

fun stories about all of those actors: Demi Moore, Judd Nelson . . . living in Malibu, etc. But I chose not to be a part of those movies or that culture. That was a tough choice but I wanted to stick to my goal.'

Those inside the Brat Pack had their goals of longevity and sincerity too – who wouldn't? – but now they had been reduced and generalised by a magazine article they feared the worst. Even the cover photo beneath the headline was over-simplified: a snap of Lowe, Nelson and Estevez in a bar, drinks in hand, pulling faces and playing up to the camera; a picture that *appeared* to be from the night out Blum had shared with them yet which actually was just an official promotional shot from Joel Schumacher's newly released ensemble drama *St Elmo's Fire*, in which the three guys starred alongside Sheedy, Moore and McCarthy. To the casual observer this was a glimpse of spoiled hedonists on another mindless night out even if in reality they were actors in character. 'They were definitely not brats,' remembers Schumacher, 'although some were better behaved than others. They weren't a pack either.' Still, as one of the directors most associated with the films of the Brat Pack, Schumacher could at least appreciate this new brand's marketability: 'The term, I think, added to the success and the popularity of the film.'[1]

Columbia released *St Elmo's Fire* at the end of June 1985, just three weeks before sister company TriStar put out teen drama *The Legend of Billie Jean*, the next Peter Guber and Jon Peters production after *Vision Quest*. *The Legend of Billie Jean* didn't feature any of the Brat Pack but story-wise it couldn't have been more pertinent. Twenty-one-year-old Helen Slater starred as the title character, a trailer park high-schooler from Texas who accidentally becomes an outlaw pin-up when she stands up to local bully Hubie Pyatt (Barry Tubb) and his sleazy father (Richard Bradford). The older man calls the police and claims she tried to rob his shop (she didn't), leaving Billie Jean to go on the run with her brother Binx (Christian Slater) and her best friends. When the gang start feeding the media with homemade video tapes detailing their plight, their fame goes through the roof but it's middle-aged

---

1 Author interview, BBC Radio 1, 6 January 2005.

antagonist Mr Pyatt who cashes in by shamelessly selling Billie Jean posters and T-shirts to local kids in awe of her rebel attitude and cropped blonde haircut. The teenage outlaws, meanwhile, balk at such profiteering. They just want what they always wanted: for Pyatt to apologise and for Binx's scooter, trashed by his son, to be repaired. They crave respect.

In the same way that the subjects of Blum's article complained about its manipulation and advantage-taking,[1] *The Legend of Billie Jean* played out a similar clash on screen: these teenagers just wanted to be taken seriously, treated fairly[2] and not to be double-crossed by adults. As a glossy Guber–Peters production, however, it wasn't as truly alternative as similarly themed stories such as *Over the Edge, Times Square* or even Terence Malick's ethereal 1973 teen-outlaw pic *Badlands*.[3] Helen Slater's image – from early scenes in the skimpiest of bikinis through to her Joan of Arc makeover into a boyish renegade – sometimes feels as fetishised by director Matthew Robbins as Jennifer Beals was by Adrian Lyne in *Flashdance*; in other words, a story about youngsters being exploited by adults was occasionally itself an example of youngsters being exploited by adults. If that wasn't exactly a new situation – countless B-movies from the late '50s had come up with their own shallow takes on teen delinquency in order to capitalise on the success of *Rebel Without a Cause* – *The Legend of Billie Jean* still seemed calculated in comparison with the more honest teen stories from the early part of the '80s, such as those from the S. E. Hinton stable, before the genre became aware of its own power. When Billie Jean's young female fans in the movie start to copy her haircut, you get the sense that's exactly what the film's producers wanted ticket-buyers to do too, exactly as they had copied Alex's slouchy *Flashdance* sweatshirts and legwarmers.

Yet just as the story begins to feel disingenuous, it hits back with something genuinely startling, such as Billie Jean helping her young friend Putter (Yeardley Smith) with her first period. 'It's wonderful,' she tells her, smiling. Whether that's just older male

---

1 Several of them appeared on TV talk show *Donahue* and laid into Blum.
2 Bille Jean's motto was also the film's original title: *Fair is Fair*.
3 That had starred Sissy Spacek and Emilio and Charlie's dad, Martin Sheen.

film-makers blatantly trying to appeal to a young female audience or not, Slater – in only her second movie, her first being the flop comic adaptation *Supergirl* – delivers the line with such calm honesty it's impossible not to believe her. *The Legend of Billie Jean*, for all the artfully casual outfits and the MTV-friendly theme song by Pat Benatar, is a rare teen-movie feminist, in need of no help from men.

Meanwhile, one grown-up in the movie does at least seem to understand the misjudging and misrepresentation that Billie Jean and her friends are going through: Peter Coyote's nice guy cop, the appropriately named Lieutenant Ringwald.

David Blum's article on the Brat Pack enlightened as much as it supposedly manufactured. Actors who had previously been unknowns, once cast in pictures that relied on a strong concept rather than a famous name, were now famous names themselves, undeniably getting movies green-lit in a way that was previously reserved for the iconic likes of Jane Fonda and Robert Redford, stars twice their age. It also highlighted how the opposite had happened to Timothy Hutton, a leading man in the decade's first youthful ensemble hit *Taps*, but who was now struggling to follow up that success, leaving his contemporaries to apparently gossip about the actor's future. Perhaps most pointedly Blum described Matt Dillon as 'the one least likely to replace Marlon Brando', seeing as the actor had somewhat tarnished his original cool by making PG-13 fluff such as *The Flamingo Kid*, a moderately successful movie from the end of 1984 but undeniably a long way from *On the Waterfront*. Blum's point was clear: awareness of their new found influence hadn't always led these young stars to the most noble projects, opportunities rather wasted. Giving an inexperienced twenty year old the power of a forty year old might not have been the wisest idea.

More subtly, the feature hinted at the many differences in these young stars' backgrounds. Whilst a unifying factor might be their relative lack of acting training and stage experience, Blum was careful to separate the showy LA kids with their movie-making families (Estevez, Penn, Cage) from the quieter east coast members who don't fit so easily into the group (Broderick, Modine, McCarthy).

And on a more general level, Blum's exposé was also an eye-opening glimpse into what was hot at the time, what everyone was into. Emilio Estevez appeared desperate to watch Matthew Broderick's romantic fantasy *Ladyhawke* at the cinema. Judd Nelson wanted to go to punk clubs.

Making a brief – somewhat reluctant – appearance in the story was thirty-year-old New York author Jay McInerney, then staying at the Chateau Marmont whilst he wrote the screenplay of his 1984 novel *Bright Lights, Big City*. McInerney's book had been infamous; a blistering portrayal of drugged-up Big Apple over-achievers that resulted in declarations of a literary Brat Pack to match Hollywood's.[1] *Bright Lights, Big City* seemed like a natural fit for Estevez and his pals to turn into a movie, with Joel Schumacher already scheduled to direct and Tom Cruise to star but, as McInerney hung out with the guys that night, talk of who would grab the co-star role was rife: Nelson, Lowe or Estevez himself? The latter was also musing on who would star in his own movie *Clear Intent*, a script he'd written about two garbage men who uncover local corruption and murder. Again, Estevez wanted to keep things amongst friends, mentioning Penn, Cage or Broderick as potential cast members.[2] Penn, meanwhile, was in the middle of his new high-profile relationship, something not lost on his colleagues.

'You seen Sean?' Blum reported Hutton asking Estevez when he bumped into him in Westwood, an affluent LA suburb neighbouring Beverly Hills.

'No,' replied the oldest Sheen brother. 'I heard he was at a party for Madonna the other night . . . '

Ultimately though, Estevez, Lowe and Nelson – 'these young studs, all under twenty-five years old, decked out in *Risky Business* sunglasses and trendish sport jacket and designer T-shirts' – didn't come out of the article well. Rob Lowe, as he hung out in the bar with Blum that night, was apparently only interested in charming girl after girl with his smile (though going home to Melissa Gilbert). Estevez was portrayed as more innocent looking, maybe

---

1 A group that featured McInerney, twenty-one-year-old *Less than Zero* author Bret Easton Ellis and former Warhol groupie Tama Janowitz.

2 It was eventually released in 1990 as *Men at Work* and starred Estevez and his younger brother.

more in control of his fame thanks to his family background, but who still pursued a *Playboy* Playmate. And then there was Judd Nelson. In Blum's eyes Nelson was the most difficult of them all, annoyed when fans came to join him at his table, equally annoyed when no one recognised him in a club. Blum didn't hold back with his description of the twenty-five-year-old: 'The over-rated one'.

In turning down the chance to join the boys, perhaps Ally Sheedy and Demi Moore dodged similar character assassinations at Blum's hand but actually it was their absence that really said the most. Whether the guys were deliberately showing off that night or not, the Brat Pack became a byword for a very male cockiness. 'The guys went out and the guys did what the guys did, and none of the women were included,' Sheedy later explained. 'The only women that were included were the ones that showed up in the restaurants and climbed up under the tables to get in their laps.'[1]

Watch the films though and it was often the female voices that were most groundbreaking. After all, there had been plenty of feisty bad boys in cinema before; nearly every article referred to Estevez, Penn, Lowe and co as throwbacks; new Brandos or Deans. Ambitious, smart, everyday young women, on the other hand, were a newer cinematic breed; especially when created by someone with the visual strength and contemporary sincerity of a film-maker like Joel Schumacher. So whilst the SaMoHi jocks made the noise, there was a quieter revolution happening behind the front page: the rise of female stars, film-makers and executives getting their voice heard, not to mention a more feminine-skewed sensitivity and design palette, more fashion-led than Francis Coppola's neo-expressionism or Adrian Lyne's sultry smokiness ... but more sincere too.

Still, sincerity just didn't make for quite such dramatic headlines as tales of Judd Nelson's ego or Rob Lowe going on the prowl.

Family was to John Hughes what murder was to Alfred Hitchcock; questions of it were nearly always there in his films, whether at the centre or subtly hovering in the background. In his trademark teen movies – films that saw him celebrated alongside Joel Schumacher

---

1 *Musicians, Mensches, and Muff-Diving: Ally Sheedy,* Amy Sohn, New York Press, 1998.

as the pre-eminent writer/director of the Brat Pack era – young characters negotiate family and gender roles with the fluency of youth. They're adolescents; questioning traditions is what they do. Hughes' first success, however, had come with scripts that singled out older people – specifically adult males – as a type more confused than teenagers by the demands of contemporary life. *Mr Mom* and *National Lampoon's Vacation*, both released in the summer of '83, put thirty-something husbands and fathers under the microscope of modern life and watched them squirm. Their success at the box-office gave John Hughes his subsequent career.

Even before his time in advertising had brought him into the *National Lampoon* office in New York, where his talent for writing bagged him a job with Matty Simmons and the team, Hughes' own family life had been colourful. It was what gave him the blueprint for his stories. Growing up in Chicago's conservative Northbrook, the suburb in which he would later set most of his movies and just an hour east from the North Shore of *Risky Business*, the teenage Hughes ploughed his own furrow; a Beatles fan as passionate about the optimistic romance of Frank Capra movies as he was sending in gags to TV shows for comics to use.[1]

Snobbery was in the air, both at home and at school, with John's mother still annoyed at having moved to North Shore from their previous home in a more affluent suburb of Michigan, whilst in class the teenage Hughes went to great lengths to divorce himself from the preppy one-upmanship so associated with high-school cliques. After graduation a career in art beckoned – John could paint a mean abstract mural – but fizzled when he dropped out of the University of Arizona after just a year. Despite a hippy attitude that chimed with the era, by the early '70s the wannabe John Lennon found himself in a suit and working at Chicago ad agency Needham, Harper and Steers. By twenty-one he was already married to his high-school girlfriend Nancy. As a baby boomer, Hughes couldn't help but join the throng in looking back fondly on his formative years of rock'n'roll in the '60s. As a young father, however, he was also experiencing first-hand the complexities of modern family life.

---

1 Rodney 'I don't get no respect!' Dangerfield was an early client.

During the snowbound winter of '79 Hughes wrote *Vacation '58*, a short memoir about a family holiday that so impressed Simmons over at *National Lampoon* that he asked the writer – who'd never before penned a screenplay – to turn it into a script for Warner. If the studio weren't initially sure about involving such a newcomer on the project, the *Lampoon* brand was on such a post-*Animal House* high that they couldn't really refuse Simmons' demands. Plus, the sceptics at Warner didn't know the whole truth, that Hughes was really no novice. Behind the scenes he was already pushing more of his stories to film companies, with Fox moving forward on both another *Lampoon* movie he'd written – *Class Reunion*[1] – and *Mr Mom*, a comedy about a businessman who has to cope with becoming a house-husband.

Mr Mom had been developed by Hughes and Lauren Shuler, a former camerawoman who'd turned producer over at Motown's film arm in the late '70s. *Thank God It's Friday* was one of her early credits, a disco-heavy ensemble movie that Motown made with Casablanca Filmworks about fictional LA club The Zoo, released a few months after *Saturday Night Fever* with little acclaim or box-office. A few months later it was that Michael Jackson-featuring *The Wizard of Oz* remake *The Wiz* that put an end to Motown's movie-making aspirations for good (although Shuler had struck up a good relationship with its writer, Joel Schumacher). Audiences, it seemed, really didn't want to see the thirty-four-year-old Diana Ross play a teenage Dorothy. Shuler left Motown and went out on her own. Like Matty Simmons at *National Lampoon*, it was John Hughes' writing for the magazine that quickly came into her mind when she was looking for projects. She called him up.

Hughes and Shuler had backgrounds that weren't dissimilar – she from Cleveland, just an hour's flight from Hughes' beloved Chicago – and the producer was only a few months older than the film-maker. But when Shuler told Hughes about an idea she had for a film he didn't bite. Instead he wanted to tell *her* about a few days in his life when he'd had to stay at home and look after his young kids – with disastrous consequences. Shuler loved it: 'It was

---

1 *Class Reunion* was later disowned by Hughes.

hilarious! I was on the floor laughing. He said, "Do you think this would make a good movie?" And I said, "Yeah! This is really funny!" So he said, "Well, I have about eighty pages in a drawer. Would you look at it?" So I looked at it and said, "This is great! Let's do it!" We kind of developed it ourselves. There's a whole complicated story about how we set it up but ultimately we did set it up.'[1] Those eighty pages became *Mr Mom*.

That *Mr Mom*'s original script had been significantly tweaked by others by the time it eventually released in the summer of '83 – partly because Hughes refused to leave Chicago and work on rewrites in LA – didn't make its story feel any less prescient. Hughes and Shuler had made a film whose easy laughs were underpinned with genuine questions about gender equality in the suburbs, the story of a once-traditional businessman whose recession-era job loss forces him to re-evaluate his role in the world and his family. Several elements in *Mr Mom* would even later become Hughes trademarks: beginning a story at the start of a day, the audience thrust into the chaos of family life in the morning; the affectionate ribbing of the nine-to-five office world, something of which Hughes had once been a part; wise-ass little kids; plus a *Tom and Jerry*-style battle of wills between two men each looking to be alpha male.

Mr Mom's lead was a thirty-two year old from Pittsburgh called Michael Keaton, cast just as he was getting great reviews for his first film *Night Shift*, a comedy that co-starred Henry Winkler and had been directed by his *Happy Days* colleague Ron Howard. *Mr Mom* was even bigger – around sixty million dollars at the US box-office – and Keaton was pushed on to the radar of Amy Heckerling,[2] whilst Hughes himself was now being eyed up by Universal, where Thom Mount had heard good things.

That a studio would want to sign up Hughes made sense. At the same time as *Mr Mom* was paying dividends for Fox that summer of '83, Warner were also hitting big with Hughes' adaptation of that *Vacation '58* short story – by now rechristened *National Lampoon's Vacation* – directed by *Lampoon* regular Harold

---

1 ign.com, Kenneth Plume, 30 November 2000.

2 Heckerling went on to cast Keaton in the middling *Johnny Dangerously* (1984), a Mel Brooks-esque gangster movie spoof.

Ramis and starring *Saturday Night Live* favourite Chevy Chase as another bumbling father, Clark Griswold; a middle-aged dad just one beat out from the rest of the world. Like *Mr Mom*, it also featured ideas later to become Hughes standards, most obviously the road movie format. Squash a family into a car for a long time and something funny *always* happens. With two hit stories under his belt over just one summer, Hughes was duly snapped up by Universal for a three-picture deal.

But how to start? Hughes was eager to begin this new life with his pet project *The Breakfast Club*: a high-school chamber-piece set over the course of one Saturday detention that featured a small cast of characters and was set mainly in one location (the school library). Best to kick off his directing career on something modest and low-budget, he reasoned. Plus, *The Breakfast Club* was already in the planning stages with A&M Productions, with whom Universal had a good relationship and Hughes had even begun to try out young actors in Chicago in a search for the right group of kids.[1]

The studio, however, had other ideas. Hughes had succeeded with family comedies like *Mr Mom* and *Vacation* so of course, *that* was what they wanted more of; something straightforward rather than stagey to kick things off. So it was *Sixteen Candles* – the story of a teenage girl's birthday getting forgotten by her family – that became Hughes' first for Universal whilst *The Breakfast Club* was put on the back-burner. Both would be produced by Ned Tanen, now the ex-boss of Universal having recently left to form Channel Productions, where he was working with former Francis Coppola assistant Michelle Manning.

'I'd been with Francis about three years and that's usually your lifespan with him,' said Manning. 'I'd done *The Outsiders* and *Rumble Fish* . . . and the executive at Universal for *Rumble Fish* was Sean Daniel . . . he said, "I want to introduce you to Ned Tanen, who's starting a company."'[2] That first meeting with Tanen was tough – Manning had become used to working outside of the Hollywood bubble with the unconventional Coppola – but she

---

1 Alan Ruck – from *Class* and *Bad Boys* – was in those original auditions, considered for the role of John Bender.
2 Author interview.

recommended John Hughes to Tanen, having overheard a couple of Warner executives (Lucy Fisher and Mark Canton) discussing him whilst they were all on a private jet one day. Tanen, a supporter of first-timers, was intrigued and Manning got the script for *Sixteen Candles* sent over. Tanen read it that night, and by the next day Channel Productions had worked out a deal to produce Hughes' first film for Universal. When he later showed *The Breakfast Club* script to Channel, they agreed to produce alongside A&M too.

If *Sixteen Candles* saw Hughes temporarily depart from collaborating with his original female muse Lauren Shuler, their relationship was far from over. What's more, this was the film on which he first worked with the fifteen-year-old girl he would turn into the heart and soul of not just his directing debut but also two more of his subsequent teen pictures. A headshot of Molly Ringwald – still a student at west LA's Lycée Francais – which Hughes had been sent from the ICM talent agency was pinned above his desk as he scripted *Sixteen Candles* one weekend; he wrote it for her even though the two had never even met.

'[He saw] a kindred spirit, I think. He also liked my face,'[1] Ringwald would later reason, perhaps never entirely understanding exactly why a thirty-three-year-old man would want to write a story for a teenage girl. But her bond with Hughes was about more than just the two of them sharing a birthday.[2] This was hero worship: 'I feel like we sort of mutually idealised each other from the get-go.'[3] In the space of just a couple of years Molly saw her connection with Hughes turn her into the queen of the Brat Pack, despite being younger than many of the guys and not even a key player in the very article that spawned their much-discussed, much-despised name.

'Chronologically, you're sixteen today. Physically, you're still fifteen.' The first words ever spoken by Molly Ringwald in a John Hughes film cut straight to the chase: this was pure teenage angst.

---

1 'Molly Ringwald on life after teen angst', *CBS News* interview with Mo Rocca, 12 June 2012.
2 18 February – also the birthday of Matt Dillon and John Travolta.
3 'John Hughes' Actors on John Hughes', *Vanity Fair*, David Kamp, 10 February 2010.

So whilst *Sixteen Candles* might on occasions have been a film as much about a whole family – as requested by Universal – as their adolescent daughter Samantha (Ringwald), chronicling the stress they *all* felt in the run-up to a big wedding, it was via her emotions that Hughes created his world. It's Samantha who really misses out when she loses her bedroom to visiting grandparents and when everyone in her loveably eccentric family forgets her birthday. Ringwald, for one, appreciated taking that kind of sensitive approach to a young character: 'Usually the kids are portrayed as very one-dimensional. Like these mindless animals that just have three things on their minds: getting laid, getting drunk, and driving real fast over Mulholland Drive. Oh, and hating their parents. I can't stand films that make out kids to be heroes and parents to be imbeciles.'[1]

Hughes' real strength, though, wasn't just writing about those issues. It was also in directing them in a style that was distinctive and sincere rather than thrown together like any number of cheap teen comedies. Capturing adolescent frustration via artfully messy bedrooms and clique-infested school halls and with a soundtrack infused with British new-wavers who were simultaneously breaking through on MTV, Hughes made sure his words had visuals that would both appeal and impress to accompany them. His camerawork was slow and controlled – a static shot of an exterior, a slow zoom on to a face – but each frame was packed with the ramshackle paraphernalia of contemporary teenage life, where a poster for the ballet on Sam's wall mingles incongruously with one of the Stray Cats. If the moves were calm, what went on inside each frame was bristling with as much decorative and inspiring conflict as could be found in an everyday teenager's head.

And *Sixteen Candles* was certainly a celebration of the everyday. Samantha might have felt she was unusual because of her odd family, her nerdy freshman stalker Farmer Ted (Anthony Michael Hall) and her under-developed body but it was precisely those things that made her relatable to an audience. Really it was all about what she *wasn't*: the high-school super-babe Caroline (Haviland Morris), with her movie-star physique and hot senior

---

1 'Molly Ringwald', *Interview* magazine, Margy Rochlin, August 1985.

boyfriend Jake (Michael Schoeffling). Caroline takes her privilege too far – partying too hard, drinking too much – and it doesn't end well for her. It's Sam's sensible normality, emerging from the shadows, that's ultimately the winner.

Central to that averageness was Hughes' *other* muse: Chicago. If LA was seriously showbiz-focused and culturally influenced by its Pacific location, whilst New York felt like the whole world in one location, then Chicago was the biggest 'regular' city in the States. It was its everyday comfort and sense of humour that Hughes so cherished and wanted to get across; this meeting place of beautiful suburbs and prosperity that had avoided much of the recession endured by the rust-belt west[1] (a problem that had been the backdrop of Tom Cruise's Pennsylvania sports drama *All the Right Moves* in 1983). John Hughes' own youth growing up in Northbrook echoed in every scene of *Sixteen Candles*, like a mix of the aptly named *Ordinary People* with the anarchy of *National Lampoon*.

Normality was also exactly what Hughes saw in Molly Ringwald: an average girl, unaware of her own allure, 'something in me that I didn't even see in myself', according to the actress[2]. Yet Ringwald's actual Californian childhood – growing up with her blind musician father Bob, singing with his Fulton Street Jazz Band, even releasing her own album aged six[3] – was far more cosmopolitan than that of Samantha. Aged thirteen she'd appeared in Paul Mazursky's *The Tempest* with John Cassavetes, nominated for a Best Newcomer at the Golden Globes in the process. By the time of *Sixteen Candles* she liked to read Salinger, writing down her thoughts about life and dream of heading to Berkeley; hardly outrageous teenage activities but certainly more intellectual than Sam.

'I'd been acting professionally since I was a child; I was pretty well-travelled and a lot more urban. Most of those characters were in small suburban towns outside of Chicago, really sort of

---

1 Much of *Sixteen Candles* was shot in Skokie, Illinois – aka 'the world's largest village'. Chicago wasn't all middle-class comfort though. Thirty minutes south took you to regions such as Englewood and Riverdale, which suffered from high crime rates and low incomes.

2 Spoken during the tribute to Hughes at the eighty-second Academy Awards, 7 March 2010.

3 *I Wanna Be Loved By You: Molly Sings.*

representative of a certain type of girl in the United States at a certain moment. Not necessarily representative of me.'[1] What was more, if *Sixteen Candles* was a hymn to what Hughes considered normal, then its 'comical' approach to Chinese exchange student Long Duk Dong (played by Gede Watanabe, a twenty-nine-year-old Japanese American) suggests a hardly enlightened approach to race relations[2] whilst Jake and Farmer Ted's treatment of a drunk Caroline – where they essentially admit that she's so out of it, they could do anything to her – was no less problematic.

Still, in the middle of a spate of male-led teen sex comedies, *Sixteen Candles* gave a regular teenage girl her own personality and depth, her own feelings. Even better, it did so with moments of a casual, teenage earthiness; talk of sex, periods and well-placed swearing in lines such as, 'They fucking forgot my birthday!' that had previously been reserved for the boys. Nineteen-eighty's trio of *Foxes*, *Little Darlings* and *Times Square* had come close but were still in either their style or their seriousness (or both) distinctly of the previous decade. The girls in *Fast Times at Ridgemont High*, meanwhile, felt more believably commonplace but were only part of a large ensemble. Come 1983 and with the fresh, florid femininity of new wave music and fashion at its disposal, plus a knowing cheekiness[3] that Hughes had perfected with his work at *National Lampoon*, Samantha's position at the centre of *Sixteen Candles* felt truly pioneering. Ringwald herself might not have been the type to hang out with the guys at the Hard Rock Café – even by the time of Blum's article in 1985 she was still too young to drink – but her association with the Brat Pack, factual or not, would at least infuse the often belligerent brand with some easygoing and relatable feminine charm.

How did the thirty-something John Hughes manage to make movies for people half his age that felt so authentic? A promotional

---

1 'Molly Ringwald: your former teenage crush', *Observer*, Mark Blackwell, 11 August 2012.

2 A gong sound accompanies his every appearance. Unfortunately, Hughes' depiction of urban St Louis in *National Lampoon's Vacation* hadn't been much more enlightened.

3 Exemplified by Hughes' tongue-in-cheek use in *Sixteen Candles* of retro TV theme tunes – *Peter Gunn*, *Dragnet* – and cartoonish musical stings; a postmodern wink that would resurface in later films.

photo taken on the set of *Sixteen Candles* goes some way to explaining. In it Ringwald, Hughes and Schoeffling sit together in deliberately the same pose: legs crossed, hands on knee, the two guys in jeans and plaid shirts with sleeves rolled up. The age difference is clear but still, Hughes looks at ease with the two teenagers, like he's part of the gang. The mid-'80s popularity of British music certainly helped him, the first time the UK had been at the centre of pop for twenty years and something which drew Hughes back to his own adolescence as a Beatles fan. The pop scene was a way in, a shortcut into the life of the contemporary high-schooler and he would talk passionately with Ringwald about current favourites such as New Order and The Cure, each of them making mix-tapes for the other ('One of my favourite things to do when I was doing movies in Chicago would be to go to his office at his house and go through his record collection,' she remembers[1]).

What Hughes felt – and Hughes was very much a writer of feeling – about their friendship he fed into his scripts, many of them churned out Jack Kerouac-style in single sessions, unfiltered emotion favoured over careful construction, at least in the early drafts. In an era where the teen film had become increasingly calculated and crafted for the mainstream, at least Hughes – himself no slouch in the marketing department – kept his heart and soul in his stories. And it's all there in that photo, a writer/director as close to his characters as he could be without actually starring in his movies himself. Yet in some respects he really *was* in those films – his personality in every song, every declaration of love, every poster on a wall – less a father figure, more a cool older brother or wise uncle who never left the adolescence he so enjoyed back in the '60s.

Whilst shooting this film about family, Anthony Michael Hall had brought a member of his own – his aunt – on to the set with him. Like Ringwald, he was still only fifteen and so needed a guardian; one of the downsides to filling a movie with genuine teenagers. Also like Ringwald he was the offspring of a jazz musician (his mother was the singer Mercedes Hall) and he'd been

---

1 'John Hughes's Actors on John Hughes', op. cit.

working for several years like her too, in commercials and on stage. When *Sixteen Candles* had wrapped the young stars with so much in common did their best to date one another, despite living on opposite sides of the country. But as their director, Hughes saw plenty of differences in the two – 'Molly is a little more precise, Michael is a little wilder'[1] – and it was Hall who he'd encouraged to improvise at the *Sixteen Candles* auditions in New York, to bring in some of his own humour. Hall didn't do Method; a couple of weeks studying at the Actors Studio had taught him that. His approach was far more down-to-earth and he played geeky Farmer Ted as simply 'a typical freshman'[2], also avoiding the nerd stereotyping – thick glasses, hair parted, pens in breast pocket – that was prevalent in other teen comedies. Hughes had first noticed Hall's easy charm when he'd played Rusty Griswold in *National Lampoon's Vacation*, stealing scenes from Chevy Chase with his casual chattiness; unguarded but not loud, goofy but not off-puttingly so. Impressed, Hughes subsequently signed up Hall to be in all three films he'd agreed to make for Universal.

Sixteen Candles was a hit, making back nearly four times its 6.5-million-dollar budget, but the second picture in Hughes' deal with the studio was the one he'd wanted to make first; the one that really fired his heart. And if *Sixteen Candles* had used the single central figure of a teenage girl as a way to get emotional, then *The Breakfast Club* would inject her feminine sensitivities into all its characters. It even began with a quote from the most famous gender bender in rock: David Bowie.[3]

Hughes gave *The Breakfast Club* script to Ringwald as filming on *Sixteen Candles* was coming to a close and she signed on to the story of teenage-bonding-during-Saturday-detention to play high-school princess Claire; all surly pouts and Ralph Lauren outfits. The rest of the group was made up of Anthony Michael Hall as naïve whizz-kid Brian, Ally Sheedy as mop-haired and

1 '*Sixteen Candles*' Sweet Teens Graduate to Stardom by Acting Their Own Ages', *People*, Jeff Jarvis, 4 June 1984.
2 Ibid.
3 Quoting lyrics from Bowie's 'Changes' over the opening credits had been – according to the film's DVD commentary – Ally Sheedy's idea.

mousey Allison (a role that Ringwald had originally wanted) and Emilio Estevez as wrestling jock Andrew. But at the centre of it all was the story's real transformation, the fifth cog in the wheel: Judd Nelson as angry tough guy John Bender, who goes from anti-social to anti-hero as he and his fellow detainees learn to share their feelings during that long day[1] in the school library. The five schoolkids start out the story as individuals, all stamped with their own brand – a brain, a beauty, a jock, a rebel, a recluse – even arriving for their punishment at Shermer High School in a way that succinctly sums up their personality (Andrew's burly father drops him off in a pick-up; Allison gets out from the back of her parents' luxury Cadillac and they drive off without a word; John turns up on foot). But by the end of the day they are a group: 'Five strangers with nothing in common, except each other.'[2]

Nelson's New England upbringing in a middle-class Jewish family, highly respected in the Maine legal world, was a long way from Bender's blue-collar poverty but a spell with Stella Adler in New York had taught the actor, then in his early twenties and supporting himself by working in a candy store, about the power of getting into character. He'd already appeared in Cannon's attempt at a *Trading Places*-style high-school movie called *Making the Grade* plus Kevin Reynolds' Spielberg-funded directorial debut *Fandango*. *The Breakfast Club* would see him playing younger than in either. But he relished what Hughes' script had to offer, the opportunities for his character, despite it being another of the writer's whirlwind stories conceived in just a few days.[3]

Hughes' directing style on *The Breakfast Club*, however, was anything but whirlwind; more measured than on *Sixteen Candles*, with the streamlined story and single setting allowing his camera to switch smoothly between remaining static – allowing action (if any) to enter its frame rather than go looking for it – and fluidly curling around or zooming in, gliding gently towards faces as the kids begin to unwind and open up (as when Andrew confesses to beating up a school nerd). It all makes for a calmly matter-of-fact

---

1 The film is set on 24 March 1984.
2 Tagline, used for the film's later release on DVD.
3 Early titles included *Library Revolution* and – wait for it – *The Lunch Bunch*.

experience, not like someone trying too hard to be gimmicky or fashionable, and the simple shots of empty corridors, alumni photos, hallway graffiti and trophy cabinets carry an almost documentary-style zen. At the Steenbeck editing table was legendary editor Dede Allen, approaching her retirement after years of groundbreaking work on such New Hollywood benchmarks as *Bonnie and Clyde*, *Serpico* and *Dog Day Afternoon*, now trimming Hughes' extensive raw footage into something of a manageable running time and with a distinctive, arresting rhythm.

But there was also that tension, that disquiet between the modesty of the camera and the passion of the emotions on show. And it's John Bender who sets off those emotions, all flick knife and attitude, simmering with ADHD and one-liners that explode like dirty bombs in the quiet of the library. Responding to Bender's prodding – poisonous but effective – the characters finally open up to their similarities, to their shared misery of teenage indifference and parental bullying.[1] 'We're all pretty bizarre. Some of us are just better at hiding it, that's all,' Andrew admits, a wrestler normally more interested in takedowns than heartfelt testimonies. Even Bender himself moves away from his bitterness and by the film's final moments has saved the group from further punishment by acting as a distraction for vindictive invigilator Mr Vernon whilst the others sneak around the hallways, unseen. The most uptight tough guy in the school has learned self-sacrifice.

After such a breakthrough in the plot – a turning point no doubt helped along by everyone taking a puff on Bender's weed – there can be only one way to celebrate: an impromptu dance (to 'We Are Not Alone' by Chicago vocalist Karla DeVito). Andrew's jerky moves might look more at home in the gym whilst Allison's are as erratic as her personality but it's a pure music video moment, film-making indulgence meeting youthful optimism. It confirms pop's power to unite all backgrounds, for boundaries to melt away. Together, they can get through this. It's MTV bottled.

After ninety-seven minutes, *The Breakfast Club* concludes with a shot that tells everyone what it is *really* about. Detention

---

1 The film was shot in sequence, a fairly unusual practice but one which can only have helped with genuine cast bonding.

finally over, John Bender walks back home across the football field, still feisty but now softened by the day's events and feeling an opposites-attract tenderness towards princess Claire. As the group's punishment essay for Mr Vernon is read aloud in voiceover – 'You see us how you want to see us, in the simplest terms, with the most convenient definitions. But what we found out is that each one of us is a brain and an athlete and a basket case, a princess and a criminal. Does that answer your question? Sincerely yours, The Breakfast Club' – Bender raises his right hand and punches the air, victorious. It was an ad-libbed move by Nelson but it hit the perfect note. Bender has had the biggest transformation over the day, the craziest emotional roller-coaster, confirmed when he – the bullish bruiser, in leather gloves and a lumberjack shirt – put Claire's delicate diamond stud into his own punky earlobe. He finally felt like a winner.

The Breakfast Club released through Universal[1] in February 1985, four months before David Blum's article gave a name to the Brat Pack gang, yet Nelson's performance as Bender was the ultimate statement of their boisterousness even before it was saddled with the term. Here was a good-looking but troubled tough guy whose virile bravado was impossible to ignore. No journalist could miss someone like *that*.

Nelson had even raised eyebrows during his audition, deciding to arrive in character and full of Bender's attitude, frustrating others who waited with him in the process. Tensions were also reportedly high during filming between Nelson and Ringwald – their approaches to acting so different – and even between Nelson and his boss, John Hughes. Yet what's often forgotten about John Bender is that way that he changes ('bends', if you will). He's not all bombast. To end the film a victor with his arm raised he needed to discover compassion and understanding too, Hughes only giving him closure after he gets in touch with his sensitive side. If Blum's article hardly portrayed the boys from the Brat Pack as emotional, at least one writer had given them characters who were.

* * *

---

1 Co-produced by Tanen and Manning's Channel Productions and A&M.

John Hughes' visual style was never as intimidating as *Flashdance* director Adrian Lyne's – for him it was less about harking back to film noir as it was about judiciously capturing contemporary teenage life – and *The Breakfast Club* placed emotional sincerity over any fashionable techniques from the advertising world. But Hughes' musical passion led to soundtracks as carefully chosen as any of Lyne's artfully lit silhouettes or shadows. Music inspired Hughes' writing too, even those scripts that didn't get off the ground. One was a vague idea for a script set very specifically in 1962, chosen because it was the year just before The Beatles invaded the charts and changed everything (although *American Graffiti* had kind of already done that). Then there was a possible story based on one of the '80s most idiosyncratic hits – and a favourite of Molly Ringwald: 'When *The Breakfast Club* ended, he started writing a script called *Lovecats*, because I played him that song by The Cure, "The Lovecats". I was obsessed by The Cure – still am. I think Robert Smith is an under-rated songwriter. Anyway, I played this song for John, and he started writing a script, and he gave me a mix tape of what the soundtrack was gonna be.'[1] Neither movie surfaced but the music in Hughes' first two films as director had already paid its own homage to British pop, filling them with outsider bands with whom Hughes – and in turn, his characters – found himself identifying.

Ira Newborn worked as a composer with Universal on movies such as *The Blues Brothers* and *Into the Night* and teamed up with Hughes on *Sixteen Candles*: 'He was very intelligent. And he also had, I must say, really excellent taste in rock'n'roll. I don't see it that much. Usually musicians, maybe. But for a director to actually have, like, right-on sharp taste, especially in English rock'n'roll, it was kind of amazing that he actually had that. He was a very interesting, special kind of guy.'[2] Hughes was also helped music-wise on several projects by industry veteran David Anderle, a former producer and A&R man whose similar passion for British acts made him – briefly – the director's closest ally. Their *Sixteen Candles* soundtrack featured, in various forms, David Bowie,

---

1 'John Hughes's Actors on John Hughes', op. cit.
2 Author interview.

Billy Idol, The Specials, Altered Images and – most prominently – Thompson Twins with their closing love song 'If You Were Here'. The London-based band had once been squatters, then heavily rhythmic post-punks before honing a more radio-friendly new wave sound. Circa '83 they teamed with American producer Alex Sadkin to come up with something even slicker, something more funk-based; they were still futuristic-looking in their boiler-suits and dandily teased hair but now they were influenced as much by US black musical culture as US culture was by their English eccentricity. It was the so-called 'second British invasion' working both ways: dissident America had latched on to these quirky bands from Europe early on, helped by a still rebellious MTV and the passion of outsider film-makers such as Hughes. But when those acts wanted to grow their popularity across the mainstream US they had to make changes. Or to the purists, concessions.

It seemed as if concessions were everywhere in 1985, from Crispin Glover's unhappy time in *Back to the Future* to Sean Penn agreeing to make *Shanghai Surprise*. Now that teen movies and young stars were money-makers, really it was inevitable. Concessions were also something Simple Minds knew all about. When *The Breakfast Club*'s musical composer Keith Forsey – the British drummer who'd worked with Giorgio Moroder and Harold Faltermeyer at Casablanca Records – approached the band with a song for the movie, they had to make a decision. It's true, the former Glaswegian punks[1] had been gradually heading closer to mainstream success, morphing from a prominent UK new wave act with a minimalist sound into something more sonically commanding with 1982's 'Promised You A Miracle'; a bigger stadium sound masterminded by former Thompson Twins producer Steve Lillywhite. But did they really want to aim for the American heartlands with a rock song that had already been turned down by Forsey's regular associate Billy Idol, as well as Roxy Music's dapper frontman Bryan Ferry and which they hadn't even written themselves?

The band were shown a rough cut of *The Breakfast Club* in London and lead singer Jim Kerr hardly responded favourably:

---

1 Originally known, oh-so-romantically, as Johnny and the Self Abusers.

'We didn't give a toss about teenage American schoolkids.'[1] They needed to though. Despite tours in the States – *and* Kerr being married to an American, Pretenders' chief Chrissie Hynde – Simple Minds' US label A&M were struggling to get the band to crossover. Everyone knew that something *had* to give. So after some arm-twisting from label, management and Hynde – herself once considered for vocal duties on the track – the group met with Forsey and found themselves bonding with him over krautrock, Donna Summer and alcohol. The deal was on.

The song was reworked from Forsey's sketchy demo and magnified into a huge chunk of power-pop with a video[2] shot in an old British mansion for added grandeur. Guitarist Charlie Burchill, like the rest of Simple Minds, was initially sceptical: 'So you've got this movie about US high-school kids, with a song by a band from Glasgow in a manor house in England. It was the thinnest of concepts, but it became huge.'[3] 'Don't You (Forget About Me)' was a US No. 1 in May 1985, after Madonna's *Vision Quest* hit 'Crazy for You' and ahead of other UK acts such as Dire Straits and Duran Duran, also reworking their originally esoteric British sounds into melodies significantly more grand in scope. Like Thompson Twins, Simple Minds had made concessions to their sound . . . and were now in the big league. The track by English duo Tears for Fears that knocked 'Don't You (Forget About Me)' from the American summit even had a title which seemed to say it all: 'Everybody Wants to Rule the World'.

So whilst *The Breakfast Club* soundtrack stuck to Hughes' faith in British bands of the time, it was also significantly rockier – more mainstream American in sound – than that of *Sixteen Candles* and much of what he would curate after. It was a direction in which a lot of Brit bands were headed, after all. What's more, for a film about simmering anger, perhaps tougher tunes made sense? John Bender – diamond earring or not – hardly looked like someone who would listen to The Smiths.

Nevertheless the dandyism of the British new wave still got a

---

1 'Simple Minds: How We Made "Don't You (Forget About Me)"', *Guardian*, Dave Simpson, 15 November 2016.

2 Directed by Daniel Kleinman, later best known as creator of many iconic James Bond title sequences.

3 *Guardian*, op. cit.

look-in on *The Breakfast Club*, courtesy of London band Wang Chung, originally an independent three piece called Huang Chung[1] but who'd found fame in the USA on Geffen Records with 'Dance Hall Days' at the start of 1984; a song later featured in that year's *Bachelor Party*. Wang Chung – Jack Hues,[2] Nick Feldman and Darren Costin – played it quirky in the 'Dance Hall Days' video, posing campily in chunky-knit sweaters and playing violins. They weren't exactly Bon Jovi. *The Breakfast Club*'s dorky Brian, you'd guess, would have been a huge fan.

Elsewhere, an American act on *The Breakfast Club*'s soundtrack also had European musical connections. Elizabeth Daily was a twenty-three-year-old singer and actress[3] signed to A&M and dating actor Jon-Erik Hexum at the time of his death in October 1984. Her track 'Waiting' was, like much of the music for *The Breakfast Club*, co-written by Giorgio Moroder stalwarts Keith Forsey and Steve Schiff, with Daily's resulting album largely produced by Harold Faltermeyer. By the time of *The Breakfast Club*, Daily had lined up a cameo to sing during a school dance scene in A&M's next movie – teen comedy *Better Off Dead* – and would soon be seen acting alongside squeaky man-child Paul Reubens in Tim Burton's feature debut, *Pee Wee's Big Adventure*, released in the summer of '85. Daily was pure California – born in LA and sporting the city's archetypal big blond hair of the mid-'80s – but her sound on 'Waiting' was the perfect blend of American rock with chic European synths and echo. It was Team Moroder's trademark,[4] after all, and 'Waiting' played out like sultry west coast rockers Heart mixed with Germany's electro-futurists Alphaville; a style that wouldn't have seemed out of place on the award-winning *Flashdance* soundtrack on which Forsey had worked. 'That's what got us *The Breakfast Club*. I had just come off that Oscar win with Moroder and I guess people thought that I had the credibility to compose a score. Whether I did or not was

---

1 The first note of the Chinese classical musical scale, in case you didn't know.

2 Yes, that's right: '*J'accuse*'.

3 *Valley Girl* was an early acting credit. *Fandango* and *Streets of Fire* followed.

4 In a 2015 interview, Steve Schiff listed the artists he listened to in the early '80s as 'Psychedelic Furs . . . The Associates . . . Roxy Music, all those Brit art school groups and – what the hell? – Aerosmith and Cheap Trick too,' micki-steele.net, 29 January 2015.

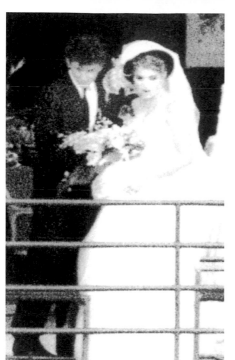

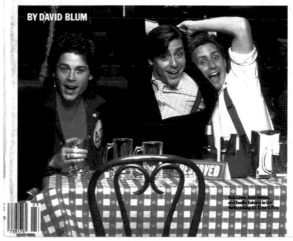

$1.75 • JUNE 10, 1985
Ronald Reagan's Great Right Hope, by Laily Weymouth
Fashion: Easy, Breezy—and Priced-Right—Summer Style

NEW YORK

HOLLYWOOD'S BRAT PACK

BY DAVID BLUM

Rob Lowe, Judd Nelson, and Emilio Estevez in the forthcoming St. Elmo's Fire.

The Malibu wedding of Sean Penn and Madonna, 16 August 1985 (paparazzi helicopters out-of-shot). Madonna was the epitome of '80s celebrity, a ruthless ambition that outshone even pop rivals Prince and Michael Jackson when it came to cultural ubiquity. The spotlight-shunning Penn suddenly found himself making headlines for all the wrong reasons. (Topham/AP)

David Blum's 1985 article for *New York* magazine coined a phrase but seriously pissed off its subjects. The front cover used a photo from Joel Schumacher's *St Elmo's Fire*, featuring Rob Lowe, Judd Nelson and Emilio Estevez, selling the Brat Pack as a bunch of boys with too much attitude and not enough talent.
(© New York Media LLC)

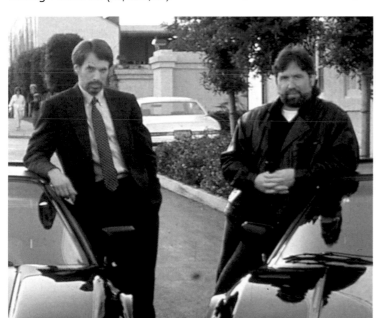

Jerry Bruckheimer *(left)* and Don Simpson *(right)*: sharp-suited, Ferrari-driving, high concept-loving, soundtrack-shifting super producers. Working with British ad man Tony Scott on the shamelessly ballsy *Top Gun* (1986) turned Tom Cruise from a teen pin-up into a megastar, just as they had done with Eddie Murphy in *Beverly Hills Cop* (1984). (Henry Groskinsky/Getty images)

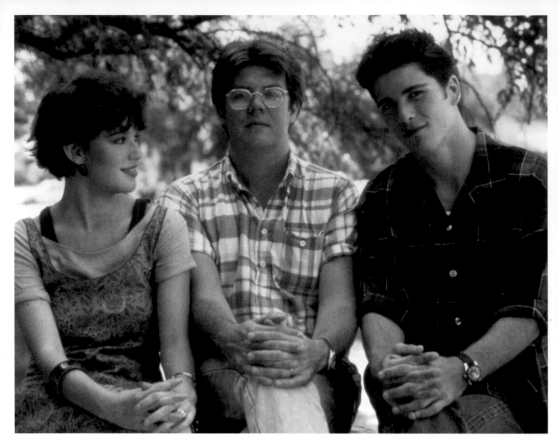

John Hughes worked with many members of the Brat Pack but his stories of teenage family life often brought with them a more female-skewed sensitivity. It was sophisticated teen actress Molly Ringwald who became the thirty-four-year-old film-maker's muse (pictured here with the director and her *Sixteen Candles* co-star Michael Schoeffling). (Universal/Kobal/REX/Shutterstock)

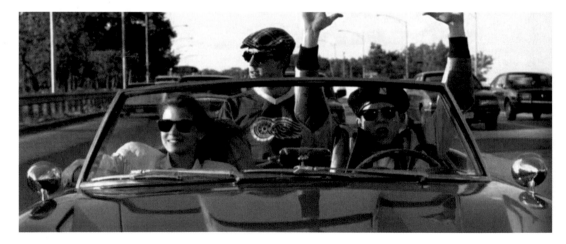

Cameron (Alan Ruck) doesn't look quite as happy to be bunking school as Ferris (Matthew Broderick) and Sloane (Mia Sara). *Ferris Bueller's Day Off* was John Hughes's 1987 teen movie swan song and his most accomplished yet: an anything-goes hymn to young friendship, first love and a cool guy who could do it all. (Paramount/Kobal/REX/Shutterstock)

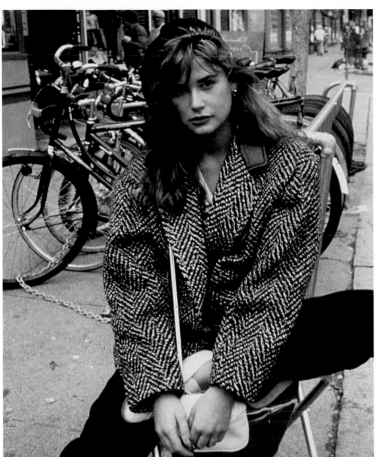

Like her contemporaries, Demi Moore hated her Brat Pack tag but a colourful adolescence and an engagement to Emilio Estevez made it difficult to shake, not to mention her scene-stealing as wild child Jules in *St Elmo's Fire*. Time out to work in theatre and a marriage to Bruce Willis helped Moore change her image from sulky teen to powerful modern lead. (© Columbia Pictures/Courtesy Everett Collection/Mary Evans Picture Library)

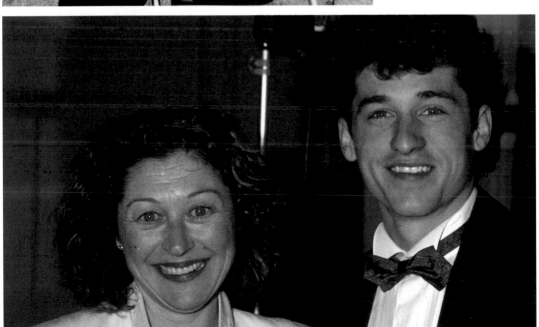

With many teen stars determined to move on by the mid-'80s, Patrick Dempsey briefly found himself a leading pin-up thanks to the success of the Hughes-esque *Can't Buy Me Love* (1987). Dempsey's private life was anything but adolescent though. In 1986, the twenty-year-old married Rochelle Parker, an acting coach over twice his age. (Jim Smeal/Getty Images)

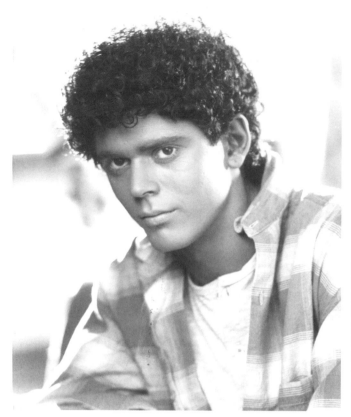

C. Thomas Howell had one of the more interesting post-Brat Pack outings with 1986's cult thriller *The Hitcher*. However, trying to do his bit for the African-American community by 'blacking up' a year later in *Soul Man* proved a big cultural – although not financial – mistake. (© New World Pictures/ Courtesy Everett Collection/Mary Evans Picture Library)

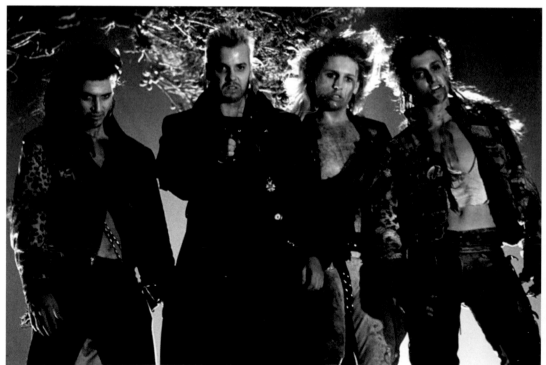

Four of the *Lost Boys (left to right)*: Billy Wirth, Kiefer Sutherland, Brooke McCarter, Alex Winter. Joel Schumacher hadn't wanted to direct what was originally a spiritual sequel to *The Goonies* but signed on when the script was made dirtier and sexier. The cast and crew made sure they all lived up to the tagline: 'Sleep all day. Party all night'. (Ronald Grant Archive/Mary Evans Picture Library)

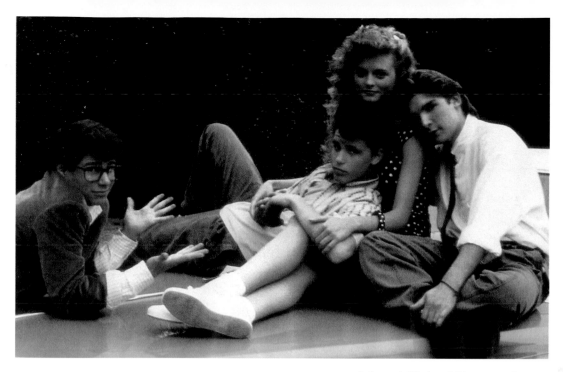

A SERIOUSLY SEXY COMEDY

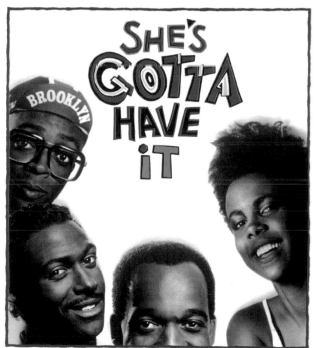

SHE'S GOTTA HAVE IT

BROOKLYN

ISLAND PICTURES PRESENTS
A SPIKE LEE JOINT
"SHE'S GOTTA HAVE IT" STARRING TRACY CAMILA JOHNS
REDMOND HICKS · JOHN CANADA TERRELL · SPIKE LEE · RAYE DOWELL · MUSIC BILL LEE
PHOTOGRAPHY ERNEST DICKERSON · PRODUCTION SUPERVISOR MONTY ROSS
PRODUCTION DESIGN WYNN THOMAS · ASSOCIATE PRODUCER PAMM JACKSON
PRODUCED BY SHELTON J LEE · WRITTEN, EDITED, & DIRECTED BY SPIKE LEE

ISLAND PICTURES

(above) Michael Manasseri, Corey Haim, Heather Graham and Corey Feldman pose with that most essential of '80s teenage commodities: a car. *License to Drive* (1988) saw the Two Coreys promoted to leading men but the inoffensive story masked the real troubles they faced growing up in the limelight. (© 20thCentFox/Everett Collection/Mary Evans Picture Library)

(left) Spike Lee took the urban youth drama away from hip-hop cash-ins such as *Breakin'* (1984) and into classier, independent realms with *She's Gotta Have It* (1986). Nola (Tracy Camilla Johns) was a young woman who lived life on her own terms, bewitching Jamie (Tommy Redmond Hicks) and Gree (John Canada Terrell) in the process. *She's Gotta Have It* was unflinching, Lee's college-set follow-up – *School Daze* – even more so.
(A Mule Filmw/REX/Shutterstock)

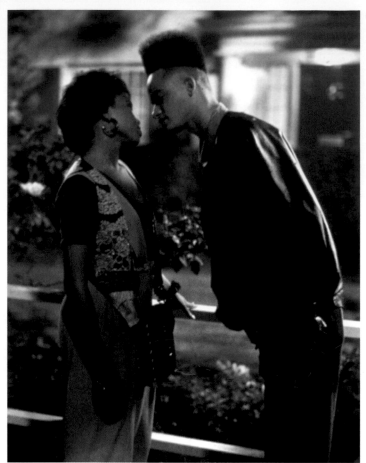

Reggie Hudlin's *House Party* (1990) didn't shy away from social issues but was bright and funny with it, the lighter side of new black cinema. Christopher 'Kid' Reid (pictured with Tisha Campbell) was the breakout star, although his high-top fade haircut almost stole the show. Such was *House Party*'s crossover success that Kid and his partner Christopher 'Play' Martin got their own kiddie-friendly TV cartoon. (Moviestore/REX/Shutterstock)

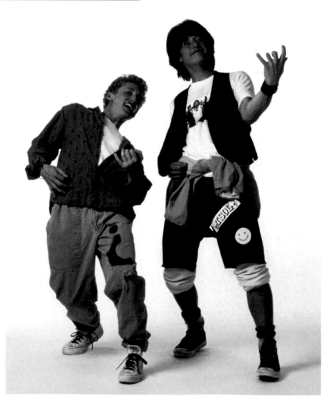

1989's *Bill and Ted's Excellent Adventure* (starring Alex Winter and Keanu Reeves) took the heavy metal slacker culture so bleakly portrayed in *River's Edge* a few years earlier on a knowing and comedic spin through history. The result was a teen movie that both winked to the genre's past and nodded to its future. (© Orion Pictures Corp/Courtesy Everett Collection/Mary Evans Picture Library)

Winona Ryder at the New York premiere of *Great Balls of Fire*, 26 June 1989. *Heathers* had been another cult teen hit for her and co-star Christian Slater earlier that year but meeting fellow bohemian Johnny Depp (just after this photo was taken) would see Winona go from being Hollywood's favourite gothic girl-next-door to half of its coolest couple. (Ron Galella/Getty Images)

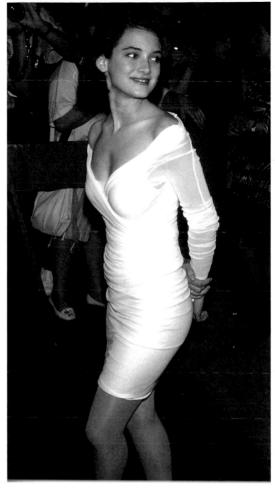

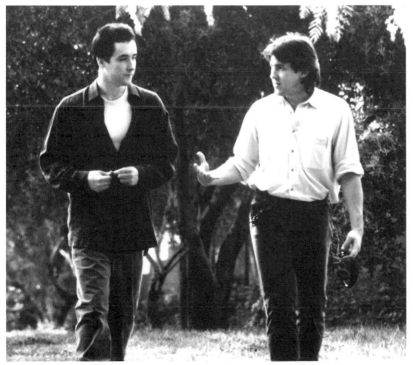

John Cusack *(left)* was a teen movie veteran by the time of *Say Anything* in 1989, but the reluctant star was proud of only a few of them. Here he discusses playing *Say Anything*'s gentlemanly oddball Lloyd Dobler with the film's writer/director Cameron Crowe. It was Cusack's last film in the genre and – finally – one he was truly happy to be part of.
(© 20thCentFox/Everett Collection/Mary Evans Picture Library)

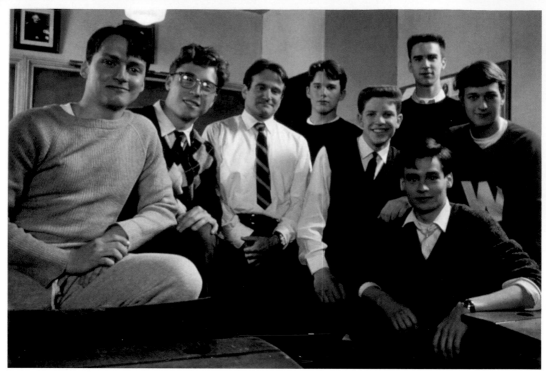

The decade ended with a journey back to 1959 in *Dead Poets Society*, but this coming-of-age tale was far from cosy. Its hints at the alternative pop culture of the '60s mirrored what awaited music and film in the '90s. *(left to right)* Gale Hansen, Allan Ruggiero, Robin Williams, Ethan Hawke, Dylan Kussman, James Waterston, Josh Charles, Robert Sean Leonard *(seated)*.
(© Buena Vista Pictures/Courtesy Everett Collection/Mary Evans Picture Library)

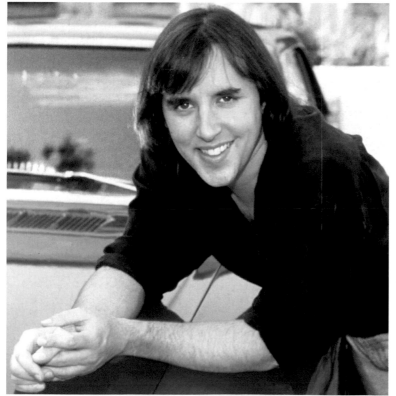

Richard Linklater shot *Slacker* in Austin, Texas, during 1989 for a budget of $23,000. He was influenced by the 'movie brats' of the '70s but *Slacker* nevertheless gave a contemporary name to a burgeoning alternative youth movement. Indie cinema had exploded in the mid-'80s with films by Spike Lee and Jim Jarmusch but Linklater – along with contemporaries Gus van Sant and Quentin Tarantino – was about to make it even hotter.
(Ronald Grant Archive/Mary Evans Picture Library)

something else.'[1] Forsey's insecurity aside, his blend of musical styles was an ideal match for the film's plot. The five members of *The Breakfast Club* started out their day as sturdily individual American archetypes but they ended it as a group of open-hearted outsiders. It was a story about getting in touch with emotions. What better way to express that awakening than with songs that blended old-school, muscular, homegrown US rock with hi-tech, rather feminine Europop?

As much as *The Breakfast Club* relied on Hughes' distinctive direction, it still had a healthy distrust of *too much* style. What's underneath – we're told – was what really counted. It was why, for many, Allison's late-in-the-day makeover by Claire felt like one concession to the mainstream too many, a cop-out plot point where the characterful oddball apparently only becomes attractive to Andrew once she's lost her distinctive couldn't-care-less look and is turned into someone more traditionally 'girly'.[2]

But look closer and it's maybe not quite so simple. There's actually no suggestion that Allison's eccentric *personality* will completely change with a dash of mascara; she's still the same kook, just with a different façade. If anything, what the makeover really shows is the superficiality of fashion, how *easy* it is to change. That's not a bad thing; indeed it's the first chance most kids get to express themselves and get creative. But as *The Breakfast Club* makes abundantly clear, thinking you know people based on their image is a bad idea and Allison is living proof that looks can so easily change. Even John Bender, for all his new found sensitivity, will at some point probably take out Claire's earring and go back to how he started. That's just adolescent life, kids regularly switching from look to look just like they were flipping through TV channels. And it's that tension that lies at the heart of all Hughes' high-school pictures: if teenagers find image changes so easy then relationship changes will probably be just as simple.

---

1 'Slow Change May Pull Us Apart: The Oral History of Simple Minds' "Don't You (Forget About Me)"', *Spin*, Andrew Unterberger. To my ear, 'Waiting' seems to owe a lot to *Flashdance*'s 'He's a Man'.
2 Sheedy had herself questioned Hughes about the makeover, wanting it to be more about Allison simply losing her heavy gothic look rather than Claire turning her into a dollish girl-next-door, complete with Alice band. She lost the argument.

Nothing lasts forever. So 'Don't You (Forget About Me)' wasn't just a sentence that scanned nicely when Keith Forsey originally wrote it. It was an emotional plea for this one thing the group felt they had by the end of detention – sincere friendship – to not be just another fashion or fad, but to last. Yet deep down, we all knew it couldn't.

The cast themselves were changing fast. Anthony Michael Hall turned sixteen in April 1984 whilst filming *The Breakfast Club*, receiving the requisite razor, after-shave and condoms as presents from his cast mates and prepping for his third movie with Hughes. Molly Ringwald, meanwhile, wanted to broaden her horizons after filming in Illinois and headed with a bunch of her friends to summer camp in the south of France. Emilio Estevez, six years older, had more grown-up things to deal with: his then girlfriend Carey Salley gave birth to their son Taylor in June and Estevez initially struggled to face up to the responsibility, whilst career-wise he had those pet projects of which Blum would be so disparaging. Meanwhile, Ally Sheedy, an actress who had always felt her literary New York background left her at a slight remove from other up-and-coming stars – and who had battled bulimia in varying degrees since her days as a ballerina – finally began to get comfortable: 'It was enjoyable there for a while. I felt like I had this network of friends, all doing the same thing, all very young, all of whom had managed to realise their dream. It was the first time in my life that I really felt I belonged somewhere.'[1]

Then there was Judd Nelson. In playing John Bender with an intense individualism straight from the De Niro school of acting, he brought dissidence into a fun '80s teen movie hit in a way that even Penn hadn't managed.[2] And – also unlike Penn – he seemed quite happy to publicise his work, doing TV interviews about *The Breakfast Club* looking more like someone from Duran Duran than a detention room, all suave slicked-back hair and sharp jacket.[3] Here was someone whose face carried both a powerful sadness and a clever determination, a look that promised the best

1 'On the Upswing', *LA Times*, Richard Natale, 10 June 1998.
2 *The Breakfast Club* made over twice as much as *Fast Times* at the US box-office.
3 Check out his 1985 interview (alongside Ringwald) with NBC's Bobbie Wygant for sartorial evidence.

of the past *and* the present ('Ally and I were like, "He's Al Pacino for our generation",'[1] remembers producer Michelle Manning). With a tailwind behind him after filming with Hughes (Nelson 'creates the strong center of the film' Ebert would later write in his review[2]) the actor left Chicago and headed to Washington to reunite with Estevez and Sheedy but this time playing someone closer to his age. In *St Elmo's Fire* he was still a young buck, full of attitude and big ideas, but this time his character hadn't just left high school, he'd actually left college too.

As stylised as Hughes' films were, on set he would often be found hanging out with his teenage stars rather than debating technical decisions with his colleagues. He trusted the right people to make it work.[3] For Joel Schumacher, however, cinematic detail had always been everything: 'I started as a two-hundred-dollar-a-week costume designer in Christmas of 1971. But I wanted to be a movie director since I was seven. I grew up on a poor neighbourhood in New York and my father died when I was four and my mother was out at work six days a week and three nights a week so I was a pretty wild child out on the streets from the age of seven on. I grew up in the shadow of a big movie palace. The fire doors I could literally see from my bedroom window; they were across the street. And I lived in that movie theatre, snuck in many times. I was one of those kids that had to be dragged out many times. This was . . . before television. Being a visual sensationalist, there were only comic books and the movies. I just lived in the movie theatre.'[4]

Joel moved around the worlds of costume and production design in the '70s, impressing Woody Allen with his work on comedy sci-fi *Sleeper* and austere character study *Interiors*: 'Woody really encouraged me to write because, of course, that's how he came to directing, through writing.'[5] Scripts for soul music

---

1 Author interview.

2 Where he also complained about *The Breakfast Club*'s unnecessary R-rating (for swearing), writing that it should really be PG-13, *Chicago Sun-Times*, 15 February 1985.

3 Ally Sheedy mentions this during a Q&A celebrating the film's twenty-fifth anniversary at Lincoln Center, New York, 20 September 2010.

4 Author interview, broadcast on BBC Radio 1, op. cit.

5 Ibid.

drama *Sparkle* (Tagline: 'From the ghetto to superstars') and urban comedy *Car Wash* followed for producers Robert Stigwood and Art Linson, positioning the gangly Schumacher – with his fashion degree and Swedish heritage – as the somewhat unlikely voice of the black movie musical; an image that saw Motown's film boss Lauren Shuler hire him for her disco remake of *The Wizard of Oz* too. If neither that nor a directing debut, with 1981's cheekily feminist *The Incredible Shrinking Woman* starring Lily Tomlin, were blockbusters, then Schumacher had at least proven one thing: he might now be in his forties but he could still stylishly tap into a trend.

It was watching local college kids in Georgetown, a suburb of Washington in which he was living whilst shooting Guber and Peters' comedy *DC Cab* for Universal, that inspired Joel Schumacher to write *St Elmo's Fire*. And it was another zeitgeist-tapper: 'This was the middle of the '80s and during "Reaganomics", as they called it in the States, and it seemed to me there was so much pressure on young people. You had to come out of high school or university having a twenty-five-year plan and they were recruiting all these kids into corporate jobs. Everyone was dressing up and looking very "yuppie-fied" and having BMWs and being glamorous and socially unconscious and I thought, They're kids! This is tough. There must be a lot of pressure right now to be an adult and what a pressure it must be on a group of friends who have vowed to be friends forever. So I wrote *St Elmo's Fire*.'[1]

Schumacher's Motown friendship with Lauren Shuler saw her agree to produce *St Elmo's* along with Ned Tanen's Channel Productions[2] but its content, cast and title didn't make for an easy ride. Pre-production was in 1984 – the blockbusting year of *Ghostbusters* and *Gremlins*, *Red Dawn* and *Purple Rain* – and Schumacher had scripted young adults more coldly career-focused and shockingly self-centred than had been seen before. Shuler and Tanen's casting recommendations from their relationship with John Hughes – Estevez, Sheedy and Nelson – had also yet to break out as box-office stars.

---

1 Ibid.

2 By the end of 1984 Tanen had gone back into the safety of the studio world, becoming head of motion picture production at Paramount.

Then there was that title. St Elmo's was the bar in which the characters liked to gather, itself named after a natural phenomenon in which coloured light appears in the air after a thunderstorm – a metaphor used in the film to indicate life's problems as just a mirage – but it was so obscure that audiences would think (executives at distributor Columbia told Schumacher) that this was a story about a fire or a saint. Ultimately, the film-maker had to use the movie's outsider status to his advantage: 'It was only because the film was relatively cheap that I was allowed to get away with so much.'[1]

And what Schumacher 'got away with' was hardly subtle. Hughes had contrasted the simplicity of his camera moves with the maelstrom of emotions going on in each shot, but Schumacher was more bluntly grandiose and gimmicky with his lighting, sets and cinematography. Why contrast when you can just throw everything into the pot? So after its opening credits – titles in blood red, obviously – *St Elmo's Fire* began with big drama: a group of friends hurry to a hospital emergency room to be with two of their own, bad boy Billy (Rob Lowe) and clean-cut Wendy (Mare Winningham), who have been involved in a drunk-driving car crash. Neither are badly hurt and Billy shows off his swagger by sitting in the back of an ambulance, bathed in the film's already favourite shade of red light, playing saxophone and flirting with an orderly; a moment of pure Schumacher posing.

Meanwhile, inside the hospital, the turmoil continues to heat up with puppyish Kirby (Emilio Estevez) realising his old college crush Dale (Andie MacDowell) is now a doctor . . . and he's head-over-heels in love all over again. When the friends – including sullen writer Kevin (Andrew McCarthy), suited yuppie Alec (Judd Nelson), trainee architect Leslie (Ally Sheedy) and party animal Jules (Demi Moore) – then head to their beloved drinking den to let their hair down, Schumacher captures the night-time bustle of a Georgetown bar with a probing camera which floats grandly through the crowds, more of that red lighting soaking every shot in anguish, capturing the drama in Cinemascope to give it some grown-up stature. As opening salvos to films about

---

1 Author interview, op. cit.

youngsters went, it was exhausting but undeniably earnest and exhilarating; a long way from the wacky domesticity that began many a John Hughes story. 'The heat this summer is at Saint Elmo's Fire' ran the tagline, with the theme tune more of a straightforward scorching rock anthem than anything Hughes would use.[1] The drama had moved from bashfulness in the classroom to zealousness in the bar. Schumacher wasn't messing about.

Demi Moore's Jules Van Patten was as vacuously ambitious in *St Elmo's Fire* as Judd Nelson's John Bender was angrily pessimistic in *The Breakfast Club*. 'This is the '80s,' she proclaims, defending an affair with her middle-aged boss. 'I bop him for a few years. Get his job when he gets his hands caught in the vault. Become a legend. Do a black mink ad.[2] Get caught in a sex scandal. Retire in a massive disgrace. Write a bestseller and become a fabulous host of my own talk show!'

It's Jules who gets hooked on coke, Jules who finds herself massively in debt and Jules who drinks too much and ends up in a hotel room with strange, MTV-watching Arab businessmen. In a movie where style was everything, Jules had the most distinctive: her outfits all power suits and pearls, her new apartment – decorated on credit – a roar of reds and pinks, complete with a giant mural of pouting Billy Idol on one wall. For the 'visual sensationalist' Schumacher, *St Elmo's Fire* was a story that conveyed its message as much through differing interior designs as dialogue, from Jules' high-fashion condo to Kevin and Kirby's boyish basement and from Dale's settled suburban comfort to Lesley and Alec's grown-up minimalism. Meanwhile, Billy – wayward and unsettled, with a wife and baby he's reluctant to acknowledge – seems to just sleep wherever he can.

It's when the characters invade each other's worlds – Lesley sleeping with Kevin in his studenty bedroom, Kirby turning up on Dale's doorstep – that the already heated drama really explodes.

---

1 A US No. 1 for the admittedly British singer John Parr, albeit one produced by Canadian power ballad specialist David Foster and with members of Californian soft-rockers Toto on session duties. This was *not* sensitive English electro. Parr had originally written the uplifting, anthemic song about inspirational Canadian Paralympian Rick Hansen – the 'man in motion' mentioned in the lyrics.

2 A black mink fur coat. The Blackglama brand had been using iconic stars such as Barbra Streisand, Judy Garland and Joan Crawford since the late '60s.

Clashing design tastes are shorthand for clashing attitudes to marriage, to politics, to careers. Suddenly a group who thought they could be friends forever find that such big claims – whilst manageable at college – aren't so easy to maintain in the real world. When Jules can take no more it's in her high-end flat that she decides to end her life; a home now emptied by debt collectors of much of its furniture. As she sits against a giant red wall and watches the curtains billow dramatically from an open window, the only decor left a huge toy Pierrot doll, it's the moment when this little girl finally realises she's tried to grow up too quickly. And it's her desperately opulent decor that's always given her away.

Moore's casting was somewhat of a fluke. Schumacher spotted her in his office block on the Universal lot, the actress in a strop because she'd been waiting for a meeting with another film-maker who had his set-up there: a certain John Hughes. It was an impetuousness that caught Schumacher's eye and even Moore herself realised she couldn't have been better-suited to the role of an impulsive party girl, telling a Kansas newspaper at the time of *St Elmo*'s release: 'Jules lives on the edge; something I know very well. I moved out of my mother's house when I was fifteen. I travelled a lot as a kid – my dad was in advertising – and I never felt I had any roots, any friends. So I became obsessed with the idea of being liked. And I did things which got me acceptance . . . when I hit big with [daytime soap opera] *General Hospital*, I wasn't sure how to deal with the sudden burst of fame. I was a little girl and, like Jules, I didn't know how to cope. I didn't know how to say "No".'[1]

St Elmo's Fire had premiered to much buzz at the Palladium in New York, having already had its release date moved up from the autumn by Columbia when they sensed a post-*Breakfast Club* hit. Around the same time as it hit theatres – early August 1985 – Demi finalised her divorce from Minnesotan rocker Freddy Moore. He was lead singer with The Nu-Kats and the pair had met in an LA club in 1979, she aged sixteen, he in his late twenties and already married. The start of the '80s had been monumental for the teenage

---

1 'Demi Moore learns to accept change', *Lawrence Journal-World*, 11 July 1985.

Demi: just after she discovered that the man she'd called dad – Danny Guynes – wasn't actually her biological father, he ended his life through carbon monoxide poisoning. Five years later and with *St Elmo's* playing in cinemas across America, the girl born Demetria Guynes might now no longer have been married to Moore but she had decided to keep her ex-husband's surname. She was also already in another relationship too, albeit a rather casual one with Emilio Estevez, himself 'on a break' from the mother of his child, Carey Salley.

But at least Moore was now clean; only a few weeks before *St Elmo's Fire* had started shooting she had come out of a spell in rehab for substance abuse.[1] So if Nelson had tapped into Method acting for his portrayal of John Bender, Moore's ability to play Jules Van Patten was much more natural. She was almost playing herself. And even though Moore had missed Emilio's fateful night out with David Blum, when *St Elmo's Fire* hit big she nevertheless found her place in the Brat Pack well and truly cemented. Ally Sheedy and Molly Ringwald might have been more sensitive in their lives on screen and off, helping Hughes and Schumacher to inject the movement with its intriguing feminine sincerity, but Demi Moore was playing it like one of the boys.

---

1 As detailed in 'Eye of the Tiger', *People*, Gregory Cerio, 24 June 1996.

Chapter Thirteen

BRAND HUGHES

The John Hughes empire expands with Weird Science; Ferris Bueller's *(fantastical)* Day Off; Some Kind of Wonderful – *the last gasp?; and back to the past with* Dirty Dancing.

Teenagers had long been sensitive. That was nothing new. What was more novel was a film-maker showing those kids on screen, seeming to tap into their everyday concerns with a mix of comedy and reverence. And even if John Hughes couldn't give every high-school subculture a voice,[1] it was clear to Molly Ringwald that there were plenty more simmering beneath the surface: 'I feel like [he] was writing a lot of gay archetypes. But at that time it really wasn't sort of acceptable – you know, a character in high school couldn't just be gay. But I mean, c'mon . . . the way that Duckie [in *Pretty in Pink*] treats me, he's written totally as the gay best friend – there's no sexual chemistry between us!'[2]

'Feminising' men in some way, from Jack in *Mr Mom* to John in *The Breakfast Club* had long been of interest to the film-maker, chiming neatly with a time in pop music and fashion where the glamorous, androgynous New Romantic movement that began in London's underground clubs at the turn of the decade – a reaction to the earthy violence of punk – had crossed the Atlantic and morphed into something that could now be seen daily on MTV

---

1 Ethnic diversity, for example, is virtually non-existent in his teen pictures.
2 'Molly Ringwald: your former teenage crush', op. cit.

via gender-bending synthpop bands such as Culture Club, Depeche Mode and A Flock of Seagulls.[1] But not everything John Hughes wrote was so open-minded. *The Breakfast Club* had originally included a *Porky's*-style scene featuring the gang spying on Shermer High's unusually sexy female PE teacher as she got ready in the locker room for synchronised swimming training, before complaints from Michelle Manning, Molly Ringwald and Ally Sheedy led to its removal.[2] A female shower scene in *Sixteen Candles did* make it into the final cut and, whilst shot from Sam's point of view and not overtly sexual, its intentions never felt entirely noble. Considering Hughes' background at *National Lampoon*, perhaps these moments of questionable bawdiness shouldn't be surprising. Their brand had broken new ground with its blend of nostalgia and anarchy fifteen years earlier but it was still a mainly male set-up that couldn't resist a smutty joke or flash of female flesh among the satire. And before Hughes' most sensitive, open-minded teenage love triangle hit the big screen – Andie, Blane and Duckie in 1986's *Pretty in Pink* – his own brand still had a little more of that randy, teen-boy naughtiness to get out of its system.

Weird Science was Hughes' third film for Universal, shot back-to-back with *The Breakfast Club*, with Anthony Michael Hall playing alongside former teen ballet dancer Ilan Mitchell-Smith as Gary and Wyatt, nerdy sophomores who dream of hanging with the cool crowd. To make their fantasy a reality, the pair 'create' the perfect girlfriend on Wyatt's computer one night which, when mixed with a little bit of hacking and a whole lot of fantasy, results in super-babe Lisa (Kelly Le Brock) appearing from nowhere, complete with both a superior brain *and* a willingness to do anything the boys want. Naturally their first choice is to watch her take a shower.[3]

---

1 Although just like the Brat Pack, the New Romantic movement was one that few bands actually wanted to admit being part of.

2 As mentioned in *John Hughes: A Life in Film*, Kirk Honeycutt, Race Point, 2015.

3 Teen sex-comedies owe a surprising amount to the popularity of the shower. What had started out as a communal bathing device in the military and sports worlds, briefly becoming a place of sexual danger via *Psycho, Carrie* and *Dressed to Kill*, it was soon the de facto setting for naked female flesh in teen boys' fantasies; *Porky's, Risky Business* et al.

Hughes' producer on *Weird Science* was Joel Silver, a thirty-three-year-old former New Jersey boy who'd worked his way up the ladder at Lawrence Gordon Productions from being the boss's driver to exec-producing on movies such as *The Warriors*, *Xanadu* and *48 Hrs.*, his passion for big-spending leading to frequent clashes with studios.[1] *Weird Science* was his second movie out on his own, in charge of Silver Pictures, but what would later become familiar attributes of his output – namely brash action and cultish fantasy/horror[2] – were already visible in the teen comedy, lending the story a cartoonish, shouty style a long way from the contemporary cool of *The Breakfast Club*.

Ira Newborn – on composing duties once again following *Sixteen Candles* – knew Joel Silver of old, from working on live music shows when Joel had been a gofer to showbiz impresario Jack Good. In fact, Hughes and Newborn had only met in the first place thanks to an introduction from the larger-than-life Silver: '[Joel] was constantly getting into trouble, constantly having people from the studio after him to skin him, because he did one thing or another that they couldn't stand,' remembered Newborn.[3] The chalk-and-cheese partnership of Silver and Hughes seemed odd on paper but the composer saw in practice how they learned to deal with their differences: 'There are so many unlikely partnerships in Hollywood that turned out well that it's ridiculous . . . yes, Joel was a motormouth; he would talk to everybody, do everything, run in fourteen directions, his emotions would go up and down, up and down. John was definitely quiet. He was funny and had a lot of enthusiasm but it was contained. I heard them say more than once, "I'll never work with that guy again," but I've seen it before, it's nothing new. It's like a loud husband and a quiet wife or a loud wife and a quiet husband; they can deal with it. And in Hollywood there's always something down at the bottom of it all: it's called money.'

Hughes brought the teenage emotions to *Weird Science*, of course, but it was Silver who had bought the rights to the sci-fi

---

1 Expertly detailed in 'The Epic Saga of Joel Silver: Money Struggles, Feuds and (Another) Second Chance', *The Hollywood Reporter*, Kim Masters, 29 April 2015.
2 cf. *The Matrix* and *Lethal Weapon* franchises.
3 Author interview.

source material, a pulpy '50s comic with the same name. Hughes had spotted piles of copies in Silver's office one day and loved the title, one issue in particular featuring a story called 'Made of the Future' in which a newly single man travels forward in time and makes use of a service dubiously known as 'Construct-A-Wife': a conceit that may have influenced Hughes when coming up with his film.[1] The original creator of that and many other strips for *Weird Science* comic, Al Feldstein, had eventually found his love of risqué topics – including his trademark statuesque women characters – curtailed after the stifling Comics Code Authority came into being in 1954, formed in an attempt to cut back on the juvenile delinquency authorities believed to be caused by such cheeky publications. But in a post-*Porky's* world Hughes would have no such problems with *his* version of the story.

Put one of Feldstein's '50s Amazons into an '80s aerobics outfit and you'd get Kelly Le Brock; a big-haired, pillow-lipped pin-up who looked as if she'd come straight from the latest flesh-filled heavy metal music video. The twenty-four-year-old Anglo-American model had needed convincing to take the role of Lisa, being by this time married to businessman Victor Drai – producer of her breakthrough movie *The Woman in Red* – and already living the high life. 'I had actually turned down *Weird Science* initially because I was in the south of France with Sting. I was with my first husband, he was doing a movie there. I was like, "Work . . . or play with Sting?" and I decided not to work.'[2]

When Le Brock said 'No', Hughes instead signed up another Kelly, Texan *Sports Illustrated* model (and then partner of Rod Stewart) Kelly Emberg. After three weeks of shooting, however, he was back on the phone to Le Brock to try and persuade her to take over from a clearly miscast Emberg – and this time she accepted. When the brunette arrived in Chicago shortly after, she found a shoot that was over-running so much no one even had the time to give her new outfits. She wore Emberg's clothes, secretly pinned and cut to suit her different body shape, for the rest of filming.

---

1 A popular idea although there is no confirmation.
2 mediamikes.com, Adam Lawton, 20 December 2010.

As well as an unusually brassy film-making partner in Silver[1] and a hurried shoot, *Weird Science* was saddled with other quirks. Here was a story where unexplained 'magic' made anything possible, most obviously when Wyatt and Gary's computer tinkering appears to go beyond mere zeroes and ones and accidentally sets off some kind of supernatural electrical storm that directly leads to the birth of their very own *Playboy* bunny. Such 'magic' even made outfits change as the boys walked from one room to another, could alter the letters on a car number plate in the blink of an eye and wiped Gary's folks' minds of any memory of their son's high-jinks. These new-fangled computers, eh? It all made a film such as *Frankenstein* – Universal's 1934 classic that's frequently referenced in both *Weird Science* and its theme song – seem almost grittily realistic in comparison to the teen picture's flights of fancy. And while those fantasies are certainly funny, they couldn't help but interfere with John Hughes' usual focus on 'normal' life that he'd honed so perfectly in *Sixteen Candles* and *The Breakfast Club*.

Interfered, but didn't ruin. Away from the pyrotechnics the trademark Hughes' family dynamics were present and correct: Wyatt's older brother Chet (Bill Paxton) terrorised him like a psychotic army sergeant would a rookie recruit, whilst Gary's bland parents were clearly indifferent to what was really going on in the head of their beloved son. Wyatt's bedroom was also styled straight from the director's heart, complete with posters of The Human League and Chicago (the city, not the band) whilst the soundtrack slipped British new-wavers Orchestral Manoeuvres in the Dark and Killing Joke, plus bonkers American art-rockers Oingo Boingo, into a more generally boisterous soundtrack.

Even the location of *Weird Science* is familiar, set once again in Hughes' made-up Chicago suburb of Shermer, exteriors shot using the same (derelict) Niles East High School in Skokie as both *Sixteen Candles* and Paul Brickman's *Risky Business*. And most significantly there's the central message of *Weird Science*, something reassuringly down-to-earth: Gary and Wyatt should forget trying to be popular and just be themselves. As Lisa gets

---

1 The gregarious Silver was also, incidentally, one of the originators of the ultimate frisbee competition.

to educate her two charges, her role slowly progressing from mere eye-candy to life coach, she even spells it out to the boys: 'People like you for what you are, not what you can give them.' It's only by realising their worth that they can woo classmates Deb (Suzanne Snyder) and Hilly (Judie Aronson) away from egocentric brats Ian (Robert Downey Jr) and Max (Robert Rusler). 'I think Gary and Wyatt are going to cause everyone to redefine their terms,' predicts Lisa; and she is right. Get past the bullying Chet being magically transformed into a giant turd and *Weird Science* was still a recognisably Hughesian story of sensitive outsiders coming out of the shadows and finding their moment in the spotlight; of guys understanding the need to be more sensitive in order to be better people. It's just that it has to jump over a whole bunch of unintelligible trickery and pseudo-science to get there.

Weird Science released at the start of August 1985, up against a surprisingly large number of other teen-boffin movies such as *Real Genius* (a campus comedy directed by Martha Coolidge), *My Science Project* (students discover a portal to another dimension) and – still on release – *Back to the Future*, as well as the *National Lampoon* sequel *European Vacation*, turned down by Anthony Michael Hall so that he could work again with Hughes.[1]

Ghostbusters had no doubt helped make science sexy the year before – and would itself get a big-screen re-release come the close of summer 1985 – but *Weird Science* only posted half the box-office of *The Breakfast Club*, making a decent – if hardly spectacular – twenty-four million dollars in the US. Home video proved to be a more forgiving market. If critics noted that Hughes might be somewhat stretching himself with his third outing as writer/director in just over a year – the dreaded 'compromise' seeming to affect even the teen movie world's poet laureate – at least Hall's performance came in for praise, his series of funny voices and facial expressions providing the effortless animation that some of the story's more outrageous moments sorely lacked. Hall also enjoyed working with the gregarious Joel Silver. 'He

---

1 *European Vacation* saw Jason Lively replace Hall as Rusty Griswold.

schooled me on many topics.'[1] Who needed real education when you had a party animal producer to teach you about the good life?

When John Hughes' next teen rom-com, Paramount's *Pretty in Pink*, followed in February 1986 it was a return to what the poster boasted was 'the real world',[2] away from the fantastical high-jinks of Wyatt, Gary and a strangely powerful home computer and back to the film-maker's more recognisable territory. Molly Ringwald, fresh from her post-*Breakfast Club* stay at a summer camp in France,[3] was also back to keep things resolutely normal, playing a character that she saw as being the closest yet to her own personality.

Paramount had reportedly wanted Hughes to sign their glamorous *Flashdance* star Jennifer Beals as *Pretty in Pink*'s lead. Beals had made just one movie during her time at college – horror film *The Bride*, co-starring Sting and the very reason for Kelly Le Brock hanging out in Europe pre-*Weird Science* – but Beals had fielded lots of offers of vacation work, including the chance of a part in *St Elmo's Fire*. Despite the studio's approach, she once again plumped for Yale over Hollywood.

Yet even with Hughes' favourite girl-next-door Molly Ringwald in *Pretty in Pink*, exactly what constituted 'the real world' could now no longer just be as simple as a bunch of kids earthily complaining about their parents. The film-maker, his stars *and* his favourite bands were heading ever closer towards mainstream stardom, success in the previous year now challenging their previous outsider status. Plus, whilst John Hughes was still sensitive to everyday teenage emotions, he was also a businessman. And he wanted his business to grow.

It was with *Pretty in Pink* that the building really began. Although Hughes was writer and producer, his prolific creativity saw him already committed to direct another project, thus leaving the day-to-day helming duties to a protégé, a stand-in who could

1 Hollywood Spotlight, realhollywood.com, 15 July 1989.
2 'The laughter. The lovers. The friends. The fights. The talk. The hurt. The jealousy. The passion. The pressure. The real world.'
3 Where she had actually felt very out of place since it turned out to be a camp for orthodox Jews. She left early, desperate to return home to her parents.

help double the brand's output: thirty-five-year-old New Yorker Howard Deutch. Really, Hughes had always preferred the writing process to the minutiae of directing and he simply wrote too much to be able to be behind the camera every time. Deutch was looking for a break too – he was a former music industry advertising man who'd cut his teeth shooting videos for Billies Idol and Joel as well as working on promo material for films including *Rumble Fish* and *The Breakfast Club*. Handily, he shared his boss's approach to creating a story, strongly based in finding laughs in the everyday: 'If you're able to put humour into something, just like it happens in life, you might get away with it. And we did.'[1]

Yet *Pretty in Pink* never scrimps on showing a tougher side of city life, a poverty not so blatant in other Hughes scripts, and a world in which lead character Andie (Molly Ringwald) must eke out her existence: a life of train tracks, garbage trucks and a crumpled, unemployed father (Harry Dean Stanton) who sits on a deck chair in his front yard and sips beer. It was a long way from the 'richies' who dominate Andie's life at high school, adolescent yuppies such as the louche Stef (James Spader[2]), a suited Aryan man-child whose cruise through life is so unencumbered by anything approaching effort that he seems to be permanently leaning, lounging or lolling, his expensive white clothes baggy on his slack body, his cigarette hanging limply from his lips, as if he can't even be bothered to make the effort to puff properly.

Pretty in Pink brought these opposing lifestyles together by centring on Andie's unconventional romance with Stef's best friend Blane (Andrew McCarthy), a relationship that leads to plentiful culture-clash moments; from clueless posh boy Blane mistakenly buying an unhip album at the indie record shop in which Andie works to Andie finding herself in a thrift store outfit at a rich kids' party, where Stef and his sometime girlfriend Benny (Kate Vernon) have ditched most of their clothing altogether. As a statement about the gap between the rich and the poor in Reagan's America, Deutch made sure that *Pretty in Pink* couldn't have been more clear.

---

1 '*Pretty in Pink* director Howard Deutch on why he owes everything to John Hughes', ET Online, Stacy Lambe, 25 February 2016.
2 Who auditioned for the role in character, obviously.

Yet without Hughes at the helm, the style that had been so prevalent in *The Breakfast Club* was somewhat diluted in *Pretty in Pink*, his unusual angles and bold, music video-style cuts watered down by Deutch into a more conventionally told tale. Interiors still helped to enrich the story, from Andie's wildly cluttered and creative bedroom that apparently mirrored Ringwald's own to the sadly minimal den of her best friend Duckie (Jon Cryer), the simple mattress on the floor and graffiti on the walls saying more about his troubled home life than any dialogue could. But there's always a sense that, had Hughes himself been behind the camera, it would have probed and pushed the cacophony of inspirations that infuse Andie and Duckie's punkish lives a little more. Instead, they are in the background rather than celebrated.

Ringwald and Paramount's Dawn Steel shared doubts over Hughes handing over responsibility to a first-timer, concerns that were somewhat allayed when it became clear that Hughes would still be a presence on set. Ultimately the biggest issue Deutch was confronted with came from the general public, those young fans of teen pictures who'd by now latched on to the power of Brand Hughes. When a test audience of kids saw *Pretty in Pink* for the first time, they loved most of it but disagreed – vocally, by booing – with perhaps the most important moment of any movie: the end.

In the original cut, closely following Hughes' script, Andie *doesn't* end up with the sensitive preppie Blane but rather childhood friend Duckie, her fellow indie kid who's been secretly in love with her for years. After a brief falling out over Andie's relationship with a richie, the two comrades are reunited at the senior prom, both in their homemade outfits, both feeling out of place and both realising that they were meant for each other as they dance together, aptly, to Bowie's 'Heroes'.

Yet when that first version unspooled in front of its test audience, Deutch saw a teenage crowd far from happy about watching yet *another* celebration of outsiders sticking together: 'The girls [that were asked their opinion] wanted her to get the boy she wanted. It was that simple . . . '[1] Far from conforming with expectations,

---

1 'Howard Deutch on John Hughes, Shooting Sex Scenes, and How *Pretty in Pink* Prepared Him for *True Blood*', Vulture, Jennifer Vineyard, 18 August 2014.

the public demanded a fairytale, a slice of wish fulfilment where Andie gets to choose who she's with rather than social cliques forcing her hand. 'It's the girl who makes the choice. It's always the woman who makes that decision. And that was my lesson from this movie,' recalled Deutch. Panicked, John Hughes took a few weeks to work out a way to get Andie back into the arms of Blane. Finally, he realised that Blane would have to make a surprise appearance at the prom, on his own, and would need to ask for both Andie *and* Duckie's forgiveness. Then, finally, Andie can make up her mind and Duckie can let his sweetheart go.

Jon Cryer, in only his second major film role[1] but having been allowed a fair amount of input into his character, wasn't immediately convinced by the need for a reshoot: 'I was disappointed. You sorta go, "Oh, I guess I'm not the leading man."'[2] That Ringwald had been ill during the initial shoot had also, perhaps, not exactly injected that original Andie/Duckie hook-up with the passion and energy that it required. So whilst they had chemistry as friends, they didn't as lovers – and audiences could see it. Eventually Cryer came around – 'I think it was kind of appropriate. Duckie always thought he was the leading man and that was his fatal flaw' – and when the trio came to reshoot the scene in LA's Biltmore Hotel, Andie's new finale with Blane was certainly infused with more optimism, showing that class lines can be crossed and that no one – especially women – should just accept the status quo. So even though Jennifer Beals hadn't appeared in *Pretty in Pink*, its conclusion ultimately made it somewhat reminiscent of *Flashdance*. In many ways, it's the more empowering ending.

That Molly Ringwald had fought for the gently tortured Andrew McCarthy to play Blane, rather than Hughes' more intense first choice of Charlie Sheen, certainly helped. McCarthy's Blane might have been privileged but at least he seemed kinda *nice*. So despite the reshoots coming at a time when the actor was performing alongside Matt Dillon on Broadway in Vietnam drama *Boys of Winter* and thus required a wig to cover up a recent

---

1 Following the little seen *No Small Affair*, a 1984 *Risky Business* clone co-starring Demi Moore.

2 'Reminiscing with Jon Cryer about *Pretty in Pink*', *Entertainment Weekly*, Mandi Bierly, 24 August 2006.

crewcut, it wasn't enough to stop the new payoff sewing in seamlessly to the original story.

But still, not everyone was a fan.[1] Hughes' original vision – perhaps based on his own life as a Duckie-style outsider, a victim of snobbery but who finally won his dream girl in wife Nancy – had been to once again celebrate the dweebs and the kooks. Had Ringwald's suggestion to play Duckie, *Weird Science* bad boy Robert Downey Jr, been cast instead of Cryer then maybe a fiery romance between the two poor kids would have felt more convincing. That way Andie's partner-in-poverty might have seemed more like a heterosexual charmer than a gay best friend? Who knows. But certainly, with beige Blane ultimately winning the girl, market demands had made sure that Hughes' more provocative ideals had been compromised. But he couldn't blame studio executives for the change. This one came straight from the mouths of his teenage audience.

The music to *Pretty in Pink* brought with it even more concessions. For starters, Deutch didn't share the same taste as Hughes and needed his arm twisted to use his producer's favoured British new wave over more traditional American rock. Molly Ringwald, meanwhile, pushed for her favourites The Rave-Ups to feature – succeeding to a degree – when they appeared playing live in the film's club scenes but not, to her annoyance, on the accompanying album.[2]

Then there was the *sound* of the bands themselves. Tim and Richard Butler were brothers from England's leafy Teddington who'd formed The Psychedelic Furs in the late '70s, influenced by the raw sound of punk and the art-school pretensions of Bowie, Roxy Music and The Velvet Underground. When they first released their single 'Pretty in Pink' in 1981, from the Steve Lillywhite-produced album *Talk Talk Talk*, it boasted a melody more poppy than was usual for the group – but it still didn't crack the charts.

---

1 According to Shuler it was around sixty per cent of the test audience who wanted the ending changed. Deutch, Shuler and editor Richard Marks all voiced regret over the forced alterations, op. cit. *You Couldn't Ignore Me If You Tried.*

2 In *You Couldn't Ignore Me If You Tried* Susannah Gora also notes how The Rave-Ups' lead singer Jimmy Podrasky was dating Ringwald's sister Beth.

The band would go on to shed members and reboot their sound courtesy of, amongst others, Keith Forsey but to most they were still a campus radio kind of outfit, not hit-makers. And then Molly Ringwald got on board. 'The song ["Pretty in Pink"] was about a girl who kinda sleeps around and thinks it's really cool and thinks everybody really likes her, but they really don't,' Richard Butler explained. '[Then] Molly Ringwald took it to John Hughes and said, "I love this song, we should use this for a movie." He took it away, listened, and wrote *Pretty in Pink*, which totally got the whole thing wrong. It was nothing like the spirit of the song at all.'[1] The band agreed to releasing a smoothed-out re-recording of 'Pretty in Pink' to coincide with the Hughes movie, giving them their biggest hit in the US so far, but deep down they weren't sure about either this new version of their old song or the sudden pressure to capitalise on their mainstream success. For a band determined to be alternative, riding the teen movie wave proved to be a mixed blessing.[2]

They weren't alone. Merseyside's Orchestral Manoeuvres in the Dark had started life with the innovative Factory record label in the UK, then headed to Richard Branson's Virgin, but in the States (where Virgin had no foothold) they were farmed over to Epic and found themselves under-promoted. Keyboard player Paul Humphreys finally saw their profile increase in America when they signed, just like fellow British Virgin artists Simple Minds, to A&M: 'That was when things started to take off. And that was also when we were consciously writing poppier songs, because it was specifically for things – like 'If You Leave' was written for *Pretty in Pink*. And of course that was our really big hit.'[3]

But was 'If You Leave' what the two self-confessed synthesiser geeks had always dreamed of? It had been cooked up quickly, requested at the last minute amid the changes being made to *Pretty in Pink*'s finale[4] and written swiftly since the band were about to go on tour. In the hurry, Humphreys and his bandmate Andy McCluskey also had to make sure the song fitted perfectly

---

1 'Welcome Back! The Psychedelic Furs', *Mojo*, November 2010.
2 The Furs were over by 1991, only to re-form in 2001.
3 The AV Club, Sean O'Neal, 28 July 2008.
4 Hughes had originally wanted their already recorded track 'Goddess of Love'.

tempo-wise with all the footage of kids dancing at the prom.[1] So whilst *Pretty in Pink*'s big-screen success powered the plaintive 'If You Leave' into the US Top 5 – a huge radio hit and popular MTV video – it also suddenly repositioned OMD as mainstream chart stars rather than the electro pioneers they had once been. And, just like The Psychedelic Furs, the band found that kind of success stifling: 'One of the reasons we broke up[2] was because I wanted to get back to more experimental stuff and we were kind of stuck in this electronic-pop thing,' Humphreys has admitted. 'I thought we'd gotten too conventional and really let go of why we got into this, which was to be experimental, but do it in a palatable way.'[3]

Back in the acting world, the reluctant members of the Brat Pack – finally successful but undoubtedly pigeonholed by that very success – couldn't have put their frustrations any better. *Pretty in Pink* released just a week after Mickey Rourke and Kim Basinger brought arthouse S&M to the masses in Adrian Lyne's much-discussed blockbuster *9½ Weeks* but even with such competition *Pretty in Pink* still managed a powerful forty million dollars of its own, pushing Ringwald on to the cover of *Time* magazine that spring (headline: 'Ain't She Sweet') and confirming the eighteen year old as the nation's favourite clean-cut daughter. It's just that this clean-cut daughter was in real life dating Dweezil Zappa, the hipster VJ and guitarist son of 'Valley Girl' rocker Frank and younger brother of Ringwald's friend Moon[4]. Getting into a serious relationship with someone like Zappa was probably not something any of her characters would ever have done, only adding to the feeling that the image Hughes had created for Ringwald – the image that now featured on the front of *Time* and countless other magazines, projected around the world – was something the actress was more than ready to leave behind. If *Pretty in Pink* was the genre's ultimate tale of being yourself and not changing for anyone, Ringwald found that having a celebrity image which

---

1 Due to the way 'If You Leave' was ultimately slotted into the scene, the effect was actually the opposite: the kids looked as if they were dancing out of time with the music.

2 Humphreys left OMD in 1989.

3 The AV Club, op. cit.

4 Dweezil was also briefly in *Pretty in Pink*, playing Andie and Jena's friend Simon.

clashed with your real personality didn't make things quite so simple. She *had* to change for herself.

Even before getting cast in *Pretty in Pink*, Andrew McCarthy was also wanting to move on. He took the role without reading the script and had been somewhat disappointed to find it *another* high-school romance when he did, perhaps explaining a performance as Blane that treads a fine line between deliberately bashful and just plain embarrassed.[1] The lesser known Jon Cryer had no such reservations about playing flamboyant Duckie, the leading men's different demeanours rumoured to have led to some conflict during filming, but it was nevertheless a role that Anthony Michael Hall had already rejected because he also wanted to distance himself from John Hughes High School.

Then there was the film-maker himself, leaving behind the deal with Universal to start again with arch-rivals Paramount, now headed by Ned Tanen after his brief flirtation with independence at Channel Productions. Tanen's return to being a studio boss shocked Hollywood insiders, not least his producer Michelle Manning: 'He had said, "I'll never be an executive again, I'll never wear a suit and tie again, I love producing" . . . [then] one day Dede Allen and I were getting on a plane to go to Chicago where John was shooting *Weird Science* to show him the latest cut of *The Breakfast Club* and Ned said, "I've just made a deal to run Paramount." And I was like, "What?! You said you'd never be a suit again. You'd never do that!" And he goes, "Well, I don't have to wear a suit and tie. That's what Paramount said. And I don't have to go to any of those stupid board meetings!"'[2]

Tanen had a questionable reputation but was still an undeniable draw for many film-makers. 'He was a person who wore this kind of cloak of, "Oh, I'm just a cranky curmudgeon," but it was totally and completely not who he was,' remembered Joel Schumacher, a colleague from all his early work at Universal. 'He was very nurturing and loving to all of us who were under his tutelage.'[3]

---

1 McCarthy has also suggested – to ABC News in 2004 – that his rather mellow *Pretty in Pink* performance might have been because he was hungover for much of the shoot.

2 Author interview.

3 'Ned Tanen dies at seventy-seven; former president of Universal and Paramount', *LA Times*, Dennis McLellan, 8 January 2009.

'Ned Tanen was a genius,' agrees Michelle Manning, 'and brilliant and passionate and the best guy to work for . . . his relationship with John Hughes was great. It was like a father/son kind of thing. Ned so believed in John that he made this huge deal with him when he went to Paramount. That was actually the first deal he made when he went there.'

With his new distribution deal, Hughes literally moved closer to the establishment by no longer working exclusively in his favoured Chicago but in Los Angeles too. The teen auteur and his troupe were up-and-comers no more. With their increasing sway they were now virtually the normal to which they had once provided an alternative.

As if he knew exactly what this new status meant, Hughes started work on his next film before *Pretty in Pink* had even completed shooting; a film ostensibly about a boy playing truant from school but really dealing with so much more. In *Ferris Bueller's Day Off*, Hughes was determined to smoothly unite the outsiders and the cool kids – his past and his present – once and for all. This wouldn't be a film about cliques and clashes but instead one about the sweet spot where populism and radicalism overlap; a celebration of everyone.

Ferris Bueller's Day Off might have been the story of 'one man's struggle to take it easy'[1] but that one man was doing what countless teenagers dreamed of doing: bunking off school so that he and his friends, Cameron and Sloane, can have one last great time together, especially with adulthood looming. But dreams were bigger than reality in *Ferris Bueller*. Everything about the title character was highly idealised, from his clothes to his behaviour and vocabulary; an impossible teenage work of art who borrowed from a range of styles and subcultures before offering them back as a little of something for everyone.

'The sportos, the motorheads, geeks, sluts, bloods, wastoids, dweebies, dickheads – they all adore him,' school secretary Grace (Edie McClurg) had to admit. 'They think he's a righteous dude.' Ferris can, in the words of Cameron, 'do anything' – and indeed

---

1 So the tagline ran. Another was simply 'Leisure rules'

does pretty much that during his day off in the sunshine, mixing up an array of seemingly opposed experiences covering sport to art to fine-dining in a timescale that, in reality, would just never work. But Ferris's fetishised lifestyle makes few concessions to plausibility. Even though their truancy is being tracked by school dean Edward Rooney (Jeffrey Jones), the trio never really come *that* close to being rumbled. When you're with such a hero, how could anyone ever catch you out?

Hughes and his casting team of Janet Hirschenson and Jane Jenkins picked Matthew Broderick to breathe life into the title character, his stage experience a valuable asset in portraying Bueller's out-of-this-world cool ('He wasn't being Ferris. He was playing Ferris. His performance – it's a performance. It wasn't supposed to be real'[1]). Next on the list of possibles, Chicago native and *Sixteen Candles* bit-parter John Cusack, just didn't have that same kind of presence. Broderick was twenty-three by now but still looked younger, on Broadway at the Neil Simon Theatre in the writer's military training drama *Biloxi Blues* when he got the gig with Hughes, turning down a film version of Simon's *Brighton Beach Memoirs* in order to work with the teen movie auteur[2].

Leading *Biloxi*'s stage cast was *Saturday Night Fever* and *Fame*'s Barry Miller, but it was Alan Ruck, in a supporting role as another of the story's army recruits, who'd especially bonded with Broderick during the run and he pushed for a role alongside him in *Ferris Bueller's Day Off*. Ruck had, after all, already worked with Hughes back in those early workshops for *The Breakfast Club*, before the director decided to make *Sixteen Candles* his first movie instead. But Ruck was even older than Broderick, edging towards thirty and already married, and Hughes was concerned he would just seem too mature to be Cameron. The director sought out Emilio Estevez (who said 'No') until, in the audience of *Biloxi Blues* one night and seeing the undeniable chemistry between these two men both pretending to be twenty-year-olds, Hughes couldn't

---

1 John Hughes on the DVD commentary for *Ferris Bueller's Day Off*.

2 The movie of *Brighton Beach Memoirs* was released through Universal at the end of 1986 with Jonathan Silverman eventually taking the lead role of Eugene. It was helmed by its stage director, Gene Saks – a Broadway legend whose distinct voice Matthew Broderick and co-star Alan Ruck knew well, inspiring Cameron's comedy drawl when he pretends to be Sloane's father in *Ferris Bueller's Day Off*.

help but be impressed. Broderick and Ruck were asked to officially audition together[1] and it was there that Ruck saw the penny drop for the director, that the boys' friendship wouldn't need to be faked: 'We didn't have to make that stuff up'. The actor might have been long out of high school but he was still keen to explore this surprisingly sensitive story of young male bonds, especially as it would be with a mate who made him laugh so hard with perfect re-creations of Richard Pryor comedy routines: 'I didn't really think of it as reliving my teenage years as much as just going on an adventure with Broderick.'[2]

In a film where reality is heightened, it for once made sense that the leads should be older than the characters they played. With their background know-how, Broderick and Ruck could infuse Ferris and Cameron with a blend of bravado and brains – a *knowingness* – that younger actors might have struggled with.[3]

'I couldn't have done it when I was actually [that age]. I sorta didn't have the technical chops. I had some ability, I had some talent but I kinda just didn't know what I was doing ... I just think in terms of experience and maybe a little knowledge I did a much better job [aged thirty] than I could have when I was twenty,' Ruck admitted.[4]

Indeed, as Bueller's girlfriend Sloane – a character named after Ned Tanen's young daughter – eighteen-year-old Mia Sara was the only principal actor still a card-carrying teenager. So if Sloane seems to look up to Ferris, wide-eyed and in awe, it's no surprise. Molly Ringwald initially hinted to Hughes that she'd want the role but her mentor had told her she was too experienced for such a supporting part. Sara, on the other hand – despite having already co-starred with Tom Cruise in Ridley Scott's troubled *Legend* – truly felt like a novice. Even her own secondary education experience had been at a highly alternative college in Brooklyn,

---

1 With them at the time, auditioning for Rooney, was Peter Michael Goetz – an experienced stage actor who had appeared with Broderick on stage in *Brighton Beach Memoirs*.

2 Author interview.

3 A situation that probably wouldn't happen today. With the proliferation of social media and online self-expression, kids in the twenty-first century are comfortable with performing to camera from a much earlier age.

4 Author interview.

nothing like the movie's everyday Shermer High;[1] attractive for an actor looking to stretch herself but nevertheless a real challenge: 'The cast were all lovely but mostly my experience was feeling very out of my depth and, you know, flailing. That's just the honest truth. I wish I could say it was a lot of fun but it wasn't for me. I know it's a bummer – but it was a bummer to me at the time!'[2]

Luckily, it's Matthew Broderick, not Mia Sara or Alan Ruck, whose character really needed to seem confident and a natural performer, Ferris dressing up in a variety of costumes that range from the Hawaiian shirt of a man of leisure (complete with cocktail in hand) to the suit and tie of business life when he pretends to be Sloane's father in order to get her out of school. He finally settles on his daywear of white T-shirt, grey trousers, leopard-skin waistcoat, white lace-ups and a leather baseball jacket. They don't especially go together, of course, but, like his personality, offer something to everyone; a mix of styles and signs that could be traced – *should you have the means* – back to Oscar Wilde's flamboyant dandy of late nineteenth-century London, all theatricality and a passion for new experiences.

And like Wilde, Ferris's influences are decidedly British, from his bedroom posters of art-rock fop Bryan Ferry, New Romantics Cabaret Voltaire and English icon Henry VIII through to the Union Flag draped by the door. That Ferris was stereotypically American in some respects, displaying a go-get-'em resourcefulness and determination that supposedly made the film a favourite of then US Vice President Dan Quayle, was one thing. But Hughes making his lead's surname Germanic and his ride of choice an Italian supercar reiterated once again the film-maker's fascination with a more fanciful European culture.

Music-wise, Hughes and music supervisor Tarquin Gotch peppered the film with a sound more eclectic than ever: Mick Jones' post-Clash project Big Audio Dynamite, electro punk dandies Sigue Sigue Sputnik (produced by Giorgio Moroder and with whom Jones had also worked), quirky Swiss experimentalists Yello and two tracks from a band managed by Gotch himself:

---

1 The interiors of which were actually shot in Hughes' alma mater, Glenbrook North High School.
2 *Total Film*, 27 October 2010.

ethereal London trio The Dream Academy.[1] Crucially it's at Chicago's Von Steuben Day parade, held to celebrate German immigrants in America and with Ferris miming to Wayne Newton's über-kitsch 'Danke Schoen', that the teenager truly wows the multicultural crowd. If you can't appreciate the melting pot of influences in today's world then, he hints to Cameron (and to us), you're really missing out.

Fashion-wise, Ferris Bueller and *Pretty in Pink*'s Duckie could almost have been soul brothers but, taking his idealism further than ever before, Hughes made Ferris a character celebrated and loved by everyone – a man totally in control – unlike the downtrodden Duck. Where Duckie gets just one cheeky look-to-camera, after his 'Duckette' (Kristy Swanson) gives him the eye at the prom, Ferris breaks the same fourth wall on numerous occasions, playing to the audience as if it's actually him calling the shots on the whole story, not John Hughes.

Broderick had initially balked at such arch asides, since he'd been required to do something similar onstage in his roles as Neil Simon's Eugene and feared repeating himself. He agreed after conceding that Ferris and Eugene were widely different characters, going on to make chatting to an invisible audience look like a breeze. And that was the point: *everything* worked for Ferris. If Duckie's wildly OTT performance of 'Try a Little Tenderness'[2] turns off Andie, his dream girl seemingly looking for a boyfriend with a little more maturity, then Ferris miming to 'Twist and Shout' has the opposite effect: effortlessly uniting the whole of Chicago.[3] He might have worn the motley clothes of a goofy outsider but, with his appeal to all, Ferris was actually the ultimate *insider*. There wasn't even any doubt about whether he would get the girl or not since he already had her.

Ferris Bueller's Day Off never got overtly political but if proof was needed of how much easier the middle classes have it, it's in

---

1 One was a cover of The Smiths' 'Please, Please, Please Let Me Get What I Want' which had already appeared – in its original form – in *Pretty in Pink*.
2 Cryer had originally shown Hughes his rendition of the duet 'State of Shock' where he sang as both Michael Jackson and Mick Jagger. The latter's Rolling Stones' track 'Start Me Up' was then considered as an alternative before they settled on the Otis Redding classic.
3 Both were choreographed by *Xanadu*'s Kenny Ortega.

those differences; the startling gap in self-confidence between the settled and suburban Ferris and the hard-up and nervy Duckie. Although Ferris complains, 'I asked for a car. I got a computer,' there's no real sense that his parents – a real estate agent and an advertising exec[1] – couldn't afford one (unlike Duckie, bumming lifts with Andie or riding around the backstreets on his BMX). Yet there's also another layer of wealth. The Buellers are nowhere near as moneyed as the parents of Blane, Stef or even Cameron and, as a result, nowhere near as cold-hearted. They clearly love their son and he has no problem with them. They're neither too rich nor too poor. Despite some niggling – Ferris's sister Jeannie (Jennifer Grey) boldly proclaiming of her brother 'I hate him' – really, they're the ideal middle-class family, happily average.

In the real world Broderick and Cryer had plenty of similarities, to the point of being interchangeable. Cryer had started out in the same Broadway play – *Torch Song Trilogy* – that had made Broderick's name ('There was this whole cottage industry of young male actors who were, basically, either understudying for or taking roles from Matthew Broderick at the time'[2]) and he'd also stepped into the actor's shoes on 1984's *No Small Affair* when the original production was shut down after director Martin Ritt's heart attack and Broderick decided instead to head to Italy – amongst other places – to make Richard Donner's fantasy *Ladyhawke*. There was a three-year age gap between the two of them but both Broderick and Cryer had an appealing boyishness; all puppy-dog enthusiasm and cheeky grins.

Broderick had, at first, clashed with Hughes over improvising, something he could never get away with on stage. It's why the director had loved working with Anthony Michael Hall so much; his passion for talking fast, loose and off the cuff. But the quieter Broderick eventually learned the game, switching into a different gear when Hughes needed him to. Watch *Ferris Bueller's Day Off* and you'll see that – like Duckie in *Pretty in Pink* – he's a character that's Brand Hughes through and through: the most charming, best-dressed rebel in Illinois.

---

1 As John Hughes himself had once been.
2 *Entertainment Weekly*, op. cit.

* * *

No director had ever seemed to want to be a teen movie auteur before. Previous makers of multiple youth pictures had done so in the exploitation world, not in something semi-serious, mainstream and stylish. In *Ferris Bueller's Day Off*, however, Hughes happily elevated teenage life into an art form, aligning adolescent friendship with Picasso, Seurat and Ferrari more than with naked girls in showers (although a scene where Ferris, Sloane and Cameron visit a strip club had been in the original script, but was cut for time reasons). If such a mood baffled Paramount executives when they first saw it, Ned Tanen's faith in Hughes paid off when he returned with a new cut worked on with editor Paul Hirsch; a revised version that was not only loved by the studio but which went on to hit over seventy million dollars when released in the US. And Hughes already had another teen movie – *Some Kind of Wonderful* – waiting in the wings with Howard Deutch once again attached to direct (in fact Hughes had written the draft of *Ferris Bueller* during a cigarette-fuelled night over at Deutch's house).

Yet there was also a sense, post-*Ferris*, that this was as good as it was going to get. Hughes had made a hit movie with a new trio of actors rather than using his previous ensembles, but he hadn't bonded with them in the way he had with the much younger Molly Ringwald and Anthony Michael Hall back in the early days. He was also spreading himself and his name ever more thinly, letting the stress of too much nicotine and too many all-nighters get the better of him, not always easy to work with and not willing to compromise.

'Of course, I can't tell you everything I thought of him because I'll have an enormous crowd of fans bearing down on me, coz nobody really wants to hear the truth about Hollywood. They want to hear that it's all sweetness and light,'[1] Ira Newborn has admitted, hinting at the issues he faced with Hughes.

The director's regular musical soulmate David Anderle also fell out with him during the filming of *Ferris* when he wouldn't agree to his label A&M exclusively working on soundtracks to Hughes' movies. Many of the young actors John Hughes had worked with

---

1 Author interview.

were now stars too, wanting to move on from his world although quickly discovering that roles for twenty-somethings weren't so easy to come by – even if you were a twenty-something yourself: 'After [*Ferris Bueller*] it became apparent that, "Oh, he's really not a teenager any more!"' remembers Alan Ruck. 'I was twenty-nine when I did that one . . . but I didn't look old enough to play the kinds of roles that TV was filled with at that time, which were lawyers and doctors and cops, y'know. So I was kind of in a little bit of a gap after my teen comedies.'[1]

Broderick himself was coming to the end of his high-school movie career and he followed up his work alongside Hughes with a film adaptation of *Torch Song Trilogy* and a role in Oscar-winning Civil War drama *Glory*. Even teaming up again with *WarGames* duo Lawrence Lasker and Walter F. Parkes on another thriller about military secrets – *Project X*, directed by *Over the Edge*'s Jonathan Kaplan – saw him as a fully fledged airman rather than a student. Meanwhile the princess of Hughes' Chicago suburbs, Molly Ringwald, turned down the opportunity to work with her mentor again on *Some Kind of Wonderful*, citing a fear of repetition. Yet she didn't leave the high-school film arena altogether, working with *Karate Kid*-helmer John G. Avildsen on teen pregnancy drama *For Keeps* in 1988 in a deliberate move away from the adoring way that Hughes wrote for her, its story significantly less idealised. Her biggest fan, this film-maker who had catapulted her on to countless front pages and bedroom walls, was hurt by her decision, as sensitive as the fragile teen characters he had made his name creating. John Hughes, the man fascinated by family and a father figure to his stars, wouldn't speak to Molly Ringwald again.

Really though, Molly Ringwald was right. *Some Kind of Wonderful*, released in February of 1987, *was* just another teenage love triangle with a message about being true to your feelings whose attempts at twists never entirely convince; essentially *Pretty in Pink*'s identical yet slightly less attractive twin. This time it was a boy at the centre of the drama, oddball and hard-up artist/mechanic Keith (Eric Stoltz) dreaming of romance with his high

---

1 Author interview.

school's upper-class beauty queen Amanda Jones (Lea Thompson) whilst unaware of the feelings his tomboy best friend Watts (Mary Stuart Masterson) has for him. However, Amanda isn't a true 'richie'; she only plays at being one whilst in reality living just around the corner from Keith. Furthermore, after Keith does manage to score a date with glamorous Amanda, he eventually realises – in a nod back to *Pretty in Pink*'s original ending – that it's actually lowly Watts he's really in love with.

Ringwald's turning down of the Watts role was just the beginning of casting woes on *Some Kind of Wonderful*, issues that ended up affecting the whole production. Mary Stuart Masterson – the daughter of Peter Masterson, who had found huge success as a writer of stage smash *The Best Little Whorehouse in Texas*, and Carlin Glynn[1] – took over the part following her appearance in *At Close Range* with Sean Penn but filling the other two leads proved problematic. So problematic, in fact, that Deutch quit the project when he found the central male role turned down by both Andrew McCarthy and Michael J. Fox. Jon Cryer wanted it – he even knew Masterson from their days at drama school in upstate New York – but Deutch couldn't settle. He told Hughes he'd had enough.

With Deutch out of the picture, Hughes hired *Valley Girl*'s Martha Coolidge to move the project forward, the new director believing she'd found her lead in Eric Stoltz, back from his exile following the *Back to the Future* debacle. She also then cast TV soap actress Kim Delaney (last seen in Emilio Estevez's adaptation of S. E. Hinton's *That Was Then... This is Now*) to play the heavenly Amanda Jones and Kyle MacLachlan as her hellish boyfriend Hardy, turning what had been an almost *Bueller*-esque comedy about a school geek on a date with a prom queen into something more soul-searching. Sign up Eric Stoltz and that's what *always* happened.

But John Hughes still wasn't happy. He didn't like this moodier approach that Coolidge was taking and went back to Deutch to ask him to reconsider. He also needed to get Ned Tanen on board to agree to the change. They both eventually did, but what might have – at last – seemed like some kind of security for *Some Kind of*

---

1 Glynn played Samantha's mother in *Sixteen Candles*.

Wonderful was anything but. The problem was, the cast – many chosen by Coolidge – had liked their director and her ideas and now found John Hughes reworking the script back into something lighter. They also saw cherished colleagues such as MacLachlan and Delaney swiftly dismissed as the project underwent another complete overhaul; MacLachlan was replaced by Craig Sheffer, star of Paramount's recent flop teen drama *Fire with Fire* (and who was then dating Andie MacDowell). An early read-through of this new version even saw Stoltz and Hughes butt heads but, after taking a deep breath, they agreed that they would have to move forward. Stoltz couldn't afford to be let go from another high-profile movie after all, so instead he offered his help. In a rare moment of cooperation, he told Deutch and Hughes that he knew the perfect person to play Amanda Jones.

Lea Thompson, Stoltz's comrade from *The Wild Life* and – at least for three weeks – *Back to the Future*, hadn't initially been interested in playing a supporting role like Amanda Jones. Her role in George Lucas's as-yet-unreleased *Howard the Duck* would – she was sure – propel her to bigger things than secondary parts in teen movies. That film's subsequent critical and commercial mauling, however, led Thompson to reconsider her plans. She was feeling fragile and needed something, anything, to revive her confidence. Stoltz's suggestion had come at just the right time. With just a week to go before filming was set to begin, Lea Thompson signed up to *Some Kind of Wonderful*.

The situation was still far from perfect. As shooting began in LA, Deutch continued to search for the right tone and several scenes had to be scrapped and reshot. Stoltz also clashed with bosses on exactly how much of an outsider Keith should be, the actor favouring a longer-haired, more intense performance than Deutch was looking for ('I thought [Stoltz] should have been a poet or a writer. It was like he didn't enjoy himself acting. It was a struggle and he was miserable'[1]). If Mary Stuart Masterson learned the drums fanatically to play Watts – the crop-haired gender-bender with her dog tags and boxer shorts, named after Rolling Stones drummer Charlie – then Stoltz wanted to go full Method,

---

1 Howard Deutch in *You Couldn't Ignore Me If You Tried*, op. cit. p.224.

frustrating himself all the more as he realised that this just wasn't the kind of script that would give him space to do that.

Now fully delegating to Deutch, John Hughes himself was less obviously on set than during *Pretty in Pink*, working as he was in Chicago on other projects. He found time to curate the soundtrack with Tarquin Gotch, an album that tellingly was released on his new label Hughes Music,[1] but which actually seemed even more leftfield than before, including Buzzcocks' Pete Shelley and The Jesus and Mary Chain (the only tune approaching hit status was the gloriously deadpan 'Brilliant Mind' by west London five-piece Furniture, a Top 30 curio in the UK). That there was nothing to match the MTV success of Simple Minds or The Psychedelic Furs was maybe a good thing artistically, meaning the process of marketing avoided what was already a formula. Yet *Some Kind of Wonderful* needed all the help it could get.

Released at the end of February 1987, a year after *Pretty in Pink* and with an almost identical poster (shot by Annie Liebowitz), *Some Kind of Wonderful* suffered from seeming like a genre ending with a whisper not a bang. Keith might have seen beyond traditional sex-appeal in choosing punkish Watts over girly Amanda but it was difficult to see what someone so spiky as Watts (sample line: 'Break his heart, I'll break your face') would ever see in Stoltz's vanilla interpretation of Keith. In the film's opening montage, Keith is seen walking home from work and playing chicken with an oncoming train, avoiding its path only at the last minute. Stoltz spent the rest of the film looking as if he really wished he hadn't moved out of the way.

Howard Deutch was more enthusiastic, in no small part due to his leading lady. Lea Thompson had noticed how her director had spent a particularly long time making sure that the portrait Keith paints of her character Amanda was a perfect reflection of her spirit, turning down several attempts by commissioned artists before settling on the ideal one. Take a look at how he shoots Amanda when she's getting changed in the locker room and you'd be similarly tough-pressed not to suspect this guy had feelings for

---

1 *Wonderful* was also credited, for the first time, as a production of the grandly named Hughes Company.

his subject. The timing was certainly right. Come the end of 1987 Thompson's relationship with Dennis Quaid was on the skids with his drug misuse spiralling. Quaid had enjoyed a big hit that year – *Innerspace*, with Meg Ryan – and was about to shoot a remake of film noir *DOA* with Ryan once again co-starring, but by the time *Some Kind of Wonderful* was being promoted Thompson and Quaid had announced the end of their engagement and the break-up of their relationship. Howard Deutch – like Keith in his film – could finally get together with the girl whose soul he had tried so hard to capture on film. And this time, it would last.

As the Hughes brand of teen movie showed signs of saturation with *Some Kind of Wonderful* and with Ringwald moving out of his orbit, it was left to another of the actresses he had helped make famous to take on the mantle of America's girl-next-door. Some recognisably Hughes traits would be on offer in her monster hit of 1987: a female-skewed romance, a soundtrack brimful of pop and a coming-of-age tale set over just a few weeks of one vacation.

Yet whilst Hughes wrote scripts heavy with heart-searching, his characters readily expressing their fluctuating feelings and growing nous, here was a movie that favoured choreography as much as conversation; a nod back to *Footloose* and *Flashdance* from the first half of the decade. It was also a marked return to the nostalgia that both John Hughes and Cameron Crowe had studiously avoided. Still, whilst it was set in a supposedly more innocent time – 'the summer of 1963, when everybody called me "baby" and it didn't occur to me to mind' – this dancing was anything but innocent. Indeed, it was proudly labelled 'dirty'.

Dirty Dancing's star was Jennifer Grey, best known as Ferris Bueller's little sister Jeannie and who had, in fact, come close to starring in *Flashdance*, auditioning 'eight or ten times' by her reckoning.[1] Losing out to Jennifer Beals was tough; Grey was a born dancer and performer, daughter of *Cabaret*'s Oscar-winning MC Joel Grey and actress Jo Wilder and a former student at Manhattan's prestigious Dalton Academy. Small parts in *Red*

---

1 As mentioned in an interview on the *Dirty Dancing: Ultimate Edition* Blu-ray.

Dawn and Francis Coppola's *The Cotton Club* went some way to stem the disappointment, along the way dating Michael J. Fox before he met her school friend Tracy Pollan, but even getting the bigger role of Jeannie Bueller – beating Meg Ryan – was hardly a dream gig. The thing was, Grey just didn't find John Hughes' *Ferris Bueller* script that funny – something she retrospectively put down to smoking too much pot at the time.[1] But working on *Ferris Bueller's Day Off* with John Hughes did at least hook her up with Matthew Broderick, the pair playing warring siblings on-screen but secretly dating off. Mia Sara's crush on Broderick would have to go nowhere. Meanwhile, Grey, slowly warming to the Hughes script, suggested her *Red Dawn* co-star Charlie Sheen for a key scene where Jeannie's heart is melted by a bad boy at the police station. He ended up almost stealing the whole film.

But *Dirty Dancing*? Grey *really* wanted to get that movie. She'd spent her teenage years sneaking off to dance at Studio 54 so understood the dualities of lead role Baby, the clean-cut girl on holiday with her parents who secretly sambas – and more – with resort ballroom coach Johnny Castle (Patrick Swayze). Expectations might not have been high for the film. *Dirty Dancing*'s distributors Vestron were, after all, primarily known as a video company who'd found success in partnership with Cannon and who were now looking to branch out into getting their own productions into cinemas. They were no Paramount, Universal or Fox. Yet when Grey danced in her audition to an old Jackson Five song, losing herself in the music, she trusted her instinct that the story's celebration of emotions would outweigh business logic: 'That's part of what this girl's journey was like – just a natural feeling.'[2] Four years after *Flashdance* had exclaimed something similar – 'What a feeling!' – *Dirty Dancing* was about to bring the emotional exhilaration of cutting loose back into the foreground.

John Hughes had given young women a modern voice but *Dirty Dancing* – a story partly based on writer Eleanor Bergstein's own experiences – gave them old-fashioned *longing*. The way that Baby

---

1 *You Couldn't Ignore Me If You Tried*, op. cit. p.180.
2 *Dirty Dancing: Ultimate Edition*, Blu-ray.

looks at Johnny – performed by Jennifer Grey with an appealing, lip-biting awe as she gawps at a man who, nine times out of ten, has omitted to put on a shirt – wasn't about being an outsider or hanging with the right crowd. Like dancing, it was all about pure instinct. 'The steps aren't enough,' Castle tells her. '*Feel* the music.'

Dirty Dancing might have had a name that sounded contemporary – and, indeed, was set to be retitled *I Was a Teenage Mambo Queen* because some thought that name *too* provocative – but it is charmingly retro in so many ways. Set specifically, like *American Graffiti*, at a time on the edge of change – just before both The Beatles coming to America and the assassination of President Kennedy[1] – Bergstein was cheeky about the dated family holiday resorts of upstate New York where her story was set but never disparaging. Sure, we're on Baby's side when she dreams of breaking away from their twee card games and magic shows to hang out in the smoky, sexy, red-light-soaked world of Johnny and the entertainment staff but still, when hotel owner Max Kellerman (Jack Weston) complains at the end of another season, 'It feels like it's all slipping away', there's a sadness for him too, unable to keep up with fashion.

That's the power of *Dirty Dancing*: it is remarkably careful not to shut out anyone. So whilst it is definitely the story of a seventeen-year-old girl it aims – unlike many teen-themed stories, those of John Hughes especially – at the grown-up remembering their own first love as well as the kid wondering when theirs might come along. Even the credits blend modern and old, a casually contemporary *Risky Business*-style red italic typeface clashing with the movie's vintage opening song: The Ronettes' 'Be My Baby', released that August of 1963.

It makes for an incongruous mix that's most obvious in the soundtrack, Alfie Zappacosta's synth-slapping 'Overload' rubbing shoulders with Bruce Channel's creaky 'Hey! Baby' – a Billboard No. 1 from March 1962 – without any consideration for historical accuracy. But then, that was never the point of *Dirty Dancing*. Just as Johnny reminds Baby that dancing isn't only about the steps,

---

1 The Beatles first started getting US radio airplay just a few months after *Dirty Dancing*'s summer of '63. Kennedy, meanwhile, was shot dead in Dallas on 22 November that year.

plenty of the songs also remind us that *feelings* are ultimately more exciting than facts. 'I've never *felt* like this before,' sings '60s Righteous Brother Bill Medley on the movie's signature song, '(I've Had) The Time of My Life', whilst Eric Carmen admits, 'I've got this *feeling* that won't subside' in 'Hungry Eyes'. Merry Clayton's jubilant, 'Yes', sums up the movie's guiding theme once and for all: 'We're gonna fall in love and it *feels* so right'. It all makes for a perfectly universal story. *Everyone* has feelings, whatever their age.

Such is *Dirty Dancing*'s love of heart-on-sleeve emotion, even brooding Johnny Castle is given a sensitive side, a Danny Zuko-like bad boy on the outside but more of a John Bender inside; accepting bitterly that the chattering classes will always see him in a certain way yet too afraid to try and show them otherwise. For Patrick Swayze, still trying to prove himself at thirty-four years old and beat the insecurities that haunted him, there were definite overtones of his own life as the misunderstood beefcake, although that didn't make the role any more immediately appealing for him. Swayze was now hot from the TV mini-series *North and South*, but to the point where he was getting unwanted attention from female fans, a situation that led him to give up his favourite pastime of showing horses in competition. His presence simply caused too much of a stir and he was warier than ever of not being taken seriously. Simultaneous with his leading-man breakthrough, Swayze's longtime mentor and manager Bob LeMond died of AIDS-related health complications, leaving the actor and his wife Lisa Niemi to deal with fame on their own. So when Swayze first read *Dirty Dancing*, he saw it only as a fluffy summer romance movie, really not the kind of thing he needed in his life. And as a dancer desperately trying to show the world that he was an actor too, a role in which he was required to mambo, salsa and rhumba for the best part of a hundred minutes didn't seem like the best idea.

But two things in the script piqued Swayze's interest. One was the attached director, Emile Ardolino, a Broadway man who'd just won an Oscar for his documentary *He Makes Me Feel Like Dancin'* about ballet star Jacques d'Amboise and his pioneering work teaching children. Second were those raw emotions burning at the heart of *Dirty Dancing*: class inferiority, family conflict, adolescent angst. If those could give him some drama to work with alongside the choreography then it might just be worth doing.

After auditioning with dancers who weren't actors, and actors who weren't dancers,[1] when Grey tested with Swayze the team of Ardolino, Bergstein and former *Xanadu*/John Hughes choreographer Kenny Ortega could tell they had the right couple. For a film entirely reliant on sexual chemistry, these two had it. Yet the difference in approach that had been evident back when they both starred in *Red Dawn* remained. Swayze threw himself into the physical side of playing Johnny, often exhausted and with his left knee injured, in no state to deal with Grey more's emotionally precarious take on life that would waver from giggles to tears and lead to multiple retakes.[2] Ultimately, she and Swayze forged a satisfactory relationship ('Despite any little irritations I felt, I have to say that overall, Jennifer did a truly phenomenal job'[3]) but what with the dancing, the friction *and* the claim by Swayze that he and Lisa had to rewrite a lot of his dialogue to make it believable,[4] the shoot up in Lake Lure, North Carolina, proved an exhausting one. If Lisa had failed in her own audition to win the role of Johnny's best friend Penny – ultimately played by *Flashdance* and *Staying' Alive* star Cynthia Rhodes – then at least a song that Swayze had co-written a few years back called 'She's Like the Wind', originally meant for his film *Grandview USA*, found its way on to the soundtrack.

And what a soundtrack. *Dirty Dancing*'s music became an industry in itself, not just focused on getting on to MTV but compiled by supervisor Jimmy Ienner (for just 200 thousand dollars) by blending new tracks with Eleanor Bergstein's favourite oldies – a mix of business and intuitive honesty that perfectly matched the film's simple emotions. As a compilation, it didn't try to be cool . . . but it worked. And after Vestron noticed tracks

---

1 Including future *Titanic* star Billy Zane.

2 Although her giggles when practising the famous concluding dance scene did, when left in the final cut, provide the film with one of its most enduring montages.

3 *The Time of My Life*, Patrick Swayze and Lisa Niemi, Simon & Schuster, 2009, p.141.

4 The actor claims in his autobiography that he and Lisa were up the night before shooting the big final scene, working on Johnny's dialogue.

from the album starting to get airplay, they sensed an opportunity and changed their release strategy for the movie, upping its opening weekend screen count from a platform of two hundred to a wide thousand or so.

Still, no one really expected *Dirty Dancing* to be a phenomenon. Even Bergstein was bluntly told to prepare for the worst: 'Everybody hated it. The producers hated it, the exhibitors hated it, the distributors hated it . . . they thought Jennifer was ugly, they thought Patrick was too old, they thought it was a stupid story.'[1] Jennifer Grey's agent, meanwhile, told her client the best thing to do would be to forget *Dirty Dancing* altogether and move on.

Yet through judicious shaping alongside editor Peter Frank, Ardolino had actually managed to create something that so many of the film's insiders didn't spot: a masterpiece of heart-over-head feelings that appealed to all ages. Plot points such as Penny's abortion[2] or Moe Pressman's missing wallet were plentiful but ultimately meaningless in comparison to the musical montages, sequences in which learning to dance becomes a substitute for a growing mutual trust between two people still trying to work out who they really are. In short, it was a story about the sensation of growing up – a sensation that everyone knew about. After many years of teen films where just such a feeling had been exploited to the point of cliché, *Dirty Dancing*'s trick was to make it seem personal, truthful and romantic all over again. Like it was the first time.

It's true, many things in *Dirty Dancing* didn't make sense. With all the entertainment staff who work at Kellerman's, why is the completely inexperienced holidaymaker Baby chosen as the best person to be Johnny's temporary dance partner? Why does Baby's medic father (Jerry Orbach) have his doctor's bag with him whilst he's taking a three-week vacation? And, when Johnny can at last dance just how *he* wants at the closing-night party, why does his choice of record – '(I've Had) The Time of My Life' – sound suspiciously like something recorded in 1987 rather than 1963?

---

1 'Eleanor Bergstein wants you to have the time of your life at the live stage version of *Dirty Dancing*, now headed to Cleveland', cleveland.com, Andrea Simakis, 2 March 2015.

2 Bergstein was asked to remove the abortion plot, for fear of controversy. But, as she rightly pointed out, the whole set up of the film hangs on Penny's pregnancy. Without it, there's nothing.

And what about tomorrow? *Dirty Dancing* ends with a moment of elation, everyone united by the liberated style of music and movement that Johnny and Baby are finally allowed to introduce, but the next day the Houseman family will return home, Kellerman's will close up for the winter season and Johnny will . . . who knows?

A sequel was mooted to answer that very question, *Dirty Dancing*'s sixty-three million dollars at the box-office and sales of thirty-two million soundtrack albums too irresistible not to follow up, but with key players adopting a one-for-all, all-for-one policy, scheduling got the better of them.[1] And really, it's better without it. For a story that rests on the fairytale of raw emotions, why let logic get in the way?

Still, as Vestron waited hopefully on all parties agreeing to a *Dirty Dancing 2* they hurriedly released a tie-in TV series to stop the gap, attempting to impose some rationale on proceedings by making Baby (Melora Hardin) now the daughter of resort owner Max Kellerman (McLean Stevenson) rather than just a holidaymaker, thus explaining how a seventeen-year-old with dreams of travelling the world might still be hanging out in the Catskills with Johnny (Patrick Cassidy). Vestron co-produced the show with *Risky Business*'s Steve Tisch but that didn't stop it being cancelled by CBS after just one series. Despite its musical anachronisms and odd jumps in reason, the original film had told the story of a very specific moment in time; a one-off. It was more than a business. It was a story of feelings that could never be repeated.

On 5 August 1987, Matthew Broderick and Jennifer Grey were enjoying their own vacation in Enniskillen, Northern Ireland; a holiday after an already busy year promoting *Ferris Bueller's Day Off* and *Dirty Dancing*, the latter about to open in the States before debuting in Europe at the prestigious Deauville Film Festival in France at the start of September. Although at the time Broderick said he had no recollection of exactly what happened that Wednesday, it was soon painfully clear: whilst behind the wheel

---

1 A soundtrack 'sequel' – simply entitled *More Dirty Dancing* – was released a year later, whilst 2004 saw partial remake *Dirty Dancing: Havana Nights* at the cinema and an Eleanor Bergstein-written musical on the stage.

of his rented BMW – Grey in the passenger seat, both listening to music on the stereo – he veered into the right-hand lane and crashed head-on with a car driven by local Anna Gallagher and her mother Margaret Doherty. Both were killed.

Broderick awoke in Belfast's Royal Victoria Hospital with injuries to his leg, ribs and lungs, Grey with whiplash. They also came face-to-face with a media not just exposing their previously secret relationship but also detailing how a pair of Hollywood movie stars had been involved in the death of two innocent members of the public. Broderick was charged with causing death by dangerous driving. Grey, meanwhile, found herself in a less serious but perhaps more surreal situation. *Dirty Dancing* was generating a huge buzz, its release just days away and her star on the rise. Now here she was, in a hospital in Northern Ireland, with feelings more complicated than any of her movie roles: 'I became America's sweetheart within five days of the accident . . . [but] the juxtaposition of that deep sorrow, the survivor's guilt and then being celebrated as the new big thing just didn't jibe. It didn't feel good to be the toast of the town.'[1] Broderick stayed in his hospital bed for the next month. If ever there was a time for a couple of teen stars to grow up, it was this.

1 *People*, Monica Rizzo and Alexis Chiu, 4 October 2010.

Chapter Fourteen

ON THE EDGE

The Brat Pack disintegrates – and the hits dry up; Tom cruises whilst Rob hits a new low; Can't Buy Me Love *and the John Hughes legacy; plus* River's Edge *takes teen movies into murky waters.*

John Hughes never seemed interested in *actual* sex. In *Pretty in Pink* it is something that the nasty rich kids do; James Spader in his louche grey suit that looks as if it's just been picked up off the floor after a one-night stand, his shirt half-unbuttoned, ready to go at it all over again.

In *Ferris Bueller's Day Off*, meanwhile, Ferris worries that Cameron will end up marrying 'the first girl he lays and she's gonna treat him like shit, because she will have given him what he has built up in his mind as the end-all, be-all of human existence'. Even in Hughes' most obviously sexual film, the wet-dream comedy *Weird Science*, its nerdy leads magically create the ultimate pin-up girl, only to be petrified of her once their fantasy becomes a reality. Sex was something to take your time with, no need to hurry. You'll have plenty of opportunity later, although even then – as Hughes showed in his 1988 twenty-something comedy *She's Having a Baby*[1] – being in a serious relationship throws up its own set of demands too.

---

1 Starring Elizabeth McGovern and Kevin Bacon, its filming overlapping with Hughes' first non-teen movie as a director, *Planes, Trains and Automobiles* (hence John Candy's cameo in the former, Bacon's in the latter).

But audiences seemed to *want* the opportunity, the relative failure of Hughes' sweetly sex-free *Some Kind of Wonderful* in early 1987 a hint that teen tastes were changing. *Wonderful* made eighteen million dollars; *Pretty in Pink*, telling virtually the same story, had done over *twice* that much exactly a year earlier. If the peak years of the *Porky's*-esque T&A comedy were over[1] then the newer, more upfront attitude to sex visible in Adrian Lyne's *9½ Weeks* and *Fatal Attraction*[2] showed that sex wasn't just something to avoid or snigger at any more. It could be enjoyable *and* serious.

The Brat Pack wanted to get serious and sexy too, to grow up and change with the times; rehashing the same '*Romeo and Juliet* with pop songs' formula just wasn't going to be enough for some of them, while others were simply now too famous to carry on in low-budget teen pics. It had to happen, eventually, and *Some Kind of Wonderful* proved to be Hughes' last high-school movie, the film-maker all too aware that his troupe were moving on without him, like children leaving home. Instead of trying to recapture their magic with other actors[3] he did something characteristically modest and simply stepped out of the teen spotlight altogether, ending the decade more anonymously as writer and producer and focusing on even younger stars in *Home Alone* and *Baby's Day Out*; little kids who wouldn't grow up so quickly. 'There's was no falling out with us, no fight,' conceded Matthew Broderick. 'He just . . . stopped being around, is the best way I can describe it.'[4]

Still, the aftermath of the Hughes-and-Brat-Pack break-up did at least see an upturn in the amount of youthful product in multiplexes, with producers trying to accommodate this host of new solo stars with their own headlining projects. Sean Penn

---

1 The third and final film in the franchise was *Porky's Revenge*, released in the spring of '85 to only a third of the original's gross.

2 Eight weeks at No. 1, grossing nearly 160 million dollars in the States – the second highest of 1987. Perhaps even more importantly, *Fatal Attraction*'s depiction of a violent affair was the pinnacle of Lyne's ad-man ability to create a talking point: who was the wronged party? Both *9½ Weeks* and *Fatal Attraction* were R-rated and hardly teen movies but the former's stars and soundtrack – Mickey Rourke, Kim Basinger, John Taylor of Duran Duran – gave it a youthful appeal whilst the latter's zeitgeist success was simply unavoidable.

3 An exception of sorts was 1991's *Career Opportunities*, a comedy about a loser (Frank Whaley) and a former prom queen (Jennifer Connolly) stuck together overnight in a supermarket. They weren't high-schoolers and the Hughes script focused on the slapstick he used so effectively in *Home Alone* as much as any angst. But it was close.

4 'John Hughes's Actors on John Hughes', op. cit.

made it look easy, brushing off the *Shanghai Surprise* debacle with a run of characteristically bullish performances, although good reviews were always more plentiful than actual box-office success. Tom Cruise, on the other hand, had both, in an enviable position post-*Top Gun* to raise his game alongside older legends such as Paul Newman in Scorsese's *The Color of Money* and Dustin Hoffman in Barry Levinson's *Rain Man*, his own youth and cockiness still integral to the stories but no longer the only selling point.[1] He was now in a league all of his own.

Between those prestige pictures Cruise gave the world *Cocktail*, again aligning himself with a more experienced and respected co-star: the forty-year-old Australian award winner Bryan Brown. At first glance *Cocktail* was a forgettable piece of teen yuppie confectionery (Cruise's Brian befriends Brown's Doug and makes it big as a flashy barman) but look closer and there's actually some impressive bitterness in amongst the sugar, the story quick to show the downside of the capitalist dream as well as the glamour. In fact, those melancholy moments are the story's only real plot points, Doug losing a lot of money on the commodities market and Brian's wandering eye at least offering some tangible drama.

Critics weren't so charitable, not least when it came to the film's subservient female characters, one – Jordan – played by *The Karate Kid*'s Elisabeth Shue: 'I think some of the reviews were kind of mean but ... there was a strong attempt at making a movie that was complicated character-wise but also fun and reflected the emptiness of only caring about financial success during that time ... it wasn't as if I was ready to lead the revolution for female driven movies ... [but] I remember being pretty sad when the reviews were not good. But then I lost my brother a few weeks into its release and movies and work took the back seat to deep grief and a long struggle to get back on my feet.'[2] That struggle included signing on to another 'girlfriend role', replacing Claudia Wells as Marty's other half Jennifer in *Back to the Future Parts II*

---

1 Newman and Hoffman won Best Actor Oscars at the 1986 and 1988 awards, respectively. Teaming with a more mature and respected colleague was a method that would also work well for Charlie Sheen in Oliver Stone's *Wall Street* and it was his co-star in that film, Michael Douglas, who won the Best Actor gong in between Newman and Hoffman in 1987.
2 Author interview.

and *III*, but the opportunity to work with Bob Zemeckis – about to break new ground by mixing live action with animation in *Who Framed Roger Rabbit?* – was a strong pull for an actress still nervous of her place in the spotlight.

Briefly though, the vortex left by the implosion of the Brat Pack created a space for a new breed of female leads with Demi Moore heading the charge as the most audacious, able to match Cruise's success in finding grown-up roles as hotshot big dreamers. She and Rob Lowe scored early in 1986's David Mamet adaptation *About Last Night*, both helped by striking physical strengths that meant neither had ever particularly looked or sounded like school kids even when they were playing them.[1] Nevertheless, Moore finished up 1986 failing to capitalise on the success of *About Last Night* by appearing in *Wisdom*, the directing debut of fiancé Emilio Estevez. David Blum's Brat Pack article in the *New York* magazine had described an Emilio who was so confident of his film-making skills but *Wisdom* tanked both at the box-office and with critics. Even forgetting its questionable script – with Estevez and Moore as Bonnie and Clyde-style outlaws on the run – the film's financier David Begelman was himself a controversial executive who'd embezzled money whilst at Columbia and whose subsequent career was dogged by financial impropriety, despite backing – in various guises – *WarGames* and *Mr Mom*.[2]

To make matters worse, the couple's proposed December 1986 marriage was called off at the last minute, with hectic schedules cited. Moore had never been comfortable with the teen label she'd ended up with ('I hate it! I find it embarrassing, hateful and demeaning'[3]) and the autumn of 1986 had been spent showing off her mature acting prowess on Broadway. Following the split with Estevez she never took on movies to associate herself with the Brat Pack again. Like Cruise, her steely determination always felt as much adult as adolescent anyway; in the case of troubled Jules in *St Elmo's Fire*, a screwed-up combination of the two. In November

---

1 'This is the movie *St Elmo's Fire* should have been', *Chicago Sun-Times*, Roger Ebert, 1 July 1986.
2 Begelman eventually committed suicide on 7 August 1995, at LA's Century Plaza Hotel.
3 *Lawrence Journal-World*, 14 July 1985.

1987, less than a year after calling off her wedding, the twenty-five-year-old Demi Moore married someone from way outside the group she'd once been an integral part of: the thirty-two-year-old star of TV's *Moonlighting*, Bruce Willis.

Despite her career uncertainty, Elisabeth Shue went on to lead 1987's *Adventures in Babysitting*[1] to considerable success. The story focused on a teenage girl's eventful night looking after her neighbour's children and was the directing debut of *Gremlins* and *The Goonies'* writer Chris Columbus. Columbus would soon work with John Hughes[2] and the influence of the *Ferris Bueller* writer was clear in *Adventures*: the tight timescale – one evening in the Chicago suburbs – where youngsters illicitly pass through the adult world of the big city. To add to its pedigree, *Adventures* was the first film to be made by *Flashdance*'s Lynda Obst in her new partnership with fellow producer Debra Hill. Shue admits, 'I was pretty clueless about the business . . . I didn't have a publicist. I didn't go to red carpet events or even own a dress. I lived back east and was slowly still making my way through college,' but the opportunities *Adventures in Babysitting* presented sparked her enthusiasm. 'I know Molly Ringwald led some important movies at the time as well but I am not sure if there were many outside of her films . . . I *loved* my experience working on that movie. The work was so fun, challenging . . . I adored Chris, Lynda and Debra. We were all working on our "first movie" and there was a wonderful energy and excitement every day. It came after I'd taken some time off from college and was nowhere in my career. I screen-tested with probably ten other major actresses at the time . . . Jeffrey Katzenburg, who was at Disney at the time, was wonderful to me and encouraged me to take things more seriously . . . there are some moments that transcend work and become a part of your life in a visceral, more meaningful way. *Adventures in Babysitting* was one such moment.'[3]

Meanwhile, Ally Sheedy had teamed up with Judd Nelson for the directing debut of their *Breakfast Club* producer friend

---

1 aka *A Night on the Town*.
2 Most successfully as director of another Hughes story where kids play at being grown-ups, *Home Alone* (1990).
3 Author interview.

Michelle Manning; someone so close to the Brat Pack that she had even been mentioned in Blum's infamous exposé and who, in its aftermath, struck a defiant pose: '[The article] didn't break the group up or anything. If anything it probably made us stronger.'[1]

Blue City was released by Ned Tanen's Paramount, although Manning found his second-in-command at the studio, Dawn Steel, hardly supportive. Perhaps Steel was right? Despite the pairing of Sheedy and Nelson, and a tagline more than nodding back to *St Elmo's Fire* ('It's the coolest heat you'll ever feel'), this story of a man returning to his home town to avenge the death of his father underperformed. Briefly, though, it looked as if Sheedy might break out as a solo star in Amy Holden Jones' *Maid to Order* – a *Cinderella* in reverse rom-com – released in 1987. 'We offered the lead first to Demi Moore, who passed,' remembers Holden Jones. 'Then after we cast Ally, she [Demi] came back and asked to do it, saying her managers had passed for her. Now that she'd read the script, she wanted the part. This was a coup, as both stars were used to far higher budget studio movies. But they were never leads [until] I broke that ground, creating lead parts for actresses . . . Ally was lovely, talented, helpful and dear. She could not have been nicer.'[2]

Unfortunately for Sheedy, this new focus on her as a leading lady only meant more pressure from the industry to 'pile on the make-up, wear tight, short dresses, go to parties, do provocative photo spreads on magazines, have my teeth straightened, my breasts enlarged, change my weight – either up or down, depending on who I was talking to'[3]. Her friendship with Moore foundered as a result, since that was exactly what *she* was prepared to do. Sheedy, on the other hand, refused – although a relationship with Bon Jovi guitarist Richie Sambora would lead to an unexpected moment when the bookish, yoga-loving actress became a hard-living rock girlfriend and ultimately found herself in rehab for addiction to anti-depressants.

---

1 Author interview.
2 Author interview.
3 'On the Upswing', *LA Times*, Richard Natale, 10 June 1998.

Maid to Order was another commercial disappointment, as was Atlantic's attempt at repeating the success of *Valley Girl* with the similarly titled *Modern Girls*, the story of three friends and their passion for the LA nightlife which starred *Electric Dreams'* Virginia Madsen and *Kids from Fame* star Cynthia Gibb. On the plus side, at least these smaller production houses were trying to champion female roles. According to Holden Jones, 'It was in a time when few in the mainstream wanted movies where the leads were women.'[1]

Others simply discovered their dream of convincing in more mature parts was tough to achieve, both audiences and film-makers – and perhaps even the actors themselves – unsure of the Brat Pack's new place in the world outside its teen bubble. Molly Ringwald's reunion with Andrew McCarthy in *Fresh Horses* – playing a poor Kentucky teen romanced by a clean-cut college boy, based on the play by Larry Ketron – would have been a dream pairing a couple of years earlier. Indeed its culture clash romance even had echoes of *Pretty in Pink*,[2] with McCarthy once again looking uptight and distracted, although Ringwald's ruffled hair and trailer park drawl as enigmatic drifter Jewel was a deliberately bold move away from her girl-next-door image. Still, come 1988 this reconvening of two Hughes superstars was one of the year's biggest losers, Columbia barely grabbing back half of its fourteen-million-dollar budget. Michael Wilmington in the *LA Times* might have recognised its relative class – 'There's a lot to admire ... especially compared to other recent American movies on young love. Ketron's dialogue is fresh, sad and funny; the film digs into American society more perceptively and compassionately than most'[3] – but dismissed Ringwald's attempt to play a sexy, capricious, bad girl and wished the movie hadn't been restricted by a Hughes-style PG-13 rating. *Fresh Horses* just wasn't enough of one thing or the other. Ringwald's hopes of playing tragic Andy Warhol muse Edie Sedgwick, whose story rights were owned by Warren Beatty, also came to nothing.

---

1 Ibid.
2 Also *Some Kind of Wonderful*, with the impish Molly Hagen playing 'rich bitch' roles in both.
3 21 November 1988.

As Jennifer Grey took time away from acting following her accident in Northern Ireland, her boyfriend Matthew Broderick returned to a movie world where low-budget movie adaptations of his earlier stage successes (*Biloxi Blues*, *Torch Song Trilogy*) gave him leading roles. His personal life, however, proved more problematic. He still faced a legal case for driving the car that had killed two in the summer of '87 and the accusation against him – of causing death by reckless driving – required him to appear in Enniskillen's magistrates' court in February 1988, just a few weeks after a Golden Globe ceremony in LA that saw Grey, Patrick Swayze and '(I've Had) The Time of My Life' nominated.[1] Grey didn't attend. Broderick's charge did, after all, carry with it a possible five-year jail term and the couple weren't in the mood to celebrate either awards nods or *Dirty Dancing*'s continued success as it moved on to home video and became the year's biggest VHS rental and a record-breaker on sell-through. But in a somewhat controversial decision over in Northern Ireland, Broderick was instead found guilty on the lesser conviction of careless driving and walked away paying a fine of less than two hundred dollars. By April, Grey had made a public appearance at the Oscars, re-teaming with Swayze to present the Best Original Score to David Byrne, Cong Su and Ryuichi Sakamoto for their work on *The Last Emperor*. Her date that night wasn't, however, Matthew Broderick but William Baldwin, a twenty-five-year-old fashion model with plans to become an actor like his older brother Alec, a regular on TV. Within a few weeks, and in no small part due to the anxiety they both suffered following that fateful night on vacation, Broderick and Grey had officially announced their break-up.

Broderick's lookalike Jon Cryer no longer had to make do with his doppelgänger's cast-offs but he still flopped alongside *The Breakfast Club*'s Paul Gleason in *Morgan Stewart's Coming Home* (a political comedy disowned by its directors), then as Lex Luthor's son Lenny in Cannon's cut-price 1987 reboot of the *Superman* franchise, *The Quest for Peace*. Meanwhile, his *Pretty in Pink* love

---

1 Grey lost Best Actress in a Musical or Comedy to Cher, for the performance as *Moonstruck*'s feisty Italian-American widow Loretta that would also win her an Oscar. Swayze, meanwhile, was beaten by Robin Williams in *Good Morning, Vietnam*. '(I've Had) The Time of My Life' did, however, win Best Original Song.

rival Andrew McCarthy did manage a hit in the spring of '87 with *Mannequin* but the story of a man falling in love with a shop dummy possessed by an ancient Egyptian princess hardly screamed progress. In fact, it had never even intended to.

Mannequin was overseen by marketing executive Joseph Farrell, a pioneer in audience research and the use of demographics in getting a film made. His numbers had suggested McCarthy for the lead because of his supposed inoffensive appeal to young women (despite the actor in real life now dealing with a burgeoning drinking problem). So if McCarthy in *Mannequin* looked as if he was just doing what he'd done before, it's because that's all he was required to do. It seemed that Kim Cattrall and James Spader had been asked to do just the same too, co-starring on autopilot as a ditzy sex-kitten and a sneering yuppie respectively.[1]

Anthony Michael Hall found himself a perhaps unlikely fan in the form of Stanley Kubrick, the *Clockwork Orange* director having loved him in *Sixteen Candles* but, after protracted negotiations, the actor had to turn down Kubrick's upcoming Vietnam drama *Full Metal Jacket* for personal reasons. If Hall was still determined to move away from Hughes-style teen movies – 'I had done three films with him and I felt like I wanted to grow: you know, the mind-set of an 18-year-old kid. I didn't know what it was all about yet. Maybe that was something he never forgave me for'[2] – what he actually made were just more teen movies that were nowhere near as insightful. Sports comedy *Johnny Be Good* (1988) was directed by *Flashdance* and *Some Kind of Wonderful* editor Bud Smith and began with a joke about a cheerleader not wearing any panties, before moving on to dog poop being smeared on a football; hardly groundbreaking stuff. In fact, *Johnny Be Good*'s highlight was the pairing of *The Breakfast Club*'s Paul Gleason with helium-voiced Chinese American Jennifer Tilly, as Johnny's school coach and his wife. Hall had admittedly beefed up for the role but neither *Johnny Be Good* nor thriller *Out of*

---

1 Farrell would later use his research to alter the conclusion of *Fatal Attraction*, released that autumn. Director Adrian Lyne wanted 'bunny boiler' Alex (Glenn Close) to end her own life as the payoff of the film and had shot the necessary scenes. Farrell's audience polling, however, suggested dissatisfaction with something so downbeat and a new climax was shot with wronged wife Beth (Anne Archer) saving the day.

2 'John Hughes's Actors on John Hughes', op. cit.

Bounds – made a couple of years earlier and, like *Johnny Be Good*, co-starring Robert Downey Jr[1] – made little impact. Hall even spent an unsuccessful year alongside Downey Jr on *Saturday Night Live* as a regular cast member in the 1985–86 season,[2] as the show tried to move forward after losing big names such as Eddie Murphy and Billy Crystal.

Ralph Macchio, meanwhile, interspersed *Karate Kid* sequels with flops *Distant Thunder* and *Too Much Sun* (reuniting with his *Up the Academy* director Robert Downey Sr and, again, co-starring Robert Jr) whilst Judd Nelson mixed further forgettable movies *From the Hip* (Razzie nominated) and *Relentless* with stage and TV work. 'I wouldn't have followed up *The Breakfast Club* with *St Elmo's Fire*,' he later admitted when asked how he would plan his career differently, if given a chance to avoid the so-called 'curse of the Brat Pack'. 'I'd have tried something alone rather than becoming part of another young ensemble cast. Better to dip my foot in there instead of diving all the way in.'[3]

Tommy Howell at least chose well with *The Hitcher* (February 1986) a cat-and-mouse horror movie with more style and Hitchcockian atmosphere than the many slasher movies on offer at the time, although the original script had been significantly more gory than the final film. But it was Rutger Hauer as the psychotic title character who was the real draw in *The Hitcher*, co-star Jennifer Jason Leigh apparently only agreeing to her role because of his involvement. *The Hitcher* was produced by HBO/Silver Screen and released through their deal with TriStar but its reviews showed it wasn't just the Brat Packers themselves who were struggling for identity. 'Was this gory slasher pic or something more?' critics asked of the film's split personality, scratching their heads.

And then there was Rob Lowe, struggling more than most to work out his place in the post-Brat Pack world. He could only follow *About Last Night* with more modest hits: the well-received

1 One scene in *Johnny Be Good* features Hall and Downey Jr at the drive-in watching the film *Putney Swope*, a cult 1969 satire directed by . . . Robert Downey Sr.

2 Both only lasted a year, the attempt to introduce new blood into the comedy institution generally deemed to have been a failure. Hall remains, however, *SNL*'s youngest ever cast member.

3 'Right Now: Judd Nelson', www.portlandmonthly.com, Colin W. Sargent, 2 October 2015.

but little seen *Square Dance* (1987), playing a man with learning difficulties alongside a fifteen-year-old Winona Ryder in her second film and *Masquerade*, a dour erotic thriller co-starring Kim Cattrall and Meg Tilly where he played up to his smooth image as a yacht-racing yuppie with a dark side.

But there were bigger problems for Rob Lowe than mere box-office. In 1988 he found himself the centre of a high-profile scandal; a headline-grabbing tale of sex, lies and videotape involving a sixteen-year-old girl at Atlanta's Hilton and Towers hotel. Lowe was in the city to attend the Democratic party convention and the night before had decided to hang out at the Club Rio bar and have a few drinks with his *St Elmo's Fire* friends Ally and Judd. It was there that a teenage hairdresser called Jan Parsons approached him with her friend Tara Siebert. Within a few hours he was taking them both back to his suite and setting up his camcorder.

Early the next morning Parsons and Siebert secretly left the hotel with both a videotape and some cash, setting in motion a few months that saw Parsons' mother take Lowe to court with a personal injury claim on behalf of her daughter and Lowe become the target of tabloid infamy as copies of the recording became publicly available, also featuring extra explicit footage that had been captured during his time in Paris. 'For a Brat Packer who was trying to recast himself as an artiste-slash-activist, it was humbling to realise that America had seen his moon-white backside moving in monotonous rhythm atop a moaning female,' reported *People* magazine.[1]

'I learned that you must accept the consequences of your actions,' explained Lowe in the same article. 'That's part of being the man that I want to be.'

But redemption wasn't immediate for Rob Lowe. The following March, at the Shrine Auditorium, Lowe found himself front-and-centre at a disastrous Oscar night show that included an opening number where he sang and danced with Snow White to – for no apparent reason – old blues hit 'Proud Mary'. The end result of the evening was a lawsuit from Disney and a letter from several industry dignitaries who branded the event an 'embarrassment'.

---

1 'Rob Lowe's Tale of the Tape', *People*, Michelle Green, 19 March 1990.

Lowe's friend Jodie Foster could only look on in sympathy as she collected her first Best Actress Oscar.[1]

The real blame, however, lay with the show's producer. Allan Carr had just wanted to give the proceedings a little of his old-fashioned pizazz, the same sparkle that the veteran had given to *Grease* so successfully ten years earlier. In fact, Carr's attempt to turn Hollywood's biggest night into a frothy musical, with the hope of regaining his Tinseltown popularity in the process, merely led to the one-time hit-maker barely ever working again.

John Hughes' retreat from the spotlight was more deliberate but gradually stepping back from the genre in which he had found most success simply led to that age-old Hollywood phenomenon: imitation. His teen films still had appeal and other producers weren't about to let their spirit go. Hence 1987 saw the release of two movies so similar in style to John Hughes productions, they were part of his brand in all but name.

Can't Buy Me Love felt both fresh and familiar on its release that August, a film without a direct connection to Hughes but which was produced by Thom Mount, an exec at Universal during the time of *The Breakfast Club*. He was now in charge of his own company after being fired by Universal's new bosses in the wake of Ned Tanen's departure. Its 'rich girl/poor boy' plot was also firmly in the mould of earlier Hughes hits.

Despite the Brat Pack's omnipresence over the previous couple of years, former 'baby mogul' Mount, by now in his late thirties, hadn't seen his own appetite for such teen movies wane – 'People at that age are sorting their lives out, trying to figure where their values lie. It's a wonderful crucible for comedy and also for things that matter'[2] – and it was an incident from his then wife Nicolette's own high-school years that inspired him to push forward with *Can't Buy Me Love*. 'Her parents had gone out of town for a long weekend. Her mother had just purchased a very expensive suede dress that she wanted to wear to a party but her mother said,

---

1 For her performance in rape drama *The Accused*, directed by *Over the Edge* and *Project X*'s Jonathan Kaplan.

2 Author interview. Mount's most recent project (as of 2016) continues his fascination with the genre: *Jungle La La* is a teen road movie.

"Whatever you do, *don't wear the suede dress.*" She, of course, wore the suede dress and went to the party and someone spilled wine on it. So she had to replace this dress costing two thousand dollars – an unimaginable amount of money for a high-school kid. She ran around for two very frantic days and finally found a replacement and put it back in her mother's closet and nobody ever knew.'

Can't Buy Me Love brings into that story the character of Ronald, a cash-poor nerd so in love with this girl that he donates his hard-earned savings to her to replace the dress – on the proviso that she'll pretend to be his girlfriend. Mount had set up *Can't Buy Me Love* with the newly formed TriStar but after they put the film into turnaround, he teamed up with former Fox chairman Dennis Stanfill to fund the picture.

Shot in Tucson for a little over a million dollars, the movie was in profit before it had even been released thanks to pre-selling it to Disney's Buena Vista for over four million. Mount's one condition for the deal? Disney would have to pay The Beatles' Apple Corps a not insubstantial amount to license the song after which the film was named.[1] It paid off. *Can't Buy Me Love* made over thirty million dollars in the summer of '87, well over twice that of *Some Kind of Wonderful*. And if the formula seemed familiar, *Can't Buy Me Love* also had an ace up its sleeve to make it stand out in the form of a non-Brat Pack leading man: twenty-one-year-old Patrick Dempsey.

Dempsey had been originally noticed (like Jon Cryer) in the same stage roles that had worked for Matthew Broderick: Harvey Fierstein's *Torch Song Trilogy* and Neil Simon's *Brighton Beach Memoirs*. 'Matthew Broderick is an actor I looked at and thought I would like to follow in his footsteps,'[2] Dempsey has fully admitted. Still, despite appearing in 1985's Catholic school comedy *Heaven Help Us*[3] with Andrew McCarthy, Matt Dillon's brother Kevin and Mary Stuart Masterson – plus starring in the requisite teen sex comedy (*Meatballs III: Summer Job*) – Dempsey didn't

---

1 Thought to be around half a million dollars.
2 Author interview.
3 aka *Catholic Boys.*

have any particular connection to a youthful movement: 'I don't think I felt any bond at the time. I feel tremendous nostalgia now, looking back at it, realising what a special time it was. [But] I wasn't thinking about the kind of work other actors were getting at the time. I didn't feel any sense of competition.'[1]

Can't Buy Me Love nevertheless put him in their league. 'I was walking in a mall after it opened and I never had the level of attention that I got that day. That was when I first realised my life had changed. After that day, I had no real understanding of it all. I would have been more thoughtful [about the fame] if I was wiser and more experienced as I am now.'[2]

If Dempsey appeared removed from the world of Estevez, Sheedy and Lowe, his personal life backed up that idiosyncratic image: in 1986 he had married Rochelle 'Rocky' Parker, an acting coach twenty-six years his senior. Parker was a widow with three children, an experienced but struggling actress who claimed to have sacrificed her own dreams of performing in order to help Dempsey with his.[3] They met during the tour of *Brighton Beach Memoirs*: 'I started talking to him about acting. We would work after the show. He started getting auditions then. During the time that we were together, I went with him everywhere; to sets, anywhere he had to go. If there was going to be a camera there, I would make sure I was there for him. I did script analysis and coached Patrick on set . . . '[4]

After *Can't Buy Me Love*, Dempsey starred in *In the Mood*,[5] the true – and hugely apt – story of Sonny Wisecarver, a teenager with a taste for older women. He followed it with more movies – coming-of-age romance *Some Girls*, college comedy *Loverboy* – that created a leading man image apparently not far from his real life with his older wife: naïve yet charming beyond his years, as willing to be mothered as he was to seduce. None were theatrical hits like *Can't Buy Me Love*, yet no one else had what he had: the

1 Author interview.
2 Ibid.
3 Claims made in divorce papers filed at LA's superior court on 23 September 1994, denied by Dempsey's reps. Parker's CV included much stage work, modelling and as an extra on *Midnight Cowboy* and *The Godfather*. She died in 2014.
4 Rochelle Parker interviewed by her son Corey, memphisactor.blogspot.co.uk, 16 September 2013.
5 aka *The Woo Woo Kid*.

looks of Sean Penn but not the anger, the sensitivity of Andrew McCarthy but not the furrowed brow. Dempsey's was a likeable boy-next-door routine yet he was also charmingly strange enough to be unlike any boy-next-door you actually knew.

Three O'Clock High, released in October of the same year, failed to match *Can't Buy Me Love*'s success in finding a new teen leading man but, like the Dempsey movie, it was another attempt to be both familiar and new, to move on from Brat Pack regulars by casting unknowns yet still to nod back too. Steven Spielberg's involvement in the production, made via his long-standing association with Universal, was one such connection, the mogul eager to repeat his teen movie success with *Back to the Future*. He instructed director Phil Joanou – a USC film school grad who'd just helmed a couple of episodes of Amblin's much-hyped *Amazing Stories*[1] – to find 'a new Michael J. Fox' to play *Three O'Clock High*'s nervy lead, Jerry. After much deliberation, the role went to twenty-five-year-old Casey Siemaszko, a fresh face to many but who was in truth already an experienced supporting player from *Class*, *Stand by Me*, *Amazing Stories* and *Back to the Future* itself. Meanwhile, for the soundtrack, Joanou looked back to *Risky Business* and hired German electro soundscapers Tangerine Dream.[2]

As for the plot – a day in the life of Jerry Mitchell as he faces up to a schoolyard fight with classroom tough guy Buddy Revell (Richard Tyson) come the final bell – here was another concept whose deceptive simplicity and rigorous timescale could have come straight from John Hughes' desk drawer. Even the picture's style – full of creative angles and deliberately jarring cuts, its set design showing off Jerry's bedroom as an artfully curated museum of adolescent paraphernalia complete with poster of James Dean – was a carbon copy of the equally considered art direction in *The Breakfast Club* and *Ferris*.[3]

---

1 *Amazing Stories* was a series of individual, half-hour fantasy dramas for which Spielberg recruited many big-name directors: Eastwood, Scorsese, Zemeckis. Despite running for two seasons, the show was not a hit.

2 From their studios in Berlin, the band initially took *Three O'Clock High* entirely seriously and composed a score that was far too bombastic. Joanou then worked with them to tone things down.

3 Joanou had planned every shot in advance.

Joanou, however, claimed different inspiration: 'Basically I watched *After Hours* about ten times and stole everything from that! I watched *After Hours* . . . and *Road Warrior*[1] for the fight scene.'[2] Spielberg unsurprisingly noticed, slightly bemused by the film that Joanou turned in – he'd pictured it more of a *Karate Kid* – and wryly commented that perhaps it might be more to Scorsese's tastes. *Three O'Clock High* didn't perform well on the big screen, perhaps cursed by its own duality: to some it looked like yet another high-school film, to others it wasn't obvious enough. Certainly its thin set-up feels stretched – even over ninety minutes – in a way that the characterful Hughes or Scorsese would never allow. Popularity on TV and video provided some recompense but *Three O'Clock High* never became the new *Back to the Future*. Far from time-travelling, it felt stuck.

Other post-Brat Pack outings through 1987 and 1988 did, however, move things forward. The Hemdale Company had originally been co-owned by businessman John Daly and actor David Hemmings, the sleepy-eyed British star of swinging '60s classics *Blow-Up* and *Barbarella*, set up to invest in entertainment product as varied as the original *Grease* stage show, supplying cable TV to hotels and, after a high profile merger, Ozzy Osbourne's metal band Black Sabbath. By the '80s, and with Hemmings no longer involved, Hemdale focused its attention on films and it was Liverpudlian Derek Gibson – who'd been at Canada's Astral during its *Porky's* days – who oversaw a push to compete with the big guns. What films emerged were a long way from the bare boobs and dick jokes of *Porky's*.

Hemdale's work with Orion resulted in James Cameron's trailblazing *The Terminator* and Sean Penn's double dose of teen noir, *At Close Range* and *The Falcon and The Snowman*. Even bigger was *Platoon*, Oliver Stone's Vietnam drama that starred a post-*Red Dawn* Charlie Sheen and picked up the Best Picture Oscar at the Dorothy Chandler Pavilion in March 1987. Then, just a couple of months later, Hemdale released *River's Edge*, a teen

---

1 aka *Mad Max 2*.

2 Joanou made these comments during a post-screening Q&A at the Seth Green Film Fest in 2007.

movie bravely unimpressed by the genre's recent ubiquity. As a result it blew the teen movie apart, finally creating a new template for its future.

At the helm of *River's Edge*, however, was a name from the past. Tim Hunter had followed his astute work with Matt Dillon on *Over the Edge* and *Tex* with 1985's *Sylvester*, a girl-and-her-horse drama starring Melissa Gilbert back in the time when she was still dating Rob Lowe. *Sylvester* had been moderately well-received – 'a sincerity that only the owner of a glue factory could hate'[1] – but showed few signs of the new territory into which Hunter would head: daringly investigating the dark recesses of teenage aimlessness.

Writer Neal Jimenez was still a student when he wrote *River's Edge*, based on a real life incident: the 1981 murder of fourteen-year-old Californian Marcy Conrad by Anthony Broussard, her fellow high-schooler who went on to brag to his friends about what he'd done but whose crime wasn't reported for two days. Yet Jimenez took *River's Edge* beyond the basic brutality of its origins and crafted something pertinent about the confused role of teenagers in mid-'80s society. In one scene we see characters learn in a history lesson about the impact of counterculture protest in the '60s. In another, ex-hippy Feck (Dennis Hopper[2]) recounts his own stories of 'flower power' rebellion. But without those goals just what do the troubled kids of today have to focus on? The way the gang in *River's Edge* – lank-haired buddies Matt and Layne, BMX-riding tearaway Tim, wide-eyed Clarissa – react to the murder of their friend Jamie reveals all: none boast the urgency and despair of people certain of their moral guidelines. They are all just drifting.

River's Edge's portrayal of the remote and the feckless, the disillusioned and dope-smoking, earned Jimenez, Hunter and The Hemdale Company a Best Picture gong at the Independent Spirit Awards, a ceremony only a couple of years old but which had already championed Scorsese's *After Hours* and David Lynch's *Blue Velvet*. The latter looms large in *River's Edge*, not just in its

---

1 *New York Times*, Vincent Canby, 15 March 1985.

2 A role that on more than one occasion nods back to his iconic turn as *Easy Rider*'s wayward biker Billy.

casting of Hopper but also with its stark, often grotesque, depiction of small-town psychotics, where melodramatic orchestral cues mix with the bleak and sexually surreal (Feck is in a 'relationship' with his blow-up doll).

But it's the depiction of a mumbling and moody heavy-metal culture in *River's Edge* that really stands out, the rage of Californian thrash band Slayer the only outlet for teenagers being offered little else. *Back to the Future*'s Crispin Glover headlined *River's Edge* as Layne (much more his kind of envelope-pushing project than the money-making mainstream of a Bob Zemeckis movie), but it was newcomer Keanu Reeves who really convinced as disenchanted headbanger Matt. Where Glover went for maniacal theatrics, Reeves modestly squinted his way through the movie; a new kind of teen movie leading man, both vacant and sensitive, ramshackle yet loyal.

Reeves was a twenty-two-year-old Canadian more into Joy Division than heavy metal but his startling presence filled *River's Edge* with a strange beauty amongst the fog and alcohol and boredom. Unique looks were part of it – Reeves was born to a British mother and a Chinese-Hawaiian father – but his early life fed into his image too. His childhood was wandering – from Beirut to Sydney, New York to Toronto – and what would be anomalistic to some became his norm. Reeves' mother, Patricia, was a former dancer who designed costumes for musicians and his father – more errant, a drug user – left them when Keanu was still a toddler ('The story with me and my dad's pretty heavy. It's full of pain and woe and fucking loss and all that shit'[1]). Like Tom Cruise he went from school to school, like Tom Cruise he was dyslexic. And like Tom Cruise he found more peace on the sports field than in the classroom.

But Reeves also had connections to acting via his stepfather Paul Aaron, a stage and screen director and, after some initial theatre work in Toronto, he headed to California to live with Aaron and make a go of performing. Reeves was immediately faced with a problem when he met producers: 'The day I landed in LA, they wanted me to change my name.' Keanu Reeves briefly

---

1 'The Quiet Man: The Riddle of Keanu Reeves', *Rolling Stone*, Chris Heath, 31 August 2000.

became K. C. Reeves[1] but the actor would always follow his own path rather than the one he was told to pursue: '[The name change] only lasted for a couple of months. It's so not who I am. Other people say, "If you want to do what you want to do, you have to do this." And the lesson being – you know what? You don't. You don't.'[2]

Reeves had made his debut as a hockey goalie in Peter Guber and Jon Peters' *Youngblood*, another attempt to rehash the *Flashdance* formula, this time with ice skates, pucks, Rob Lowe and Patrick Swayze. *River's Edge* gave him not just an opportunity to take a lead role, but was also something that chimed with his own free-spirited existence as a biker, bass-player and occasional drug taker. If the story didn't have easy answers or neat conclusions then that was the point, since neither did Reeves' own troubled life. Matt's drug-addled relationship with Ione Skye's Clarissa made the clean-cut world of Ringwald and McCarthy suddenly seem like something from a different age, so tame and twee.

Like Reeves, Ione Skye's early life was similarly peripatetic; from London to Los Angeles, via San Francisco and Connecticut, the daughter of folk-singing '60s folk singer Donovan and model Enid Stulberger. In LA she'd attended the Immaculate Heart High School in Los Feliz, famous for its entertainment world alumni (and Heidi Fleiss) and her family mixed in artistic circles: 'My mom knew a lot of people. It was LA in the '80s. It was this sort of chic, gay, English crowd. There were musicians and actors . . . I had a very expansive, creative upbringing.'[3] George Harrison and Jefferson Airplane's Grace Slick were part of her circle and hard-drinking Red Hot Chili Peppers' frontman Anthony Kiedis was her boyfriend. It was no surprise that Skye couldn't wait to get out of traditional education, feeling stifled by its rules. At first glance, she had a fresh-faced innocence about her, a look certainly played up in *River's Edge*, but Skye's dreams were headstrong: 'I remember sitting on the steps of the school thinking,

---

1 His middle-name is Charles. 'Keanu', incidentally, is Hawaiian for 'cool breeze'.
2 *Rolling Stone*, op. cit.
3 'Ione Skye Remembers *Say Anything* and *River's Edge*', thehollywoodinterview.blogspot.co.uk, Terry Keefe, 16 November 2012.

Get me out of here. God, please let me get this part [in *River's Edge*] so I can get out of high school. And I never went back.'[1] And with the impact of *River's Edge*, teen movies were never quite the same either.

---

1 Ibid,

Chapter Fifteen

LOST BOYS, YOUNG GUNS

At home with the Downey-Parkers; Corey, Charlie and Lucas; *Joel Schumacher's appetite for destruction; teenybop returns (and gets a* License to Drive); *plus, six reasons why the west was wild.*

For some stars, a move into wilder, darker movie-making territory sparked in part by *River's Edge* spelled trouble: no one would ever believe that suave Rob Lowe or timid Andrew McCarthy could be disillusioned metal fans or spaced-out party animals, whatever decadent pursuits they might have got up to in their private lives. For others, though, it seemed less of a hurdle and more of a boost. Now they could finally be themselves.

Over in a rambling, two-storey Hollywood coach house, once home to John Lennon, the twenty-year-old Sarah Jessica Parker and Robert Downey Jr had set up home. 'When the phone rings, Downey is apt to answer, "House of decadence",' reported *People* magazine in a glossy article,[1] the feature accompanied by photos of the couple mocking the usual serious poses you see in all those 'at home with' lifestyle articles. Parker and Downey Jr had actually first met back in Manhattan in 1984, when both were filming family drama *Firstborn* in New Jersey for director Michael Apted. Within just a few weeks they were dating. Downey Jr – who'd dropped out of SaMoHi to try and make it on Broadway, championed by casting director Shirley Rich – revelled in being

---

1 Gioia Diliberto, 30 September 1985.

feisty, close in spirit to his counterculture film-maker father: 'I had very much this post-adolescent, faux nihilistic, punk-rock rebellious attitude. I thought my way was so much cooler than people who were actually building lives and careers.'[1] S. J.'s mum, understandably, wasn't so keen on her young daughter's serious relationship with Downey, even if the spiky-haired actor proudly claimed that marriage was on the cards.[2]

But Downey's partying was a problem. Introduced to drugs by his dad, excess – and its after-effects – had become part of his everyday life: 'I was making money. I was mercurial and recklessly undisciplined and, for the most part, I was happily anesthetised. Sarah Jessica would pull me out of a hangover and we'd go pick out furniture together.'[3] Downey's *Weird Science* co-star Kelly Le Brock was more blunt: 'He was a little shit.'[4]

Parker was the complete opposite of her boyfriend, even on screen. In 1985's *Girls Just Want to Have Fun*, a bubbly cash-in from New World on the Cyndi Lauper hit of the same name, she'd played a coy Chicago convent girl encouraged to enter a TV dance contest by her gregarious best pal (played by a twenty-one-year-old close friend of Matthew Broderick's called Helen Hunt). Meanwhile, in *Footloose* she'd been the bouncy best friend of the movie's real wild child, Lori Singer's Ariel.

But if Parker's relationship with the extroverted Downey Jr was already one of chalk and cheese, it wasn't helped by the couple's frequent house guest. Kiefer Sutherland was a year younger than Downey, another kid from the movie world who'd grown up in the midst of a divorce, to-ing and fro-ing between Toronto and LA as the son of Canadian actors Donald Sutherland – *Animal House*'s Professor Jennings – and Shirley Jones.[5] He'd already been an extra in *Max Dugan Returns* – in which his father appeared – after befriending star Matthew Broderick on visits to the set and he'd received critical acclaim for the low-budget Canadian movie *The Bay Boy*. In LA,

---

1 *Parade* magazine, Dotson Rader, 20 April 2008.

2 *People*, op cit. In the same article S. J.'s mum is quoted as saying: 'At their age they should be having fun and trying different relationships instead of getting so serious.'

3 *Parade*, op. cit.

4 'Why *Weird Science* Pin-Up Kelly Le Brock Left Hollywood', Yahoo! News, Ben Falk, 31 July 2015.

5 Jones and Sutherland divorced after he began a relationship with fellow actor Jane Fonda.

however, things were more of a struggle. He lost out on *A Nightmare on Elm Street* to Johnny Depp and his role alongside Sean Penn in *At Close Range* didn't actually include any lines of dialogue.

Things were so tough for while that Sutherland even lived, as had Nic Cage a couple of years earlier, out of his car (a '67 Mustang). Hooking up with the fun-loving Downey, however, saw a meeting of minds. 'I have a few drinks,' Sutherland admitted, 'and I'm not so worried about tomorrow and not thinking about yesterday. I am in this moment and I don't give a shit about anything else and that's that. It's right out of the textbook of problem drinkers.'[1]

Downey Jr's wild charisma that emanated from his Hollywood home was a magnet to other young stars too: Anthony Michael Hall and Billy Zane – the former had starred with him in *Weird Science*, the latter had failed to get *Dirty Dancing* but managed a small role in *Back to the Future* – were close friends. An awestruck Jodie Foster would later remark of Robert, 'His beautiful brain has no "off" switch and no caution button.'[2] But it wasn't just older teens and twenty-somethings that hung out with the Downey-Parkers. Back when they were still in New York and filming *Firstborn*, S. J. and Robert had helped their twelve-year-old co-star to cope with his parents' divorce.

He was called Corey Haim; a Toronto-born hockey and comic book fanatic who'd fallen into acting after accompanying his older sister Cari to auditions. But if Haim wasn't the usual child star with dreams of making it big then that only helped his on-screen appeal. He was a natural, seeming to have been plucked from being cocky in the classroom and dropped straight into the movie world. It was exactly that kind of charm that saw him offered a role in *Firstborn*. Then came another, this time as one of four mouthy-but-naïve twelve year olds hunting for a corpse in the 1986 adaptation of Stephen King's *The Body*. *This is Spinal Tap*'s Rob Reiner was set to direct after Adrian Lyne had turned it down but first *The Body* had to be retitled to make it sound less threatening. Reiner plumped for *Stand by Me*.

---

1 'Kiefer Sutherland: Heart of Darkness', *Rolling Stone*, Erik Hedegaard, April 2006.

2 At a ceremony honouring Downey Jr with the American Cinematheque Award, 14 October 2011.

Corey Haim, however, decided to say 'No'. *His* preferred choice of film was *Lucas*, another coming-of-age drama that – like *Stand by Me* – took early teen characters as seriously as Hughes had his high-school seniors. What *Lucas* didn't have on its side, however, was a respected director or author behind it, or even an iconic song as its title. *Stand by Me* sailed past fifty million dollars on its release during the summer of '86 – its nostalgia for the '60s as pertinent to adults as its coming-of-age thread was to kids – after *Lucas* stalled at around eight million dollars that spring. It really shouldn't have done. *Lucas* – too quickly an almost forgotten movie – features some of the most compelling scenes in teen cinema of the era.

Corey Haim's *Lucas* is a fourteen year old with brains and heart but no swagger. As a prodigy he's in class with students two years his senior but his weedy body and speccy gawping make him the butt of the cool kids' jokes. Whilst they flirt and party, he prefers to study insects or spout forth on the superficiality of social cliques and materialism. When new girl Maggie (Kerri Green) joins the school, however, she gets to know Lucas without being bogged down by received wisdom, leading him to – for what we can only presume is the first time – fall entirely in love.[1]

Lucas was written and directed by David Seltzer, a middle-aged film-maker who'd hit big in the '70s with demonic blockbuster *The Omen*. But he'd only done the horror for the money. *Lucas*, set in the Chicago suburbs he knew so well, was something Seltzer really believed in: a story of not judging a book by its cover (or, indeed, a nerd by his glasses). If the tone occasionally seems uncertain, Dave Grusin's score sometimes at odds with what's happening on screen, the film still gave Haim a chance to shine with a heartbreaking enthusiasm. Lucas is ever the optimist, uncynical even when he's being – in perhaps the film's most affecting scene – humiliated by jocks in front of everyone during assembly.

And school never looked more intimidating than it did in *Lucas*. Seltzer captured the vastness of the student body with countless extras pushing and shoving their way down halls and through

---

1 Haim claims that he also fell for Kerri Green in real life too.

locker rooms, filling up the bleachers at sports games. All the time there's Lucas's puny frame in the middle of things, the lone oddball swimming against the tide, standing out in the crowd, secretly loved by tomboyish Rina (a fifteen-year-old Winona Ryder, in her debut). In the equally packed lunch hall there's talk of a teacher who'd committed suicide when his love for a woman wasn't reciprocated, a dark undercurrent to the film that suggests things don't get any easier once you're an adult. But we never find out the exact details; *Lucas* focuses solely on the children rather than the grown-ups, not even parents getting much of a look-in. Instead it's Charlie Sheen who provides a fatherly shoulder for Lucas, being the one football player (Cappie) who respects the geeky outcast for his untainted kindness, yet who ultimately upsets the boy's sensitive disposition when Maggie chooses to date him instead. A few weeks later, Sheen would be seen in that cameo role in *Ferris Bueller's Day Off*. In *Lucas*, though, he gave a performance of surprisingly mellow grace.

Despite *Lucas* underperforming, Charlie Sheen was truly breaking through. He was another that had starred in an episode of Spielberg's *Amazing Stories* at the start of the year and would end 1986 with the lead in Hemdale and Oliver Stone's *Platoon*, full of a maturity and tenderness unusual in a twenty-one year old. He was, however, already the father of a toddler – Cassandra, with his high-school girlfriend Paula – and, like Sutherland and Downey Jr, balanced his quiet gentlemanliness with bouts of outrageous partying. His actor father Martin had done the same, something Charlie and Emilio had both witnessed when their dad's mental and physical state imploded during the *Apocalypse Now* shoot in the Philippines. At fifteen Charlie lost his virginity to a hooker called Candy in Las Vegas, paid for with his father's credit card. At sixteen he was arrested for being stoned at the wheel of his BMW. At Santa Monica High, meanwhile, he found himself expelled for non-attendance just a few weeks prior to graduation. In a way, it all made sense. Charlie had seen what fun Emilio was having with his success and he didn't just crave the same; he wanted *more*.

'The thing about Charlie is, he wrestles with all his demons in public. Most of us would go away and hide when we deal with that stuff,' believes Alan Ruck,[1] who had celebrated Sheen's twenty-first birthday with him while shooting *Three for the Road* in 1986 – also co-starring Kerri Green – having briefly crossed paths with him on *Ferris Bueller* (and who would again on *Young Guns II*[2]). Janet Templeton, meanwhile, liked to recall the moment her son was born, almost suffocated by the umbilical cord during delivery: 'Charlie started screaming and he hasn't stopped since.'[3] And by his side during the film of *Lucas*, the impressionable fourteen-year-old Corey Haim, his own taste for partying starting to dangerously mirror that of his older co-star.

Back at Parker and Downey Jr's house, it wasn't Charlie Sheen, Corey Haim, Anthony Michael Hall or Billy Zane who ultimately found themselves in the middle of the couple's romantic issues but Kiefer Sutherland. The intimidating gruffness he shared with his father Donald had won Sutherland the part of *Stand by Me*'s older antagonist 'Ace' Merrill, the adolescent snarl in a story that aims younger than many of its contemporary teen movies yet which also carries beneath its nostalgia[4] a fascination with the macabre (as with so much of Stephen King). He had also – like Charlie Sheen and Casey Siemaszko – recently excelled in an episode of *Amazing Stories.*[5]

Despite Sutherland being in a committed relationship with Camelia Kath (widow of Chicago guitarist Terry Kath, who had died from an accidental gunshot wound to the head in 1978), it's been suggested that his presence at the Downey-Parker house sometimes made things complicated: '[Kiefer] was probably staying with us for a while and then I was having some trouble with Sarah Jessica and he was looking after her. It was all rather incestuous back then . . .'[6] Downey Jr has admitted. But he has

---

1 Author interview.

2 And then, most significantly, on '90s TV hit *Spin City*.

3 'Decadence that destroyed Prince of Hollywood Charlie Sheen', *Daily Mail*, Alison Boshoff, 18 November 2015.

4 *Stand by Me* is narrated by lead character Gordy as an adult, looking back on his Oregon childhood in 1959.

5 Sutherland's episode from late 1985 was the same as Siemaszko's: 'The Mission'. It was directed by Spielberg himself and also starred Kevin Costner.

6 *Howard Stern Show*, Sirius XM, May 2016.

also remained realistic about the situation: 'He didn't steal my girl, he remained in the relationship he was in ... He is, and remains, a very disciplined guy despite whatever habits either of us had ... he was a shoulder ... better him than some stranger.' And, after all, the party-loving Robert never claimed to be easy to live with: '[S. J.] was normal and I was out of my mind.'[1]

Still, despite his busy house and even busier social life, Downey Jr remained working. He had been considered for the lead roles in both *Top Gun* and *Ferris Bueller's Day Off* and, as the careers of Kiefer, Corey and Charlie began to take flight in 1986–87, he also scored two lead roles, albeit in high-profile flops. *The Pick-Up Artist* had the influential writer and self-confessed hedonist James Toback directing,[2] Woody Allen regular Gordon Willis shooting and Warren Beatty – a figure equally deified and debated – producing but the romantic comedy about a commitment-phobic ladies man failed to attract an audience.

Molly Ringwald co-starred in *The Pick-Up Artist*, playing the one woman – museum tour guide Randy – who was a match for Downey Jr's hyperactive Jack Jericho and remembers a shoot where the modernity of the Brat Pack style clashed with Toback and Beatty's grounding in the authenticity of another era: 'There were lots of cooks in the kitchen. Warren would take Robert Downey and me into a room and make us break down the entire script. He made us delete all the adjectives. He would even delete stage direction because that was how Stella Adler, his acting coach, trained him.'[3] *The Pick-Up Artist* ended up with an uneven tone and a heavily edited running time (just eighty-one minutes) that hardly invited critical acclaim although Ringwald's single-minded Randy showed a sexual confidence impressively unusual in a female lead. Still, its meagre thirteen million dollars at the box-office was noticeably less than its budget.

Downey Jr's next film *Less Than Zero*,[4] meanwhile, could have been a contender. Directed by London-based Pole Marek Kanievska

---

1 Ibid.

2 Toback has recently (late 2017) been the subject of several well-documented accusations relating to his womanising.

3 theatlantic.com, John Meroney, 19 August 2010.

4 Its title came from Elvis Costello's 1977 anti-fascist single of the same name.

and based on Bret Easton Ellis's *cause célèbre* novel about drug-addled rich LA kids,[1] the Fox release was packed with John Hughes alumni looking to prove themselves: Andrew McCarthy, James Spader and Jami Gertz (a former child star from Chicago who had appeared in *Sixteen Candles*). Yet its production history was one of confusion, its concept endlessly tinkered around with by filmmakers uncertain exactly how to deal with remnants of the Brat Pack in a shadier, more cryptic drama. No wonder audiences were bemused.

Less Than Zero had originally been optioned by producer Marvin Worth for only 7500 dollars in the summer of '85, before it had even been published, with the understanding that Twentieth Century Fox would back it. The story needed work though. This was no conventional tale, consisting of not so much a plot as a series of extreme situations, sleaze-filled moments capturing college rich-kid Clay's return to his native LA for the Christmas holidays and his experiences as a bisexual cocaine user. Any screenplay would need to tidy up its deliberately explicit approach. However, a first draft by Pulitzer prize winning writer Michael Cristofer was deemed still too risky by Fox, leading them to give it to *Risky Business* producer Jon Avnet for a reboot ('I felt it was so depressing and so degrading. A crucial element of the American Dream had gone haywire and you had to put it in a recognisable form in a movie, not just shock people,' Avnet said of the first draft[2]).

But there was trouble at the top. Fox's president Larry Gordon had quit the company in 1986 and new boss Leonard Goldberg – one-time producer of *WarGames* – didn't like what he'd been left. At least industry veteran Barry Diller, now chairman at Fox after his years at Paramount, championed *Less Than Zero* and screenwriter Harley Peyton was brought in to do more work on the script, although that still didn't entirely allay certain fears. Was the story's gay sex too prominent at a time when AIDS was in the headlines? Was Downey Jr's character of Julian too wayward for McCarthy's teenage girl fanbase? Staying true to the downbeat

---

1 Published in 1985 when he was only twenty-one.
2 'Sanitizing a Novel for the Screen', *New York Times*, Aljean Harmetz, 18 November 1987.

mood of the novel would be laudable but hardly lead to box-office fodder, yet losing the brutal power of the book would mean the whole point of the story would be gone too. Messages were mixed. Fox executive Scott Rudin tells of a new scene added to soften the story, where Gertz's character Blair – a drug-user herself and in a love triangle with Julian and Clay – throws cocaine down the sink in front of other partygoers ('What a waste!' 'Well . . . call a plumber!'); a moment at odds with the hedonism of the original but greeted with cheers by a surprisingly conservative teen test audience. Another scene featuring the Red Hot Chili Peppers was then heavily edited – against Kanievska's wishes – as the funk rockers were deemed to look too intimidating.

Such mixed feelings from all sides about where to go with *Less Than Zero* ultimately – and inevitably – left the finished product neither one thing nor the other, a mix of the indulgent and the uneventful. There's a surprising shot of McCarthy's bare bottom early on but pretty soon Clay is as bland and wimpy as *Pretty in Pink*'s Blaine or *Mannequin*'s Jonathan. Ultimately, as in both of those films, it's James Spader in support who ends up way more appealing than anyone, playing Julian's drug-dealing nemesis Rip with his usual twitchy and distracted lip-licking relish.

Less Than Zero's soundtrack at least had hints of something different, managing an edge courtesy of producer Rick Rubin, then co-owner with Russell Simmons of the New York record label Def Jam that had been breaking down boundaries with hip-hop acts such as Beastie Boys, Public Enemy and Run DMC, blending rap with heavy metal. He gave jangly girl band The Bangles a tougher sound – one they preferred – on their cover of Simon & Garfunkel's moody 'Hazy Shade of Winter which opened the movie whilst early rap pin-up LL Cool J also got a spot on the album with 'Going Back to Cali'.

Downey Jr also came out of the film well; what's left of Ellis's original sleazy rich-kid appeal in the flattened-out adaptation really belonged to him. Julian is a young man already lost, his puppy-dog eagerness mixing with tragic desperation whilst Clay and Blair run around after him, trying to do the good thing and save their friend from his self-destruction. It's no wonder Downey Jr was so convincing. In his real life, he could see that S. J. was doing exactly the same thing: 'She provided me with a home and understanding. She tried to help me. She was so miffed when I didn't get my act together.'[1] *Less Than Zero* posted decent reviews thanks largely to his performance and Edward Lachmann's modish night-time cinematography but, like *The Pick-Up Artist* before it, struggled at the box-office. Was this a teen film or an adult one? Downey Jr was equally confused, liked and respected but without a hit. So he kept on partying.

If *Dirty Dancing* was feminine and romantic, about a more innocent teenage time – summer 1963, perhaps the *last* innocent teenage time – a film released alongside it in 1987 celebrated the opposite: the laddish, the outrageous and the modern. It would also be the film to finally turn Downey Jr's house guests Kiefer Sutherland and Corey Haim into superstars. In fact, Joel Schumacher's rock'n'roll teen horror movie *The Lost Boys* boasted a whole *host* of braying young actors, as well as a loud and lairy soundtrack, plus the kind of strutting tagline that proved both apt and irresistible: 'Sleep all day. Party all night. Never grow old. Never die. It's fun to be a vampire.' No more John Hughes and his sensitive teen dandies.

Nineteen-eighty-seven was a year of cultural contrasts, a cross over period of decency versus temptation not just in the opposing moods of *Dirty Dancing* and *The Lost Boys*. If it wasn't the smiley Whitney Houston making waves in the charts, then it was the depraved Mötley Crüe. At the cinema the super-sweet *Three Men and a Baby* made millions but then so did the devilishly sexy *Witches of Eastwick*. Alan Parker's artfully demonic *Angel Heart*, meanwhile, joined the dour *River's Edge* as one of the most controversial. In the news, previously clean-cut figures such as televangelist Jim Bakker and Senator Gary Hart found their careers in tatters after exposés of extra-martial affairs while the always delicate Michael Jackson tried to go the other way and deliberately get in on the debauchery, his *Bad* album from September a little unconvincingly boasting a cover full of black leather and graffiti and song titles such as 'Smooth Criminal' and 'Dirty Diana'.

---

1 *Parade* magazine, op. cit.

At the close of the year the name of one high-profile legal case succinctly summed up this battle of the raucous against the romantic: *Hustler* vs Falwell. The Moral Majority preacher Jerry Falwell had taken Larry Flynt's porn magazine to court over a parody article from 1983 that caricatured him as a drunk and a letch. After a lengthy and detailed case *Hustler* ultimately won, its spoofing of a public figure protected by the First Amendment and it was the kind of liberal ruling that ran through Schumacher's own output: 'I think that a lot of our culture is set up for people to deny who they really are. I'm not saying that all people are inherently evil but we spend so much of the time wanting people to think that we're perfect, that we don't have bad thoughts or do bad things, that we're all really perfect people ... and we are. We're perfect in our imperfections.'[1]

That same summer of *The Lost Boys* had also seen the debut studio album by west coast party animals Guns N' Roses hit record stores. It was called *Appetite for Destruction* although *Perfect Imperfections* would have worked just as well. *Appetite's* opening track began with a lycanthropic howl and a bold invitation: 'Welcome to the jungle, we've got fun and games / We got everything you want honey, we know the names / We are the people that can find whatever you may need / If you got the money honey we got your disease'. In the era of AIDS panic, a virus spread by 'fun and games' that had provoked incendiary moral debate, that last word couldn't have been more pertinent.

After much touring and eventual MTV airplay, G N' R's *Appetite for Destruction* – released on Geffen Records, other labels apparently too scared to sign band members Axl, Izzy, Duff, Steve and Slash[2] – slowly worked its way to the top spot of the Billboard album chart and into the spotlight. Critics were swift to deconstruct its success, its popularity deemed a two-finger salute to several years where sex, drugs and rock'n'roll had become taboo and rebellious youthful energy stifled by the conservative Reagan-Bush administration, campaign groups such as the Parents' Music

---

1 'The story behind *The Lost Boys*', from www.totalfilm.com
2 Lead guitarist Slash had been at Beverly Hills High with Nic Cage.

Resource Center[1] and uncertainty about HIV. At a time in need of an emotional release *River's Edge* explored the bleak consequences but *Appetite for Destruction* and *The Lost Boys* took a more upbeat approach: both welcome come-ons to a free-spirited party.[2] The dress code was low-key too: punky rips and thrift shop leathers, dirty clothes that shrieked of dirty minds way more than even the dandy spandex and poodle hair of Kiss and Twisted Sister. Or as Axl Rose so eloquently put it: 'People like Paul Stanley from Kiss can suck my dick!'[3]

Not that *The Lost Boys* was meant to be so riotous. The story had originally been conceived by producer Richard Donner as a companion piece to his kids' film from 1985, *The Goonies*, another of exec-producer Steven Spielberg's pre-teen adventure stories that had starred Sean Astin, Martha Plimpton, Josh Brolin and Kerri Green, in a script by Chris Columbus. Donner liked what original *Lost Boys* writers Janice Fischer and James Jeremias had come up with – a family-friendly vampire take on *Peter Pan* that matched *The Goonies'* spirit of youthful adventure – but when he pulled out to make buddy movie *Lethal Weapon* instead and after false starts on *The Lost Boys* with Australian thriller director Richard Franklin and 'Material Girl' video helmer Mary Lambert, Donner's wife Lauren Shuler recommended her old friend Joel Schumacher for the job.

Schumacher wasn't sure; he was hot from *St Elmo's Fire* and certainly not keen to just make *The Goonies Part 2*. Kids' films weren't his thing. Instead he suggested that *The Lost Boys* get tweaked into something with adolescent attitude, something to make him more keen to be involved. Jeffrey Boam's rewrite gave him just what he was after. Look closely and there are still some nods to *Peter Pan*[4] but mainly Boam had produced something

---

1 *Appetite for Destruction* carried one of the PMRC's infamous 'Parental Advisory' stickers.

2 Beastie Boys' '(You Gotta) Fight for Your Right (to Party)' had blended rock and rap in the spring of '86, in what appeared to be an earlier, grungy ode to teenage hedonism with a video that saw the oikish trio invade a nerds' party (the nerds in glasses, bowties and reading *Popular Science* magazine). Actually the Top 10 hit was written as a spoof of the prancing macho hair metal of Mötley Crüe and Twisted Sister, although few realised the joke. Guns N' Roses, however, were entirely serious about their commitment to snarling, no frills rock'n'roll. It was what made them stand out.

3 Shouted to the crowd at the Paradiso in Amsterdam, 2 October 1987. Some older rockers – such as Kiss – hadn't exactly been supportive of Guns N' Roses.

4 e.g. Nanook the dog, similar to J. M. Barrie's Nana.

much more sexy: a grubby celebration of teenage outsiders and the misunderstood.

Schumacher had certainly never hidden his own troubled past: 'Back in the late '60s when I was in fashion and working for Halston,[1] I'd walk around the city at night on drugs like a ghost. I was shooting speed. I had blankets over my windows and went out around midnight and would walk around in the freezing cold, with some adventure along the way. I was in another world, what Joan Didion called, "You're out there where there is nothing".'[2]

If the film-maker had written *St Elmo's Fire* because he was fascinated by how earnest college leavers had become in the early '80s then his interest in *The Lost Boys* was the logical flip side. The demonic title characters – a leather-clad teen biker gang led by Kiefer Sutherland's David, terrorising the Californian seaside town of Santa Carla[3] – might have officially been the bad guys but their openly debauched lifestyle was at least a lot more honest than the suit-clad yuppies who hid their hedonism behind desk jobs and officialdom. It also looked a hell of a lot more fun. Who wouldn't rather be Axl Rose than Phil Collins?

Horror movies had, of course, utilised vulnerable teenagers as lead characters for many years. After all, the genre plays on an audience's uncertainties and fears; what time in life has more of those than adolescence? But it was the VHS boom of the '80s that really gave horror another lease of life, this new outlet allowing independent producers to make gorier films for video than a studio might for the big screen and still get plenty of viewers.[4] Unsurprisingly, the success of such slasher franchises wasn't without controversy. It was an open secret that, despite restrictive MPAA ratings, many young teenagers would watch these movies in the comfort of their front rooms. 'I think after *Friday the 13th* and its imitators there

---

1 American fashion label, luxurious but simple, worn by the likes of Liza Minnelli, Elizabeth Taylor and Bianca Jagger.

2 Vulture.com, Tim Murphy, 9 August 2010.

3 A fictional place. Most of the film was actually shot in Santa Cruz, California, but the locals only agreed to let Warner shoot there if they changed the name.

4 Although the majors such as Paramount were in on the act too, releasing eight *Friday the 13th* films during the decade.

was a feeling that horror was bad and bad for kids,'[1] *A Nightmare on Elm Street* creator Wes Craven mused. 'It was during that period when video games were being looked at as causing kids to be violent and there were all sorts of made-up stories about kids killing their sisters wearing *Friday the 13th* masks and whatever. The far right was starting to rattle these cages, and I think the studios were afraid of making a film that had blood in it.'

The Lost Boys certainly didn't have the Moral Majority in mind when it lowered the gore and upped the style of its horror but it was an acknowledgement that since so many youngsters devoured scary movies, why not give them something with a modern, MTV aesthetic? To achieve it, Schumacher infused his film with the spirit of Gothic rock; a movement first popular in the psychedelic '60s but which, by 1987, boasted a rockier British spin that was beginning to crack the States courtesy of bands such as The Mission and The Cult. The latter were produced by Rick Rubin – his first non-rap act – and they toured North America that year with Guns N' Roses as support. The rumour was the band's frontmen, partners-in-crime Ian Astbury and Billy Duffy, had trashed so much equipment on the road that no company would lend them any more.

The Lost Boys was also where Corey Haim – cast as lead Sam Emerson, young newcomer to Santa Carla – would meet *his* future sidekick and lifelong collaborator. It made sense since the two had a lot in common, sharing both a life of excess and – in a coincidence perfect for a teen market always looking for an accessible hook – a first name.

Corey Feldman had appeared in bigger movies than Corey Haim – the aforementioned *Gremlins*, *The Goonies* and *Stand by Me*, plus regulation horror *Friday the 13th: The Final Chapter*[2] – not to mention countless commercials and TV shows, but his family life with his manager father wasn't always happy; something that really struck home when working with Joel Schumacher on *The Lost Boys*. '[Joel] was a high-tempered man so he did tend to raise his voice a lot, which was a bit startling for me because I was

---

1 '"I Don't Feel Like I Gave Birth to Jesus": Wes Craven on *A Nightmare on Elm Street*', *Filmmaker* magazine, Jim Hemphill, 31 August 2015.

2 Feldman had also auditioned for the title role in *Lucas*, whilst Haim went for what would become Feldman's role of Mouth in *The Goonies*.

around a lot of violence and anger and things like that as a kid,' Feldman has said of his director. 'But he was never violent with us or anything like that.'[1]

Others in the industry were not so considerate. Both Coreys, just in their early teens when making *The Lost Boys*, partied like rock stars in their downtime mainly as a way to forget horrific incidents from their pasts. Feldman's mother Sheila, a former *Playboy* model with drugs issues, had obsessively controlled his diet as a toddler, calling him fat and even before his age was in double figures the young star was repeatedly reminded by his parents of his position as the family's breadwinner[2]. He also claimed that an assistant hired for him by his father had repeatedly abused him sexually – an experience he had in common with Haim. 'He [Corey Haim] had more direct abuse than I did. With me, there were some molestations and it did come from several hands, so to speak but with Corey, his was direct rape, whereas mine was not actual rape. And his occurred when he was eleven.'[3] He believed the pair of them were 'being passed around' Hollywood circles in the mid-'80s, that 'the number one problem in Hollywood was, is and always will be paedophilia'[4], and as he publicly attempted to 'divorce' his parents, claiming they were 'both very abusive and very selfish and were more interested in what was happening with themselves than what was happening with my life'[5], Feldman was also spending more and more time with Michael Jackson, one of the few people who could understand what it was like to grow up in the spotlight as a child star. The two had been introduced by mutual friend Steven Spielberg and bonded over a shared fear: their fathers.

Thankfully, not all the partying behind the scenes of *The Lost Boys* came from such a dark place. Alex Winter was a twenty-one-year-old Broadway child actor-turned-NYU film student who'd got the role of vampire teamster Marko straight after playing another gang member on the very different *Death Wish 4*, another

---

1 *The Hollywood Reporter*, Seth Abramovitch, 25 May 2016.

2 The publication of Feldman's 2013 memoir *Coreyography* (St Martin's Press) led Sheila to deny many of his claims.

3 Ibid.

4 'Underage and Famous', NBC's *Nightline*, 10 August 2011. Feldman has never named names and Haim's mother has generally distanced herself from his claims.

5 *The Hollywood Reporter*, op. cit.

Charles Bronson exploitation pic produced by Cannon and directed by series regular Michael Winner: 'Michael was crazy and sadistic and probably psychotic; not altogether talented but *really* entertaining. It was an extremely entertaining experience. He was just batshit crazy and the movie was godawful.'[1] Moving on to work alongside Kiefer Sutherland, Brooke McCarter and Billy Wirth as *The Lost Boys* proved to be another entertaining time for Winter, albeit for rather cooler reasons: 'We were basically a rock band, y'know. The four of us were basically a rock band, in a party town, working nights. So you can fill in the dots on that . . . I didn't really have much to do so I had an enormous amount of down-time and it was without a doubt the most debauched and memorable summer of my life. Usually on a movie it isn't that glamorous – it is pretty hard work and arduous and it can even be boring. *Lost Boys* was none of those things. It just wasn't. It was fun, it was a giant party. Joel created this extremely familial environment, like you feel like you're really part of this tight-knit family. He's very inclusive like he really brings you in. I made a lot of friends. Kiefer and I went nuts. A bunch of us went nuts. I had a really great time; definitely the most fun I ever had working on a film.'[2] For a gothic rock horror all about the allure of life in the fast lane, it shouldn't have been any other way.

Yet even as *The Lost Boys* was shooting, Joel Schumacher's exact *raison d'être* was still a mystery to many. Songwriter Gerard McMann had attracted the director's attention with his regular LA gigs, plus tracks for *Fast Times* and *All the Right Moves* and was now approached to contribute to the brooding *Lost Boys* soundtrack: 'I asked Joel if I could view the film first to get a vibe on what it looked like and its flow [but] he told me that would be impossible at that time as they were still shooting.' McMann had to rely on hints in the script rather than any visuals to get inspired, drawing on 'enough dark things going on in my own life at the time, living in gothic New York'[3].

---

1 Author interview.
2 Ibid.
3 Author interview.

Alex Winter had read the script too but also couldn't yet see exactly what Schumacher had in store: 'I found it amusing and entertaining and funny and all that but nowhere in there was his game plan ... no indication of what he wanted to do ... But I began to realise he was up to something when I could see the crew he was building around him like Michael Chapman. I was like "Why is the DP [director of photography] of *Raging Bull* shooting this movie? Like, what the fuck is going on, y'know?!"'[1]

Even Kiefer Sutherland, cast by Schumacher after seeing his brief and silent role in *At Close Range*,[2] remembers being – perhaps aptly for a vampire movie – in the dark: 'I wish I had known what we were doing when we were doing it. You know? It's been such a part of my life, and I wish in the process of making it I had enjoyed it a little more.'[3]

Bemused executives, meanwhile, kept asking Schumacher for details but even he didn't yet have a definitive answer: 'Nobody really knew what we were making. And in many ways *we* didn't know what we were making!' Queried by Warner as to whether he was directing a horror or a comedy, Schumacher simply replied, 'Yes.'[4]

Composing a song with only a vague idea of what was needed nevertheless paid off for McMann: 'Within three days Joel rang me on a very hungover morning and was raving about the song and that they were playing it on set and how everyone was blown away. [But] I probably never would have written "Cry Little Sister" if I'd watched the film.'[5]

Meanwhile, as *Lost Boys* went into post-production Schumacher's dual worlds in fashion (Ralph Lauren came to visit the set) and comedy started to come together, *The Lost Boys* edited into a perfect mix of style and humour. The penny finally dropped for Alex Winter: 'That material could have just been shot like a straight-up horror comedy, which the '80s was rife with. But I don't think anyone had come at a teen horror comedy with the

---

1 Author interview.

2 'He's a born character actor,' Joel Schumacher said of Sutherland in the DVD feature *Casting Kiefer*. 'His presence is extraordinary.'

3 The AV Club, Will Harris, 7 March 2016.

4 Joel Schumacher on *The Lost Boys* DVD commentary.

5 Author interview.

approach of a Nicholas Ray '50s teen exploitation movie like *Rebel Without a Cause*; just gave it all of that style and, with a tongue in cheek, took it really seriously ... I just figure that was really a stroke of genius on Joel's part [to do that]. That's just my impression. When I made that movie I'd just come out of NYU Film School so I was steeped in that cinema ... It was sort of like doing grad school. I just shut up and watched. Thankfully, I don't say a damn thing in the movie so I had plenty of time to watch!'[1]

And along with the jokes and the blood, *The Lost Boys* was seriously sexy. Seductive dry ice floods the town's carnivalesque boardwalk, pouting punks and rabble-rousers loitering bewitchingly in the shadows, a huge change to the conventional city life that lead characters Sam and Michael knew from their previous home in sunny Phoenix. 'They're the only monsters that are really sexy ... they can be sultry and sexy and have real intimacy because there's an exchange of body fluids,'[2] Schumacher said of the vampires at the centre of the story, having captured that seductive quality with a distinctly contemporary palette: 'Music videos educated a whole generation to surreal images and non-sequitur storytelling. A lot of the things we did in this movie would have seemed too odd to people before MTV, actually. That gave us a lot of licence to play with things.'[3]

But even Schumacher's modish eye hadn't initially clocked Jami Gertz as a possible to play Star, the story's free-spirited and beguiling half-vampire beauty queen who entices Jason Patric's Michael into her blood-sucking world. Casting her was actually Patric's idea, the eighteen year old having starred with Gertz in the previous year's megabomb sci-fi *Solarbabies*, and who hadn't been able to get her off his mind. If Kiefer Sutherland and his gang were the dark heart of *The Lost Boys*, with Coreys Haim and Feldman the comedy relief, then Jason Patric and Jami Gertz were the eye-candy. Schumacher had initially wanted someone petite and blonde to play Star but when he took on the raven-haired Gertz at Patric's suggestion, he was happy to be proven wrong.

---

1 Author interview.
2 DVD commentary, op. cit.
3 Ibid.

Nevertheless, *The Lost Boys* had its budget cut when Schumacher made the decision not to cast major names. So if much of its horror comes from what *isn't* shown as opposed to what is, such modesty was initially only because of financial restraints rather than a clever, long-standing vision. The vampires were rarely seen flying simply because it was just too expensive to show.

Still, by using mainly newcomers, *The Lost Boys* also felt like a step forward; a move clearly appreciated by audiences since the movie opened at No. 2 at the box-office, eventually taking over thirty-two million dollars from a budget of around eight million dollars. Sam has posters on his bedroom wall of Rob Lowe and Molly Ringwald but the fresh-faced appeal that was so big when the movie shot in 1986 was already looking tired by the time of its release a year later; things had moved into sexier, more sinister territory.

'People Are Strange' sang Echo & The Bunnymen on *The Lost Boys'* huge-selling soundtrack, the track a cover of a 1967 single by goth-rock pioneers The Doors, whose lead singer Jim Morrison featured on another poster in the movie, this time in David's bohemian bat cave. 'I felt that the lost boys would be big Doors fans because The Doors to me had the perfect combination of nihilism and sultry sexuality and poetry. It always seemed that Jim Morrison in his lyrics was haunted by death,' said Schumacher.[1] Such nihilism and death had certainly never been part of Lowe and Ringwald's kids-next-door routine.

'Joel was and is the most creative and open-minded director I've ever worked with. He takes risks that he knows can ultimately make the difference,' remembers Gerard McMann, but it was the lyrics to one of INXS's two songs on *The Lost Boys* soundtrack that perhaps best sum up its hedonistic appeal: 'Gonna have a good time tonight / Rock'n'roll music gonna play all night'[2]. INXS lead singer Michael Hutchence had wanted to get more involved with the film world, having already appeared in low-budget Aussie punk scene biopic *Dogs in Space* and, as news of Oliver Stone's upcoming Jim Morrison biopic circulated around Hollywood,

---

1 *The Lost Boys* DVD commentary.
2 'Good Time' was a duet with fellow Australian rocker Jimmy Barnes, a cover of The Easybeats' 1968 hit.

both he and The Cult's Ian Astbury were mooted as possible leads. First, though, INXS had to follow *The Lost Boys* with a new album, October 1987's *Kick*, with Joel Schumacher himself directing one of the music videos: a smokey, biker bar-set four minutes for the auspiciously titled US No. 2 hit, 'Devil Inside'.

The aftermath of *The Lost Boys* saw a regime change in teen Hollywood, most notably for Corey Haim. Suddenly he was no longer someone with other people's posters on his wall. He was a poster boy himself. Nineteen-eighty-eight's *License to Drive* re-teamed Haim with Feldman – the Two Coreys – as names-above-the-title best friends Les and Dean, the former (Haim) a boyish charmer trying to woo high-maintenance babe Mercedes (Heather Graham) despite his humiliation at flunking the school's driving course. But if *License to Drive* heralded the new headlining power of two young stars (both Coreys were just sixteen at the time of filming) its execution was decidedly familiar.

Produced by Davis Entertainment, run by the son of infamous Twentieth Century Fox boss Marvin Davis, writer Neil Tolkin's *License to Drive* script featured such John Hughes staples as an eccentric family in the middle-class suburbs, an eventful teenage house party and the frustration felt by a kid without a car. Mercedes was like a teenage Lisa from *Weird Science*, both erotic and erratic, whilst Les's decision to 'borrow' the family's wheels to impress her was reminiscent of both *Ferris Bueller* and Paul Brickman's *Risky Business*. From the latter there was even Richard Masur; once Joel's suspicious Princeton admissions officer, now playing Les's off-the-wall father.

The Two Coreys' real-life hangout of choice back then had been Alphy's Soda Pop Club, an exclusive underage night in the Hollywood Roosevelt Hotel, sponsored by twenty-two-year-old soft drinks magnate Randy Miller. It was there that Haim mixed with fellow young stars such as Frank Zappa's niece Lala Sloatman, *Who's the Boss?*[1] actress Alyssa Milano – a professional performer since touring in *Annie* aged seven – and her former TV co-star,

---

1 In which Tony Danza played a former baseball star now working as a live-in housekeeper to a high-flying female divorcee (Judith Light).

fifteen-year-old Nicole Eggert, about to feature alongside Scott Baio in his small-screen comeback *Charles in Charge*. Haim was there every week: 'I was going out with Alyssa at the time and kind of going out with Nicole. We were all seeing one another off and on. We were young. It was the '80s and it was different times. We were all friends. We were like the Brat Pack, but we had our own people. It was Ricky Schroder, Alfonso Ribeiro, Feldman, me, Nicole, Alyssa, Scott Grimes. We were like our own team.'[1] Nights at Alphy's were eventful, one even seeing Randy Miller jump from the eleventh floor as a stunt for a New York Seltzer commercial.[2] But the party only lasted a couple of years. 'By the end it was dying out and everyone was on drugs! I was on drugs. Feldman was on drugs. At the end of it, we were sixteen or seventeen years old! *Lost Boys* was done, and we were going to other clubs and doing drugs. So at that time a lot of people were getting messed up.'[3]

None of which you would notice in *License to Drive*. Haim's onscreen charm was his sweet goofiness, a charmer but not a player, and the film plays young; a remarkably conservative follow-on from his roles in *The Lost Boys* and *Lucas*. There was even a streak of casual jingosim in there, with both Les's sister's 'loony' left-wing leanings and a 'slimy foreigner' called Paulo things of ridicule.[4] The soundtrack, meanwhile, steered clear of raucous rock and focused more on poppy R&B. At the film's close, Billy Ocean's jovial 'Get Out of my Dreams (Get into my Car)' plays over the end credits; the very song that a few months earlier had kept INXS's 'Devil Inside' from the US top spot.

Haim's personal life might not have been quite as sweet-smelling as his baby-faced outward appearance but the twenty-two million dollars that *License to Drive* made in the US was a testament to

---

1 'Him, Himself and He', *Vice* magazine, Jennifer Stratford, 13 May 2012. Ricky Schroeder had won a Golden Globe for 1979 boxing drama *The Champ* when he was just nine and then featured in TV sitcom *Silver Spoons* that also starred Alfonso Ribeiro. Scott Grimes was a sixteen-year-old actor and singer who'd been in TV films, horror pic *Critters* and *Who's the Boss?* as Milano's love interest, Chad.

2 Miller – a frustrated danger man – also owned tigers, jaguars and bobcats.

3 'He, Himself, and He', op. cit.

4 'Who cares what your commie boyfriend thinks?! I say it's great to be raised in America!' shouts Les to his sister Natalie at the dinner table. She was played by Nina Siemaszko – the sister of *Three O'Clock High*'s Casey.

his unthreatening appeal. A couple of weeks after *License to Drive* released, Boston bubblegum poppers New Kids on the Block placed their first single inside the US Top 50, more R&B-lite called 'Please Don't Go Girl' with a lead vocal by fourteen-year-old Corey Haim lookalike Joey McIntyre. New Kids had been put together by impresario Maurice Starr in an attempt to repeat the early '80s success of his boy band New Edition and Corey Haim could have come straight from the same stable; apparently playful, cheeky and carefree. Both New Kids and Haim box-ticked teen problems such as first love and friendship in their output, but only in the most superficial of ways, whilst seventeen-year-old singing stars Tiffany and Debbie Gibson scored hits as their slightly more earnest female counterparts.[1] Teenybop pop stars hadn't been big since the '70s but now, after a run of issue-laden songs and movies – 'We Are the World' to *WarGames* – and with the inevitable change of national mood that came with a new president,[2] this younger breed of teen stars began to replace the politicised with the peppy. And Corey Haim was at the helm, the logical alternative to the macho brooding rage of *The Lost Boys*, Kiefer Sutherland and Guns N' Roses, perfect for young teenage girls.

Yet behind the smiles Haim continued his own, very dark struggle. On the advice of his *Lost Boys* friend Brooke McCarter they filmed a thirty-five-minute documentary together, calling it *Corey Haim: Me, Myself and I*, a video diary of the actor that was sold in stores, produced after his first stint in rehab to show what a great place he was now in. What it actually exposed was a young man with a huge house and car . . . but no joy. When Haim wasn't talking in voiceover about the inane minutiae of his life ('You are what you wear. I wear something different every day') he was looking distracted on camera, his attention span short as he hopped around from one thing to another – hockey, tennis, keyboards, modelling – always looking for fun but never seeming satisfied. He wanted to grow up in his films, he announced in a

---

1 Tiffany had US No. 1s with 'I Think We're Alone Now' and 'Could've Been' at the end of 1987 whilst Gibson's 'Foolish Beat' from spring 1988 made her the youngest person ever to write, produce and sing a US No. 1 single.

2 George H. W. Bush would beat Democrat Michael Dukakis in the 1988 presidential election. Whilst Bush was a familiar Republican, having been Reagan's VP, he arrived at a time when relations with the USSR were thawing under the more open leadership of Mikhail Gorbachev.

more serious moment and he looked up to the *Three's Company* sitcom actor John Ritter for his comic ability. Music-wise, Haim declared he was into that 'funky, hip, pop jam thing'. But he also came across as someone desperately searching for something – *anything* – to give his life some meaning.

Joel Schumacher looked on: 'There is a part of you that wonders, "Well, did I innocently, inadvertently, by matching [Haim and Feldman] together, create an atmosphere where this all happened for them?" . . . you don't know if you'd contributed to this in some way by actually casting them.'[1]

Plus, of course, Schumacher was going through his own struggles at the same time as his teenage stars. 'I started drinking when I was nine, doing drugs in my early teens. I'd shot drugs in my arms from 1965 to 1970. When I got off "the needle", as we say, I didn't think I had any problems any more because my denial was, "As long as I'm not putting a needle in my arm I don't have any problem." But as my life in Hollywood became more complex and more successful – which was happening by 1986, 1987 – then definitely the old demons came back. And whilst I was not shooting drugs I was certainly getting into recreational drugs at way too frequent a level. I never thought drinking was a problem so, of course, I was an alcoholic who didn't realise he was an alcoholic . . . [But] you become so busy you're not really dealing with your problems. You can fill your time with stuff and you don't have to think about it.'[2]

Perhaps most interestingly though, Corey Haim's *Me, Myself and I* revealed as much about a cultural change as it did about a single star. Increasingly user-friendly video technology meant that cameras were no longer just for professional film shoots; now they were for fun at home too, allowing anyone to film, document and analyse their life. If some paid the price for that – from James Spader in 1989's lauded drama *Sex, Lies and Videotape* to Rob Lowe in real life – Haim was utilising a camcorder in *Me, Myself and I* to put across the image he wanted his fans to believe in: he was just a cool, happy-go-lucky guy.

---

1 Author interview, BBC Radio 1, 6 January 2005.
2 Ibid.

Yet the scenes of his posing in fashion shoots and pouting on a pool inflatable also show a less casual side; an awareness of image that came from growing up on camera and not knowing any different. Now that technology had moved from the film studio into the home, performers like Haim could carry on their show even when officially off-the-clock. The explosion of internet-based social media and its use as personal publicity was still a long way off, of course, but really *Me, Myself and I* played like an early piece of YouTube self-love; trying to make a life seem carefree and innocent when it was clear that something so manufactured could actually never be *that* innocent. 'Stay on course. There are so many obstacles in life,' Haim told his fans in the film. 'There are a lot of feelings growing up, a lot of questions you have while you're growing up . . . everything should work out fine as long as you keep in touch with yourself.' But with an ever-growing army of cameras pointed at him, lenses both invited and unwanted, working out exactly what his 'self' was proved difficult.

Whilst Corey Haim's legion of young fans meant he had to mask his troubled side, older teen stars openly continued their journey into darker territory. Kiefer Sutherland repeated his bad-boy act as supporting actor in April 1988's controversial *Bright Lights, Big City*, a noble stab at complex drama by baby-faced star Michael J. Fox. *Bright Lights* was based on the novel by Jay McInerney and had been optioned by Columbia after publication back in 1984, the adaptation memorably referenced in David Blum's Brat Pack article as a potential vehicle for any number of the group.[1] Tom Cruise was originally attached, with Schumacher directing but, after many delays at its second home of United Artists – and with Judd Nelson, Emilio Estevez and Rob Lowe all at times considered for roles – the movie finally got made with a heavily rewritten script, new director and unlikely star in the former Marty McFly.

Michael J. Fox had become a megastar post-*Back to the Future*, although he'd struggled to follow up the franchise with mature leading roles, pushing him like so many others to drink. 'Those

---

1 'The last book I read on my own was *Bright Lights, Big City*,' Molly Ringwald told *Interview* magazine in August 1985. 'It reminded me a lot of *Catcher in the Rye*, because it was so specific and you really felt like you went through it with him.'

times I wasn't pressing the flesh, promoting one project or another, politicking or otherwise busy, I was applying the third component of my three-part strategy for survival in Hollywood: partying my ass off.'[1] Marriage to his *Family Ties* and *Bright Lights* co-star Tracy Pollan, recently split from Kevin Bacon, helped Fox find some stability yet attempts to branch out – working with Paul Schrader on *Light of Day*,[2] Brian De Palma on *Casualties of War* – got him decent reviews but negligible audiences. Why was this clean-cut kid from *Back to the Future* suddenly trying to be cool?

Bright Lights, Big City, with its incendiary source material about a cocaine-snorting Big Apple journalist,[3] was another way of showing his range but the first director attached after Schumacher left, Joyce Chopra, was fired by executives concerned she was taking too long on a tight shoot that had to fit in with Fox's *Family Ties* schedule. McInerney, meanwhile, saw a lot of the drug-taking from his original story toned down so as not to completely ruin Fox's clean-cut image; a repeat of what had happened to his friend Bret Easton Ellis's *Less Than Zero* adaptation. McInerney was then rehired to work on the script with new director James Bridges, who now had only seven weeks to complete the film and had made the bold move of sacking many of the original supporting cast.

After much disruption, *Bright Lights, Big City* was released with the right soundtrack (Prince, Depeche Mode, New Order) but with the wrong reputation; considered to be, according to *Time* magazine, 'like something that has been kicking around too long in the dead letter office'. Like *Less Than Zero* before it, *Bright Lights* flopped badly – a pity since the end product had its positive points: Sutherland's turn as Fox's devilish best friend was straight from the James Spader school of appealing sleaze, whilst Dianne Wiest's flashback performance as Fox's mother gave the film some much needed emotion. Donald Fagen's bluesy score, meanwhile, combined with Gordon Willis's melancholy cinematography to effectively capture the hollow partying of moneyed young

---

1 *Lucky Man*, op. cit., p.133.

2 *Light of Day* was originally called *Born in the USA*. Springsteen worked on the soundtrack and was subsequently inspired to write a rather famous song with the same title.

3 Also one of the few novels to be written in the second person.

Manhattanites. It's all so feverish and rambling, it's like a sequel to *St Elmo's Fire* written by Jack Kerouac.

Still, *Bright Lights, Big City* was also difficult to love. A one-dimensional role for a now pixie-haired Phoebe Cates felt like an opportunity wasted and whilst Michael J. Fox tried hard, his trademark puppyish enthusiasm just made audiences want to see him leave the bars and clubs of cold-hearted yuppie New York and get back into the DeLorean.

When Fox did find box-office success outside of the *Back to the Future* franchise it only came courtesy of the more family-friendly comedy *The Secret of My Success*, playing a college graduate who quickly loses his first Wall Street job after a corporate takeover, then takes a role in the mail-room of another and moonlights as a trader. *The Secret of My Success* was huge, five weeks at No. 1 and with *Footloose* director Herb Ross again showing a lightness of touch that could make even the most unlikely story seem credible. But Fox was back as the clean-cut nice guy, his character of Brantley Foster essentially Marty McFly in a sports jacket. Kiefer Sutherland, on the other hand, looked as if he didn't even *own* such a thing.

With a grubbier charm now roughing up parts of the entertainment world, even the previously unfashionable macho western was getting a second lease of life. *Young Guns* boasted the tagline 'Six reasons why the west was wild' and told the story of Billy the Kid's youthful troupe of gun-slingers during the Lincoln county war of 1878, with original Brat Packer Emilio Estevez headlining as the infamous outlaw. Emilio's flop *Wisdom* hadn't helped with his quest to be taken seriously but the surprise success of buddy cop movie *Stakeout*[1] in the summer of '87 was some compensation. Now his move to dirty up as Billy the Kid alongside cutting-edge colleagues – six renegades described as 'the flotsam and jetsam of frontier society' – saw Estevez cooler than he had been since the mid-'80s. Kiefer Sutherland was a natural co-star as 'Doc' Scurlock but it was Emilio's little brother Charlie, still only twenty-two,

---

1 Directed by *WarGames* and *Saturday Night Fever* helmer John Badham and co-starring Richard Dreyfuss. *Stakeout* took a whopping sixty-six million dollars in the late summer of 1987.

who boasted the credibility after his second film with Oliver Stone – *Wall Street* – had been an Oscar winner a few months earlier. For a brief time Charlie seemed to be the only one who might stop Tom Cruise – Sheen was similarly chiselled in the looks department but with a slippery, less trustworthy air that made him more interestingly tortured than most of Tom's showmen. In *Wall Street* he'd acted opposite another relative – his dad, Martin – and his money-grabbing character's slow realisation that big business wasn't everything chimed fatefully with the global financial crash that hit markets in the autumn of '87.

Young Guns also featured *Three O'Clock High*'s Casey Siemaszko as Charlie Bowdre; Dermot Mulroney – a twenty-five-year-old, upscale, cello-playing Virginian who seamlessly morphed into 'Dirty Steve' Stephens – plus, as racially abused Mexican gang member Jose Chavez y Chavez, Lou Diamond Phillips. Phillips had generated plenty of heat for his performances as late Latino rock'n'roller Ritchie Valens in 1987's *La Bamba* and Hispanic student Angel Guzman in 1988's classroom drama *Stand and Deliver*[1] and was seen as a star on the rise. It was only a couple of years earlier that he'd had to make do with playing an anonymous 'Sidewalk Thug' in an episode of TV's *Dallas*.

Young Guns boasted rock on its soundtrack and a snarl in its Stetson and real-life parallels weren't difficult to make. Emilio was friends with New Jersey hair-metal god Jon Bon Jovi, who'd hit big with the outlaw ballad 'Wanted Dead or Alive' in the spring of '87 and would later sing the theme to *Young Guns II*, but the gang warfare of *Young Guns* mirrored the growing unrest in contemporary urban America as much as it nodded back to the old guitar-plucking wild west. Street battles between rival gangs such as the Bloods and the Crips in rundown south-central Los Angeles, their anger exacerbated by both claims of police brutality and the increasing popularity of crack cocaine, were more and

---

1 Phillips' heritage was not, in fact, Mexican. His father was Cherokee American, his mother Filipina. The lead in *Stand and Deliver*, playing real-life teacher Jaime Escalante, *was* of genuine Mexican descent: Edward James Olmos had already won a Golden Globe for *Miami Vice* and was Oscar-nominated for the movie – the first American-born Hispanic to get such a nod. At a time when much emphasis was being placed on 'new black cinema' (see next chapter) Olmos and his *Stand and Deliver* co-star Andy Garcia were doing much to push the representation of Latinos in movies too.

more discussed both in the news and on rap records[1] and what both the historical gunslingers and the modern hip-hoppers represented was a dissatisfaction with social injustice and with those in charge, all pushing them to take the law into their own hands by any means necessary.

Really the *Young Guns* were more akin to the riotous rebellion of Guns N' Roses than they were the preening power pop of Bon Jovi, G N' R themselves having been likened more to hip-hop than traditional rock: '[They] have less in common with metal acts than with rap artists like Public Enemy, which project a lethal toughness while urging self-improvement,' wrote *Q* magazine in a profile piece of the band. 'They are young, foolhardy, stubborn, cynical, proud, uncompromising, insolent, conflicted and very candid about their faults.'[2] It could equally have been describing the *Young Guns*, the film element of an emerging movement that saw rebel music, racial injustice and badass desperadoes occasionally cross into one another's territory.[3] All were, like the *Lost Boys*, officially the bad guys. To most though, they were maverick heroes.

Young Guns producer Joe Roth was certainly a maverick. After graduating from Boston University he initially wanted to be a sportswriter but fell in with an improv comedy group led by Chevy Chase and instead produced their 1976 low-budget spoof of TV programming, *Tunnel Vision*, co-written and co-directed by future *Police Academy* scribe Neal Israel. It made money, leading Roth to a career as an independent producer, working with Israel again on *Bachelor Party* and *Moving Violations*. 'He understood what worked, how to sell our new wave youth comedies to the studios and how to promote them,' remembers Israel.[4] But what Roth really wanted to do was *direct*.

---

1 NWA's album *Straight Outta Compton* – released August 1988 – was gangster rap's breakthrough moment, eventually selling over three million copies.

2 Q, Rob Tannenbaum, March 1989.

3 New York thrash-metal band Slayer would put that crossover on record in 1991 when they collaborated with Public Enemy on a new version of their single 'Bring the Noise'. The rap band's original had appeared on the soundtrack of *Less Than Zero*. The early '90s also saw director Mario van Peebles follow his era-defining urban drugs thriller *New Jack City* (1991) with the 'black Western' *Posse* (1993).

4 Author interview.

Joe Roth raised six million dollars and got a second mortgage on his house in order to helm a pet project: 1986's boxing drama *Streets of Gold*. It flopped. Undeterred, Roth – now with a directing agent – got the gig helming *Revenge of the Nerds II* and managed to pay off his debts in the process. Deep down he knew that, despite his best intentions, he was a better businessman than an artist – something he had in common with his father-in-law, beach party B-movie king, Samuel Z. Arkoff – but in 1987 he founded Morgan Creek Productions so he could at least still give himself some directing work. Yet that sportsman's competitive streak soon took over. Joe Roth wanted to take on the studios as a hit-making money-man and directing suddenly became less important to him than producing the goods. His business partner in Morgan Creek, James Robinson, knew how to make it happen, if necessary in unconventional ways. He had started as a Subaru parts salesman, making his name in Hollywood by providing companies with bridging loans – money used to get a film made before a studio comes in with distribution deal.

With *Young Guns*, Morgan Creek's first film and one set up with then-revolutionary private financing arrangements, the enterprising Roth and Robinson struck gold. The story felt like the perfect fit for its young stars to grow up yet still celebrate the reality of their wild boy lifestyles. Sutherland relished the experience: 'The first *Young Guns* was the most fun I've ever had on a film. We were shooting in Santa Fe, New Mexico, most of our stuff was in the day and it was winter, so there was only eight hours of daylight, so we had a very quick schedule. I had never gone to college, I left school at a really early age and all of a sudden I've got six really great friends hanging out with me every night. And we were a really tight group and we just had an absolute blast.'[1]

Young Guns' lack of major female characters and a deliberately unreconstructed setting confirmed one retrograde step: despite the best attempts by *The Breakfast Club*, *Pretty in Pink*, *Some Kind of Wonderful* and *Dirty Dancing*, teen-movie sensibility had not won the day. The lads were back. In the week of *Young Guns'* release in August 1988, just a year after *The Lost Boys* had been

---

1 The AV Club, interview by Will Harris, 7 March 2016.

unleashed, the No. 1 album in the States was Def Leppard's heavy metal behemoth *Hysteria*, replacing the raucous *Appetite for Destruction*. Both records – different in approach but deliberately boisterous – had plenty of fire left in their tanks too. Each would be back at the top spot before 1988 was out.

Chapter Sixteen

HIP-HOP AND HAIR

Hip-hop's Wild Style *goes global; the rise and rise of Eddie Murphy;* Soul Man; *Spike Lee uplifts (and upsets); the filthy get furious in John Waters'* Hairspray *and* House Party *dances into the '90s.*

Back in December 1983, Matt Dillon had noticed a new trend:

Matt Dillon:	I was at the Roxy all last night.
Andy Warhol:	Who was there?
MD:	Some really good band, but I forget the name. I was just basically checking out the breakdancers.
AW:	They haven't made a movie of breakin' yet . . .
MD:	Yeah, I know, it may just be too on the nose to make a movie about it.[1]

On the nose or not, Matt and Andy wouldn't have to wait long for a breakdancing film. For the couple of years when Dillon was white teen America's favourite bad-boy pin-up, the closest many urban kids got to their own adolescence on the big screen was in a spate of low-budget musical dramas that captured the early days of hip-hop with varying degrees of realism. Whilst not teen pics in the sense of being set in school or college, these were films aimed at the primary consumers of this new hip-hop lifestyle – teenagers – and their storylines were often secondary to the authenticity

---

1 *Interview* magazine, December 1983.

they boasted by having real rappers and graffiti artists star. They made money too.

Nineteen-eighty-two's *Wild Style* kicked things off, a film about Brooklyn graffitiing so rough it was almost fly-on-the-wall. Directed by underground film-maker Charlie Ahearnes, *Wild Style* was a loosely plotted eighty-two minutes that starred genuine street artists Lee Quiñones and Lady Pink, requiring them to do little more than be themselves: 'Pink and I were, in a word, turbulent,' admits Quiñones of their real-life relationship. 'We were very young. She was younger than me; I was twenty-one, she was sixteen or seventeen years old. Geez. We were an item – before we even met there were already rumours that we were sort of the royal couple. When I first met her, I was like, "What is this pretty little girl doing with us dirty-ass painting motherfuckers? What's wrong here?" But I looked in her eyes and was like, this girl is talented and driven. Hey, maybe we can paint together. I think Charlie saw the beauty in our young love.'[1]

And despite the rawness of *Wild Style*'s early South Bronx hip-hop, there *is* something beautiful about witnessing real members of the scene improvising in their natural habitat. Names from the underground art world also appeared – Niva Kislac, Patti Astor – and local legend Fab 5 Freddy's involvement got Blondie's Chris Stein on board for the soundtrack, a friend from their time together working on New York's experimental Public Access TV.[2] If the 'acting' in *Wild Style* was stilted then the performances were anything but, the novel bravado of early hip-hop acts such as Kool Moe Dee, Double Trouble and Rocksteady Crew[3] earning director Ahearnes interest from unlikely places (some funding came from Germany's ZDF and the UK's Channel 4 television networks). Eventually *Wild Style* even headed to the Cannes Film Market and was sold around the world. It was actually Japan that got the world

---

1 'Wild Style: An Oral History', complex.com, Alex Gale, 11 October 2013.

2 On Glenn O'Brien's *TV Party* show. Freddy also worked alongside fellow underground artists then breaking into the mainstream such as Madonna's Mudd Club and Danceteria associates Jean-Michel Basquiat and Keith Haring. He was also namechecked in Blondie's 1981 US No. 1 'Rapture' – the first chart-topper to feature rap.

3 Rocksteady Crew's dancer Richard 'Crazy Legs' Colón also appeared as a street dancer in the background of *Flashdance*. He was occasionally in the foreground too: for more complex dance moves he was heavily disguised as Jennifer Beals' body double.

premiere, introducing hip-hop to locals at that point still into the retro-greaser sound of homegrown rockabilly bands such as the Black Cats and The Cools. After *Wild Style* arrived in Tokyo, that soon changed.

Back in the States, the Big Apple went crazy for *Wild Style*, Philadelphia too, but it was never going to be a countrywide blockbuster. Rap culture was still too new and too niche to appeal to the mass teen market quite yet, plus *Wild Style* was far from glossy. But it was a film whose success came more through how it influenced others rather than just box-office. *Wild Style* got noticed by the right people. Chris Stein watched it happen: 'I remember telling Charlie, as soon as this thing comes out Hollywood is going to copy it. [And] *Beat Street* came out right after. It's pretty bad.'[1]

Nineteen-eighty-four's *Beat Street* in fact had a similar story to *Wild Style*, of making it big in New York's graffiti and music scene, plus – in Doug E. Fresh, Melle Mel and the Rocksteady Crew (again) – more of the hottest talent showcasing their moves and rhymes. But despite *Beat Street* being an independent film heavily influenced by a recent cutting-edge PBS documentary,[2] critics felt its substantial sixteen million dollars at the box-office, its production credit for fifty-seven-year-old singer Harry Belafonte *plus* its backing from Orion Pictures lent it a mainstream feel;[3] a sign of things to come.

Hip-hop movies might have started out as cult curiosities but when exploitation specialists Cannon unsurprisingly cashed in on their growing popularity, what was once local and rudimentary morphed into a widespread teen phenomenon. The company's sunny, smiley, LA-set *Breakin'*[4] came out in June 1984, with its sequel – the marvellously titled *Breakin' 2: Electric Boogaloo* – released only seven months later. The first film told the *Flashdance*-esque story of Kelly (Lucinda Dickey), an LA jazz dancer who discovers breakdancing. Dickey had just made *Ninja III: The Domination* for Cannon, a film that somehow managed to

---

1 'Wild Style: An Oral History', op. cit.
2 *Style Wars*, from 1983.
3 Belafonte also oversaw the two soundtracks, along with electro pioneer Arthur Baker.
4 aka *Breakdance: The Movie*.

combine the dual crazes of martial arts and aerobics (she played a dance instructor possessed by a ninja spirit) and she'd also shown off her moves in *Grease 2*. With *Breakin'* part of Cannon's much-discussed distribution deal with iconic studio MGM,[1] a contract that had surprised Hollywood but which kept alive Menahem Golan and Yoram Globus's dream of being taken seriously, *Breakin'* had the clout to hit nearly forty million dollars in the US – early hip-hop's biggest hit so far.

Lucinda Dickey's co-stars were nineteen-year-old Shabba Doo Quinones and seventeen-year-old Boogaloo Shrimp, dancers who'd appeared in music videos and ads, helping to popularise the body-popping style of dancing[2] that was a more colourful, child-friendly, even funny counterpoint to the aggressive moves of B-boying and the harder hip-hop sound championed by Run-D.M.C. on their self-titled debut album.[3] Really, *Breakin'* used classic golden-age musicals as its template way more than anything politicised and edgy. When Turbo (Boogaloo Shrimp) breakdances with a broom it's not hard to imagine Gene Kelly doing something similar thirty years earlier, albeit with tap rather than rap.

The studios were now on board. Warners followed the trend with their own *Krush Groove* in October 1985, Michael Schultz's fictionalised story of the Def Jam label that was essentially a showcase for the Russell Simmons business empire and which starred Kurtis Blow, seventeen-year-old LL Cool J, the afore-mentioned Run-D.M.C., The Fat Boys and – somewhat contro-versially – singer Sheila E. The twenty-seven-year-old Prince collaborator (and occasional girlfriend) wasn't herself integral to the Def Jam story but was added solely as high-profile love interest, much to the consternation of hip-hop purists. But it could have been worse: Golan and Globus over at Cannon had originally approached Russell Simmons with the idea of a film, as had Harry Belafonte. It was only *Car Wash* director Schultz who finally got the rap mogul's attention.

---

1 A deal that came to an end at the close of 1984 when MGM disagreed with the explicit content of Cannon's erotic Bo Derek drama *Bolero*.

2 A dance that utilised jerky, robotic movements, reportedly influenced by Sally Anne Howes pre-tending to be a doll in the movie *Chitty Chitty Bang Bang*.

3 That 1984 debut was the first hip-hop album to achieve gold sales in the States.

Russell Simmons was desperate for Fab 5 Freddy to portray him in *Krush Groove* but ultimately had to concede to a twenty-one year old called Blair Underwood instead. He did, however, get his wish when it came to the plot. Along with the casting of Sheila E., Simmons made sure that *Krush Groove* – originally called *Rap Attack* – was a significantly softened interpretation of the real Def Jam story, something more palatable for the masses. It worked. *Krush Groove* made back its entire three-million-dollar budget in a week.

Such bandwagoning meant overkill was inevitable. *Electric Boogaloo* made less than half the box-office of the original *Breakin'* and a loosely connected third film called *Rappin'* even less, whilst New World's *Body Rock* from late 1984 saw pretty boy Lorenzo Lamas, the star of TV soap *Falcon Crest* and *Grease* (where he played jock Tom Chisum) as the unlikely lead in what was essentially a hip-hop take on *Saturday Night Fever* (Big Apple street dancer dreams of making it big). *Body Rock* might actually be a guilty pleasure, boasting an ebullient Phil Ramone-curated soundtrack, shiny night-time cinematography from Wim Wenders regular Robby Müller and more eye-watering dance moves, outrageous outfits and neon lights than you ever thought possible. But in the space of just a couple of years *Body Rock* showed how urban teen movies had gone from fact to fiction, a genuine cultural milestone quickly milked dry. Maria Vidal's theme tune to *Body Rock* climbed the charts but the film itself suffered the dual indignity of flopping *and* garnering Lamas a nod at that year's Golden Raspberry Awards.[1]

Nineteen-eighty-seven: Michael Jackson is America's biggest pop singer, Bill Cosby its most famous TV star and Eddie Murphy the number one actor.[2] In some respects their blackness meant everything, in others nothing. Parts of popular African-American culture were unarguably now mainstream but that was also the

---

1 He 'lost' to Sly Stallone, playing alongside Dolly Parton as cabbie-cum-country singer in *Rhinestone*, a comedy that also saw the muscly star clash with the director, *Porky's* main man Bob Clark.

2 Michael Jackson released *Bad* in August of that year and spun off a record five US No. 1 singles; Bill Cosby's eponymous TV sitcom topped the ratings; and Eddie Murphy had the biggest opening weekend of the year – thirty-three million dollars – with *Beverly Hills Cop II*.

problem: to some mainstream meant unchallenging and watered-down, a missed opportunity.

The Cosby Show had premiered three years earlier, would run for another five, reviving both the sit-com genre and NBC's ratings.[1] Yet the Huxtables were an upper-middle-class Brooklyn family, seven in total; Cosby's Cliff Huxtable a doctor, wife Clair (Phylicia Rashad) an attorney, plus five children. Producers Marcy Carsey and Tom Werner had been ABC execs who'd hit big with *Mork and Mindy* and Travolta's *Welcome Back, Kotter* in the previous decade and who needed a show for their new independent production company. They'd loved Cosby's stand-up act, hugely popular on record for its folksy, home-spun anecdotes that avoided the confrontational humour of fellow '70s comedians such as Richard Pryor and George Carlin, and thought it was the perfect base for a series. Cosby's manager wife Camille had one demand though: as the highly educated daughter of university-schooled parents herself, she wanted Bill's TV family to be the same. Make them aspirational, not blue-collar.[2]

It was both a masterstroke and a miscalculation. As the show pulled in massive primetime audiences, the jumper-wearing Bill becoming known as 'America's dad', some critics complained it was setting race relations back rather than progressing them. '*Cosby* exposes more white Americans than ever before to the most nobly idealised blacks in the history of entertainment, yet social and economic conditions for the average black American have not been bleaker in a very long time,' wrote Henry Louis Gates Jr in the *New York Times*.[3] And what the show subliminally suggested, Gates argued, is that if you're in poverty it's your own fault, crucially ignoring the social and political squeezing on many ethnic minorities of the time. In other words, if Dr Huxtable could live that life, why couldn't anyone?[4]

---

1 CBS's black *All in the Family* spin-off *The Jeffersons* actually ran for longer than *The Cosby Show*, but without the huge ratings.

2 *Blue Collar*, incidentally, had been a Paul Schrader-directed Richard Pryor drama in 1978, about a black man working on a car production line in Detroit. Cliff Huxtable wouldn't have gone near such a place.

3 'TV's Black World Turns – But Stays Unreal', 12 November 1989.

4 NBC had another hit – *Diff'rent Strokes*, about a small black orphan 'rescued' and brought up by a white family – that was criticised for playing up to antiquated notions of the white master 'saving' the poor black slave.

Over in the Billboard charts, racial issues were similarly swerved. Jackson's nine times platinum album *Bad* saw the pop star mature with his songwriting in ballads such as 'Man in the Mirror' but his lyrics had become more personal than political. Meanwhile Prince – once a possible guest vocalist on *Bad* – released the glorious *Sign O' The Times* double-album, whose title track was certainly socially charged, although in general terms – drugs, AIDS, gangs – rather than in the specifics of race. That same year the twenty-four-year-old Whitney Houston – a former gospel singer and model from New Jersey, originally considered for the role of oldest Huxtable daughter, Sondra – scored the first-ever album by a woman to debut at No. 1 with *Whitney*. Yet she did so amid accusations that the songs were simply safe and formulaic; half bubblegum pop, half sappy ballads.

At the movies, Eddie Murphy didn't do sappy. Yet to make the blockbuster hits that Richard Pryor never had in the '70s he'd certainly had to curtail the charged comedy he'd shown in his 1983 HBO stand-up special *Delirious*, complete with its own 'Strictly for adults only' warning on the video box. Indeed, Murphy made a conscious choice to favour mainstream movies over stand-up, realising there was less chance of debate and outrage over their content.

Still, Murphy's popular success on the big screen shouldn't be diminished. Unlike Cosby, Houston and Jackson, his blackness *was* often front and centre in his performances; his 1982 breakthrough film *48 Hrs.* entirely relied on the chalk-and-cheese frisson between him and co-star Nick Nolte, as convict and cop, in an early take on the '80s buddy movie. If 1984's *Beverly Hills Cop* pushed fewer racial buttons, Murphy's being black still hovers in the background of a fish-out-of-water story originally intended for Mickey Rourke's rough-and-ready bad-boy charm, then retooled by Sly Stallone into a more straightforward action movie when it looked as if the *Rocky* star might be taking the lead.

When *Beverly Hills Cop* was finally handed to Murphy, the script was rewritten again and jokes added back in, but the point remained: Axel Foley's no-nonsense Detroit policing methods are out of place in the land of the rich and famous. Ultimately, *Beverly Hills Cop* is a film about snobbery in general, the hoody-wearing

Axel sneered at by old men in suits at a private members' club and suspiciously eyed up when checking in at a posh Beverly Hills hotel. If no one actually racially abuses Axel it's only because *Beverly Hills Cop* has got a whole host of other pretensions to prick first.

It wasn't as brutally authentic as real-life street artists and rappers putting on a block party, but to many young movie-goers it didn't matter. Murphy's big-budget pictures were simply fun and uplifting. Here was someone fast-talking and good-looking, taking control of any situation whatever his surroundings, more akin to Cruise's Maverick or Broderick's Bueller than the hapless, older comedy figure Pryor cut in movies such as *Stir Crazy* or *Superman III* (or, for that matter, Cosby's laidback, mumbling Dr Huxtable). However diluted Murphy's on-screen persona was compared to his stand-up, he was certainly never dopey or cosy. *Beverly Hills Cop* began with a spectacular, ridiculously over-the-top truck chase with The Pointer Sisters 'Neutron Dance' thumping on the soundtrack, the director Martin Brest – once deemed too serious for *WarGames* – creating a film that's the very opposite of mild-mannered. So whilst Foley certainly inhabited a gap in society in which skin colour played a part, that wasn't the whole story; a commercially smart sidestep that Don Simpson and Jerry Bruckheimer's *Flashdance* had already made. Instead, both films are about being bright, ballsy and excessive in the face of *all* kinds of prejudice; cheeky and creative rather than out-and-out angry.

Murphy's mid-'80s pictures weren't teen movies in the sense of their characters, plots or settings reflecting adolescent issues played out in high school or college but they were pop-laden, high-concept joke fests whose sassiness was aimed squarely at the youth market. And in terms of young, black movie stars he was all there was; alone and on a pedestal.

Despite being the same age as many of the Brat Pack,[1] Murphy was significantly never cast in the rash of teen movies from the time; never even put in an educational setting, surely an area where his swagger could have been put to explosive use. Conversely, of

---

1 Murphy was born in 1962, the same year as Michael J. Fox, Ralph Macchio and Lea Thompson.

course, that did allow him to enjoy proper adult roles, playing his real age – something many similarly aged actors could only dream of – yet it's notable that he made mainstream teenage audiences laugh only in films set far away from their own school environment; e.g. in jail cells, police departments and on the streets. Was his confident blackness – all wisecracks and perfectly groomed moustache – potentially too confrontational for some producers to cast him in 'safer' settings? That Murphy had no black Brat Pack to hang out with spoke volumes. Instead, he spent time with John Belushi and Robin Williams, noticeably staying away from the drugs that were taking over their lives. 'I know if I would have fucked around with that, I would have been in all the way. I'd have made a million headlines.'[1]

In being sensitive to racial equality in casting – but by also not making a big deal of it in the plot – Simpson and Bruckheimer found huge success, yet it was surely an opportunity missed.[2] If high school or college isn't a good place to ignite social debate then where is? Mainstream '80s teen movies used the genre as a place to highlight unemployment (*Pretty in Pink*), gangs (*The Outsiders*), the Cold War (*Red Dawn*) and extreme right-wing conservatism (*Footloose*) – but not racial inequality. And even though there was one exception in 1986 – a near thirty-million-dollar hit too – it's one teen movie about skin colour that no one really wants to talk about.

Soul Man was directed by Steve Miner – his first teen comedy after horror hits *Friday the 13th Part II*, *III* and *House* – from a script by Carol Black, starring C. Thomas Howell and with *Risky Business*'s Steve Tisch on production duties. So far, so normal. What made *Soul Man* stand out from the crowd though was its plot: pubescent white playboy Mark decides to black up by deliberately overdosing on bronzing tablets in order to qualify for a Harvard scholarship reserved for African-Americans. Suddenly *Soul Man*'s place as the *persona non grata* of '80s teen films starts to make sense.

---

1 *Rolling Stone*, Brian Hiatt, 10 November 2011.

2 One they partially made up for with 1995's urban classroom drama *Dangerous Minds*.

'The film makes fun of the things we have to struggle with every day: the jokes, the hassles, the preconceptions and the demands. The notion itself – that some white kid can . . . all of a sudden understand all the things we have to deal with – is very offensive to us,'[1] explained Van Scott, spokesperson for the Black Student Alliance of UCLA as he and two hundred others protested outside a cinema in Westwood on the day that *Soul Man* opened. It's hard to disagree. Yet however misjudged its story, *Soul Man* was at least full of good intentions, naïve but well-meaning.

'This is the '80s, man. This is the Cosby decade. America loves black people!' Mark proclaimed after coming up with his bright idea, the film setting itself up as a witty takedown of modern hypocrisy. But if *Soul Man* wanted to do for race relations what *Tootsie* had done for gender – just with tanning pills instead of a dress and wig – its teen-movie restrictions never allowed for the insight and introspections that had so enriched the Dustin Hoffman film a few years earlier.

Tommy Howell had certainly seen *Soul Man* as an opportunity to make a point: 'I'm shocked at how truly harmless that movie is and how the *anti*-racial message involved in it is so prevalent . . . this isn't a movie about blackface. This isn't a movie that should be considered irresponsible on any level. This is a movie that is quite the opposite for me.'[2] Howell followed his turn in *The Hitcher* with *Soul Man*, the role of Mark more charismatic and plain horny than he'd ever played before but also someone who does actually learn things on his journey through college. 'But when I made the movie, I didn't go into it with the idea that I had a responsibility to sort of teach America a lesson. I went into it because it was a great script. It was so well-written, so funny and – sadly – very true.'

Eddie Murphy himself had 'whited-up' for a *Saturday Night Live* sketch about how much easier life as a Caucasian was ('White Like Me' from December 1984), sending up earnest undercover reporting along the way. Yet *Soul Man*'s script lacked both Murphy's knowing wink and centuries of maltreatment to justify its behaviour. Without those there was just too much controversial

1 'NAACP, Black Students Protest Film *Soul Man*', *Los Angeles Times*, John Voland, 29 October 1986.
2 'C. Thomas Howell on *The Outsiders*, blackface and how Marlboros got him cast in *E.T.*,' The AV Club, Will Harris, 13 February 2013.

history behind Carol Black's concept for any message, however well-intentioned, to come out unscrambled. Yes, the jokes about privileged white kids' misconceptions of black guys were sometimes cheekily funny. Mark's fellow students stupidly presume he'll be good at basketball, for example. Meanwhile, the ditzy Whitney (Melora Hardin) claims to feel 'four hundred years of oppression and anger in every pelvic thrust' after their one-night stand. Then there's the scene – half-hideous, half-hilarious – where Whitney's family sit with Mark at the dinner table and picture him in a variety of grossly stereotypical black guises such as pimp, jungle native . . . and Prince.

But *Soul Man* never earned the right to be so playful. The first time it showed Mark – before his extreme 'suntan' – he was waking up in bed with a female conquest whose name he couldn't even remember. He goes on to recite his yuppie dream with best friend Gordon (Ayre Gross): 'We make our first mill' at thirty, retire to the islands at thirty-five.' It's a big ask to then see this braggart as a subversive icon for the black struggle.

Soul Man did good business in the US but its opening weekend position behind *The Color of Money*, Tom Cruise's hook-up with legends Paul Newman and Martin Scorsese, revealed plenty about the huge gulf between the projects on offer to former members of the Brat Pack. Howell would never lead another theatrical hit but remains fond of what *Soul Man* set out to achieve: 'It was a great lesson for me just as a person, because it made me much more aware of the issues we face on a day-to-day basis and it made me much more sensitive to racism . . . I think it's a really innocent movie with a very powerful message and it's an important part of my life. I'm proud of the performance, and I'm proud of the people that were in it.'[1]

Howell met his first wife through the film, co-star Rae Dawn Chong, the twenty-five-year-old daughter of comedian Tommy Chong who'd just appeared in another film about black oppression, very different in tone but which had also received criticism for being told through a white man's lens, Steven Spielberg's first grown-up movie, *The Color Purple*. Michelle Wallace in *The*

---

1 Ibid.

Village Voice argued, 'Spielberg juggles film clichés and racial stereotypes fast and loose, until all signs of a black feminist agenda are banished, or ridiculed beyond repair.'[1]

Roger Ebert, on the other hand, named *The Color Purple* the best movie of 1985. As Reagan battled even those within his own party over sanctions against the infamously segregated South Africa (he didn't support embargoes or boycotts), debates about racial equality in his own country – and on the big screen – raged on.

Over in Fort Greene, Brooklyn, a twenty-nine year old out of film school called Shelton Lee wasn't happy. It's why his mother had given him the nickname 'Spike'; the small and bespectacled Lee was always prickly about something, certainly not accepting the success of *Breakin'* or *Beat Street*, *The Color Purple* or *The Cosby Show* – even that of Eddie Murphy and Michael Jackson – as evidence of a new racial tolerance. Rae Dawn Chong's involvement in *Soul Man* had especially irked him.[2] 'Spike loves to fight,' the film-maker's friend and business associate Nelson George told *Vanity Fair*. 'There's a gleeful look he gets, a certain kind of excitement in his eyes when shit is being stirred up.'[3] The man himself was even more blunt, 'I bet the Klan watches Bill Cosby at eight o'clock every Thursday night.'[4]

Raised on the films of the movie brats and the son of respected jazz bassist Bill Lee, Spike wanted to make films about young African-Americans that unflinchingly dealt with tough issues whilst avoiding the usual stereotypes: dancers, chancers, entertainers. And he did it with his 1985 debut *She's Gotta Have It*,[5] a monochrome drama starring twenty-two-year-old Tracy Camilla Johns as streetwise and sexually adventurous artist Nola, turning the traditional idea of the demure woman on its head.

Made on a shoestring 175,000-dollar budget in just twelve days, and based on Lee's hour-long thesis film *Joe's Bed-Stuy Barbershop:*

---

1 18 March 1986.

2 *Spike, Mike, Slackers and Dykes*, John Pierson, Faber & Faber, 1995, p.62.

3 Quoted in *The African American Almanac*, seventh edition, Gale, 1997.

4 'My talk with Spike Lee', *Chicago Sun-Times*, Roger Ebert, 7 June 1991.

5 An earlier film – *Messenger* – had fallen through before shooting started.

We Cut Heads, *She's Gotta Have It* was shot in Brooklyn with a limited cast and edited on a rented machine in Lee's apartment. By the time it was completed, pulling in funding from a variety of sources, Lee – who also co-starred – was so deeply in debt that one production house threatened to auction off the film's negative unless he reimbursed them. But the gamble paid off. In just ninety minutes *She's Gotta Have It* took the urban youth movie out of the hands of well-meaning white guys and music moguls and boldly pushed it into more audacious realms.

She's Gotta Have It proudly displayed a new view of urban New York, an artful and articulate space, one that might have suffered with social issues but which wasn't defined by them. After several years of bad acting and breakdancing, it was a blessed relief. From its opening black-and-white photos of Bedford-Stuyvesant locals, accompanied by a melancholy, jazzy piano soundtrack, Lee showed a world view more akin to Woody Allen[1] than *Wild Style*, more *À Bout de Souffle* than *Electric Boogaloo*; although, as Nola states early on, 'I don't like labels.' It makes sense. The three men in Nola's life – motormouth Mars (Lee), bland Jamie (Tommy Redmond Hicks) and poseur Greer (John Canada Terrell) – were all possessive, unable to handle her free-spirited behaviour which, in a man, would barely warrant a mention. The more they demand, the more she pulls away. Ultimately, the dream of perfect Hollywood romance, expertly parodied in a Technicolor song-and-dance number, just isn't her. If guys can't handle that, more fool them. So whilst Nola might not have liked labels, it's easy to define what she *isn't*. Here was no romantic princess of the suburbs. She was no Molly Ringwald.

She's Gotta Have It screened at several festivals and was seen by a number of potential distributors, including Atlantic and Vestron, before it was eventually released by Chris Blackwell's Island Pictures – the theatrical film division of his iconic record label – who paid 400,000 dollars for domestic and international rights, the movie picking up prizes with bold names such as the New Generation Award and the Award of the Youth[2] along the way.

---

1 Lee would quickly tire of the Woody Allen comparisons but they're unavoidable.

2 From the Los Angeles Film Critics Circle and the Cannes Film Festival respectively. But Lee was still pissed off not to win the big prize – the Caméra D'Or – at Cannes.

Most of all, though, it ignited a revolution in independent cinema where micro-budget character studies broke free from their humble origins and became arthouse hits.[1] If they weren't teen movies in the traditional sense, that was the point. The student crowd lapped up their counterculture sensibilities as something different from the gloss and polish of the mainstream; a revolution akin to the impact of *Easy Rider* back in 1969. Just as Dennis Hopper hadn't been anything like '60s leading men Charlton Heston or Kirk Douglas, Spike Lee was certainly no Spielberg or Zemeckis.

Hip-hop was moving forward too, with 1987 seeing Def Jam release Public Enemy's debut *Yo! Bum Rush the Show*, bringing a new blunt anger to what had previously seemed like – with the Beastie Boys and LL Cool J – more posturing than being genuinely pissed off. Eric B and Rakim followed that summer with *Paid in Full*, a long-player that brought a fresh artistry to lyrics and sampling, whilst over in Long Island three teenage friends formed a rap trio with the intention of blending '60s flower-power ideals with hip-hop. They called themselves De La Soul and – like Lee in *She's Gotta Have It* – weren't afraid to throw a jazzy fluidity into their music as well as contemporary sampling.

But if both Spike Lee and hip-hop were bringing young black issues to the fore with a new parlance, not everyone joined in. Yes, Eddie Murphy made occasional stands, refusing to take part in Paramount's seventy-fifth anniversary photo in 1987 as he would have been the only black man there. He would also later claim that his success laid the groundwork for hip-hop's growing popularity: 'It's similar to when James Dean came out, and the town realised, "Hey, you'll go see movies where kids are the story." Young and fresh and street; all those things became a part of hip-hop. I embodied all those things, it's the soil for all that came afterward. They didn't even realise you could make money in those areas.'[2]

---

1 Jim Jarmusch's starkly arresting *Stranger Than Paradise* is generally thought to have started the indie trend, breaking through in 1985, with *She's Gotta Have It* next and then Steven Soderbergh's debut *Sex, Lies and Videotape* closing the decade by giving James Spader's career a credibility boost and setting up Miramax for their dominance of the market in the '90s.

2 *Rolling Stone*, op. cit.

But even in his mid-twenties and as the biggest movie star around, Murphy didn't align himself with the new youthful hip-hop culture. When he made his own records – such as 1985's million-selling 'Party All The Time' – they were with glitzy early '80s funk sensation Rick James rather than up-and-coming rappers. Murphy didn't, he claimed, need rap to look up to: 'Black folks never had anything like hip-hop, but I already had my own thing when the hip-hop wave jumped off. They weren't my heroes, because I was running with them.'[1]

Even Spike Lee initially only mirrored hip-hop's new social debate rather than specifically filling his films with rap tunes. For his next movie – 1988's *School Daze* – he again used jazz and classic musical traits instead of contemporary styles, this time to tackle college life directly by dissecting fraternity and sorority prejudices at an historically black school, the fictional Mission College – based on his own experiences at Atlanta's Morehouse. The six-million-dollar budget for *School Daze* reflected the success of *She's Gotta Have It* although Lee still felt this was an insult; the average cost of a picture in the mid-'80s, he liked to remind people, was eighteen million dollars. He also struggled to find collaborators since the script was unflinching in its depiction of discrimination within the black community.

Nineteen-eighty-four's first black Miss America, Vanessa Williams, turned down the lead female role of Jane, not wanting more controversy after being stripped of her crown over unauthorised nude photos being published in *Penthouse* magazine (Lee cast twenty-year-old *Little Shop of Horrors* chorus girl Tisha Campbell instead). Meanwhile, the authorities at Morehouse and other black colleges back-peddled after studying the script, deciding they didn't want the film shot on their campuses. Even Island Pictures – champions of *She's Gotta Have It* – got cold feet just before shooting, leading David Puttnam at Columbia to pick up the funding before himself having concerns. On 12 February 1988, with Puttnam now ousted from the studio, Columbia released *School Daze* with virtually no promotion.

Lee's vision in *School Daze* was huge in its scope, as much about

---

1 *Billboard*, Jeff Weiss, 6 February 2015.

the history of black America as it was 'just' a college picture, its story told through multiple perspectives and unafraid of soap-boxing both between musical numbers and during them ('Good and Bad Hair' places the oft-ignored but highly contentious debate about skin tone and hair type within a Busby Berkeley-esque framework). To some critics that meant *School Daze* bit off more than it could chew, Janet Maslin in the *New York Times* citing the film as a prime example of how promising directors often disappoint with sophomore efforts. Lee fought back with his own characteristically confrontational response: 'Ms Maslin probably considers the numbers in *Chorus Line, Flashdance* and *Footloose* great cinema.'[1]

But by now Spike Lee had an audience, young fans that wanted engaging depictions of contemporary black youth rather than just hurried cash-ins or stiff historical prestige pictures ('That's some bullshit right there,' Lee told *Slant Magazine* of the cosy *Driving Miss Daisy*'s 1989 Best Picture Oscar win[2]). *School Daze* broke new ground as the first 'black musical' directed by an African-American and even managed a significant profit despite the battles it faced just to get seen. From the sidelines, Lee's opinions were also starting to get noticed by the mainstream. Just a few months before *School Daze* came out the sitcom *A Different World* made its debut on NBC, the story of young students at a predominantly black college that mingled serious social issues with regular jokes and featured some of the same actors that had starred in *School Daze*: Jasmine Guy, Kadeem Harrison. The title was significant too. Whilst *A Different World* wasn't as charged as anything Lee would ever put his name to, it was still a lot more youthful and dynamic than the series from which it was a spin-off and after which it aired on a Thursday night: *The Cosby Show*.

The explosion in new indie cinema post-*She's Gotta Have It* also saw the return of an icon of old independent film-making: John Waters. Nineteen-eighty-eight's *Hairspray* was as camp, retro and

---

1 Lee expressed this opinion in a letter to Maslin's employers, printed by the paper. The whole argument is well covered in Aline Brosh's article for *The Harvard Crimson* entitled 'Spike's Dislike', 9 March 1988.

2 R. Kurt Osenlund, 27 November 2013.

thoroughly Baltimore as any of his '70s counterculture classics but, following a seven-year hiatus, Waters' comeback was now released by a more mainstream-looking New Line Pictures. What had once been a cult outfit had changed into something much more slick thanks largely to the financial success of its *A Nightmare on Elm Street* franchise. As a result, *Hairspray* was Waters' familiar teen kitsch but now for the mass market as much as the college circuit. He even waved goodbye to his usual X rating when *Hairspray* was rewarded by the MPAA with a modest PG.

Hairspray still had a social objective that much of teen cinema had studiously avoided. As the 'Free South Africa' movement swept across American university campuses, Waters' movie re-created a time only twenty-five years earlier when segregation had been similarly prevalent at home in the States. So whilst feisty teen Tracy Turnblad (Ricki Lake) might have been another of Waters' trashy outsider eccentrics – all overweight brassiness and tawdry home-life – her open-minded, youthful exuberance cut through the director's trademark frou-frou to highlight a 1962 issue that still had searing contemporary relevance. Tracy wanted to end racial discrimination on her cheesy local TV music show but she could equally have been campaigning for harmony in a number of late '80s communities both in America and across the world. *Hairspray* might have been full of arch dialogue and preposterous beehives but when, during a protest scene at an amusement park, a handcuffed Tracy cries out 'Police brutality!' it could barely have been more topical. Waters' place in independent cinema lacked the artistry of Lee but the sidelines they both still occupied, however different, remained the only place for pertinent debate told through the eyes – and haircuts – of frustrated teenagers.

The Hudlin family from East St Louis knew both sides of the story. On the one hand their home was big and their family life secure but on the other their city was buried deep in the southern tip of Illinois, just across the Mississippi from Missouri, nearly three hundred miles from the affluent Chicago suburbs of *Risky Business* and *Sixteen Candles*. Part of America's rust belt, East St Louis had suffered badly in the latter part of the twentieth century, a decline which mirrored that of the steel and railroad industries that once provided the locals with so many jobs. By the late '80s the infrastructure was broken, with crime figures some of the worst in the country. 'The blackest city in America,'[1] as youngest Hudlin son Reggie called his home,[2] had little reason to celebrate.

Yet with their debut film, that's exactly what Reggie, twenty-seven, and his older brother Warrington did. After all, they'd grown up being taught the importance of education and manners and it had taken them to Harvard and Yale respectively. Their background was privileged compared to many – father Warrington Sr ran an insurance company – although even from their bedroom windows in the relatively affluent Virginia Place they could see the city crumbling from lack of investment and apparent government indifference. Ike and Tina Turner were locals made good, but other homegrown role models were increasingly hard to find.

So as *House Party* shot in 1989 – written and directed by Reggie (based on his student short), produced by Warrington – it was as a mix of two styles: part biting urban politics, part optimistic musical comedy, a slick blend of *School Daze* and *Breakin'*. *House Party* brought the young black experience out of 'the ghetto' and into the forgotten suburbs, focusing more on the fear of getting grounded than the fear of race riots and drugs, whilst still dropping in hot social issues such as police harassment. Its story was certainly streamlined – a guy tries to sneak out of his home on a school night to get to his friend's house party, his path blocked by bullies, an overbearing father and the cops – but in fusing froth with authenticity, positivity with punch, *House Party* packed a lot into its teen-movie framework.

Will Smith's childhood had been in the more ethnically diverse, middle-class neighbourhood of Wynnefield, West Philadelphia, but for a while it looked as if the young rapper – only recently out of his teens – and his DJ best friend Jeff Townes might be just the guys Reggie Hudlin needed for his leads in *House Party*. Professionally known as hip-hop duo DJ Jazzy Jeff and the Fresh Prince (and managed by Russell Simmons), Townes and Smith had just been recipients of the first ever Grammy for Best Rap

---

1 Around ninety-eight per cent of the population were black or African-American.
2 *Rolling Stone*, Peter Travers, 9 March 1990.

Performance for 1988's 'Parents Just Don't Understand', virtually a teen movie on record,[1] so their profile was perfect.

What's more, the rappers owed *House Party*'s backers New Line a favour. Their follow-up single to 'Parents' had been called 'A Nightmare on my Street', riffing on the horror film that was one of Smith's favourites. The track had been sent to New Line for inclusion in their fourth Freddy Kreuger outing, *The Dream Master*. Unimpressed, the film company instead threatened a lawsuit for copyright infringement of the name, offering Smith and Townes a choice as payback: star in two movies for New Line and we'll take some of the money you owe us from your fee or forget the films and just pay up. Ultimately, the duo chose the latter, not wanting to be tied down. They had empty wallets and no movies on their resumés, but at least they had their freedom.

Still in need of two leads for *House Party*, Reggie Hudlin then considered Long Island act Groove B Chill – Daryl 'Chill' Mitchell and Gene 'Groove' Allen – for whom he'd directed some music videos but they didn't convince. Frustrated, he called up music industry insider Hurby 'Lovebug' Azor for advice. Azor was a big deal, then working with Salt-N-Pepa, the female hip-hop trio who'd landed with a bang by sampling *Revenge of the Nerds* on 1985's 'Showstopper' before going global a couple of years later with 'Push It'. Azor told Hudlin that he was managing an act who were old friends of the Salt-N-Pepa girls; two guys not actually a million miles away from DJ Jazzy Jeff and the Fresh Prince and who'd just made a splash with their debut album *2Hype*. They even had the right names to fit perfectly into *House Party*'s youthful spirit. In real life they were Christopher Reid and Christopher Martin from the Bronx and Queens respectively, but on record they were Kid 'n Play. Hudlin loved what he saw. Even though he also decided to hang on to Daryl Mitchell and Gene Allen and cast them in supporting roles, in Kid 'n Play he'd finally found his stars.

Reid, in particular, was superb in *House Party*. Whilst both were really too old to be playing high-school wide boys (Reid was

---

1 At the beginning of the second verse, Will raps about his folks leaving him at home for a week and going for a joyride in their Porsche – very *Risky Business*.

twenty-five, Martin twenty-seven), Reid's performance is one of boyish innocence, a wannabe rapper whose wide-eyed look helps us to believe in his naivety, that he wouldn't drink or deliberately get into trouble. To add to the sweetness, Hudlin filled his frames with cartoonish camera angles and child-like, bold colours.[1] So whilst *House Party* doesn't completely ignore contemporary social issues (such as Sharane's frequently referenced upbringing in 'the projects') it broached those topics with a vivacious humour rather than anger: 'Why in God's name did you call his mother a garden tool?' asks Kid's bemused, middle-aged principal whilst he's getting his knuckles rapped for fighting.[2]

Grown-ups in *House Party* just didn't get what it was like to be a teenager – the language, the emotions, the music (Public Enemy are frequently referred to by mistaken older folk as 'Public Enema') – and that was funny. If it wasn't hugely *original* to make a movie about high-schoolers wanting to have a good time, then at least *House Party* rehashed those teen-movie tropes with a vibrancy and verve that made it feel like it was. And seamlessly woven into that quest for a good time was hip-hop, by now as much part of everyday teenage life as wearing the right clothes and getting annoyed about homework.

On Saturday 20 January 1990, *House Party* made its unlikely debut at the Sundance Film Festival in Utah. The Robert Redford-championed event out in the snow of Park City had found itself the home for the celebrated new wave of indie cinema following *Sex, Lies and Videotape*'s debut there the year before, so to many the laughs and lightheartedness of *House Party* looked out of place. What's more, with its New Line backing, *House Party* also had a distribution deal in place; a rarity for a film at a predominantly arthouse festival.

Yet there was plenty of crossover between the froth of *House Party* and the more cerebral questioning of contemporary indie output. Both Robin Harris (who played Pop to Kid) and Martin Lawrence (Kid's friend Bilal) had just appeared in Spike Lee's third and most lauded film yet, *Do the Right Thing*, a blistering

---

1 By the end of 1990, Kid 'n Play would in fact have their own eponymous children's cartoon series that aired on NBC.
2 A ho/hoe, in case you didn't get it.

portrayal of racial tension in Brooklyn, whilst *House Party*'s female leads Tisha Campbell and Adrienne Joi-Johnson (Sidney and Sharane) had featured in *School Daze*. Reggie and Warrington Hudlin, meanwhile, had been involved in the production of *She's Gotta Have It* at its inception, via their interest in the Black Film-Maker Foundation.[1]

The judges at Sundance 1990 relished *House Party*'s innovative approach too, the comedy confounding initial expectations and wowing the crowds on its way to both the Film-Makers' Trophy and a gong for its cinematography. '*House Party* is first of all a musical and best approached in that spirit,' wrote Roger Ebert. 'To call it a teenage movie would confuse the characters with the subject . . . the plot is an excuse to hang a musical on and the movie is wall-to-wall with exuberant song and dance.'[2]

House Party left Sundance's ski-slopes that January at the forefront of a so-called 'new black cinema', sharing the awards spoils with other groundbreaking portrayals of African-Americans: Wendell B. Harris's *Chameleon Street* and Charles Burnett's *To Sleep With Anger*. By the following year Sundance had become the official home of youthful-but-smart, angry-but-funny racial drama, winners including nineteen-year-old Matty Rich's portrayal of a New York City housing project, *Straight Out of Brooklyn*, and Joseph Vásquez's rap-infused coming-of-age tale *Hangin' with the Homeboys*, also released by New Line.

After a release in the spring of '90 – that saw *House Party* clean up with twenty-six million dollars (over ten times its budget) – a sequel was quickly readied, scholars already deeming its style the 'urban, black, folk comedy'; a type of film-making that subverted certain racial stereotypes whilst still gleefully parading many sexual and religious ones and causing plenty of debate as a result. Despite being R-rated, *House Party*'s overriding air of levity also fed into a cultural appropriation of hip-hop culture by an ever younger and more mainstream market, exemplified in the pop charts when acts such as New Kids on the Block, Vanilla Ice and

---

1 Reggie even appears in *She's Gotta Have It* as one of the 'talking heads', a succession of men reeling off their favourite chat-up lines.

2 *Chicago Sun-Times*, 9 March 1990.

MC Hammer sold millions to a white teenybop audience.[1] Meanwhile, at the movies, New Line's 1990 kiddy-friendly adaptation of the *Teenage Mutant Ninja Turtles* comics saw the four reptiles strut around the sewers like an ostentatious rap group, the film's theme tune 'Turtle Power' a US Top 20 hit for hip-hop duo Partners in Kryme. *Electric Dreams'* Steve Barron directed, Corey Feldman voiced smartass leader Donatello and children lapped up its underlying, unthreatening urban bravado to the tune of 135 million dollars in the States.

Such a dilution of hip-hop lifestyle led some critics to complain of stereotypes being perpetuated and preconceived notions being enforced, all masking a dominant white culture's claims of superiority. Others, however, were simply fixated by the likes of Christopher 'Kid' Reid's trademark high-top fade haircut: 'The stuff just sits up there, proud and indestructible,' wrote Hal Hinson in the *Washington Post*. 'If a nuclear blast wiped out the rest of the world, that hair would still be standing.'[2]

---

1 Vanilla Ice and MC Hammer had actually been rapping long before their pop success but they only went platinum after committing to a playful, novelty image on 'Ice, Ice Baby' and 'U Can't Touch This' (both 1990). New Kids' 1988 breakthrough album, meanwhile, boasted an audacious hip-hop title that attempted to mask its harmless bubblegum sound: *Hangin' Tough*.

2 9 March 1990.

Chapter Seventeen

1989: SEIZE THE DAY . . . AND PARTY ON

From Fast Times *to* Excellent Adventure – *Bill & Ted bring new colours to the high-school slacker; the knowing charm of Winona, Christian and Johnny; John Cusack becomes a reluctant star; Dead Poets Society defies the establishment (politely); and the '90s arrive . . . with long hair and familiar faces.*

On the cusp of a new decade, 1989 felt like the year that knew too much. Director Tim Burton gave DC Comics' *Batman* a sophisticated gothic moodiness and bizarre Prince soundtrack that was a long way from memories of clean-cut Adam West and child-like '*Pow!*' speech bubbles. Big budget sequels to *Back to the Future*, *Ghostbusters* and *The Karate Kid* all tried to recapture lightning in a bottle, each financially successful but inevitably less fresh and well-loved as their predecessors. Meanwhile, *Look Who's Talking* – a commercial if not critical comeback for John Travolta – showed that even babies had now become smartasses.

A continued love, perhaps even a need, for some kind of apparent innocence prevailed, of course, seen in everything from the incongruous *Driving Miss Daisy* Oscar win that had so infuriated Spike Lee to the brief popularity of teen TV star Kirk Cameron, an evangelical pin-up more genuinely clean-living than The Two

Coreys.[1] But the success of Public Enemy and Guns N' Roses proved that kids wanted something more pugnacious too. The '80s were coming to an end but new things were also beginning, a fresh decade where a more astute pop culture was ready to repackage and reuse its past in novel ways.

Bill & Ted's Excellent Adventure was made in 1987 but, due to the collapse of its original backer De Laurentiis Entertainment, it wasn't until two years later that it got a release. Coming out in February 1989 actually made more sense though. This was a film that played like a melting pot of the teen movies which had come before it, a blatant celebration of the kind of outsiders who'd once been on the sidelines but who now, as unlikely heroes, were an indicator of where things were headed.

Bill & Ted was where *River's Edge* met *Back to the Future* . . . and then some; a mix of heavy metal and time-travel told with a knowing cheekiness that could only come from an independent feature wanting to shake up the decade's clichés. The title characters were dopey for sure, but what they were enthusiastic about – rock music, girls – they were *really* enthusiastic about. More to the point, *Excellent Adventure* was damn funny, the boys at first seeming to owe much to *Fast Times'* beach bum Spicoli but on closer inspection being much more childlike . . . and a lot less stoned. Kid 'n Play would be the black alternative, two cartoonish teenagers as simple-minded as ten year olds revelling in their surprising leadership qualities, but *Excellent Adventure* perhaps owed even more to the urban music scene's love of sampling and scratching than even *House Party*. It boasted an innocent cut-and-paste approach to school learning where key figures from the past are brought together, out of context, by the power of technology (in this case, a time-travelling telephone box). It was history, remixed; as gloriously shambolic and unpretentious a clash as Aerosmith teaming up with Run-D.M.C. on 'Walk This Way' or MARRS sampling Eric B and Rakim on 'Pump Up the Volume'. This was postmodernism with a smile.

But *Bill & Ted's Excellent Adventure* was also more than just some comedy experiment. It had real heart. Alex Winter followed

1 Popular for his role as teen charmer Mike Seaver in ABC's family sitcom *Growing Pains*.

his supporting turn in *The Lost Boys* with a title role: 'It's not really, at the end of the day, a movie about dumb Valley guys. It had a sweetness, an idiosyncrasy, it didn't have a lick of cynicism in it and I think that was really refreshing ... it's a movie about friendship and I think that connected with people.'[1]

The originators of *Bill & Ted* had also been friends. Scriptwriters Ed Solomon and Chris Matheson were buddies from their days at UCLA, the latter the son of famous science-fiction novelist Richard Matheson, and it was in the early '80s that they'd performed together in improv shows on Sunset Boulevard playing charmingly ignorant schoolboys trying to discuss current affairs; characters they nicknamed Bill and Ted. Encouraged by Matheson Sr, Ed and Chris then turned their routines into a full-length script, written over just a few days in local LA coffee shops, 'giddy optimism' their buzz phrase as they fleshed out these guys from suburban San Dimas, California, who blindly ploughed into any situation with just a smile and a whole lot of self-belief. Bill and Ted used words they didn't really understand, found themselves in situations they couldn't possibly comprehend, but it didn't matter. Their sweet-natured desire to 'be excellent to each other' and a total faith in the power of rock would always get them through.

Both Interscope and Warners were initially interested and Matheson and Solomon were asked to do rewrites, cutting back on any *Back to the Future* similarities (originally Bill and Ted used a time-travelling '69 Chevy van instead of a telephone box) and playing up the child-friendly elements of the story. Teen movies, several executives feared, would soon be on their way out. To direct, twenty-something helmer Stephen Herek was approached, industry insiders knowing he'd made a hit out of New Line's cheap horror flick *Critters* the year before.

Yet pretty soon *Excellent Adventure* lost its momentum. In the middle of a fad for time-travelling teen flicks, what new things – producers asked – did *Bill & Ted* really have to offer? At least Herek stayed committed. His formative years were spent in the legendarily counterculture city of Austin, Texas (motto: 'Keep

1 Author interview.

Austin weird') and he knew kids like Bill and Ted, those benign drifters who hung out in malls out in Nowheresville, Suburbia, dreaming of jamming with Van Halen. When De Laurentiis Entertainment eventually saved the film financially the project finally moved forward and, after many auditions, Stephen Herek found like-minded souls for his cast.

Diane Franklin had followed *The Last American Virgin* with *Amityville II* plus several TV movies but in *Excellent Adventure* she found her fresh face and pre-Raphaelite curls put to good use as mediaeval Princess Joanna, even if the role was hardly burdened with extensive dialogue.[1] Franklin had thought she was auditioning for the part of Joan of Arc, one of Bill and Ted's many new friends from their time-travelling exploits, but that role eventually went to former Go-Gos guitarist and singer Jane Wiedlin. In the lead, alongside Alex Winter as Theodore 'Ted' Logan, was *River's Edge* star Keanu Reeves as his best friend, Bill S. Preston Esq. Then, just to keep things fresh after extensive auditioning, the boys swapped roles.

When the De Laurentiis Entertainment Group filed for bankruptcy in 1988,[2] scuppering not only the just-finished *Excellent Adventure* but also Julien Temple's new retro musical *Earth Girls Are Easy*, neither Keanu Reeves nor Alex Winter expected the movie they'd worked so hard on, shot in and around Phoenix, to now get a release let alone be a hit. By the time it got rescued and the release date of February 1989 set, hopes were even more faint: there hadn't been a significant teen hit since *The Lost Boys* two years earlier (since *Ferris Bueller* in 1986 if you were looking for a traditional high-school setting). As the gigantic *Back to the Future Part II* readied itself for release later in the year, there seemed to be little room for any more time-hopping teenagers.

Yet as much as critics tried,[3] that friendship at the heart of *Bill & Ted* – a sweetly earnest bond held together by the most surreal

---

1 Her fellow princess – Elizabeth – was played by eighteen-year-old Kimberley LaBelle.

2 Dino De Laurentiis had worked with Fellini in the 1950s, built his own film studio in Italy and produced American movies as varied as *Serpico* (1973), *King Kong* (1976), *Conan the Barbarian* (1982) and *Blue Velvet* (1986). The failure of novelty 1987 thriller *Million Dollar Mystery* – where audiences were given real clues to the whereabouts of a buried bag containing a million dollars – was briefly his undoing though.

3 'Painfully inept,' wrote Vincent Canby in the *New York Times*, 17 February 1989.

of circumstances – couldn't be easily dismissed. 'Not since *Crocodile Dundee* has a sleeper come as such a surprise to the industry,' wrote Anne Thompson in an article for the *Chicago Tribune* a month after the film's launch. 'This underscores how much Hollywood executives are wired to this week's conventional wisdom. A few years ago, when youth comedies were king *Bill & Ted* would have been taken more seriously. Now that the business has focused on grabbing older moviegoers, the studios aren't that interested in appealing to the relatively "narrow" youth segment. But that's the very group that turned *Beetlejuice* into a hit this time last year. And now kids are turning out in droves for Stephen Herek's irreverent history lesson (written by Ed Solomon and Chris Matheson), which Orion Pictures agreed to release in partnership with Nelson. After the first Los Angeles research screening, Orion refused to believe how good the results were and ordered another preview in Secaucus, New Jersey. "The numbers were even higher," recalls co-producer Michael Murphey. "It appeals to ages sixteen to twenty-four." Luckily that age range doesn't read movie reviews . . . '[1]

The joy on screen wasn't put on. Winter bonded with Reeves from the time of their auditions; they were of similar age, similar background, had a similar outlook: 'It's the kind of role that's just really, really joyful to play . . . It was a lot of labour, it wasn't stress-free, it wasn't kind of a romp like *Lost Boys* was but we really did have a good time doing it . . . thankfully they hired two guys who came out of theatre . . . we're both just very physical actors and we really saw the roles as very, very physical.'[2]

Performing with that kind of naïve gusto also proved eminently quotable, a great way to appeal to a youthful audience: 'The guys [Ed and Chris] had done such an amazing job with the language, we didn't mess with the language. We enjoyed trying to wrap our mouths around it, it's really fun stuff to say and it is very declarative and they are proclamations so I always felt it lent itself to physical proclamations with your body . . . I think what works about what Chris and Ed do with the *Bill & Ted* movies is that for all their

---

1 16 March 1989.
2 Author interview.

absurdity, both from the language standpoint and the time and science standpoint, they follow really specific rules . . . they make sense . . . once you get into the rules of that language you can ape it yourself and it's fun.'[1] Like Kid 'n Play over on NBC, by 1990 *Bill & Ted* were the subject of their own kids' cartoon series on CBS.

But if *Excellent Adventure*'s boldly innocent leads meant it played to children as well as teens – an extra-young audience who responded to its dumb jokes and lack of serious angst – Winter still believes the movie wasn't without political opinion. Whilst some critics debated if *Bill & Ted* celebrated or satirised stupidity, its star played it as a clever mix of both: 'I don't want to impose politics where it doesn't exist but . . . the '80s were not unlike the time we find ourselves in now [with Donald Trump as Republican president], where Reagan had taken office and America had retreated into this very jingoistic, nationalistic, protectionist environment. It was definitely not lost on Keanu and I that part of what we were doing was representing that kind of child-like, sheltered, ignorant view of being an American – but with heart. What if you took that attitude out into the world? What would that look like? It becomes this great act of unification and everyone learns from each other which is simplistic but works for a comedy. That was not lost on us at all. We're like the dumb Americans who just think that Joan of Arc is Noah's wife and then of course we really end up meeting Joan of Arc and we come to understand the world and how it functions and we all learn from each other.'[2] Look at it like that and *Bill & Ted's Excellent Adventure* might actually have been the most pro-education movie of the '80s. After all, how many others had featured quotes from Socrates? Or rather, *So-crates*.

That wasn't the case with *Heathers*, a film released a month after *Bill & Ted* and where neither students nor teachers impress with any kind of charming enthusiasm. Quite the opposite. At a time when the few successful teen pics there were – *Bill & Ted*, the *Back to the Future* sequels – popped with colour and appealed to

1 Ibid.
2 Ibid.

younger crowds, here was something equally knowing yet deliberately at odds with its contemporaries. *Heathers* was bitter and twisted, satirising a decade of high-school movies as much as high school itself. From the opening slo-mo scene of three bitchy teen princesses, all archly called Heather, hitting croquet balls at nice girl Veronica to the throes of clean-cut anthem 'Que Sera Sera', it was clear that gritty realism wasn't its main goal. This was hyper-realism.

Writer (and video store clerk) Daniel Waters had rather grandly wanted Stanley Kubrick to direct his *Heathers* script, since the legendary film-maker had engaged with teen violence so beautifully and brazenly in *A Clockwork Orange*. Kubrick unsurprisingly unavailable, Waters instead found thirty-year-old USC film graduate Michael Lehmann calling the shots, a former Zoetrope employee (he'd operated cameras on *One from the Heart* and *The Outsiders*) who'd just made a splash with a short film boldly titled *Beaver Gets a Boner*. And whilst Lehmann was no Kubrick, he still gave *Heathers* a distinct energy, creating a movie with an almost dreamlike incandescence, heightening every nuance and expression to outlandish levels not seen since David Lynch's *Blue Velvet*. Both movies riffed on old-fashioned, apple-pie Americana and the myths of innocence and youth, *Blue Velvet* showing a teenage boy's infatuation with a troubled nightclub singer, *Heathers* the spree of violence that Veronica and her brooding boyfriend J. D. unleash on their classmates, the results of which – it's fair to say – don't go *entirely* to plan.

Yet *Heathers* also explodes clichés that we've been fed directly from teen films and literature; the popular girls, the jocks, the wholesome friends Veronica and Betty[1] (named after girls from the salubrious '60s *Archie* comic books) and the cool rebel who even has the same initials as James Dean. If *The Breakfast Club* bravely gave such stereotypes three dimensions then *Heathers* added another layer: malice.

This is a high school of swearing ('Fuck me gently with a chainsaw') and savagery ('Are we going to prom or are we going to hell?'), a no-holds-barred destruction of an adolescence that for

---

1 Betty was played by Renée Estevez, the youngest of the Estevez siblings.

John Hughes would have been more straightforwardly appealing but in Waters' script is deliciously warped. One pertinent scene, sadly cut, showed Veronica and her classmates showering in their clothes, much to the consternation of boys spying through a peephole, a direct take-down of *Porky's* and the host of '80s movies featuring horny boys looking for some flesh. *Heathers* never wanted to be the film that gave audiences what they wanted or expected. It never aimed to just rehash Hollywood's old puberty tropes. J. D. even communicates with his dad by bizarrely swapping roles; the son talking like the father, the father like the son. The world of Sherwood, Ohio, might have seemed super-normal on the surface yet underneath it's anything but.

Heathers' leads couldn't have been more perfectly chosen; two teenagers who combined a sheen of suburban normality with an introspective underbelly. Playing J. D. was Christian Slater, a seventeen year old from Hell's Kitchen, New York, who'd been acting on stage and on TV since a child. His father Michael was an actor too but a battle with alcoholism had led to a divorce from his mother, agent-turned-casting director Mary Jo, in the mid-'70s. Still, the young Christian had already got a taste for his father's profession, watching him on stage on Broadway, so his mom started to get him gigs in ads and soap operas. He'd also already sampled champagne, quaffing his first whilst on tour with a production of *The Music Man* when he was just nine. A movie breakthrough was supposed to happen in 1985 with TriStar's tough teen vigilante pic *The Legend of Billie Jean*, Christian cast as the younger brother of ass-kicking lead Helen Slater (no relation), but the movie proved to be only a later success on video. It happened again when Slater appeared in mediaeval thriller *The Name of the Rose* a year later, this time a smash in Europe but a flop in the States. By the start of 1989 and with the skateboarding drama *Gleaming the Cube*, another underperformer, Slater had shown plenty of range but little box-office appeal. He was already a cult star at just seventeen.

Not even *Heathers* changed that, since the New World picture barely made back a third of its budget at the US box-office – but it all added to Slater's image. Here was the anti-establishment boy-next-door, smiley to look at but with the knowing swagger of a junior Jack Nicholson and the mop hair of a rock star. Really, he was just too cool for the mainstream; didn't even look as if he wanted it. He was much happier as the bad boy. 'I was seventeen, just hormones and ego and the sense of invincibility that comes with that,' he told the *Guardian* of his snarling attitude,[1] explaining further to *Interview* magazine: 'A whole world opened up to me that was shocking and weird and different and I enjoyed and, you know, took great advantage of it at times. No doubt about it.'[2]

It was what teenagers wanted too. If Bill and Ted showed the fun side of postmodern teenage playfulness then J. D. was all about the dark side of too much awareness, the dangers of being able to see through the conventions of high school. That grinning anger and lone-wolf attitude became Slater's selling point,[3] the perfect mirror of a 1989 music scene which saw lo-fi indie 'grunge' metal blossom from the outsider states of America's north-west and go global, complete with angst-filled lyrics and a blatant disregard for the usual 'rules' of rock (guitar solos, musical ability, macho bravado etc.). Seattle label Sub Pop was at the forefront, its bands Soundgarden and Nirvana then leaving for major label deals in 1988 and 1989 respectively.[4] Introverted J. D., the much-travelled teen observing high-school culture from his corner of the canteen, clad in what was probably a thrift store coat and fascinated by suicide, could easily have been their biggest fan.

Veronica was more wholesome than J. D., the voice of reason in a climate tumbling out of control, but the actress who played her had a bohemian background that made Slater's look positively conventional. Winona Ryder was named after the Minnesota town in which she was born, could boast controversial counterculture psychologist Timothy Leary as her godfather and – so the press liked to claim – spent her formative years on a commune (more accurately described by Ryder as simply a family co-operative in northern California). Yet Ryder was never simply a hippy chick.

---

1 Sophie Heawood, 9 October 2015.

2 Lars Von Trier, 6 June 2015.

3 After playing outlaws in *The Legend of Billie Jean* and *Heathers*, he would do so again in *Robin Hood: Prince of Thieves* (1991) and *True Romance* (1993).

4 Soundgarden to A&M, Nirvana to Geffen.

Her look was hollow-eyed and fragile but there was a forceful inquisitiveness too, an intelligence born from an open-minded upbringing with parents Michael Horowitz and Cindy Palmer; her father a book dealer and archivist, her mother an author and fellow '60s liberal.

Winona – Noni to her friends – grew up an old soul, serious and literary, wanting to act maturely but equally cursed and blessed with young looks. She gazed upon her lifestyle with mixed feelings, relishing the enlightened attitude of her family but still occasionally craving the security and normality of a suburban childhood. Her tastes told a similar story, as fascinated by the traditional glamour of old Hollywood stars Audrey Hepburn and Greer Garson as the free-spirited indie queen Gena Rowlands; reading comforting American classic *Little Women* one minute, bible of frustrated teens *The Catcher in the Rye* the next.

It was a complexity that confused but impressed. The teenage Winona was training at the American Conservatory Theatre in San Francisco and had signed with the Triad acting agency when *Lucas* director David Seltzer spotted her showreel and cast her as lovesick geek Rina. Filming on *Lucas* proved to be eye-opening for a novice with little experience, the long days and stop/start energy of a film set something new to her, but even in a small role – Rina is as hopelessly in love with Corey Haim's Lucas as he is with Kerri Green's Maggie – Ryder made an impact. She just did 'earnest' so well. The little-seen *Square Dance* with Rob Lowe followed in February 1987, then Atlantic's equally bypassed anti-Vietnam family drama *1969* where Ryder threw all her energy into duff lines such as, 'We have to make people understand why it's wrong!' alongside Kiefer Sutherland and Robert Downey Jr.

But it was her heartfelt solemnity in *Lucas* that so impressed director Tim Burton, offering Winona a role in a new comedy that he'd been given by David Geffen called *Beetlejuice*. Burton wanted her as Lydia, the macabre and moody daughter of a family recently moved into a haunted house, a teen outcast who proclaims, 'I myself am . . . strange and unusual'. It made sense. Winona herself was going through her 'goth' phase in real life, as regularly clad in black as Burton and her dual interest in both retro-Americana and modern spikiness made them the ideal pair. *Beetlejuice* begins with a version of Harry Belafonte's late '50s calypso hit 'The Banana Boat Song' – also featured in *Hairspray* that same year – but soon mixes Burton's *Addams Family*-style horror kitsch with Lydia's contemporary, laconic insights; she's like the cooler, more detached, older sister of *The Lost Boys*' Frog Brothers. There's no direct reference to the mainstream queen of normality Molly Ringwald in Ryder's *Beetlejuice* performance but in choosing an ingénue role such as Lydia, a character with a sardonic knowingness that Ringwald's creations for John Hughes never had, Ryder was making her point. As Ringwald made do with a nondescript supporting role in Alan Alda's middling family comedy *Betsy's Wedding*,[1] Winona Ryder was relishing characters with interests as varied as her own, a quintessential gamine who'd also fostered a cutting-edge awareness of all the clichés.

Spotting Daniel Waters' sharp-tongued dissection of all those conventions in his script for *Heathers*, Ryder knew it *had* to be her next film after *Beetlejuice*. The match was too perfect to miss out on, especially since it so much reminded her of her favourite J. D. Salinger stories. Producers had hinted they actually wanted Jennifer Connolly for the *Heathers* lead, the eighteen-year-old former model the curvacious opposite of Ryder's own tomboyish style, prompting Winona to get a glamorous makeover from Macy's just before her audition. She was single-minded: 'I just wanted to say those lines and I wanted to work with those people. I felt like if I don't do this movie, I'll never be able to live with myself. And I'll kill whoever does do it!'[2] Neither her agents nor her parents wanted Winona Ryder to take on the bleak *Heathers* role but, unlike the *License to Drive* star Heather Graham, who *did* turn down a part in the film because her mother didn't appreciate the script, Winona just went with her instincts.

Since *Heathers* so relished its knowingly exaggerated *Rebel Without a Cause*-style emotions (with more than a nod to the caustic camp of John Waters[3]), Slater and Ryder decided to continue the cheeky histrionics of their characters on the promo

1 Also featuring Ally Sheedy. Both were Golden Raspberry nominated for their roles.
2 *Winona Ryder: The Biography*, Nigel Goodall, Blake Publishing, 1998, p.74.
3 No relation to *Heathers*' writer Daniel.

trail too, pretending to journalists that they really were a lovestruck couple like J. D. and Veronica. In truth, however, the extroverted Slater was more into the idea than serious Winona. She'd never even had a proper boyfriend but Slater had already been dating fellow *Heathers* star Kim Walker. Though there *was* eventually a brief fling between Slater and Ryder, the romance fizzled out quickly.

As summer approached the actress already had another film to promote: *Great Balls of Fire*, where she played Myra, the thirteen-year-old cousin and eventual wife of rocker Jerry Lee Lewis (Dennis Quaid). Ryder befriended musician Mojo Nixon on set, the cult rockabilly star playing Jerry Lee's drummer James Van Eaton, and the actress reinforced her outsider status in the teen world by appearing in Nixon's video for the succinctly titled 'Debbie Gibson is Pregnant with my Two-Headed Love Child', playing the clean-cut teen pop star as a junk-food-eating kook in a wedding dress.

However, it was at the *Great Balls of Fire* premiere at the Ziegfeld Theatre in New York that June that Ryder's place in pop culture would really be cemented. Sporting an uncharacteristically tight, white mini-dress and arriving in a pink Cadillac, it was there that she first locked eyes with the star of the hottest teen show on television: *21 Jump Street*'s Johnny Depp. Two years into the Fox series about young police officers working undercover in schools, Depp wasn't happy with his sex symbol status and increasing showiness of the drama – 'It was a strange time because I had become this product. And it made me very uncomfortable . . . they [producers] just started to build this image and it had nothing to do with me. So it was weird.'[1] Sizeable pay cheques eased some of the pain yet ultimately frustrated him all the more.

Luckily, Depp had just been handed the opportunity to send-up those pin-up looks by shooting with John Waters on his *Hairspray* follow-up *Cry-Baby*, a musical pastiche of '50s delinquency movies where Depp had been cast as Wade Walker. Nicknamed 'Cry-Baby', Walker was a mid-'50s drape[2] rock'n'roller

---

1 *The Oprah Winfrey Show*, 2 November 2004.

2 Also known as a greaser; complete with cowlick falling artfully onto his forehead from a head of slickly Brylcreemed hair.

with the novel ability to cry a single tear when singing his songs, a trick that drives girls wild.

If *Cry-Baby* was another step by John Waters towards the mainstream – the film produced by Ron Howard's Imagine Entertainment and distributed by Universal – then his supporting cast was as motley as ever: teenage newcomer Amy Locane, punk legend Iggy Pop and Traci Lords – a twenty-one year old who herself was looking for serious roles after retraining at the Lee Strasburg Theater Institute following a brief but high-profile career in porn.[1]

It wouldn't be until a few months after the *Great Balls of Fire* premiere that Winona Ryder would see Johnny Depp again but this second meeting was more substantial than just a glance across a room. They properly hung out together with mutual friends at LA's legendary Chateau Marmont hotel. Ryder was nine years Depp's junior but she was already nonplussed by the drink and drugs habits of young Hollywood after seeing her liberal parents and friends dabble in them when growing up. Her main issue in life was insomnia, an ailment that only added to a gaunt look that was fast becoming her trademark and which, along with a contrasting candied voice, made her like a mix of *The Breakfast Club*'s Claire in both her early gothic stages *and* after her girl-next-door makeover.

Depp, however, was more of a confused party animal, moved around a lot as a child by his family and now, like Kiefer Sutherland and Robert Downey Jr, mixing shyness with the hard-living lifestyle of the rock star he'd always dreamed of being. He had divorced first wife Lori Anne, had been involved with *Dirty Dancing*'s Jennifer Grey following her relationship with Matthew Broderick, plus had dated Sherilyn Fenn, a rising star from Detroit who'd spent the '80s making the most of the low-budget, straight-to-video market (*Zombie High*, *Thrashin'* et al). Watch Depp's heavily trimmed role as Lerner in Oliver Stone's *Platoon* and it's Sherilyn's name that the actor has scrawled across his army helmet.

---

1 She had been arrested by the FBI in May 1986 after it was discovered that she'd been underage when shooting the majority of her adult movies.

But when Winona Ryder and Depp got talking at the Chateau, neither could really believe how much they had in common, both equally into the beat poets, *The Catcher in the Rye* and rock'n'roll. One outsider had found another; boho twins. To celebrate their meeting of minds, the couple not only soon got engaged but Ryder also later watched as her new fiancé sat down in a chair at the Sunset Strip Tattoo Salon and got something way more permanent than he ever had for Grey or Fenn: a fresh inking on his shoulder that read 'Winona forever'.

Gracie Films – named after vintage comedienne Gracie Allen – had been founded by *Terms of Endearment* writer/director James L. Brooks in 1986 and had already scored popular and critical acclaim with Penny Marshall's *Big* starring Tom Hanks and Brooks' own *Broadcast News*. For the former journalist Brooks it was all about the writers. He wanted Gracie Films to be recognised as a company that nurtured smartly funny scripts, stories unafraid of strong dialogue and unique characters and for a while he'd been mulling over an idea about a beautiful young girl with a crook for a father. Despite the failure of *The Wild Life*, Brooks had also been impressed by Cameron Crowe's sassy-but-sensitive writing style and the idea of collaboration stayed in the back of his mind. Crowe, for his part, was dreaming of writing 'a tribute to the first girl I really fell in love with. She fell for me, and I fell for her . . . but not at the same time.'[1] This time though, he had one stipulation: he would have to take control of whatever he wrote by directing the story himself. He'd had enough of his scripts getting altered. The resulting collaboration was *Say Anything . . .* , a bittersweet and wordy mix of both James Brooks' crime story and Cameron Crowe's autobiographical romance, produced by Gracie Films, directed by its writer and released by Twentieth Century Fox just a month after *Heathers*.

If *Heathers* angrily bore the battle scars of high-school life then *Say Anything . . .* smiled through the healing process, telling the story of an idiosyncratic post-graduation relationship between sheltered high-school brainbox Diane and sweet-natured nobody Lloyd; a romance which elevated everyday suburban Seattle life

---

1 From Crowe's website, www.theuncool.com

into a place of grand statements and true love. Playing the valedictorian was Ione Skye, her haunting appeal in *River's Edge* finding one of many fans in Cameron Crowe.

As jittery Lloyd was John Cusack. Like so many of his contemporaries, Cusack was frustrated. It was no surprise really. He'd been a regular in teen movies for the last five years, both in support to big names like Molly Ringwald, Rob Lowe and Andrew McCarthy as well as a lead himself. All of which meant Cusack knew the game well, maybe *too* well. Plenty of teen-movie work was being offered to him but with each new script he was painfully reminded of what he'd learned over his half-decade of movie-making: not all high-school pictures were created equally.

John Cusack was one of five children, born and raised in Evanston – a North Shore city twelve miles north of Chicago – to liberal activists Richard, an actor and film-maker, and teacher Nancy. Hanging out with his childhood friend Jeremy Piven at the theatre workshop run by his parents, Cusack had already appeared on stage and in commercials by the time he hit his teens, leading to Chicago's auteur John Hughes casting him in the background of *Sixteen Candles*. Cusack then lost out on the role of John Bender in *The Breakfast Club*[1] but his own unique and awkward charm – alabaster-skinned and dark-haired from his Irish roots, most believable as a strong-willed loner lead rather than in a grinning chorus – was already developing. His was a calmly deadpan refusal to play the game; uniquely appealing, although Cusack was never going to admit to it, always preferring a quietly common sense explanation for his early success: 'I was sixteen when they wanted to make films about sixteen year olds in Chicago.'[2] He wasn't about to over-analyse his roles as a geek trying to get a look at Molly Ringwald's panties (*Sixteen Candles*) or as a horny posh boy egging on Andrew McCarthy's affair with an older woman (*Class*). And that self-deprecation was all part of the allure.

Whilst it was Judd Nelson who went on to make Bender's *Breakfast Club* sarcasm and snarl iconic, Cusack took the near-

---

1 It was apparently between just Cusack and Judd Nelson.

2 'John Cusack: Hollywood Is a Whorehouse and People Go Mad', *Guardian*, Henry Barnes, 25 September 2014.

break as a chance to move to LA and work with Rob Reiner, the actor-turned-director[1] who was still a couple of years off helming *Stand by Me*. Reiner's project at the time was *The Sure Thing*, a comedy based on writer Steven Bloom's experience of a road trip from his stuffy east coast college to his friend's Californian university – a place where he was promised a great few days of partying and sex – with Cusack tapped by Reiner and casting directors Jane Jenkins and Janet Hirshenson to play mouthy lead Walter 'Gib' Gibson.

However, the fact Cusack was still under eighteen years and barely known meant that financiers Embassy Pictures needed some convincing. Reiner and his producer Roger Birnbaum stood firm, the director putting up Cusack in his house. When Embassy finally agreed and *The Sure Thing* began shooting, Cusack was at last optimistic that this was the kind of teen movie he really *wanted* to make. Forget all the other fluff. Here was a college comedy that might actually defy expectations. And he was right. Whilst *The Sure Thing* begins with shots of Gib's promised one-night-stand (Nicolette Sheridan) in her bikini on the beach, oiling herself up seductively with sun lotion, the story ultimately rejects the sex-comedy framework that it could so easily have followed and morphs into something surprisingly thoughtful; laddish Gib and his travelling partner, good girl Alison (Daphne Zuniga), forming an unlikely romantic bond on the cross-country journey. *The Sure Thing* was definitely more *It Happened One Night* than *Fraternity Vacation*.

But John Cusack soon found out not everything he made could live up to his high ambitions. *The Sure Thing* was on its way to moderate box-office success and critical acclaim when its executive producer Henry Winkler, now working behind the scenes after leaving his role as The Fonz on *Happy Days*, heard a film-maker friend 'Savage' Steve Holland was looking for a lead in his new movie. Holland's short film *My Eleven Year Old Birthday Party* had made a mark on Winkler when he saw it at the Los Angeles Film Festival, impressed by dark humour that was sometimes *so* dark you weren't sure whether to laugh or cry. He'd then encouraged

---

1 Most famous for his seven years playing Meathead in sitcom *All in the Family*.

Holland to begin work on his debut feature, lending him a desk at his office. Now that Holland's screenplay was finished and going into production, titled *Better Off Dead*, Winkler felt he knew exactly who should play the lead: John Cusack.

Just like Steve Holland's short film, *Better Off Dead* was another black comedy, this time about depressed teenage skier Lane Meyer who's been considering suicide since his girlfriend Beth dumped him. The story was loosely based on Holland's own life and, as the writer/director checked out *The Sure Thing* on Winkler's recommendation, he could immediately see what the producer had meant: Cusack had exactly the right oddball personality to carry *Better Off Dead* and play a character who was essentially Holland's alter ego. Backers A&M Films, CBS Films and distributor Warner might have needed a little more convincing – they hadn't even seen *The Sure Thing*, only knowing Cusack as a nerd in *Sixteen Candles* – but even as a first-time director, Steve Holland stood his ground: 'I was like, "You don't even know what you're getting right now. You're gonna be so ahead of the curve to get Cusack now." I really went to bat for him and they let me have him. I still think it's the best thing that ever happened to me and the movie, getting Cusack. Nobody else could have pulled that off.'[1]

Better Off Dead came out in late August 1985, just a few months after *The Sure Thing* and in a summer packed with teen product: *St Elmo's Fire*, *Back to the Future*, *The Legend of Billie Jean*, *National Lampoon's European Vacation*, *Fright Night*, *Weird Science*, *Real Genius*, *My Science Project* and *Teen Wolf*. The market was saturated, too jammed for this unconventional tale about an introverted winter sports fan and *Better Off Dead* struggled to around ten million dollars. Yet there was an even bigger problem looming than mediocre box-office. Steve Holland and his *Better Off Dead* stars Cusack and Curtis Armstrong – the latter signed after impressing in *Risky Business* – were about to shoot a second movie together with A&M and Warners over on Cape Cod called *One Crazy Summer*[2] when suddenly, out of the blue, John Cusack declared he had lost interest.

---

1 'Better Off Dead DVD extras that never were', *Entertainment Weekly*, Mandi Bierly, 2 August 2011.
2 Originally called *What I Did On My Summer Vacation* but changed by the studio. Holland had, however, won his battle to stop *Better Off Dead* being changed to the hugely generic *Out on a Limb*.

It didn't matter to Cusack that in *One Crazy Summer* he was about to lead his third movie. In his mind, after watching a preview of *Better Off Dead* and apparently walking out in disgust, he would be stuck in Massachusetts making what was almost a sequel to a film that he now realised he didn't even like. Steve Holland was distraught: 'The next day, we were supposed to start shooting [*One Crazy Summer*] and [Cusack] looked really pissed off. He just said that he hated [*Better Off Dead*] and, from the sense that I got, that I betrayed him in making a movie so stupid . . . it was just heartbreaking to me that he didn't get it.'[1]

One Crazy Summer did get made and released the following year, Cusack reluctantly gritting his teeth and starring as quirky high-school graduate and budding artist Hoops McGann, falling for wannabe rock star Cassandra (Demi Moore) during his family's east coast vacation. Shooting with a lead who didn't want to be there was no fun for Holland though. Whilst *One Crazy Summer* managed to scoop a little more money than *Better Off Dead*,[2] it was still no blockbuster, not helped by Cusack making his feelings obvious and refusing to promote it. Luckily, the headlines that August were all about George Lucas's mega-flop *Howard the Duck*,[3] released a week earlier, as well as the arrival of a distinctive voice in new black cinema: Spike Lee's *She's Gotta Have It*. All of which left both of Holland's films to find a more natural home – with significant cult success – on home video and late-night cable.

But did Cusack really have a reason to be so annoyed? In many ways *Better Off Dead*'s Lane is more like *Say Anything*'s Lloyd Dobler – sensitive and idiosyncratic – than *The Sure Thing*'s horny Gib. Gib *pretends* to be strangely charismatic, spinning such lines as, 'How would you like to have a sexual encounter so intense it could conceivably change your political views?', but he's always

---

1 *Entertainment Weekly*, op. cit.

2 Around thirteen million dollars.

3 Based on the cult Marvel comic of the same name and co-written and produced by Gloria Katz and Willard Huyck, Lucas's longtime collaborators from the days of *American Graffiti*. *Howard the Duck* should probably have been an animation but Universal wanted a quicker production so the title character – a giant, alien waterfowl – was animatronic. Cusack was an early choice to voice Howard but it instead went to Broadway actor Chip Zien. *Back to the Future*'s Lea Thompson and *The Sure Thing*'s Tim Robbins co-starred.

doing it for the same reason: to get laid. He's also got similarly rampant mates and exists on a diet of uninspired junk food; a 'wild' streak that's initially repugnant but – we're supposed to believe – ultimately attractive to the uptight Alison. *Better Off Dead*, on the other hand, never has to try hard to make a priapic teenage boy seem charming. Lane is a lovesick loner, astute and earnest, unlike anyone else around him, drawing sketches to take his mind off the weight of the world he carries on his shoulders. Cusack's hangdog does, of course, make even *The Sure Thing*'s lusty Gib more appealing than the usual randy jock but really, he's still more straightforward than unconventional. It's Lane who's the real one-off.

Nevertheless, after feeling disappointed with *Better Off Dead* and *One Crazy Summer*, Cusack was initially reluctant to take on another high-school movie. It was only on reading the *Say Anything* script that he realised that Cameron Crowe offered something more: 'Lloyd is a great American character,' Cusack happily declared of the story's lead. 'He's an individualist who marches to the beat of his own drum and trusts his instincts. He's a guy who's well aware of what is going on around him, yet he chooses to be optimistic. It's a valid and interesting approach to life. It's certainly more creative than opting for teen angst, which is boring and adolescent.'[1]

So perhaps it had been *Better Off Dead*'s obvious 'teen angst' that so quickly put off Cusack working on Holland's movies?[2] It's also true that *Better Off Dead*, unlike *Say Anything* or *The Sure Thing*, was way more *silly*: Lane's bizarre mother giving him frozen ready-meals as Christmas presents, his mute little brother building laser guns and his kooky best friend Charles sporting a variety of wacky headgear. Although some of those oddities were based on Holland's actual childhood, *Better Off Dead* undeniably played broad, boasting the wackiness of a Hanna-Barbera cartoon or – in its silent moments – retro slapstick. Realism wasn't its greatest concern, as made clear by both the casting of New York-born Diane Franklin as French exchange student Monique *and* by

---

1 From the press notes to *Say Anything*.
2 Although it's hard to believe he hadn't noticed that when reading the script.

an animated dream sequence in which Lane imagines a hamburger singing Van Halen's 'Everybody Wants Some' (obviously). Cusack, hitting twenty just before *One Crazy Summer* came out, had simply grown out of acting stupid for a quick laugh – and he wasn't afraid to let people know. Rob Reiner, meanwhile, followed *The Sure Thing* with *Stand by Me* and cast Cusack in a sensitive cameo role much more to his liking: as Geordie's heroic, ghostly older brother Denny.

Cameron Crowe had begun the decade determined to give teenagers an authenticity and respect they deserved in *Fast Times at Ridgemont High*. In ending it the same way with *Say Anything . . .* he also gave John Cusack an exit plan from the confines of the '80s high school pic that had so frustrated him. Thematically, *Say Anything . . .* could have been a John Hughes movie: another *Romeo and Juliet* love across the divide, with *Some Kind of Wonderful*'s Eric Stoltz making an appearance and Diane Court a wholesome female lead role that could easily have been played, three years earlier, by Molly Ringwald. But *Say Anything . . .*'s outlook was crucially different; the wordier, looser, more aware-of-its-own storyline style ('I am looking for a dare-to-be-great situation') that producers at Gracie Films championed yet also, by focusing on the unpredictability and confusion of life immediately post-graduation, full of realism in its grey areas. How do you move forward when everything you know is over? For Lloyd and Diane it's the end of high school that throws them. For Lloyd's sister Constance (played by Cusack's real sister Joan) and best friend Corey (Lili Taylor) it's the end of romances that they can't get past. Whilst *Say Anything . . .*'s storyline about Diane's crook father (John Mahoney) might give the plot some concrete direction, mainly it just ambles along endearingly, as free-flowing and fickle as the teenagers it portrays. Constantly questioned about his future, all Lloyd can really come up with is 'I know . . . that I don't know'.

As with *Fast Times*, Crowe's reasons for writing the movie had actually been relatively simple: 'I tried to just make it a story that had . . . young love within it. At the time people said, "Well, no one's gonna go see this movie because there's not enough teen stuff in it for teens to wanna come and there's not enough adult stuff for adults to wanna come." And the movie was sort of rescued from early oblivion by Siskel and Ebert . . . [who] decided to just pick it out and champion it and overnight we got more theatres and people acknowledged it.'[1]

That heartfelt approach led to *Say Anything* . . . making over twenty-one million dollars in US theatres, its soundtrack – unsurprisingly for a film by muso Crowe – impressing with its use of Peter Gabriel's fervent 'In Your Eyes' during both Diane and Lloyd's back-of-a-car love scene and most memorably in a later moment, Lloyd playing the song on his boombox in a bid to win her back. Even in those standout occasions though, a notch down from the excess of an Adrian Lyne montage but still deliberate and bold, Crowe retained his goal of truthfulness: 'You wouldn't remember those moments if they weren't in their context. I like that they stick out. My favourite film-makers have those moments. To be remembered for those few things that linger is really cool. [But] you can't ever go for it and say, "Oh, here's a *moment* I hope will catch on", because then the gods will just punish you immediately. What you gotta do is just have characters that feel real and then they might do something or yell something that you might remember.'[2]

No one really wanted to fit into the Brat Pack but Cusack's determined and vocal search for the 'real' and unique – alongside film-makers as varied as Rob Reiner, Steve Holland and Cameron Crowe – meant he never had to. His work with the latter two saw him create characters that were oddballs, nervily cramming more words into a sentence than you ever thought possible, but with good hearts; endearingly dry, shy *and* believable, despite his own concerns about Holland's approach. 'You have to be picky otherwise I think you get over-exposed. And I think people get sick of you pretty quick unless you, kind of, preserve some integrity,' Cusack told CNN in April 1989 in promoting *Say Anything* . . .[3] and he shunned the exposure of his private life too

---

1 Author interview, BBC Radio 1, 3 November 2005.

2 Ibid.

3 Interview with Sherry Claypool, 14 August 1989.

– rumoured romances with Jami Gertz (whom he met on the set of *Sixteen Candles*) and Melissa Gilbert (during a downturn in her relationship with Rob Lowe) never played out in the press. Cusack's image – even on film – was always looking as if he wanted to run off and hide. No wonder he found so much real-life solace in watching sports, blending into the background as he sat amongst stadium crowds.

The opportunity to leave the business came with a spell at NYU but it was only brief, ultimately losing out to a return to acting. Yet John Cusack's struggles with the industry remained, noticeable every time he agreed to do publicity, quietly and hurriedly answering questions as if he would really rather be *anywhere* but in Hollywood: 'I get so sick of the business and sick of talking about acting and going to parties where there are actors there and sick of hearing about scripts and sick of the freeway.' Like the director who gave him his first break – John Hughes – the conflicted Cusack was most comfortable away from the glare, at home in Chicago. But he still stayed a movie star.

Lloyd Dobler was an equally intriguing mix; too individual to fit into the burgeoning 'grunge' movement going on in his own city of Seattle (preferring to kickbox whilst others lazily loafed and played garage rock) but with his unusual optimism he was still part of a 'Fuck it' attitude that could be placed somewhere within more traditional counterculture.[1] In other words, like J. D. and Veronica in *Heathers*, Lloyd's lack of need to follow the crowd was in itself a new movement of independent individualism; early signs of the so-called 'Generation X' of young adults just out of education but who didn't want to immediately put on a suit and tie and make their fortune, so different to the herds of yuppies of a few years earlier. Two independent film-makers waited in the twin hubs of American alt-culture – Portland, Oregon and Austin, Texas – to further explore this new phenomenon whilst Cameron Crowe himself considered how to follow up *Say Anything . . .* with a story that would also capture the era's blossoming alternative music scene and lifestyle.

---

1 As was Lloyd's music taste: alt-rockers Fishbone, Brit agitators The Clash and the punk funk of Red Hot Chili Peppers, led by Ione Skye's boyfriend Anthony Kiedis.

Cusack, meanwhile, happily found that all that consistent anxiety about his teenage movies was paying off. He now had credibility, by 1990 working in fully mature roles alongside renowned directors John Sayles, Stephen Frears and Woody Allen; a long way from many of his struggling contemporaries and a helluva leap forward from singing hamburgers.

Over ten years after *Grease*, Hollywood went back to high school 1959-style. Welton Academy in *Dead Poets Society* couldn't have been more different to Rydell High: where the working-class, Californian T-Birds and Pink Ladies sang and danced, preening and pushy, eager to express themselves at every opportunity, the rich boys of Welton were bound by uptight rules and stifling regulations. Really, they were like a pack of sheep trapped in a holding pen, strangled by the paraphernalia of traditional private schooling – banners, boater hats and bagpipes – as stuffy educators readied them for careers in medicine and law. Whilst the kids at Rydell didn't seem to have any plans for the future, those at Welton had plenty. It's just that they were more likely to be those of their parents or teachers than their own.

Compared to its predecessors in 1989 – *Bill & Ted*, *Heathers*, *Say Anything* . . . – *Dead Poets Society* might have seemed old-fashioned and proper, a retrograde step back to 'classy', period film-making that would appeal as much to adults as their teenagers. At its heart though, *Dead Poets* is arguably the angriest statement of the lot. The criticism it levels at traditional institutions such as Welton – isolationist, conformist – were as relevant to contemporary America, after almost a decade of Republican leadership under Reagan and Bush, as a 1959 US stifled by two terms of Eisenhower. In its nods to the beatnik jazz age blossoming outside the confines of Welton and even in the suicide of a major character, *Dead Poets* also mirrors the hints of *Heathers* and *Say Anything* that something moodier and more alternative in pop culture was brewing, waiting with its long hair and guitar just over the horizon.

And then there's Mr Keating. As the Whitman-quoting new English teacher and alumnus who urgently encourages his class to think for themselves rather than follow the crowd, his cries of '*Carpe diem!*' were really no different to Lloyd's 'I'm looking for a dare-to-be-great situation' or even Bill and Ted's 'Party on, dudes!' All three celebrated the courage to live large on your own terms, unique and audacious[1]. So even if the actual *Dead Poets Society* of the title were a tight-knit group the film was quick to point out that each member was also defiantly, inspiringly individual too. And if it all occasionally looks too glossy and genteel to be provocative, plentiful shots of watery Vermont sunsets and low-flying geese artfully peppering the drama, underneath that sheen *Dead Poets* really shouts loud about the dark side of existence. *Seize the day*, it cries. *Because death is just around the corner.*

For *Dead Poets Society* we should thank, perhaps surprisingly, French acting giant Gérard Depardieu . . . or at least his hectic late '80s' schedule. Australian director Peter Weir had been eager to follow up his two breakthrough US hits with Harrison Ford, 1985's *Witness* and 1986's *The Mosquito Coast*, with a romantic comedy starring Depardieu about a Frenchman who marries an American for convenience, called *Green Card*. But Depardieu was so in demand following his crossover success with the Provençal drama *Jean de Florette* that Weir was told he'd have to wait at least a year for his dream *Green Card* lead to be available.

Over at Disney, Jeffrey Katzenberg met with Peter Weir to discuss *Green Card*'s delay. Seeing that the director wanted to get working on something, Katzenberg gave him a script of a film that had once had *Revenge of the Nerds*' Jeff Kanew attached to direct. 'Read it, see what you think, maybe we can make it while you're waiting on Depardieu,' Katzenberg told Weir. The director put the script by Tom Schulman into his bag to read on the plane back to Sydney. As the 747 took off and he looked at the unusual title – *Dead Poets Society*? – he was already hooked. Six weeks later Weir was back in LA with Katzenberg, discussing casting.

The shaping of *Dead Poets Society* caused much debate at Touchstone, Disney's live-action, adult offshoot that would be producing the movie. Notes on the script, the *bête noire* of many a screenwriter, flowed freely around the office, suggestions including making the boys' passion dancing rather than poetry

---

1 Or even 'bodacious'.

(with the questionable new title of *Sultans of Swing*) and focusing more on the character of Mr Keating than the pupils themselves. After all, Robin Williams had been cast in the role, fresh from his Oscar nomination for *Good Morning, Vietnam*, but the boys were largely unknown.

That such a change didn't happen was in part thanks to casting director Howard Feuer's rigorous recruitment process for the charismatic teenage leads, his previous success working on similar ensembles *Bad Boys* and *Heaven Help Us* – plus his expert knowledge of the theatrical world – leading to auditions with hundreds of young actors from across the country. The resulting cast weren't showy wannabes. Just like their characters they seemed to be driving for something more soulful.

Robert Sean Leonard had started out in summer rep in his Ridgewood, New Jersey home town before taking his preppy teen angst to the New York stage after being spotted: 'I was surrounded by Glee-style kids and I looked at the ground and mumbled and I think they must have thought I was Marlon Brando, when in fact I was just embarrassed!'[1] Leonard made his Broadway debut in March 1986 as Eugene in *Brighton Beach Memoirs*, the role that had made Matthew Broderick a star and had since been played by Jon Cryer and Patrick Dempsey, amongst others. His *Dead Poets Society* character, Neil, was also a theatrical fan, the last vestiges of an early draft of the script that had been set entirely at a drama school and Leonard mirrored his character by craving a life on the stage rather than in Hollywood. He didn't want to be an all-grinning movie star like Tom Cruise. He wanted to be quietly respected, naming the Shakespearian Sam Waterston – who'd also found film success with a harrowing performance in 1984's *The Killing Fields* – as a role model.[2]

Austin-born Ethan Hawke had similarities to his character too: quiet and studious in his daily life yet with a focus buried beneath the bookishness, the nervy Todd determined to write a great poem and to let Mr Keating know how much he meant to him. 'I was really, really serious about my work, and it was hard to work with

---

1 *Evening Standard*, Fiona Mountford, 29 June 2015.
2 In *Dead Poets Society*, Leonard would find himself acting alongside Waterston's son, James.

him [Robin Williams],' admitted Hawke. 'It wasn't so much that he was intimidating. It's that I didn't want to be intimidated by him.'[1] After first performing in a school production of Bernard Shaw's *St Joan*, the young Hawke – then in New Jersey following his parents' break-up – was briefly fêted as a new child star, leading Joe Dante's 1986's tween sci-fi *Explorers* alongside River Phoenix. But true to his sensitive form he'd quit acting after it flopped, the disappointment too much for him. Phoenix was a friend but also someone to be jealous of, grabbing roles as a troubled soul with an apparent ease that made it look as if he wasn't even trying. Hawke's upbringing was open-minded but Phoenix's had been something else, his parents' non-conformist tendencies reaching their peak in the mid-'70s when they'd joined David Berg's controversial Children of God cult and moved the family to Venezuela as missionaries. Relative normality had been reinstated come the next decade, the Phoenix clan having moved in with maternal grandparents in Florida, but as River moved into the world of child performers he boasted a well of radical life experiences from which to draw, something Hawke could never replicate.[2] Post-*Explorers*, Ethan Hawke decided to move on, heading to the Carnegie-Mellon University in Pittsburgh to carry on his studies well away from the industry.

Yet just like John Cusack's truncated time at college, a niggling need for the spotlight returned when Ethan Hawke heard *Dead Poets Society* had started casting. He auditioned, got a role and promptly left college. 'Until I was sixteen, I wanted to be Holden Caulfield; from sixteen to twenty-three, I wanted to be Neal Cassady,'[3] he confessed, references to *The Catcher in the Rye* and *On the Road* confirming his desires were literary and maverick . . . but also unashamedly ambitious.[4]

Gale Hansen was less well-known, yet found even his relative obscurity didn't help him escape the studio's over-zealousness

---

1 'The Payoff for Ethan Hawke', *New York Times*, Diana Kennedy, 14 April 2002.

2 Even River's fourteen-year-old brother Leaf had maturity beyond his years, endearingly troubled alongside Keanu Reeves in Ron Howard's family smash *Parenthood* in the summer of 1989. The following year he would return to using his actual birth name: Joaquin.

3 'In his own hothouse', *New York*, Vanessa Grigoriadis, 28 June 2004.

4 'You just seem to require a lot of attention,' Hawke's alter-ego William is pointedly told in the actor's first novel, *The Hottest State*, published in 1996.

during *Dead Poets Society*'s planning stages. Weir's wife Wendy had liked his audition tape and suggested him for the role of rebellious student Charlie Dalton (he had actually auditioned to play more of a background role: gangly Gerard Pitts) but when it was revealed that Hansen had been economical about his age – he was already in his late twenties and engaged to be married – he was forced to go through the casting process all over again, despite the Weirs and Howard Feuer knowing he was the right guy ('It seems there were politics back in Burbank'[1]). Hansen even had to keep quiet about his age around his co-stars, although over a shoot lasting several weeks such secrecy ultimately proved to be impossible: 'It was the anniversary of JFK's tragic death and we were all at a table in the restaurant of the hotel. The TV news was on. I mused under my breath, "I remember that day." Every head swivelled my way. Ethan said, "How old *are* you?" like it was a spit take. But by that point we were a brotherhood.'

To his credit, Jeffrey Katzenburg stuck up for Tom Schulman and Peter Weir's vision throughout the extensive casting and planning, his mantra during pre-production being refreshingly simple: 'Just make the movie.'

One major thing did change, however. In the original script Mr Keating had been ill, slowly dying of the lymphatic cancer Hodgkin's Disease, but for Weir it seemed an unnecessary addition, a slice of pathos that would leave audiences siding with the teacher more because he was unwell than because of what he stood for. After some debate, Keating was transformed into an inspirational rebel now in perfect health. If what happened *after* Keating's time at Welton is never fully explained in the film, then it was only reflecting a similar mystery in Schulman's childhood, when an unconventional teacher suddenly left after only a brief time at his school; an incident that had partly inspired him to write *Dead Poets Society* in the first place.

In the winter of 1988, Weir headed with his cast and crew to begin filming on the 2200 acres of land that made up the respected St Andrew's School in Middletown, Delaware. In real life St Andrew's was co-educational, liberal even. For the next few

---

1 Author interview with Gale Hansen.

months, turned into the obstinate Welton Academy, it would be anything but.

* * *

If 'Carpe Diem!' resonated with audiences who flocked to see Dead Poets Society during the summer of '89, Gale Hansen also saw the phrase connect with everyone during filming: 'It was the call to action for the entire cast and crew. It's quite something to be on a set with golden hour happening and union members running with equipment to get one more set-up so Peter could get one more shot. They loved him that much and believed in his vision because he included everyone, absolutely everyone, in that vision. "Carpe Diem!" has stayed with me all these years.'[1] With extensive rehearsing and in banning the cast from talking in modern slang, even off camera, this story about a teenage bonding proved to be the same in real life. The boys let their hair down on winter days off in Delaware or New York, one time the whole group taking a train to Manhattan so that five of them could audition for the role of Ted Danson's son in upcoming film Dad (Hawke got it), another time heading to the movies to see just how far Tom Cruise had come since Risky Business with the multi-award nominated drama Rain Man.

Still, even after Dead Poets Society's popular and critical success – nearly a hundred million dollars in the US and four Oscar nominations – one of its stars found himself unconvinced (again) that acting was really for him. Heading back to New York, Ethan Hawke signed up to study English at NYU, listening to alt-rock and growing his hair longer in the process. It was that same cultural shift that Bill & Ted, Heathers and Say Anything . . . had all – in their own quirky ways – hinted at: a nationwide move from the glossy focus of mid-'80s yuppiedom towards something more drifting. On the other side of the country that autumn, Portland scenester Gus Van Sant was creating waves with his second feature, Drugstore Cowboy; a movie that saw Matt Dillon return to his former status as critical darling by growing his hair too, then shooting up and robbing hospitals. Cameron Crowe liked what he saw and was inspired to make his next feature Singles, also starring

---

1 Author interview.

Dillon; a film that would capture the burgeoning and incestuous alt-rock scene on Van Sant's home turf.

For the increasingly inquisitive Hawke it seemed almost inevitable that he would one day migrate back to his laidback birthplace of Austin where Richard Linklater, a twenty-nine-year-old film-maker and founder of the Austin Film Society, was now shooting his first official feature.

Linklater's film was aptly called *Slacker*; a story eccentrically charming but also personal and raw, far removed from the buffed and polished high-concept vehicles that youth cinema had morphed into a few years earlier. *Slacker* was eventually described by Cameron Crowe's old employer *Rolling Stone* magazine as capturing 'a generation of bristling minds unable to turn their thoughts into action'[1], a mood fortuitously shared by the creatively unanchored Ethan Hawke. But for a film that defined an era, *Slacker*'s origins were modest; a budget of just 23,000 dollars and all shot on 16-mm film, even its story a meandering 'day-in-the-life' of disparate Austin residents, several of them young drifters determined to follow their own path rather than being trapped by convention. Really they were just the querying teenage minds of *Dead Poets Society* in their logical modern setting after thirty years of social change.

It was an approach Linklater had been inspired to follow after watching a film from the start of the decade and those days of New Hollywood that were now long gone: Martin Scorsese's *Raging Bull*. For Linklater, *Raging Bull* was the most influential piece of work he had ever seen and the teen movie genre as a whole featured a variety of films and performances either influenced or repelled by it – from Penn to *Porky's*. And as Linklater and Van Sant took their groundbreaking scene into the '90s with low-budget, personal tales of disaffected youth, another Scorsese fan – an out-of-work actor called Quentin Tarantino – alternated shifts at a popular video store in LA's Manhattan Beach with work on his own fiercely idiosyncratic scripts that would have an even bigger impact on the new wave of independent film-making.

---

1 Peter Travers, 11 July 1991.

Tarantino boasted an encyclopaedic understanding of countless film genres and you could see it in his dexterous and tuned-in scripts for the crime stories he cooked up with fellow employee Roger Avary. It would be a couple more years before either saw those scripts go into production but when a project they'd been tinkering with for several years – back when it was known as *Black Mask* – *did* get the green light, Tarantino was quick to use his knowledge of Hollywood to draw up a wish list for his cast.[1] *Pulp Fiction*, as it was now known, had one character – a drug-dealer called Lance – perfect for a number of young actors looking to break away from the teen film success they'd found in the 1980s: John Cusack was first choice, Christian Slater also a possibility, Johnny Depp and Nic Cage too. Ultimately though, despite the film-maker's early plans, none got the role. Their loss was Eric Stoltz's gain. Bagging the hotly contested part, Lance's long hair, straggly beard and love of breakfast cereal was the perfect chance for the serious Stoltz to dig deep into a character . . . and produce a perfect snapshot of modern slacker life.

It was Quentin Tarantino's second choice to play lead hitman Vincent Vega who really benefitted from *Pulp Fiction*'s eventual critical, cultural and box-office success though.[2] Supporting player Michael Madsen had been top of the list, having already worked with the director on the Sundance hit *Reservoir Dogs*, but the Chicago-born actor – close friend of both Roger Ebert and Chris Penn – was now tied up making *Wyatt Earp*, one of the many westerns to follow in the wake of *Young Guns*. Instead Tarantino turned to a star he'd long admired – and was even unknowingly renting a West Hollywood apartment in which this guy had himself once lived – rewarding him not only with a tough R-rated script but also, seventeen years after his first, another Oscar nomination. Miramax's Bob and Harvey Weinstein, *Pulp Fiction*'s distributors, might not have initially agreed with the director's out-of-fashion choice for Vincent but, after packed cinemas and countless plaudits, they soon forgot

---

1 A piece of paper purporting to be this typed-up wish list was leaked to the press in September 2015.
2 The first independent film to gross over 200 million dollars.

any initial disagreements. And after a decade in the doldrums, an era where Hollywood's target audience had changed beyond almost all recognition, John Travolta was suddenly cool all over again.

Acknowledgements

Thank you to:
  Matthew Hamilton at Aitken Alexander Associates
  Andreas Campomar and Claire Chesser at Little, Brown
  Lucian Randall
  My family and friends
and everyone who kindly agreed to an interview.
  Much appreciation goes to the coffee shops of Woodbridge, Ealing, Halifax, Potters Bar and Maidenhead where the majority of this book was written.

Index

Page references followed by fn indicate a footnote.